A Theory About Control

A Theory About Control

Jack P. Gibbs

Westview Press

BOULDER • SAN FRANCISCO • OXFORD

Copyright © 1994 by Westview Press, Inc.

Published in 1994 in the United States of America by Westview Press, Inc., 5500 Central Avenue, Boulder, Colorado 80301-2877, and in the United Kingdom by Westview Press, 36 Lonsdale Road, Summertown, Oxford OX2 7EW

Library of Congress Cataloging-in-Publication Data
Gibbs, Jack P.
    A theory about control / Jack P. Gibbs.
        p.   cm.
    Includes bibliographical references and indexes.
    ISBN 0-8133-2243-X
    1. Sociology—Philosophy.   2. Social control.   I. Title.
HM24.G445   1994
301'.01—dc20   94-16170
                                                                                    CIP

Printed and bound in the United States of America

The paper used in this publication meets the requirements of the American National Standard for Permanence of Paper for Printed Library Materials Z39.48-1984.

10   9   8   7   6   5   4   3   2   1

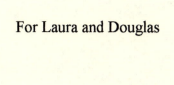

For Laura and Douglas

Contents

Tables and Figures

Tables

Figures

Foreword

Edward Shils (1985:810) argued that "the original programme of sociology"—legitimacy in the academy and on the part of the educated public—"has been achieved" in large part, though the intellectual task of "discovery of the fundamental laws of social life" remains. Today, neither the legitimacy of sociology nor its fundamental intellectual task seem secure.

There is no shortage of diagnoses as to why this should be the case. Most focus on such matters as the neglect of undergraduate teaching among academic departments of sociology, the balance between "basic" and "applied" sociology, or on other internal divisions within the discipline. But something more fundamental may be involved.

Sociology is a congeries of theoretical and methodological perspectives and substantive interests. Sociologists are contentious about such differences, and they worry about too much diversity. With rare exceptions, however, worrying has not translated into serious scholarly attention to explication of key concepts or debate as to whether sociology requires a "central notion" or what that notion might be.

Jack Gibbs is one of those rare exceptions. In *Control: Sociology's Central Notion*, Gibbs (1989) argued not only that control should be the discipline's central notion but also that failure to agree on a central notion is debilitating to sociology, retarding its theoretical power and development, and contributing to fragmentation and the lack of cumulative knowledge. Others, including the editor of the most recent (1988) *Handbook of Sociology* and co-editor of a National Academy of Sciences/National Science Foundation–sponsored assessment of "Achievements and Opportunities" of all the behavioral and social sciences (Gerstein, *et al.*, 1988), seem to forecast the demise of sociology as an "identifiable field" in the future (Smelser, 1988:13).

A reviewer of the aforementioned *Handbook* expressed his unease that the volume pays scant attention to the work of several important scholars "*because their work cannot be fitted neatly into the boxes of disciplinary subfields.* Instead, these sociologists speak to our discipline as a whole" (Powell, 1989: 493; emphasis added).

The implications of this assessment are troubling, suggesting not only that sociology lacks an agreed-upon core, but that important work of relevance to sociology *qua* sociology is less likely to influence the discipline than are more narrowly specialized inquiries that may have less relevance to the discipline as a whole. Here, again, is where Jack Gibbs weighs in.

Gibbs here returns to the central notion issue and to his candidate: control. He returns, also, to his insistence on predictive power of theories as "the issue in sociology," an argument first advanced in his presidential address before the Pacific Sociological Association (Gibbs, 1968). Here Gibbs delineates seven dimensions of predictive power: testability, range, parsimony, accuracy, scope, intensity, and discriminatory power.

The theory about control here advanced cannot be easily summarized (e.g., as Gibbs remarks, "something comparable to Marx's famous reduction of human history to class struggle"). Suffice to say, in Gibbs' words, that it identifies "several purported effects at the international level of two reciprocally related *construct* variables: (1) the extent and efficacy of control attempts...and (2) perceived control capacity." The asserted effects, "listed in the form of constructs or concepts," are the following: "the extent and efficacy" of three types of control attempts (inanimate, control of human behavior, and biotic), the amount of supernaturalism, the amount of scientific activity, concentration of biotic control, degree of division of labor, technological complexity, technological efficiency, intranational variation in death ages, the level of educational attainment, predominance of animate industries, degree of industry differentiation, degree of occupational differentiation, and amount of inanimate energy use.

After setting forth the theory in formal terms Gibbs tests 15 hypotheses derived from the theory's theorems. The result is generally positive but predictive accuracy is modest. His discussion of possible interpretations of this finding and of future work on the theory is candid and rigorous. A lengthy appendix discusses in more detail a formal mode of theory construction for sociology.

The model of theory construction developed and illustrated in this book is foreign to most of sociology and to most sociologists. Few have even begun to attempt, in their own theorizing, what Gibbs has undertaken with rigor and at great length. Indeed, the lengths to which Gibbs explains his model and its application will seem to many to demand prohibitively long exposition for that most common medium of scholarly publication, the professional journal article. And so it is. But formal theorizing need not require such lengthy presentation if its conventions are agreed upon and followed. Until that day, Gibbs' exposition is likely to be viewed as informative and illustrative, but too radical to be seriously entertained.

Skepticism concerning the validity and reliability of data, research methods, and theoretical interpretation are marks of a healthy discipline. But sociologists seem prone to excess, perhaps too willing to entertain doubts concerning attempts at rigor and quick to embrace nihilistic thinking regarding the possibility of a science of human behavior. Whether one agrees with the position adopted in this book, and in Jack Gibbs' other expositions of his position, one must admire his attempt to present an alternative based firmly on science and positivism.

In the final analysis the importance of this book is neither the power nor the substance of the theory here advanced; it lies rather in the challenge to the discipline, the boldness of the alternative it proposes, and the rigor and candor with which that alternative is pursued.

Jack Gibbs has done a great service, not only to sociology, but to all the social and behavioral sciences, with his candor, his rigor, and his persistence. We will do ourselves a great disservice if we do not take his multiple messages seriously.

James F. Short, Jr.

Preface

My critics (alas, numerous) will be delighted to learn that this book may well be my last, but they are likely to be dismayed on recognizing that I have not changed my opinions about any fundamental matter. I persist in viewing sociology as fragmented beyond description, and the fragmentation is virtually certain to increase as more and more sociologists flock to postmodernism, postempiricism, postpositivism, post *ad nauseam*. Sociology always has been a fertile ground for any intellectual movement that belittles even the idea of objectivity; and long before liberating sociology, critical sociology, resurgent Marxist sociology, hermeneutics, deconstructionism, and all of the "posts," there was no effective consensus in the field as to appropriate criteria for assessing theories. Worse, in recent decades on the whole sociologists have become less inclined to recognize that such consensus is essential for progress in a field. Indeed, the notion of progress is alien to "post" thinking, and nothing is gained by appealing to science. Numerous sociologists eagerly embraced Kuhn, and currently they can cite various philosophers and historians as evidence that science has no distinctive unity.

I have not come to the foregoing conclusions only recently (see Gibbs, 1968). The only thing I have learned over past decades is that the *new* "received view" in the philosophy of science and antipositivism in sociology promote epistemological nihilism. Mathematics and the advanced sciences may survive it, but I seriously doubt if sociology will survive should current trends continue; and, again, my pessimism antedates the fashionable (Gibbs, 1979).

Unfortunately, the problems that plague sociology transcend the epistemological. From the outset the field has been badly fragmented, in part from an incredibly diverse subject matter, but even more so in recent decades by the proliferation of contending perspectives. So the first of two principal arguments pursued in my previous book (1989)--maximum coherence in a field requires a central notion--has special significance for sociology. By a central notion I mean a notion that those trained in a field can use to describe and think about all or virtually all of the field's subject matter. I have not changed my mind on that subject, nor about the second principal argument: control could be sociology's central notion.

My previous book did not go far beyond the two principal arguments. I had to be content with an elaborate conceptualization of control and an examination of contending sociological perspectives in connection with the argument

that control could be the field's central notion. However, describing and thinking about a field's subject matter is not an end in itself. If a central notion does
not promote impressive theories, it fails for that reason alone. So this book's
primary purpose is to state a theory about control (Chapters 3-7) and report a
series of tests (Chapter 8).

The tests are important if only because they are consistent with still
another argument that I have pursued for decades (see, especially, Gibbs, 1968,
1972). Briefly, effective consensus in assessments of particular theories cannot
be realized unless predictive power is taken as the supreme criterion in those
assessments. The tests reported in Chapter 8 bear on the theory's predictive
accuracy, but there are six other dimensions of predictive power. Although all
seven dimensions are recognized in this book, it is not presumed that the
recognition of diverse dimensions will convert avowed antipositivists in
sociology. They appear reluctant to go beyond the use of the term "positivism"
as a pejorative label to a clarification of its meaning; even so, that point is
secondary to the most fundamental reason why so many sociologists reject
predictive power as the criterion for assessing theories. The rejection gives
them a license to criticize theories solely on the basis of personal opinion or
some ideology, though not making that basis explicit. If a theory is contrary to
a sociologist's preconceptions (including ideologies) of or presumptions about
human nature and social life, then so much the worse for the theory. To be sure,
many sociologists write or speak as though tests of theories are desirable, but it
is an old trick to recognize and emphasize test findings only when the theory is
consistent with one's preconceptions or presuppositions.

Unfortunately, there are several possible reasons for rejecting predictive
power as the appropriate criterion when assessing theories, and one is far from
obvious. It is difficult to apply the predictive power criterion when assessing a
sociological theory stated in accordance with the traditional discursive mode of
theory construction, which is nothing more than the conventions of some
natural language (e.g., English, German); and the outcome of an attempted
application of the criterion is virtually certain to be debatable. The difficulty
and the debatable outcome are inevitable because the logical structure of a
discursively stated theory is so obscure that divergent interpretations cannot be
avoided (for elaboration, see Gibbs, 1972). So exegetical sociology is a cottage
industry, and divergent interpretations are viewed sanguinely because personal
opinion in the assessment of theories has become sacrosanct.

And why do many sociologists cling to the discursive mode of theory
construction? One obvious reason is their familiarity with the natural language
in which they lecture and write. Because the rules of a formal mode transcend
natural language conventions, adopting a formal mode is akin to learning a
new language; hence, it is likely to be perceived by many sociologists as a

burden. Less obvious, no formal mode can match a natural language's flexibility, especially when it comes to rhetoric, the staple of conventional sociological theory. Still less obvious: because a discursive theory's logical structure need not be truly clear, the theory may run for hundreds of pages without taxing the audience's patience. Members of that audience are not expected to see whether and how the components are logically interrelated, and the theorist himself or herself may not know.

Despite recognition of the seeming permanence of the discursive mode of theory construction, the control theory in Chapters 3-7 is stated in accordance with a formal mode of theory construction, one set forth in a lengthy appendix. Why steer such a course of intractability? To do otherwise would be a tacit denial of previous arguments about formal theory construction.

Far from placating critics, the foregoing is likely to make them all the more hostile. So why make the arguments explicit and try to adhere to them throughout the book? Because in science certainty is an illusion and only candor can be the supreme value. Unfortunately, candor is not enough, but in this case I hope it will prompt critics to confront the arguments that gave rise to this book and articulate alternatives.

Most of the initial draft was completed while the author was a Fellow at the Center for Advanced Study in the Behavioral Sciences. My gratitude for support extends also to Vanderbilt University's College of Arts and Science and the College's Department of Sociology. I am grateful for three commentaries: Glenn Firebaugh's on the manuscript, Larry Griffin's on the Appendix, and Walter Wallace's on the Appendix; but all three are free of any liability. Jim Short deserves my thanks for his candid and insightful Foreword. The typing of Ms. Linda Norfleet (Vanderbilt's Department of Sociology) was an enormous contribution, and my wife Sylvia helped me in myriad ways.

Jack P. Gibbs

PART ONE

Preliminary Considerations

If a scientific field's progress must be judged by only one criterion, the most conspicuous possibility is an increase in the number, range, and/or scope of *accepted* theories. However, when a scientific field is plagued with issues and problems, that condition precludes progress. It is not just a matter of the issues and problems being such that they cannot be overcome by any theory; worse, they may be such as to eliminate the possibility of effective consensus in assessments of theories and thereby preclude progress.

Unfortunately, two particular problems and a particular issue in sociology make it extremely unlikely that any theory will be accepted by even a majority of sociologists. So this part of the book, comprising two chapters, largely pertains to those problems and that issue.

The first problem is the extreme diversity of sociology's subject matter (see Boudon, 1980:3, and Gibbs, 1989:3). That diversity makes it inevitable that each theory is limited to only a minute fraction of sociology's subject matter; consequently, numerous sociologists are not likely to be impressed by any theory, viewing it (rightly) as alien to their specialty or interests. Such judgments are not constructive, but all a theorist can do is make the limits of his/her theory explicit rather than follow the tradition of "grand" theory and create the impression of an all-inclusive theory. That disclaimer is set forth early in Chapter 1, and it is all the more needed because of the argument that control could be sociology's central notion, meaning that sociologists can describe and think about all or virtually all of sociology's subject matter in terms of control. Although the theory set forth in Chapters 3–7 pertains to control, it does not follow from the central notion argument, not even if valid, that the theory is all-inclusive. However, if the argument is valid, the theory can be expanded much more readily than can a theory not focused on the field's central notion, control or otherwise.

The second disclaimer in Chapter 1 relates to an issue rather than a problem. Sociologists have never realized effective consensus as to appropriate criteria for assessing the merits of a sociological theory, and no theory can resolve that issue. All that the theorist can do is identify what he/she takes to be

2

appropriate criteria, and in Chapter 1 one particular criterion is described at length. That criterion is predictive power, and a large part of the chapter is devoted to a description of predictive power's seven dimensions. Such treatment is justified because many sociologists ostensibly have a narrow conception of that criterion, commonly equating it with predictive accuracy, which is actually only one of predictive power's seven dimensions.

The suggestion is not that numerous sociologists reject predictive power as the appropriate criterion for assessing a theory merely because of confusion. Unfortunately, there is a plethora of reservations about the criterion, some of which are truly understandable. Nevertheless, sociology always has been fertile ground for epistemological nihilism; hence, sooner or later many sociologists will be attracted to "postmodernism" (a term used here as a generic label for all "posts"—postempiricism, postpositivism, etc.—and hermeneutics and deconstructionism). But if there is anything that sociology does not need, it is more epistemological nihilism; and its escalation can be checked only by promoting some particular criterion for assessing theories. So reduction of epistemological nihilism is the principal justification for the concern with predictive power, even though that concern diverts attention from the theory and may alienate some readers.

The second and final problem stems from recognition that a simple identification of a candidate for sociology's central notion will not do. Whether control or something else, an elaborate conceptualization is virtually certain to be needed. In that connection, contemporary sociology suffers from far too little conceptual work, perhaps in part because Weber and Parsons tarnished that line of work by confusing conceptualizations with substantive theories. Be that as it may, Chapter 2 offers an elaborate conceptualization of attempted control, including a fairly extensive typology. But the conceptualization is not offered in the naive belief that even the majority of sociologists will see the need for it; to the contrary, some sociologists appear indifferent if not hostile to conceptualizations, even to the point of believing that constructive research and impressive theories are possible without confronting conceptual issues and problems.

1

Claims and Disclaimers

As argued at length elsewhere (Gibbs, 1989), control (more precisely "attempted control") could be the central notion for the social and behavioral sciences, meaning that professionals trained in one of those fields can describe and think about all or virtually all of the field's subject matter in terms of control. If the argument comes to be accepted, it will further the integration of the social and behavioral sciences, an advance if one grants that those disciplinary boundaries are either extremely vague or arbitrary (unconstructive in either case). However, even if it could be demonstrated that the subject matter of the social and behavioral sciences can be thought of in terms of control, that demonstration would not warrant unqualified acceptance of control as the central notion.

Whatever the field or the central notion candidate—control or something else—acceptance of it requires considerable evidence that describing and thinking of phenomena in terms of the notion furthers the field's coherence. That point is consistent with a corollary argument—no field can realize maximum coherence without a central notion. Yet a central notion must do more than further conceptual integration; it must also promote the formulation of impressive theories.

The extent to which a central notion candidate meets the requirement cannot be known without using it extensively, all the more because there are at least two major ways that the use of a central notion can promote the formulation of theories. To the extent that the notion enters (directly or indirectly) into definitions of a field's terms, it promotes conceptual integration. Granted that scientists discover order, they also *create it* through conceptual innovations; and conceptual integration facilitates the formulation of theories. Indeed, what could be taken as the ultimate goal—a synthesis of all theories in a field—virtually requires conceptual integration. The second way by which a central notion facilitates the formulation of theories cannot be described without making still another disputable claim. Describing or thinking of phenomena in terms of a particular notion prompts recognition of *possible* empirical associations, possibilities that might otherwise have gone unrecognized. That claim is supported by the theory in Chapters 3–7, for it is a product of thinking about diverse phenomena in terms of control.

Although the theory might interest various social and behavioral scientists, the author's discipline, sociology, is the immediate consideration. If the argument about a central notion and control does not hold for sociology, it must be interred in the cemetery of ideas. For that matter, limited space alone precludes observations beyond sociology, and only the practitioners in a particular social or behavioral science are qualified to assess the extent to which control can be used to describe and think about their subject matter.

The First of Two Major Disclaimers

Given that the theory (Chapters 3–7) encompasses seventeen constructs or concepts, by any reasonable standard it has considerable scope. Nevertheless, the theory bears on only a minute fraction of sociology's subject matter. The theory may be expanded eventually, and some observations along that line are made in the last two chapters; but the immediate concern is a disclaimer.

The suggestion is not that control should be identified as the subject matter of any social or behavioral science, nor that the ultimate goal is necessarily an all-inclusive theory about control, let alone a synthesis of all sociological theories. It is one thing to claim that a field's subject matter can be described and thought of in terms of some designated notion, but quite different to equate that notion with the field's subject matter.

As for an all-inclusive theory, if defensible, it would provide the field with maximum coherence. Yet it could be that no theory about control, or whatever the central notion in question, will answer all of the field's questions adequately, perhaps not even the major questions. On the other hand, neither the possibility nor the desirability of an all-inclusive theory is denied.

To claim that a notion can be used to describe and think about a field's subject matter does not imply that the notion refers to some ultimate cause. Stated otherwise, the idea of a central notion is far less monistic than it may appear. Thus, should one argue that technology is the direct or indirect cause of all human behavior, including social and cultural phenomena, surely the argument would be monistic; but it would not imply that one can truly describe and think of all human behavior in terms of technology. After all, to assert that "X is the cause of Y" is not to describe and think of either variable in terms of the other; and phenomena may be described and thought of in other than causal terms.

The foregoing is consistent with the depiction of science as a vast competition in which the participants seek to discover *or* create (analytically) as much order as possible. Maximum order, however defined, may never be realized;

and it may be that in any particular field no one ever gives an acceptable answer to all of that field's questions, though eventually the unanswered questions are likely to be abandoned. In any case, the immediate point is that scientists may create as much order *analytically* as they discover, and the proposal of a central notion candidate is actually an attempt to create order analytically on a vast scale. The claim is radical only if one assumes the possibility of science without conceptualizations.

The Inexplicable

Although the search for an ultimate cause of human behavior (or of some derivative, such as society or culture) may never end, currently many scientists and philosophers appear to regard the search as sterile; and alleging that a theory does not identify an ultimate cause is destructive criticism. Nonetheless, in any scientific field certain phenomena are commonly regarded as inexplicable or simply taken as a given. Thus, physicists use the notion of force extensively; but they are inclined to take particular kinds of forces as given, and it may well be that many physicists would argue that an attempt to explain the very existence of forces is premature at best. However, far from frustrating, recognition of "inexplicables" in a field may promote consensus in assessments of theories. Rather than resort to the feckless demand that a theory identify the ultimate cause of the explicandum, a theory may be judged as commendable if it reduces the explicandum to one phenomenon in the field's subject matter, one so basic that it is taken as inexplicable or simply as a given.

At least at certain levels, variation in properties or dimensions of attempted control cannot be explained. Consider the simplest dimension of the extent of attempted control at the national level—the sheer frequency of attempts during some period (e.g., any calendar year). Even if research resources were such as to establish the values of that variable for just a few countries, there would be no prospect of explaining international variation in those values. To be sure, the variation probably reflects international contrast in population size, but how could variation in some kind of per capita rate of attempted control be explained? The question defies an answer not because there are no obvious possibilities; to the contrary, there is a multitude of possibly relevant factors. To illustrate, the U.S. "control rate" might reflect not just variation in geographic factors (terrain, weather, natural resources, etc.) but also innumerable historical factors, such as the timing of the arrival of various peoples and their sociocultural characteristics.

The foregoing should not be construed as claiming that variation in properties or dimensions of control is forever inexplicable. Rather, the problems (some purely practical, such as limited research resources) in pursuing an explanation are so formidable that taking control properties as *givens* is justified.

Second Major Disclaimer

Whatever the merits of the theory in Chapters 3–7, it will not resolve the most crucial issue in the social and behavioral sciences. Stating the issue as a question: what is the appropriate criterion or criteria for judging a scientific theory's merits? The question is rarely confronted in sociology, and the few answers given suggest negligible consensus.[1] Moreover, the trend in recent years has been an increase not just in dissensus but also in the seeming reluctance of numerous sociologists to confront the question, even those who have not fully embraced antipositivism (e.g., Boudon, 1980).

For nearly three decades the dissensus has contributed to and reflected an astonishing proliferation of schools, camps, or perspectives, with some of the more common labels being: critical sociology, emancipatory sociology, hermeneutics, and postpositivism. However, even before the 1960s there was scarcely effective consensus in sociology as to the appropriate criteria for judging theories.[2] One major source of dissensus was Talcott Parsons' sociology (especially *The Social System* [1951]). His indifference to and ostensible ignorance of systematic sociological research contributed more to dissensus in assessments of theories than has the shrillest critical sociologist. Nevertheless, at one time the "appropriate criterion" question was much better understood, if only because there was much more agreement as to the meaning and perhaps acceptance of two key terms, "scientific" and "theory." Today, nothing is gained by invoking the notion of science, because social and behavioral scientists, sociologists especially, have quite divergent conceptions of science (see, e.g., Cancian, 1990, and Geertz, 1990, for observations on feminist views of science). Then it is doubtful that the majority of social and behavioral scientists would agree when defining a theory, let alone accept both of two related arguments endorsed here: (1) that theories are the ultimate concern in any science and (2) the question about the appropriate criteria for judging theories is thus the *paramount* question.

The situation may be even worse than the foregoing suggests. Many sociologists are now so committed to reducing everything to value judgments that they appear to misunderstand arguments about sociology as a science. Contemplate David Altheide's declaration (1990:70): "I wish to challenge the basic assumption often made that sociology is not as good or as developed as physics or chemistry." Althiede may have construed the invidious comparison as somehow introducing a moral issue (hence, his use of the word "good"), but that in itself suggests a determination to view all sciences in moral terms. Yet Altheide's declaration does not exemplify the characteristic incoherence of postmodernism. Savor the quality of Stephen Pfohl's statement (1991:9), writing as President of the Society for the Study of Social Problems: "In using the word *postmodernity* I am referring to the Historical (*sic*) emergence of a terrifying new social formation structured around the dense and high velocity technological rituals of image management, informational CAPITAL, cybernetic-like mechanisms of social control, and the predominantly white male and heterosexist militarization of everyday life and culture."

Smoke Screens

Far from confronting the paramount question (*supra*), avowed antipositivists have focused on issues that divert attention from it. Only a few brief observations can be made on three such smoke screens.

The Antipositivism Mania. Since the 1960s, the term "positivism" has come to be used by many sociologists pejoratively. When so used, the term refers merely to something that the writer or speaker does not like. The term is rarely defined, and commonly no specific reason for rejecting positivism is given. Hence, the pejorative use of the term is like a dog barking in the night; hostility is clearly manifested, but the target is obscure.

The usage in question is all the more indefensible given Halfpenny's demonstration (1982) of twelve meanings of positivism, which alone suggests that the label should be abandoned. Actually, the diversity of meanings is even greater than indicated by Halfpenny's survey. He did not explicitly identify what is taken here as the pivotal meaning. Positivism is subsequently defined such that the term refers to a particular answer to the question about the appropriate criteria for judging theories; as such, the term bears directly on a crucial issue. Hence, when avowed antipositivists use the term "positivism" without defining it, that usage enables them to dodge an issue.

The Evils of Quantification. What is the major impediment to progress in sociology? The answer given here requires two statements. First, the ultimate manifestation of progress in a scientific field is an increase in the number of accepted theories or an increase in the range and scope of accepted theories. Second, far from having accepted theories, sociology is bereft even of effective consensus as to the appropriate criteria for assessing theories. But some sociologists give a quite different answer to the impediment question: the field suffers from an excessive concern with quantification and measurement.

The answer is largely peculiar to sociologists who are identified by themselves and/or others as humanists, and it is a perennial smoke screen. Specifically, in taking Lord Kelvin's pronouncement about measurement all too seriously, some humanists equate science and quantification; and their ranting against quantification merely conceals an opposition to the very idea of scientific sociology. Worse, the ranting diverts attention from the paramount question (*supra*), one that humanists in sociology never confront directly. For that matter, in castigating quantification humanists always stop short of this claim: sociologists disagree only when assessing the merits of "quantitative" theories.

The Notion of a Value-Free Science. Over recent decades the "humanist vs. scientific sociology" controversy has been eclipsed by this question: is science value-free or value-laden? Given that any activity, whether shooting craps or praying, can be interpreted as manifesting some value, the answer must be: science is value-laden. But the answer rightly suggests that the value-laden thesis is trite; and it is another smoke screen, again one that diverts attention away from the paramount question (*supra*).

Insofar as the value-laden thesis answers the paramount question, it is something like this: a scientific theory's merit should be judged in terms of the values that the theory promotes or opposes, and a scientist should accept a theory only if it furthers his/her values. Even assuming agreement as to what values a given theory promotes, no imagination is required to see why advocates of the value-laden thesis would deny the answer. It would reduce any field to a debating club; and while advocates of the value-laden thesis may have no other aspirations for sociology, their candor has limits. In particular, they appear indifferent to this disciplinary question: *entirely apart from invidious comparisons*, how does sociology differ from literary criticism, journalism, theology, social work, philosophy, social criticism, and history? Yet the indifference is hardly surprising given the eagerness with which some sociologists have embraced postmodernism (including all other "posts," hermeneutics, and deconstructionism). That eagerness indicates an inclination to think of sociology as anything but a science.

The value-laden thesis is consistent with the "externalist" view of science (for examples of that view, see references in Chalmers, 1990, or Hull, 1988, to the publications of D. Bloor, H. Collins, P. Feyerabend, and T. Kuhn). The externalist view originated largely with Kuhn (1962), but the value-laden thesis thrived in sociology long before him. Even so, if only because of the disciplines of Kuhn and Feyerabend, the common practice of equating "externalism" and the "sociology" of science is misleading.

An Answer to the Paramount Question

The paramount question is answered thus: the appropriate criterion for judging a scientific theory's merits (or adequacy or shortcomings) is its predictive power relative to that of contending theories.[3] Observe particularly that predictive power is the *exclusive* criterion. Other (contending) criteria are either so vague as to preclude their application or, if applicable, such as to preclude agreement in independent judgments of the theory. That rationale is defended following the conceptualization of predictive power, something needed because sociologists tend to equate predictive accuracy with predictive power, rather than recognize that the former is only one of seven dimensions of the latter. However, no amount of clarification will prompt even a majority of sociologists to accept predictive power as a criterion for judging theories, let alone the exclusive criterion. The immediate rationale for treating the subject here is that it bears on the second major disclaimer—that *no* methodology, research finding, theory, argument, perspective, or central notion candidate (control or otherwise) can reduce sociology's epistemological nihilism (i.e., a denial of anything akin to objectivity or truth). However, sociologists will not take predictive power seriously unless they fully understand its dimensions, especially those beyond predictive accuracy. For that matter, misconceptions of predictive accuracy abound in sociology.

Predictive Accuracy. The term "prediction" has an unfortunate connotation; it suggests statements about the future—prophecies, forecasts, extrapolations, etc. Predictive accuracy is defined here quite differently. In a real sense, every testable theory does make an assertion about the future, but only in this form: if researchers do such-and-such, they will report having observed or otherwise detected such-and-such. The first "such-and-such" would be the instructions for testing the theory, and the second "such-and-such" would be the report of a test outcome. However, what researchers report as a test outcome (i.e., the data) cannot be some future condition; obviously, researchers report past events, never future events. So a theory's predictive accuracy is the *amount* of correspondence between (1) what the theory implies in the way of statements about particular *unknowns* and (2) what individuals subsequently assert about those unknowns that are taken as the criterion for the truth or falsity of the implied statements.

To illustrate, suppose that the following conclusion (theorem) is deduced from a theory: among countries, the greater the degree of urbanization, the greater the suicide rate. Customary uncritical uses of the term "prediction" notwithstanding, the conclusion does not qualify. It is a *generalization* from which testable predictions about particular countries and times can be deduced, and a theory is untestable unless it comprises at least one such generalization. The more immediate point, however, is that the conclusion about urbanization and suicide (*supra*) cannot be construed as a forecast, prophecy, or extrapolation; but the generalization expressed in the conclusion does serve to clarify the notion of predictive accuracy.

The generalization would become testable only if accompanied by stipulations of formulas for computing a country's degree of urbanization and suicide rate, along with instructions as to requisite data and a test procedure. One procedure would be to compute the degree of urbanization and the suicide rate for at least two countries and then answer this question (any genuine question implies something *unknown*): for each pair of countries where one degree of urbanization is greater than the other, does the country having the greater degree also have the greater suicide rate? The answer is consistent with the statement deduced from the theory if and only if *affirmative*.[4] As for the series of tests in question, the theory's predictive accuracy would be the *proportion* of instances where the answer is affirmative. The alternative is a measure of ordinal association between the two variables, Spearman's rank-order coefficient of correlation (*rho*) or Kendall's *tau*.

Rather than conduct tests pertaining to *ordinal* accuracy, a researcher could compute some measure of nonordinal association between the values of the two variables, degree of urbanization and the suicide rate. If the association measure varies from −1.00 to +1.00 (as in the case of *r*), then it is a measure of the statement's *associational* accuracy (ignoring the measure's sign, plus or minus, if as predicted by the theory). The weakest possible criterion, *directional* accuracy, is introduced by this question: given two or more associational tests based on ordinal or nonordinal measures, what proportion of the signs of the measures (plus or minus) are consistent with the statement deduced from theory? A far more stringent criterion, *precisional* predictive accuracy, presumes that the statement in question has been deduced and translated (perhaps inductively but in any case as part of the theory) into an equation that permits researchers to compute an expected value of the dependent variable for each unit under consideration. In that case precisional predictive accuracy is simply the average of the absolute or proportionate differences between the predicted values and what are taken as the actual values.

The four alternative kinds of predictive accuracy (directional, ordinal, associational, and precisional) need not give rise to sterile arguments as to which one is decisive, because the ultimate goal is a theory that exceeds *all contenders* as regards each predictive accuracy criterion. To be sure, if a theory is stated such that one or more of the four criteria cannot be applied (e.g., the theory's testable generalizations are not equations), then the theory cannot be assessed with regard to some kind or kinds of predictive accuracy. However, when that is the case, the theory's testability, another dimension of predictive power (*infra*), is less than maximum. Most important, even though in the final analysis no dimension of predictive power is more relevant than any other, it is particularly important to emphasize that a theory's predictive accuracy always should be judged relative to that of *contending theories* rather than by some absolute standard, let alone one imported from another field.

Testability. This dimension of predictive power is the most difficult to explicate and the most controversial, especially in connection with sociological theories. The immediate reason is that many sociologists appear to judge theories without regard to tests; indeed, they commonly stop short of demanding testable theories, and they pay scant attention to the notion of testability itself. "Test procedure" is a typical subject in sociology methods courses and related texts, but a procedure presupposes some conception of *defensible* tests. That subject is scarcely treated in the sociological literature; and the lacuna reflects the tolerance of untestable theories, perhaps even the unexpressed conviction that a theory can be assessed satisfactorily without tests.

Even avowed positivists have done little to clarify the notion of testability. Most of them evidently presume that only operational definitions are needed to test a theory and that Popper's notion of falsifiability (1965) somehow circumvents epistemological problems. As indicated subsequently, the notion of an operational definition will not bear examination, and Popper identified only a necessary condition for defensible tests.

No theory is testable unless it comprises at least one synthetic statement (or empirical generalization or claim or assertion). Whatever the label, the statement's truth or falsity is not given by the very meaning of its constituent words or symbols. However, for several decades and especially since Quine (1951, 1960), it has been fashionable to question if not deny the distinction between synthetic statements and analytic statements (the latter being taken as true or false by the very meaning of their constituent words or symbols). Such sophistry runs contrary to something that no one really questions: millions of scientists believe that the truth or falsity of *some* statements is contingent, meaning that the statements are neither true nor false by the very meaning of the constituent terms (for a vast elaboration, see Pawson, 1989).

So Popper rightly emphasized falsifiability; but the exact sense in which some theories are more falsifiable than others is far from clear, and it cannot be the sheer number of constituent synthetic statements. Granted that a theory cannot be falsified if it comprises no synthetic statements, falsifiability is only *necessary* for tests of a theory. Whether a synthetic statement can be tested defensibly depends on the *empirical applicability* of its constituent terms or their definitions.

A term or its definition is empirically applicable *to the extent* that independent investigators (1) indicate that they either understand the term if it has been left undefined or regard its definition as intelligible; (2) in actual practice demonstrate or at least grant feasibility, meaning (*inter alia*) that research resources, including expertise, are sufficient to apply the term or its definition in *identifying or describing* events or things; and (3) realize congruent outcomes in independent applications to the same events or things. Briefly illustrating, given a definition of the term "middle class," a systematic assessment of its empirical applicability would require that at least two investigators independently attempt to apply the definition to the same set of individuals and answer this question for each individual: is he/she "middle class" if judged in accordance with the definition?[5] Should the investigators agree in their answers for all individuals, that outcome would indicate maximum empirical applicability; and should agreements not exceed chance expectation, that outcome would indicate minimum empirical applicability.[6] The example unrealistically ignores two possibilities: the investigators report that they (1) regard the term's definition as being unintelligible or (2) lack the research resources to apply the definition. Either possibility would indicate minimum empirical applicability, and the two facets of empirical applicability, intelligibility and feasibility, are reasons why empirical applicability cannot be equated with "reliability."

The foregoing example ignores the quantitative character of many sociological terms, meaning that they denote properties of an entity, be it a population or an individual, that can be described with even the appearance of ostensible precision only by reference to numerical values. In that case there is no real prospect of independent investigators offering congruent *descriptions* unless the theorist stipulates a formula and related instructions as to requisite kinds of data and the means of their acquisition.[7] Should it be argued that instructions as to *kinds of data* are not needed, imagine a theorist saying: tests will corroborate this theory regardless of the kinds of data or how acquired.

The foregoing observations on empirical applicability apply to formulas as well as to definitions. Specifically, investigators may report that they regard a formula as unintelligible, or they may report that its application is not feasible (gathering or otherwise acquiring data as instructed is impractical, given the limits of research resources or other constraints on research). Even if the formula is regarded as intelligible and its application as feasible, the numerical values reported by independent investigators for the same entity may be markedly incongruent. In a very real sense those values are descriptions of the entity, and congruent values are indicative of empirical applicability.

Congruence can be reckoned as *equivalence* (absolute agreement) or as *concordance* (correlation). In the latter case, each independent investigator or investigatory team has applied the formula in question to two or more entities (but the same ones for all investigators), and the values reported by a particular investigator constitutes a set. Given two such sets, *ordinal* concordance is expressed by a coefficient of correlation between the ranks of one set of values and the ranks of the other set, while *nonordinal* concordance is the product-moment coefficient of correlation between the two sets of values. Although the theorist hopes for equivalence or negligible disagreement between such sets of values, he/she may be willing to settle for substantial ordinal or nonordinal concordance; because if correlation coefficients are to be used in testing of the theory, the outcome will not depend on which set of values is used in the test.

Whether reckoned in terms of equivalence or concordance, empirical applicability is a matter of degree in a double sense. When two investigators describe a particular entity (as when reporting a numerical value), even though they assert that the description was made in accordance with the stipulated definition and/or the formula, it is extremely unlikely that their descriptions will be absolutely equivalent. However, whatever degree of empirical applicabillity is indicated by the reports of independent investigators about a particular set of entities, *variation* in congruence (i.e., from one set of entities to another) is also relevant when assessing a definition or a formula. In general, the greater the number of applications, the greater the average congruence, and the less the variation in congruence, the more confidence in empirical applicability is justified.

The subject bears on testability because any synthetic statement's testability is contingent on the empirical applicability of its constituent terms. However, a theory may be testable even though the theorist does not claim that *all* of the constituent synthetic statements are testable. In that case, the theorist should explicitly identify the statements that he/she regards as testable or use a formal mode of theory construction that eliminates the need for such identification (e.g., the mode could be such that only the conclusions of the theory—the theorems—are taken as testable).

So suppose that the theorist identifies only one statement in his/her theory as testable. Then suppose that reports by investigators indicate that at least one term, or a formula denoted by a term, in the supposedly testable statement cannot be applied (i.e., it is unintelligible or its application is not feasible). Those reports alone would raise serious doubts about any purported tests of the theory. Think of the matter this way: given evidence that none of a statement's constituent terms are empirically applicable, how could any purported test of that statement be credible?

Now suppose no investigator has reported that any constituent term (or a denoted formula) of the supposedly testable statement is unintelligible or that the term's application is not feasible. Even so, when two or more independent investigators use some term in the statement to describe the same set of entities (including values in the case of quantitative properties of entities), the description could be incongruent. Given incongruence, any purported test of the statement would tax credulity. The reason is simple: when descriptions of the same entity by two independent investigators are markedly divergent, how can a test based on either description be defensible?

As the foregoing suggests, judgments of a theory's testability are difficult and inherently controversial. It will not do to declare that a theory is testable if and only if tests of it have been reported. Such declaration presumes that (1) all reported tests are necessarily defensible and (2) judgments of testability cannot be made apart from actual tests. True, because testability judgments necessarily pertain to a *potential quality* of a theory, they are more conjectural than are references to actual reported tests; but a reported test may or may not be defensible, even though better than none at all.

The extent to which a reported test of a statement is defensible depends on the amount of evidence indicating that the statement's constituent terms are empirically applicable. Yet empirical applicability is always a matter of degree; and evidence of any particular degree can never be conclusive, all the more because the indicated degree is likely to vary from one pair of independent investigators to the next and/or from one set of entities (individuals or populations) to the next. For that matter, if a theory comprises two or more supposedly testable statements, it could be that tests of only some of those statements are defensible; and theories may differ in that regard.

All of the foregoing is somewhat academic. Few sociologists are inclined to assess a theory's testability as just prescribed; indeed, many of them appear indifferent to testability. While intuitive judgments of empirical applicability are better than none at all, assessments of testability are inherently questionable unless based on *evidence* of empirical applicability. Most important, unless sociologists come to take empirical applicability seriously, the notion of testability will have little relevance for the field.

The position just taken should not be confused with operationalism. Sociologists who advocate operationalism have never clarified the notion of an operational definition, and they commonly use the term in an unintelligible manner. For example, it is a practice for sociologists to stipulate a certain minimum and maximum annual income as a criterion of middle class and then refer to the criterion as an operational definition. What is "operational" about such a definition? The label merely beguiles.

More serious, operationalists appear to hold that *all* of a theory's constituent terms must be operationalizable before tests of the theory are possible. Such barefoot empiricism expunges numerous terms—those that denote purely theoretical notions—from the field's vocabulary. Moreover, a theory could be such that at least one term in each premise has no empirical applicability whatever, and yet it might be possible to deduce at least one testable conclusion (i.e., all of the conclusion's constituent terms are empirically applicable). But deduction requires explicit rules, not operational definitions. The vast majority of sociological theorists eschew explicit rules of deduction. In one theory after another there are sentences commencing with a phrase something like this: "It follows from what has been said that" (see Gibbs, 1972:102–104, for several illustrations). Close examination commonly reveals that it is not clear what follows from what, much less how. Such is the case because the deduction, if it can be called that, was made without explicit rules, let alone conventional rules (e.g., those of the classical syllogism).

The subject of deduction introduces a clear criterion of an *untestable* theory. If it is agreed that a theory's premises are untestable and that no conclusion can be deduced from the premises by explicit deduction rules, then the theory is untestable. The criterion is illustrated by purported tests of Durkheim's theory about variation in the suicide rate. Over recent decades many sociologists have reported a measure of association between church membership rates or the volume of religious publications and suicide rates (see Gibbs, 1993c, for references) as though it is a defensible test of Durkheim's theory. Yet there are no extant rules of deduction by which any relation between such variables and the suicide rate can be deduced from Durkheim's theory *as he stated it.* Indefensible though they are, such purported tests are not truly puzzling. The two key variables in Durkheim's theory, social integration and social regulation, are quantitative properties of social units; but at no point in *Le Suicide* did Durkheim (1951 [1897]) suggest a formula for the numerical expression of those variables, and it is difficult to imagine a formula that would be accepted by critics and promise more than negligible empirical applicability. True, in purported tests of Durkheim's theory, such variables as church membership are not identified as measures of integration or regulation; rather, the relevance of the variables is left obscure. But the more general point is that tests are bound to be indefensible if there is no basis for presuming appreciable empirical applicability of at least some of the theory's principal constituent terms, even if only those that appear in the conclusions (theorems).

Predictive Scope. This dimension of predictive power pertains to a notion commonly recognized by scientists and philosophers, perhaps because it bears on the idea that theories are explanatory in one sense or another but differ as to explanatory power. A theory's scope is indicative of its explanatory power if scope is defined as the number and inclusiveness of dependent variables.[8] So a theory that identifies causes of variation in the homicide rate *and* the degree of stratification (i.e., two variables) would have greater scope than a theory that identifies causes of only one of those variables or, say, the causes of only variation in human fertility.

The interpretive problem pertaining to scope is illustrated by contemplating four theories, each of which purports to explain variation in one dependent variable: theory A, the burglary rate; theory B, the property crime rate; theory C, the total crime rate; and theory D, the social mobility rate. If scope were merely a matter of the number of *explicit* dependent variables, it would be the same for the four theories. Yet no one would question that scope is greater for theory C than for A or B (i.e., the dependent variable is more inclusive in the case of C). Burglary is a subclass of property crimes and the latter is a subclass of crime; hence, the dependent variable in theory A is a subclass of the dependent variable of both B and C, while the dependent variable of theory B is a subclass of the dependent variable of theory C. So the rule: when comparing the *general* scope of two theories, an explicit dependent variable of one theory is counted if and only if *not* a subclass of an explicit dependent variable in the other theory. Accordingly, the scope of the three "crime" theories is as previously indicated ($C>B>A$), but there is no difference in the scope of D and that of A, B, or C. Should the "no difference" appear questionable, the problem is not serious. The primary concern is the comparison of the predictive power of *contending* theories, meaning those that share at least one dependent variable in common, explicitly or implicitly.

The only remaining problem is illustrated by a comparison of two contending theories: X, which purports to explain only variation in the mental illness rate; and Y, which purports to explain variation in both the schizophrenia rate and the social mobility rate. According to the rule pertaining to general scope (*supra*), X and Y do not differ (the schizophrenia rate in theory Y does not count because it is a subclass of X's dependent variable, the mental illness rate); but from the viewpoint of those interested in psychopathology, X is more inclusive than Y. The problem is avoided by recognition that the rule pertains to *general* scope, while *specific* scope always pertains to one particular class of dependent variables; and it is relevant only when comparing contending theories. The specific scope rule is this: a particular theory's specific scope with regard to a particular class of dependent variables is greater than that of a contending theory if and only if the contending theory's dependent variable is a subclass of the particular theory's dependent variable.[9] Thus, the specific scope of X is greater than that of Y, even though they do not differ as regards general scope.

Predictive Range. Although the unity of science lies in reliance on predictive power as the criterion for assessing theories, it does not follow that the appropriate terminology for describing predictive power dimensions can be the same for all sciences. Predictive range is a case in point. Whereas the most relevant terminology for the social sciences, sociology in particular, pertains to types of units, a terminology of types of conditions is relevant for all sciences, psychology and the physical-biological sciences particularly.

A sociological theory is ambiguous if it does not explicitly identify the *types* of units that would be compared when testing a constituent statement (the statement's actual testability is irrelevant). Consider this illustrative generalization: the greater the residential density, the greater the interpersonal violence rate. The reference to a rate suggests that the generalization does not pertain to individuals (i.e., they would not be compared in a test); rather, it pertains only to territorial units, because other units (e.g., organizations or associations) have no residential density. But does the generalization apply to neighborhoods, cities, urban areas, metropolitan areas, metropolitan regions, or countries? It would be ambiguous to answer "some" but tax credulity to answer "all." There is every reason to assume that no social science generalization holds for all types of units, much less equally well.

The subject is especially relevant for sociology, which has an astonishing variety of unit terms. In addition to the territorial social units mentioned previously, there are all manner of nonterritorial social units, such as occupations, age groups, marital statuses, groups, institutions, and organizations.

A theory's range is determined by the *types* of units to which it pertains. Range is difficult to judge confidently if the theorist used the discursive mode of construction (i.e., merely the conventions of a natural language, such as Spanish or English). A formal mode of theory construction facilitates assessments of range if it requires that each synthetic statement in a theory commence with a *unit phrase* that includes at least one particular *unit term*, such as "Among countries" or "For a city over time" or "Among countries and for any country over time."[10] But even if the unit terms are explicit, a rule for assessing a theory's range is needed.

A theory's range pertains to the number and inclusiveness of its unit terms. Reconsider the previous generalization about residential density and the interpersonal violence rate. If that generalization is a premise or a conclusion of a theory, the theorist must add a unit phrase to avoid ambiguity. Suppose the theorist believes that the generalization holds sufficiently (though not necessarily equally) for cities and metropolitan areas in the same country. If so, there would be two versions of that generalization in the theory, one commencing with "Among cities in the same country" and the other commencing with the phrase "Among metropolitan areas in the same country." The alternative is only one version of the generalization, commencing with the phrase "Among cities and metropolitan areas in the same country." If there are no other unit terms in the other constituent synthetic statements, then the theory's range value would be "two."

The problem stems from recognition that identification of several specific types of units (e.g., cities, metropolitan areas, age groups, organizations) is cumbersome; and the solution is to use some generic designation, such as territorial units, social units, or populations. Such designations force recognition of "inclusiveness" as a facet of range. Contemplate a comparison of four theories: A, in which the unit phrase is "Among cities"; B, in which it is "Among cities within the same country"; C, in which "Among territorial units"; and D, in which there are two unit phrases—"Among cities within the same country" and "Among organizations within the same country." If range were strictly a matter of the number of different types of unit terms, then theory D would be the greatest of the four; and the other three theories would be equal. That comparison would ignore the notion of "inclusiveness," and a rule is needed (as in the case of scope) to take that notion into account. The *general* range rule is this: when comparing the general range of two theories, a unit term of one theory is to be counted if and only if not a subclass of a unit term in the other theory. Given that "cities within the same country" is a subclass of cities and that cities is a subclass of territorial units, then the application of the rule yields the following general range differences: $A>B$, $A<C$, $A=D$, $B<C$, $B<D$, and $C=D$.

If someone were interested *only* in theories about territorial units (most unlikely), the scope equivalence of C and D would appear paradoxical. However, when the concern is exclusively with a *particular class* of unit terms or phrases (henceforth designated as "relevant"), the *specific* range rule is: a theory's specific range is greater than that of a contending theory if and only if the relevant unit term or terms of the latter is a subclass or subclasses of the unit term or terms of the former. Taking territorial units as the particular class of unit terms in question, all four of the theories in question—A, B, C, and D— can be compared as regards specific range.[11] Application of the specific range rule results in this order: $C>A$, $C>B$, $C>D$, $A>B$, $A>D$, and $B=D$.

Predictive Intensity. Defined briefly, predictive intensity is the variety of space-time relations dealt with by a theory. The bearing on predictive power should be obvious. A theory that deals with only one type of space-time relations predicts less (*ceteris paribus*) than does a theory that deals with more than one type. However, the conventional labels for designating types of space-time relations—synchronic vs. diachronic and cross-sectional vs. longitudinal—do not exhaust the logical possibilities (see Gibbs, 1982); and most statistical associations reported in the sociological literature express one particular type—synchronic and cross-sectional (two or more units of comparison, such as cities, with the values of the variables for each unit pertaining to the same time, be it a point or period).[12] So it is unfortunate that sociological theorists rarely clarify the space-time character of their empirical generalizations, and the typical generalization is ambiguous for that reason alone.

Consider a previous statement with the unit phrase added: Among cities in the same country, the greater the residential density, the greater the interpersonal violence rate. The spatial character of the assertion is clear; it pertains to all of the cities in any particular country. But what is the *temporal* character of the assertion? Does it mean that in tests the values of the two variables are to be synchronic? If so, does the statement deny the possibility of a substantial association between the variables if the values for one temporally precedes the values of the other? If the possibility of a substantial "lag" association is not denied, which variable should be lagged and what lag length (duration) would maximize the association?

The ambiguity of sociological generalizations as regards space-time considerations could be avoided readily by an explicit unit phrase in all of a theory's constituent synthetic statements and "temporal quantifiers" in the conclusions (theorems).[13] Consider this restatement of a previous generalization: Among cities within the same country, the greater the residential density at T_{0-1}, the greater the rate of interpersonal violence during T_{1-2}. The first temporal quantifier, at T_{0-1}, would be interpreted as meaning any time *point* in any historical calendar year (e.g., 1820, 1993, or 2020) and the second temporal quantifier, "during T_{1-2}," would denote the historical calendar year following whatever is taken as an instance of T_{0-1} (the calendar year prior to T_{1-2}). Sociologists are not likely to adopt such language until they abandon the discursive mode of theory construction and cease tolerating ambiguous generalizations that are supposedly testable.

The most likely objection is something like this: no theorist can deal with all types of space-time relations; hence, maximum predictive intensity never can be realized. The objection ignores the possibility of the theorist claiming that the stipulated temporal quantifiers and unit phrase *maximize* the association between the variables, meaning that the magnitude of the association will be less for *any* alternative type of space-time relation. If that claim is made, then the theory does deal with all types of space-time relations. Should the theorist be unwilling to make the claim, the theory's predictive intensity is less than maximum (how much depends on the temporal quantifiers and unit phrases).

Clarity is not the only rationale for a concern with types of space-time relations when stating a theory. If a causal assertion is made, it is not testable until translated into the language of space-time relations. The most feasible translation is to state casual premises and then deduce conclusions (theorems) in the form of *covariational* generalizations. Temporal quantifiers in the premises are not essential, but any covariational generalization is ambiguous without them. Moreover, the most common conception of causation depicts the cause as preceding the effect in time, and the immediate implication is that the magnitude of the association will be greater when the "effect" variable is lagged than when the "causal" variable is lagged. The general point is that a theorist cannot make causal assertions and yet formulate a testable theory without considering temporal quantifiers.

Discriminatory Power. Suppose that a theory comprises two testable empirical generalizations, both of which assert a positive or negative association between two variables (i.e., each generalization is bivariate). The theory may be such that the theorist has some basis for anticipating which association is the closer (e.g., if the generalizations are to be tested by computing a product-moment coefficient of correlation, the statement of theory includes a prediction as to which of the tests will yield the greatest r value). Such generalizations may be based on a principle, one possibility being something like this: the greater the number of intervening variables in the casual sequence (a path or circuit) that connects the two variables, the less the *synchronic* association between the two. The rationale is that causation entails a time lag between change in the causal variable and the effect variable; hence, if the values of the two terminal variables (one the cause and the other the effect or both mutual effects) are synchronic, the association between them will be less than it would be with the appropriate time lag.[14] Even accepting that rationale, the principle can be invoked, as part of the theory, only if it is assumed that the total "temporal length" of a causal sequence (i.e., all constituent time lags combined) is largely a direct function of the number of variables in the sequence.

Whatever the basis of the generalization about contrasts in the relative strength or closeness of particular associations, it may prove to be false. So there is a need to recognize a distinction between "potential" and "test" discriminatory power. Of course, if a theory comprises only one testable empirical generalization, discriminatory power is not a relevant dimension of predictive power; but there may be several testable generalizations in a theory and yet the theorist is unable or unwilling to anticipate differences in the magnitudes of the associations. If so, the only potential for discriminatory power lies in crude induction (i.e., test outcomes).

Parsimony. Of the seven dimensions of predictive power, parsimony most clearly illustrates why predictive accuracy and predictive power should not be equated. As defined here, parsimony has no logically necessary connection whatever with predictive accuracy.

Suppose that theory X comprises five premises and ten conclusions (theorems), while theory Y also comprises five premises but only one conclusion. As such, the conclusions/premises ratio is 2.00 for theory X but only .20 for theory Y. If the notion of parsimony (as it applies to theories) is ever to have a clear meaning, there is no obvious alternative to what is suggested by the illustration.

Should parsimony be judged in terms of the ratio of conclusions to premises, it is surely a dimension of predictive power. After all, if a theory's conclusions can be translated into predictions about particular events and things (statements about particular unknowns) and numerous conclusions are implied by one or a few premises, why deny a connection with the notion of predictive power? To be sure, some if not all of the predictions may prove false, but that possibility has to do with predictive accuracy, not parsimony.

A Complexity. Suppose that a theory clearly exceeds a particular contender with regard to, say, testability, range, and parsimony but has less when it comes to predictive accuracy, scope, intensity, and discriminatory power. Which theory should be rejected and which retained? Any choice would entail some judgment about the relative importance of the seven dimensions of predictive power, and judgments along that line are certain to generate debates that cannot be resolved. So those debates should be avoided. The ultimate goal is a theory that exceeds all contenders as regards each dimension of predictive power; hence, to avoid the premature rejection, no theory should be abandoned as long as it exceeds *all* contenders as regards at least one dimension of predictive power.

The strategy is entirely consistent with the conventional idea that scientists both create and discover order in the universe. Assuming that the nature of that order is expressed in theories, then the obvious question about any theory is this: how much order does it create? The answer comes as a response to another question: what is the theory's predictive power relative to that of contenders? The criterion's relative and quantitative character is all the more defensible if one assumes that no theory ever creates maximum order.

Nonetheless, there is a complexity concerning dimensions of predictive power. While testability is not the decisive dimension, the significance of other dimensions is greatly reduced if the theory in question is untestable. Predictive accuracy cannot be assessed at all without some defensible tests, and testability is also relevant when contemplating scope, range, intensity, discrimination, and parsimony. Indeed, if testability and predictive accuracy were irrelevant, it would be easy to formulate an awesome theory as regards all other dimensions of predictive power, though one that might appear patently absurd. Hence, unless a theory's predictive accuracy is impressive by one standard or another (e.g., it exceeds that of some contending theories), the theory should be a prime candidate for elimination.

When it comes to scope, range, intensity, discrimination, and parsimony, a distinction should be made between *ostensive* and *test* predictive power. Ostensive scope is assessed along the lines previously indicated, but in the case of test scope it is a matter of the dependent variables in the theory that have entered into one or more defensible tests.[15] Similarly, each test must be limited to instances of a specific type of unit (e.g., cities, organizations, a country over time, etc.), and an assessment of the theory's range would be limited to those types of units compared in at least one defensible test. Then in the case of a theory that deals (one way or another) with all types of space-time relations, it could be that only one type has been considered in defensible tests; if so, ostensive intensity is at a maximum, but test intensity would be near the minimum (zero if there have been no defensible tests at all). The distinction applies in much the same way to discriminatory power. A theory may be stated such that all of the testable generalizations in the theory are ordered as to expected magnitude of association between the constituent variables; if so, ostensive discriminatory power is at the maximum. Yet if there have been no tests of those expected orderings, test discriminatory power is zero. Finally, the distinction is least complicated in the case of parsimony. When reckoning *test* parsimony, untested conclusions are excluded from the calculation of the ratio of conclusions to premises.

The "ostensive-test" distinction does not apply to testability or predictive accuracy, and for the other five dimensions *test* predictive power cannot exceed *ostensive* predictive power. Nonetheless, one theory, *X*, may exceed another theory, *Y*, with regard to all dimensions of *ostensive* predictive power; and yet theory *Y* exceeds theory *X* in all dimensions of *test* predictive power. Again, however, there is no need for sterile debates over the relative importance of the two types of predictive power, ostensive or test. As before, the ultimate goal is a theory that exceeds all contenders as regards all dimensions of both types of predictive power, ostensive and test. Of course, such a theory never may be realized, but it is hardly radical to think of science as a never ending quest.

The Puzzle Concerning Predictive Power

As suggested earlier, many sociologists, perhaps the majority, ostensibly reject predictive power as the exclusive criterion for judging the merits of sociological theories. Even those who do not explicitly reject the criterion are commonly far from candid. They can be characterized as "convenience empiricists," which is to say that they accept or reject theories in light of their preconceptions or presuppositions about human nature or social life and emphasize tests only when the outcomes are consistent with their preconceptions or presuppositions.[16] Accordingly, whether or not they emphasize a theory's predictive power or lack of it depends on their *prior* acceptance or rejection of the theory for reasons (e.g., ideological) that have nothing to do with predictive power.

The notion of predictive power has been explicated at length to identify, as the second major disclaimer, an epistemological issue that no arguments or theories about control can resolve. It should be said also that the notion has been treated extensively because numerous references are made in subsequent chapters and in the Appendix to predictive power. However, the treatment would be incomplete without recognizing that the rare emphasis in sociology on the predictive power criterion is puzzling.

Alternative Criteria. The immediate puzzle is that so few sociologists make their rejection of the predictive power criterion explicit, let alone advance an alternative. Instead, they attack positivism and speak against "taking physics as the model of science," always without confronting this question: exactly what model is the alternative? The silence on the matter of criteria is puzzling if only because there are distinct alternatives to predictive power. Weberian or *verstehen* sociology is relevant because it suggests this argument: a theory has merit to the extent that it promotes understanding of the phenomena identified by the theory. That criterion is an alternative if only because Weberians are prone to deny any connection between prediction and understanding. Yet imagine a theory that generates *consistently accurate predictions* as to which individuals have engaged in robbery *and* as to the robbery rate of any territorial unit. Then imagine the theorist saying: despite the theory, I have no understanding of robbery.

The argument is not just that there is a connection between a defensible understanding of a phenomenon and predictive power; additionally, there is little prospect of agreement among those who assess the merits of a particular "understanding" unless those assessments are based on the predictive implications of that understanding. Should Weberians deny or reject that argument, they are obliged to confront two questions. First, if the understanding provided by a theory is to be judged strictly in terms of intuitive satisfaction, what basis is there for expecting agreement among sociologists in their assessments of theories? Second, if something other than intuitive satisfaction is to be the basis for judging sociological theories, what is it if not predictive power?

Essentially the same issues are generated by the proposal to judge theories in light of the notion of explanation. However, the proponents are by no means limited to some particular division of sociologists; and the "explanatory criterion" has a large following in all sciences and in philosophy, the immediate reason being the conventional belief that theories "explain." Theories do explain in one sense or another, but advocates of the explanatory criterion ignore two things. First, philosophers differ sharply when defining "explanation."[17] Second, even when two individuals agree in their definitions, they commonly differ as to what constitutes an *adequate* explanation. The second consideration introduces the present argument: judgments of the adequacy of an explanation are likely to diverge unless they are based on predictive power as the criterion of adequacy. Indeed, judgments of theories in terms of explanatory adequacy tend to be binary (i.e., the theory offers either an adequate or an inadequate explanation), but *quantitative* criteria of explanatory adequacy are more defensible and much in keeping with the present conception of predictive power.

The Puzzle Deepens. Long before the resurgence of Marxist sociology, various schools or camps of sociology (e.g., symbolic interactionists, phenomenologists, ethnomethodologists, humanists) had explicitly or implicitly rejected predictive power as the criterion for judging theories, usually as an accompaniment of an attack on positivism. However, even though Marxists are commonly avowed antipositivists, their rejection of predictive power is puzzling because they never tire of referring to "Marxist theory," which alone suggests that Marxists are more in need of a criterion for judging theories than are some other sociologists (humanists especially, because evidently they aspire to scholarly works rather than theories in the scientific sense). After all, Marxists can scarcely deny that there are contending versions of Marx's theory (or theories, as the case may be); hence, the question: by what criterion are the contending versions to be judged? An appeal to Marx himself is no answer, because exegetical Marxist sociology gave rise to the contending versions.

The present claim is that predictive power could be the criterion for judging contending versions of Marxist theory, and the same is true for all theories that are contending exemplars of some perspective or school. Of course, that claim is moot if a Marxist is determined to adopt the version of Marx that appears to be the most consistent with his/her ideology. In that case both the formulation and assessment of theories becomes irrelevant. Be that as it may, it will not do for Marxists to profess an exclusive concern with the *instrumental potential* of Marx's theory or some version of it. No assessment along that line is divorced from predictive power. Imagine someone saying: I can use this theory to such-and-such end, but that claim has no predictive implications.

At first glance there is no puzzle as to why humanists in sociology are prone to reject predictive power as the criterion for judging theories. The reference is actually always to *scientific* theories, and humanists commonly come close to a rejection of the very idea of scientific sociology. Yet they are prone to stop short of an explicit and categorical rejection, which suggests that they perhaps reject not "scientific sociology" but objectionable beliefs associated with it. There are at least three possibilities in the way of objectionable beliefs: first, that physical scientists are concerned only with predictive accuracy; second, that the predictive accuracy of sociological theories can equal that of physical theories; and, third, the assumption of determinism is imperative for all of the sciences. Actually, what advocates of scientific sociology do or do not believe is debatable; but in any event, the three beliefs have absolutely no bearing on the proposal that predictive power be taken as the criterion for judging sociological theories. Perhaps that recognition may prompt some humanists in sociology to rethink their opposition to the criterion; but, to state the major disclaimer again, no argument or theory about control can resolve the epistemological issue in question.

Notes

1. It would be grossly misleading to suggest that advocates of the "externalist" view of science answer the question. They purport to answer the question "How *do* scientists evaluate scientific theories," while appearing at great pains to ignore a quite different question: "How *should* scientists evaluate scientific theories?" The latter question goes beyond ethical considerations if one is concerned with promoting consensus in assessments of scientific theories.

2. So it is hardly surprising that a multitude of sociologists embraced Kuhn's arguments (1962) with unbridled enthusiasm. Never mind that (1) the arguments are far too vague for anything like systematic tests, (2) Kuhn himself did not view his arguments as relevant for sociology, (3) he used the term "paradigm" in a bewildering manner (Masterman, 1970, alleges 22 different meanings), and (4) most sociologists appear blissfully unaware that (Hull, 1988:111) "With hardly an exception, professional philosophers were irritated if not appalled by [Kuhn's] book."

3. Following Kuhn (1962), it has become fashionable to presume that because a theory-free observation language or datum is impossible there cannot be anything like contending theories about the same phenomena. Stated more succinctly and in Kuhn's terms, theories are "incommensurable." Pawson (1989:116–122) is one of the very few sociologists who rejects the claim that incommensurability is an insurmountable problem, but many philosophers of science have voiced doubts about the claim. Hull (1988:492–496) has treated the issue at length, and one quote expresses his judgment: "The trouble with the [argument] is that occurrences that should be impossible happen all the time." However, it should be added that Kuhn's incommensurability argument derives from his insistence on externalism, the claim being (evidently) that scientists accept or reject scientific theories because of considerations divorced from science *per se*, such as class interests. The thesis makes Kuhn vulnerable to a common criticism—that he cannot account for progress in science or science's success (see, especially, Banner, 1990:7–33). Of course, since 1962 Kuhn has restated his views (see Hull, 1988) to the point that no one can say incontrovertibly what his position is or was.

4. The internal logical consistency of a theory is not something removed from predictive accuracy. Contradictory predictions reduce predictive accuracy, and they are the most consequential manifestation of an internally *inconsistent* theory.

5. The procedure would be the same for an undefined term, and the point takes on special significance because there are some undefined terms in all theories. Note, however, that there are two types of such primitive terms: (1) empirical primitives, those that enter into the definition of other terms in the theory; and (2) theoretical primitives, those that do not enter into the definition of other terms. The distinction is all the more important because a term may have great utility and be absolutely essential for a theory even though the theorist does not regard the term as empirically applicable. Stating the matter another way, unlike operationalism, the suggestion is not that all of a theory's constituent terms must be empirically applicable; defensible tests of a theory are possible even though some of its terms are not considered by the theorist as being empirically applicable. Finally, the empirical applicability of a theory's terms has no necessary

connection with the theory's validity; rather, empirical applicability of some terms is necessary for assessments of validity.

6. No particular number of investigators could provide conclusive evidence, for the same outcomes would not obtain necessarily for still other investigators. Should that consideration engender rejection of the notion of empirical applicability, the rejection would stem from the mistaken belief that the dilemma of induction can be avoided; and it would reflect a demand for certainty, a demand alien to science.

7. Of course, a field's conventions could be such that independent investigators realize agreement without definitions, stipulations of formulas, or data instruction; but that condition is totally alien to the social and behavioral sciences.

8. An argument could be made for considering all of the variables in a theory, dependent or independent. In that case, however, the appropriate designation would be *total* scope, and scope's connection with explanatory power is more obvious if defined in terms of dependent variables. However, a variable may be both independent and dependent in the same theory; if so, it is treated as a dependent variable.

9. Although the wording becomes cumbersome and complicated, the rule can be extended to the case of more than one dependent variable in either or both of the contending theories. However, in any case, the dependent variables must be subclasses of or equivalent to the particular larger class in question ("mental illness" in the illustration).

10. Nothing precludes the use of qualifying words, such as "urbanized countries," or even words that denote a condition, such as "countries undergoing a civil war."

11. Whether two theories are considered as contenders is primarily a matter of their constituent constructs or concepts, not their unit terms. However, if two theories are considered as contenders because of their constituent constructs or concepts, one question in judging their relative merits is: which has the greater range?

12. The spatial reference is hardly esoteric; any unit term, even "individuals," denotes spatial entities. Observe also that there is no overlap between the spatial quality of the synthetic statements in a theory and the notion of predictive range. Every empirical generalization pertains to some type of spatial relation and some type of temporal relation, but the "spatial" has no connection with the variety of types of unit terms in a theory. More specifically, an empirical generalization that asserts something about change in one spatial entity over time differs from an empirical generalization about contrasts between or among two or more spatial entities (not what is taken as the same entity over time); but the nature of those entities, whether they are cities, countries, individuals, or what have you, is irrelevant as far as *types of space-time relations* are concerned. Thus, there is no necessary logical connection between the predictive intensity of a theory—the variety of types of space-time relations dealt with by the theory—and the theory's predictive range (the variety of unit terms in the theory).

13. If a theorist is unable or unwilling to clarify the space-time character of an empirical generalization, publication of the theory would be premature. However, specification of the temporal character of asserted relations (the length of lags, if any, between variables) is imperative only in the case of conclusions, which are supposedly the testable constituent statements. A premise, whether causal or covariational, need not precisely specify the temporal character of the asserted relation.

14. The theorist aims, of course, to identify the time-lag length that maximizes the association; and if he/she overestimates or underestimates the length of the lag, the observed (measured) association may be less than is the synchronic association.

15. Such is the case even when the unit term is a generic designation, such as "Among territorial units." In any test there could be a mixture of specific types of units (e.g., cities in some constituent statements, countries in others), but such a mixture might conceal a very real possibility: that the theory's predictive accuracy is highly contingent on the type of units compared in the tests.

16. Writing as a philosopher of science, Richard Miller (1987:4) characterized the social sciences as "where hypotheses are most apt to be judged on purely methodological grounds." To the contrary, many sociologists could not care less about methodology; indeed, self-avowed humanists typically argue that too much attention is paid to methodology.

17. Consider Richard Miller's assessment (1987:15) of the situation: "The dispute over the nature of explanation is one of the most heated in the philosophy of science." Yet Miller persists in making explanation central.

2

Control, Types of Control, and Power

If only because control is the principal subject of the theory set forth in Chapters 3–7, an elaborate conceptualization is needed. Such conceptualization runs contrary to a pernicious belief that is all too common in sociology: constructive research and impressive theories are possible without confronting conceptual issues or problems. Examine Tallman's commentary (1984:1121): "Efforts to explicate key concepts in sociology have generally been met with stifling indifference by members of our discipline." The commentary is misleading only in that it (1) suggests sociologists are consistently explicit in expressing their indifference to conceptualizations and (2) ignores hostility to conceptualizations.

Conceptualization of Attempted Control

Defined generically, attempted control is *overt* behavior by a human in the belief that (1) the behavior increases or decreases the probability of some subsequent condition and (2) the increase or decrease is desirable. Overt behavior is the commission *or* omission of an act; and the "subsequent condition" may either be an organism's behavior or the existence, location, composition, color, size, weight, shape, odor, temperature, or texture of some object or substance, be it animate or inanimate, observable or unobservable. The condition may or may not take the form of a change, meaning that one may act or refrain in the belief that the commission or omission increases or decreases the probability of change. Finally, the definition of attempted control may bring to mind the notion of power, particularly Weber's treatment of the notion (especially 1978:53); but the connection between control and power is a subject best left to the end of this chapter.

An alternative definition of attempted control could be something like this: overt behavior that is intended to have a specific consequence.[1] Such terminology has been avoided because the conventional meaning of intentional behavior is too narrow. An intentional act is commonly thought of as preceded by deliberation and conscious anticipation of a specific consequence. That conception differs from the present definition of attempted control because of three key terms: deliberation, conscious anticipation, and specific consequence. Think of someone driving a car. To describe his/her gripping the steering wheel as "intentional" in the sense just indicated would be misleading. Drivers are rarely aware of gripping the wheel, nor do they often consciously anticipate some specific consequence of releasing that grip. So much of driving behavior lacks the intentional quality of, say, an assassin firing a gun, but who would deny that drivers grip the wheel in the belief that the behavior decreases the probability of something *undesirable*?

One counterargument—we have beliefs only when conscious of them—is flawed. If humans could not act without consciously anticipating specific consequences, their survival would be jeopardized. Reconsider gripping the steering wheel. Although that behavior is usually habitual and unreflective, surely it is reasonable to infer that the driver grips in the belief that it reduces the probability of *some kind* of collision. Granted, the phrase "behavior-in-the-belief-that" is cumbersome and unconventional. The phrase "with knowledge of" may appear more appropriate; but it does not communicate the *affective* facet of the belief—that some anticipated consequences of behavior are desirable and others undesirable.

When identifying and classifying human behavior in connection with the present conceptualization of attempted control, social or behavioral scientists need not claim to know the *actual* thoughts and feelings of those who are being observed (i.e., to "get into the actor's mind"). In identifying and classifying a particular act in a particular social unit, the crucial question for the observer is: what related thoughts and feelings would the typical social unit member attribute to the actor? As the question suggests, no one should apply the conceptual scheme in any social unit unless he/she has extensive knowledge of that social unit, especially the kind of knowledge that anthropologists pursue in their field studies. Some disagreements are inevitable even in the case of extremely knowledgeable observers, but the conceptualization's *degree* of empirical applicability is another matter. To be sure, the degree could be increased by the development of standard observation procedures, and interpretive sociologists could lead the way if they would only curb their solipsistic tendencies and recognize the need for sociology to have a natural history tradition *as a means rather than an end*. Unfortunately, however, the argument that all terms are "theory laden" has been promoted by avowed antipositivists so much that the prospects for a natural history stage in sociology are now very dim.

Successful (Effective) Control

The concern is with *attempts at control* if only because the success-failure distinction bears on Control Principle 2–1: individuals tend to repeat those types of attempted control that they perceive as having been more successful than alternatives.[2] While the principle makes operant psychology relevant, it does not belittle vicarious learning.

Many social and behavioral scientists will have misgivings about defining control by reference to beliefs, and some of them explicitly state that control may be intentional or unintentional (e.g., Dahl, 1982:17); but without that reference the distinction between successful and unsuccessful control is lost, along with the repetitional principle (*supra*). Both are maintained here by this definition of successful or effective control: when a human engages in attempted control, it is successful *to the extent* that he/she perceives the condition in question as having been realized, maintained, or avoided. So conceived, successful or effective control is both perceptual and a matter of degree. For some purposes, it is relevant to consider also the success-failure perceptions of targets of attempted control, or of anyone who comes to know of the attempt; but those perceptions can be treated as contingent properties of attempted control rather than a success-failure criterion. In any case, the question for the observer is: what perceptions would the typical social unit member attribute to the individual or individuals being observed?

Indefensible Contenders. As for distinguishing successful and unsuccessful control *without* reference to cognitive and/or affective facets of internal behavior, the first of four possible opposing criteria (all of the "overt-behavior-only" type) is this: human behavior is successful control if and only if it has an environmental consequence. The objection is not just that virtually all overt human behavior has some environmental consequence. Think of an individual backing out of a bank with a gun in hand and being shot by a police officer. Presuming that the officer's behavior was caused by the robber's behavior, it follows that the robber "controlled" the police officer.[3] So the overt-behavior-only criterion of control invites absurdities.

Second contending criterion: an instance of overt behavior is successful control if and only if all known previous instances have been followed by an event of some particular type. But such invariant associations scarcely exist. To illustrate, because there have been instances where a police officer shouted "Halt!" without a discernible effect, then according to the "invariant association" criterion no instance is successful control, not even when someone halts. Nothing is gained by speaking of "*most* instances." Thus, if in 51 percent of past cases where a police officer shouted "Halt!" no one nearby ceased moving, it would be absurd to identify instances of halting as *unsuccessful* control. Why would shouting "Halt!" be attempted control in light of the present definition?

Because the typical social unit member would say that the officer acted in the belief that (1) such action increases the probability of an individual halting and (2) the increase is desirable.

Third contending criterion: an act is successful control if and only if it has a consequence that the actor perceived as probable. The criterion recognizes only the *cognitive* facet of internal behavior (perceptions of causation); so consider one illustrative implication of ignoring the *affective* facet. Various surgical operations are virtually certain to result in discomfort, and surgeons know it. Accordingly, accepting the third alternative criterion, should the patient feel discomfort after surgery, then the operation was successful control even if the patient dies. Why? Because the surgery had a consequence—a feeling of discomfort—that the surgeon anticipated. Why is surgery attempted control in light of the definition advanced here? Surgeons evidently operate in the belief that it increases the probability of some subsequent *desirable* condition. Would the operation be successful control? Only to the extent the surgeon perceives some anticipated desirable condition as having been realized. However, it is not denied that the "desire for control" (see Burger, 1992) may vary substantially even among members of a relatively otherwise homogeneous population, but at the same time it is not denied that people are "persistently motivated to improve their control of outcomes" (Friedman and Lackey, 1991:13).

The fourth and final contending criterion: an act is successful control if and only if repeated. Suppose that a hunter crouches near a pond for hours and returns to camp without any game but repeats the action the next day; as such, the first day's action was successful control. That astonishing implication is not the only objection; the criterion in question ignores something essential for human survival—goal persistence despite *failures* in control attempts (in this case, the failure to make a kill). The notion of a goal relates to internal behavior, both cognitive and affective; and the importance of goal persistence is not limited to human predation. Consider some observations from a psychoanalytic perspective (Tolpin and Kohut, 1989:240): "healthy human children preserve the confidence that they have the power to get what they want despite the fact that, from birth on, actual experience frequently teaches them otherwise." Similar observations can be made about human curiosity and control, especially information seeking as a consequence of control failures or control impotence (see Swann, *et al.*, 1981; and Friedman and Lackey, 1991).

The Larger Issue

The present conceptualization presumes that descriptions of overt behavior are bound to distort unless reference is made to internal behavior. Observers do not literally *see* people saluting, robbing, reaching, signaling, fighting, kissing, eating, or killing, to mention only a few acts. To be sure, in all instances there are observable ectodermic movements, as when the hand comes into contact with the forehead; but to define those acts only by reference to movement (i.e., ignoring internal behavior) is contrary to the English language and everyday experience.[4] Searle's observation (1983:105) is especially relevant: "If I am asked, 'Why did he raise his arm?,' it sounds odd to say, 'Because he intended to raise his arm.' The reason it sounds odd is because by identifying the action as 'raising his arm' we have already identified it in terms of the intention in action."

That humans continually infer the intentions, beliefs, or perceptions of others, contemplate how readily we are surprised by incomplete acts, as when someone walks to a ringing telephone but never lifts the receiver. We are commonly only dimly aware of inferring internal behavior because we do it often without surprises. However, it hardly need be said that the association between overt behavior and internal behavior may not be even remotely the same in all social units, and that consideration is the primary rationale for social and behavioral scientists relying on the inferences of what they take to be the typical social unit member. Yet that reliance is not merely dictated by the impossibility of "observing" internal behavior. Humans continually attribute internal behavior (intention, motive, etc.), and a vast literature indicates that human behavior is (1) mediated by intentions and (2) commonly determined by the actor's perception of the evaluative standards of significant others. The bulk of that literature (see, e.g., Brinberg, 1979) is associated with psychology, but indifference to it by sociologists perpetuates robotic sociology.

Some Anticipated Objections

One likely argument against accepting control as sociology's central notion stems from a presumption—that attempted control encompasses a very limited range of behavior. Extending the argument, humans rarely pursue specific goals consciously and deliberately; rather, human behavior is commonly habitual and unreflective, without rational calculation of any cost-benefit.

The key terms in the argument—consciously, deliberately, habitual, unreflective, calculation, rational cost, and benefit—suggest an instrumental, hedonistic quality of behavior, a suggestion that distorts no less than Durkheim's robotic image of humans. However, a control terminology can be used to describe the actions of instrumental hedonists; and ignoring them would reflect an indifference to human history, one crowded with grasping manipulators, whose recognition in classical sociological theory is largely limited to Pareto's ramblings (especially 1935).

Many sociological notions are lifeless in that they appear removed from an awful feature of human existence—things often go wrong: Sam has lost his job,

Debra's husband beats her, Alex is threatened with eviction.[5] Moreover, when trouble comes, people usually do not merely cringe; they try to do something about it (one of many phrases meaning "to attempt control").

It is pointless to depict social life as governed by putative norms and yet grant that things go wrong even for assiduous conformists (perhaps Sam lost his job despite his diligence). For that matter, if norms actually govern social life, why do sociologists study deviance with gusto? It will not do to answer, along with Durkheim (1938 [1895]), that deviance is normal. That answer only raises doubts about norms as behavioral determinants (see Edgerton, 1985). Finally, how can sociologists write about power without recognizing that the notion is metaphysical unless it somehow refers to control?

Should a sociologist object that previous illustrations of the inapplicability of sociological terminology are "micro," the objection misleadingly suggests that sociology is truly relevant for all human concerns at the "macro" level. Think of terrorism and nuclear arms control. Those phenomena are surely genuine human concerns and macro by any definition; but sociologists have had little to say on either subject, leaving thoughtful commentaries to others (e.g., O'Brien, 1986, and Dahlitz, 1983).

Sociological terminology, principles, and theories are commonly divorced not just from human concerns; they rarely have real bearing on purposive human phenomenon, micro or macro. If the argument appears exaggerated, examine Donald Black's ostensible conception of an ideal sociological theory (1976:7), as one that "neither assumes nor implies that [the individual] is...rational, goal directed, pleasure seeking, or pain avoiding." The suggested indifference to human behavior's purposive quality may be even greater in such sociological specialties as human ecology and demography, whose subject matter appears less cultural or symbolic than is the case for the sociology of law, Black's specialty.[6] However, Black's candor is commendable; he has made his predilection explicit, something many sociologists fail to do.

Narrow Conceptions of Control

One particular anticipated objection—control behavior is rare—reflects more than a robotic image of humans.[7] The objection is consistent with two widespread beliefs about control that most sociologists seemingly accept but seldom acknowledge, even though the beliefs are conducive to a very narrow conception of control: first, control is evil; and, second, targets of attempted behavioral control are always particular (specific) individuals.

The first belief is rejected here for a reason unrelated to the conventional argument that scientists should have no truck with the notion of evil because it entails value judgments. Rather, by any reasonable standard all manner of attempts at control over human behavior are benign, normatively neutral, or perhaps even laudatory. Picture an adult rushing into a burning house and forcibly removing a hysterical child. The adult's action would be control (indeed, *coercive* control) but hardly evil. For that matter, it is more accurate to say that "evil requires control" than "control is evil." Consider one of Liebow's observations (1967:29) on a Washington, D.C., street frequented by a group of black men in the early 1960s:

> A pickup truck drives slowly down the street. The truck stops as it comes abreast of a man sitting on a cast-iron porch and the white driver calls out, asking if the man wants a day's work. The man shakes his head and the truck moves on up the block, stopping again whenever idling men come within calling distance of the driver.

Many sociologists would rightly regard the behavior of the labor scavenger as an evil, a degrading feature of capitalism and indicative of the exploitative character of American race relations. Their indignation may lead them to overlook the obvious—that the evil is an *attempt at control.*

Now consider two other widespread beliefs in sociology that are also conducive to a narrow conception of control: (1) the control *goal* is always to manipulate the behavior of particular individuals and (2) macro human phenomena cannot be described or thought of in terms of control. The first belief ignores the controlled exercised by humans over other nonhuman organisms, as in animal or plant domestication, and over inanimate objects or substances, as when creating *or* using a tool. Moreover, even when control is limited to human targets, it is not confined to attempts at controlling the behavior of particular individuals. To illustrate, when a store owner places signs on the building's exterior, surely he/she believes that the signs increase the probability of attracting customers in general and not just particular individuals.

Then think of law and advertising. Human control is the name of the game in those institutions; but the target is an indefinite category, all potential offenders or all consumers. If the illustrations do not pertain to the "macro," that term's meaning is hopelessly abstruse.

The idea of indefinite control targets takes on special significance in light of this argument: to control someone is to thwart their will or overcome their resistance (note the connotation of "evil"). To illustrate, when someone builds a formidable wall around his/her house, uncountable individuals never had the intention to enter the house by stealth or force; therefore, so the argument goes (Oppenheim, 1961), the wall makes such individuals "unfree" but does not control them. The argument confuses two questions about a particular act. First, was the act attempted control? Second, if so, who were the targets? Agreement in answers to the second question is not necessary for agreement in answers to the first. Moreover, the house owner may have built the wall in the belief that it decreases the probability of *anyone* entering the home by stealth or force; if so, the target of the control attempt was an infinite set of individuals. Finally, there is no basis to argue that positive submission or willing compliance to a command or request makes it something less or different from a control attempt.

Some Elaborate Illustrations

Despite the foregoing, critics may persist in objecting that control attempts are for too rare for control to be sociology's central notion. Hence, more illustrations are needed.

Modes of Dress. In dressing for work, a man or woman may not think of his/her actions as avoiding punishment; yet it would be attempted control if in dressing he/she believed that public nakedness increases the probability of an undesirable condition. Do men and women dress for public appearance in that belief? No one familiar with American life would doubt it; but note the implication—dressing is countercontrol in that it is believed to decrease the probability of being controlled, such as being arrested.[8] True, the dresser's beliefs may not pertain to a legal punishment, but that point is conceptually irrelevant.

Should sociologists stoop to explain "dressing," they would have no basis for saying something more than this: the act is conformity. The implied explanation ignores deviance and reflects an insensitivity to human behavior's purposive quality. No notion furthers that insensitivity more than does "norms," even though it is another candidate for sociology's central notion. Social scientists resort to normative explanations frequently, despite the obvious problem posed by deviance (see Edgerton, 1985). Moreover, sociologists rarely actually study putative norms; instead, they blithely take norms as given and ignore this question: for this particular social unit, why are the norms what they are? If the notion of norms can be justified, an adequate answer requires reference to control.

Insofar as norms can be defined and identified defensibly,[9] they vary from one social unit to another; hence, an assessment of an adequate explanation of putative American dress norms requires reference to dress norms elsewhere. So why is wearing an overcoat a putative American norm of seasonal dress? Contemplate this reply: because the U.S. is not a tropical country. If the explanation appears absurd, note its consistency with putative dress norms in numerous other countries. However, whatever its merits, the explanation is incomplete without recognition that clothing may be worn as a means of inanimate control, a way of reducing exposure to the elements.

The reference to inanimate control suggests that humans may dress so as to avoid physical discomfort; but thinking of socio-cultural phenomena in terms of control does not necessarily lead to grotesque oversimplifications, such as asserting that all clothing is worn as "comfortable inanimate control." The very body position of clothing commonly suggests some connection with sex, but the argument that clothing has something to do with controlling sexual relations in no way implies invariant modes of dress. Nevertheless, there are some predictable objections. Polhemus and Procter (1978:10) may be quoted as stating that "climate does not always determine whether or not clothes are worn," but without recognition that *insofar as climate does determine clothing* it does only through attempts of humans to control conditions. Likewise, critics will be incorrect if they depict the present argument as assuming that humans are naturally prudish or even that clothing is universal.

To analyze dress as means of control is a far cry from a theory, though more informative than the conventional reification—society or culture "defines" proper clothing. The immediate point is that clothing facilitates controls that have nothing to do with weather or sexual relations. A few studies provide evidence that certain kinds of uniforms facilitate effective human control (e.g., Bickman, 1974), although many sociologists may be indifferent because of their preoccupation with structural variables. Be that as it may, human control in military units is furthered by uniforms that distinguish not only "hostiles" and "friendlies" but also superordinates and subordinates.

Now consider the dress of a Victorian male elite in London, complete with cape, gloves, and a cane. Veblen would speak of conspicuous consumption, but that characterization has no more explanatory value than a strictly psychological description (e.g., such dress reflects vanity). By contrast, think of the elite's dress in terms of control. It increases the probability of attention and deference, which is to say control over others (e.g., waiters).

A likely objection to the Victorian illustration: in dressing the elite did not intend to control others. "Intent" in the conscious and deliberate sense is far less relevant than this question: in dressing did the elite believe that his dress mode increased the probability of a deferential response and that such responses are desirable? If so, the elite engaged in attempted control.

Nothing has been said about why the elite wanted to control others, valued control, etc. The immediate goal is to describe an elite's behavior in terms of control rather than pretend to answer this question: why do individuals want to control behavior? Perhaps that question would have to be answered to explain an elite's mode of dress,[10] but taking control as their central notion would not commit sociologists to motivational questions or explaining individual differences. When sociologists cease chattering about structure and function, the field's generic question becomes: why is such-and-such type of behavior more frequent in some social units than in others?

So the presumption of the illustration is that male elite dress (a type of behavior) was much more relevant in Victorian London than, say, in a small Iowa town. Why? Describing "dress" as attempted control does not explain the contrast, but describing phenomena in terms of control facilitates explanations. In the case at hand, one possibility is contrast in population size and, correlatively, that London elites interacted with and attempted to control strangers more than did small-town Iowa elites. But why would either condition be relevant? An answer is suggested by recognizing that modes of dress are attempts at control, especially in anonymous, impersonal situations.

The foregoing contradicts conventional sociological wisdom, according to which humans conform to norms as an end in itself. To the contrary, humans conform *to control others* (Edgerton, 1985:9, refers ambiguously to "manipulation of rules"). Granted, once a type of behavior becomes predominant in a social unit, there is something akin to pressure for conformity; but when someone conforms in the belief that to do otherwise invites ridicule or loss or injury, conformity is attempted control.

The argument extends to Merry's allusion (1984:271) to gossip's "power to control behavior." Even accepting the reification, gossip controls behavior only when humans refrain from some types of conduct because of fear of what others will say about or do to them.[11] Williamson's observations (1984:117) on American history provides a depressing example of a different but related phenomenon: "That the number of lynchings decreased after 1892 might be attributed primarily to a rising caution among black men that led them to avoid occasions that could possibly be twisted into a semblance of rape or an attempt at rape. Almost certainly, black men came generally to avoid being alone with white women, were careful not to meet feminine eyes with a level gaze, and guarded the tone of their voices in the presence of white females." Such behavior was no novelty for blacks, who had long since learned to appear simple, docile, and manageable in the presence of whites; but "playing Sambo" was attempted countercontrol.

The argument that putative norms come into being and are perpetuated in connection with control is more informative than the conventional view: norms emerge for obscure reasons and are perpetuated by tradition.[12] Then consider the functionalist view: norms emerge and are perpetuated because they meet some societal need. Insofar as any collectivity can be said to have needs, the need of one societal division (e.g., the need of capitalists to hire labor at the lowest possible wage) may be inimical to the need of another division (the proletariat's need for more than bare subsistence).

Beyond Modes of Dress. Consider Control Principle 2–2, the *effectiveness principle*: humans tend to employ only those types, kinds, or means of control that they perceive as effective. That generalization is consistent with the argument that the putative norms of some social units exist because some or all members perceive them as facilitating control. Then there is a more general argument: sociological principles should reflect recognition that humans govern their behavior in light of beliefs about consequences (see, especially, Friedman and Lackey, 1991), and to that end no concept rivals control.

Another consideration is that humans perceive events in terms of cause and effect, often without experimentation. Thus, actual experience is not needed for individuals to perceive a connection between appearing in public naked and punitive reactions, but the how and why of causal perceptions are not *conceptually* relevant. Nevertheless, the present conceptualization of control tacitly emphasizes that humans do perceive events in casual terms.

Additional Illustrations. Now reconsider someone speaking to a friend. Observers might disagree about the response anticipated, but that is conceptually irrelevant when identifying "speaking to someone" as attempted control.

Plowing illustrates why there is no fundamental conceptual difference between attempts to control animate things (e.g., growing wheat) and attempts to control human behavior or inanimate things. Why? Humans have beliefs about causal connections and govern their behavior accordingly. However, whereas the farmer believes that plowing is *necessary* for a crop, the speaker believes that speaking is *sufficient* for altering the friend's overt behavior. Then, unlike some instances of speaking, plowing is *cumulative* control; the farmer believes that a series of different actions (e.g., plowing, planting, weeding) taken together are necessary for a harvestable crop.

When attempted control takes the form of a series of similar acts, each attempt is *repetitional* control. Thus, a homemaker rarely consciously perceives the preparation of a particular meal as necessary or sufficient for maintaining the partner's domestic behavior; but should the homemaker cease preparing family meals indefinitely and for no ostensible reason, an eventual marked alteration in the partner's behavior would not be puzzling. Such a situation indicates the actor's belief that a repetition of acts maintains or alters someone's behavior, but the homemaker is unlikely to believe that repeated preparations of family meals are sufficient to maintain the partner's behavior; rather, they are only necessary along with a series of other kinds of acts (e.g., shopping). Accordingly, preparations of family meals are more accurately labeled "cumulative-repetitional."

What has been said of the homemaker applies also to the partner trudging to work without consciously anticipating being fired for doing otherwise. The similarity suggests that cumulative-repetitional control is very common; hence, there is at least one basis for describing and thinking about the continuity of social life in terms of control.

The foregoing types of control are somewhat complex, but human behavior is too complicated for simple conceptualizations. As a case in point, contemplate the connection between social relations and human control. The behavioral manifestation of a social relation is a series of acts, and control is often realized only through serial acts; so the notion of cumulative-repetitional control is especially relevant in analyzing social relations.

Finally, in imposing a prison term on a convicted felon the judge believes that such a sentence is necessary to incarcerate the defendant, and he/she may further believe that the sentence contributes to deterrence. The word "contributes" is strategic because no judge is likely to believe that imposing only one sentence has a discernible impact on the crime rate; rather, a judge is likely to believe that each sentence is only one of numerous actions by numerous legal officials, which taken together reduce the crime rate. Such *contributory* control differs from the repetitional and cumulative in that those who engage in it believe that their actions *along with those of others* increase or decrease the probability of some condition (a kind of control akin to Power's conception [1984] of collaboration and the related notion of mutual intention).

Contributory control is only one subclass of multilateral control. Another subclass, *representational* control, occurs when two or more individuals agree that the outcome of their interactions is to be construed by them as a command or directive to themselves and/or to others. Such control is conspicuous in legislative actions, but it may be an agreement between any two individuals that either speaks or otherwise acts for both.

The foregoing distinctions do not remotely exhaust the possibilities (see, e.g., Burns, 1958), but not even a very elaborate typology of control would suffice. The variety of control attempts beggars description, and in the final analysis distinctions should depend on research or theoretical interests.

Basic Types: Inanimate Control

Attempted inanimate control is overt behavior by a human in the belief that (1) the behavior increases or decreases the probability of an inanimate thing's existence or a change in the thing's characteristics and (2) the increase or decrease is desirable. An inanimate thing is any lifeless object or substance (observable or not); and a characteristic may pertain to any property, such as location, shape, size, weight, color, composition, texture, or odor.

When the first primate threw a rock at a predator, he/she engaged in *locational* inanimate control to facilitate biotic control—to drive off an animal. Such control is rare among animals, but the primate altered only the rock's location. The next and revolutionary stage in inanimate control—the *transformational*—was the modification of inanimate things, such as stripping a twig preliminary to inserting it into a nest and pulling out insects to eat, as chimpanzees do. From that stage onward, inanimate control increasingly became technological.

Technology

Appreciable agreement is realized in identifying *some* things as technological, but what do they share in common that makes them distinctive? Little is gained by replying that they are tools or machines. The meaning of either term is too vague for consensus in answers to several questions. Are the following things tools or machines: shoes, maps, computers, gasoline, bolts, buckets, sails, eyeglasses, pencils, houses, sweaters, ropes, and gates? If so, why? If not, why not? If only some of those things qualify, which ones? Of those that do not qualify, what is the rationale for excluding them from "technology"?

Proposed Definition. For reasons just suggested, "tool" and "machine" are unsuitable terms for defining technology. So the following definition encompasses all *unquestioned* tools or machines and much more: technology includes all inanimate things made or modified by humans, excluding human food.[13] Not all features of an object or substance need be modified. If a piece of flint has been chipped in some pattern, its ensuing shape alone makes it technological, even though its composition has not been altered. Likewise, when preparing a field for planting, it is the holes or furrows that make the field technological. Once made or modified, an inanimate thing's subsequent use is conceptually irrelevant; and some things used for a human purpose are not technological, such as throwing an *unmodified* rock at an animal.

The proposed definition furthers agreement in classifying things, meaning that it promises appreciable empirical applicability. Thus, in addition to unquestioned tools and machines, technology includes (*inter alia*) shoes, maps, gasoline, bolts, buckets, sails, eyeglasses, pencils, houses, sweaters, ropes, and gates.

Anticipated Objections. For obscure reasons, some writers accept a "material" definition but only if it limits technology to things used to realize physical goals. Although that terminology is less ambiguous than "useful purpose" (Oswalt, 1976:24), difficult questions are raised. Used by whom and how many? Must the use be uniform? If not, what criteria determine predominant use?

As the questions indicate, the phrase "material things used to realize physical goals" is ambiguous; and the suggested exclusion of symbolic artifacts from technology is especially debatable. A painting is surely symbolic; but if hanging a painting in a room is not the pursuit of a physical goal, what is it? Then what of symbolic artifacts (e.g., traffic lights) that are used to control human behavior? Likewise, why display paintings in an art gallery if not to attract people? The general point is that exclusion of instruments of behavior control when defining technology (see Lenski and Lenski's definition, *infra*) greatly diminishes the notion's significance.

If technology is defined in terms of "use" rather than *origin*, the definition blurs the distinction between analytic and synthetic statements about technology. In particular, many technological items appear efficient in that their use reduces the time and/or human energy required to realize physical goals; but if technology is so defined, the claim that technology is efficient becomes tautological.

Other definitions (*infra*) suggest that technology includes not only material things but also (1) knowledge pertaining to those things and (2) the procedure by which goods, services, commodities, or benefits are produced, including the organization of production (e.g., corporations, the division of labor, assembly lines). But to designate particular kinds of knowledge as technological makes the notion extremely broad, and why not speak simply of "technical knowledge"? Moreover, if the organization of production is identified as technology, then a well-known argument—the latter determines the former (see, e.g., Marsh and Mannari, 1981)—suggests that technology determines technology. Such confusion stems from implicit rejections of material definitions of technology, such as: "A final reason that advanced technologies have more division of labor is that a high degree division of labor is *part* of an advanced technology." (Stinchcombe, 1983:89) The argument blurs the distinction between a conceptual link and an empirical association. Similarly, granted that "No tool exists apart from social organization, or from ideas and beliefs." (White, 1973:13), why establish the connection as a matter of definition?

   Some Contending Definitions. Frisbie and Clarke (1979) notwithstanding, subsequent quotations demonstrate great diversity in definitions of technology (see also, especially, Winner, 1977, and Wagner, 1979).

BARBOUR (1980:35): "Technology may be defined as 'the organization of knowledge for the achievement of practical purposes.' It is a set of skills, techniques, and activities for the shaping of materials and the production of objects for practical ends... ... We will be using the term technology to refer to a broad set of human activities, and not simply to the machines and tools that constitute the hardware of technology."

BIMBER (1990:341): "I will treat technology as physical artefact or machine, as well as the material elements of the processes by which artefacts are produced."

GENDRON (1977:23): "A technology is any systematized practical knowledge, based on experimentation and/or scientific theory, which enhances the capacity of society to produce goods and services, and which is embodied in productive skills, organization, or machinery."

HANNAY and MCGINN (1980:27): "As for...content...let us define *a technology* as the complex of knowledge, methods, and other resources used in making a particular kind of product or in creating a particular procedural system."

LENSKI and LENSKI (1987:434): "**Technology** Cultural information about the ways in which the material resources of the environment may be used to satisfy human needs and desires."

OSWALT (1976:24, 33): "An artifact is the end product resulting from the modification of a physical mass in order to fulfill a useful purpose. ... Technology may be defined as all the ways in which people produce artifacts..."

RICHTER (1982:8): "for present purposes it will be most convenient to abandon the conception of technology-as-knowledge, and to define technology to encompass *tools and practices deliberately employed as natural (rather than supernatural) means for attaining clearly identifiable ends.*"

WEINSTEIN (1982:xi): "*technology* refers primarily to a system of knowledge intended to have practical bearing—know-how."

WHITE (1975:17): "Technology consists of tools and weapons and techniques of using them."

Issues and Problems. The notion of a "real" definition notwithstanding, definitions are never demonstrably true or false; but assessments of them can transcend purely personal opinion, especially as regards empirical applicability. A definition is empirically applicable to the extent that independent investigators (1) regard it as intelligible, (2) indicate that its application is feasible, and (3) realize congruent outcomes when applying it to identify or describe particular events or things (including, possibly, the computation of numerical values).

Actual attempts by independent researchers to apply a definition are essential, but judgments about prospective empirical applicability need not be sheer opinion. No definition is empirically applicable if unintelligible because inconsistent, and Barbour's definition is an instance. The first sentence limits technology to knowledge, but the second creates doubts, and the last refers to an activity. Then some definitions can be misleading. For instance, Richter's definition indicates that technology includes tools, but he subsequently states (1982:12): "It is possible to have not only technologies that do not entail tool using, but also technologies that consist essentially of refraining from doing certain things."

Vague terminology and dubious distinctions abound in definitions of technology. For example, Bimber (*supra*) equates technology with "artefact" or "machine" without recognizing that those terms are by no means synonyms. Then examine three phrases from the contending definitions (*supra*): aspects of the pattern of activities, procedural systems, and the capacity of society. Those phrases have vague meanings, and the rationale for their use is obscure. Yet even Gendron's reification—"the capacity of society to produce"—is minor compared to two common practices in writing on technology: (1) a failure to recognize conceptual problems (e.g., Susskind, 1973, and Radder, 1986) and (2) recognition but with no attempted resolution (e.g., Winner, 1977:8–12).

The major contrast between definitions of technology is the material-nonmaterial emphasis, but two definitions may emphasize the nonmaterial and yet otherwise differ sharply. Thus, Weinstein and Gendron would limit technology to knowledge, whereas Oswalt would limit it to "ways" of producing artifacts. As for definitions that are not exclusively "material" or "nonmaterial" (e.g., evidently Barbour, *supra*) the inclusion of objects or substances, overt behavior, and internal behavior (knowledge particularly) makes technology such an unmanageably broad notion that fruitful theories about it are unlikely.[14] Then observe again that a broad definition tends to blur the distinction between analytical and synthetic statements. Contemplate Brooks' statement (1980:65): "Technology must be sociotechnical rather than technical, and a technology must include the managerial and social supporting systems necessary to apply it on a significant scale." What happens to the notion of technological determinism? The question is all but ignored in the literature.

Basic Types: Biotic Control

Although social scientists often appear indifferent to it, starvation has been common throughout history (Sorokin, 1975); and even if human starvation should cease, the importance of the food quest would remain. The quest is a study in biotic control, but that basic type of control (the second of three) is becoming increasingly important in light of new forms.

A Definition and a Typology

Attempted biotic control is overt behavior by a human in the belief that (1) the behavior increases or decreases the probability of an organism's existence or a change in any of the organism's characteristics but including behavior only in the case of nonhuman organisms and (2) the increase or decrease is desirable. An organism is a living plant or animal, human or nonhuman; and a characteristic pertains to any property, such as size, shape, weight, color, texture, composition, or odor. The definition applies to a human killing a deer or planting seeds, but various kinds of biotic control (e.g., dentistry, cutting lawns, training animals) are not food quests in the ordinary (direct) sense. Yet all instances can be assigned to one of six subtypes.

Gathering Food. Whatever Adam and Eve's indiscretion, biotic control became onerous. Short of Eden, all environments are potentially lethal for humans, meaning that they can gather enough food in the wild state to survive only by moving about, perhaps over several miles.

The spatial mobility required to gather food is a variable in the "starvation equation." Movement without technology requires human energy; and if the calories burned in the food quest exceeds the food's caloric value, starvation is imminent. However, bipedalism is only one of several evolutionary developments that warrant recognition in thinking about biotic control and the food quest. The development of a dexterous hand was also of great significance, because dexterity facilitated both gathering *and* carrying food.

Hunting or Fishing. Anthropologists commonly describe the pursuit of small, slow animals as food gathering. Nonetheless, the distinction between hunting (or fishing) and gathering food is clear only if the former is defined as the pursuit of undomesticated animals, regardless of their size or mobility.

Hunting and fishing are generally much more technologically intensive than food gathering, and there is an obvious reason. Some animals are so swift, powerful, and/or dangerous that successful control of them virtually requires technology (e.g., spears, nets). So hunting or fishing may have been the first major impetus for technological innovation.

Domestication of Plants. An indescribable variety of activities has entered into plant domestication. The earliest activity may have been only protective, perhaps driving animals from wild plants. In any case, humans can promote wild plant growth several ways, such as watering, fertilizing, or weeding.

Numerous varieties of inanimate control (e.g., plowing) and human control (e.g., supervising farm laborers) enter into contemporary plant domestication, and the basic types of control are often closely integrated. Designating control behavior as being inanimate-biotic, human-biotic, inanimate-human-biotic, or human-inanimate-biotic (to mention four examples) introduces a complexity, but sociology's conceptual apparatus must force recognition that human actions tend to be manifold, processual, and functionally integrated.

Domestication of Animals. Whenever and wherever the first human controlled an animal without killing it, he/she took the initial step in animal domestication. The second step was to extend control over and protect an animal long enough for its reproduction.

Plant domestication is conducive to sedentary spatial organization and an increase in population density, but animal domestication was a colossal evolutionary step also. Many populations came to specialize in pastoralism, and in some cases extensive plant domestication may have required earlier animal domestication. Meat is a major protein source, and animal domestication became a major impetus for technological innovations (inanimate control). Various technological items are used in animal domestication—ropes, saddles, harnesses, wagons, carts, etc.; and the division of labor is another important correlate of animal domestication. Only a few occupations, such as the veterinarian, evolved with animal domestication; but the eventual result was extensive product specialization in manufacturing (e.g., barbed wire, saddles). Perhaps most important, applied scientific research (e.g., preventive immunological measures) devoted to animal domestication is beyond estimation; and selective breeding of animals is an ancient kind of biotic control. Finally, keeping pets is a puzzling but distinctive human practice.

Try to imagine feudalism or the Spanish conquest of Mexico having taken place without the horse. Although those episodes suggest that the horse's domestication had an enormous impact on human history, certainly the first domesticator did not anticipate feudalism or Mexico's conquest. Those episodes were clearly unintended consequences of biotic control, but the horse's domestication is another reason to argue that all major episodes in human history stem from attempts at control.

Somatic Control. As the proportion of the labor force in agriculture declines, biotic control appears to become less important. Yet the necessity of food remains, and biotic control has gone far beyond domestication.

Millions of Americans make a living by altering the shape, size, weight, or functioning of human organs. Surgeons are obvious practitioners of such *somatic control*; but health care in general qualifies, and the number of related occupations (e.g., dentists, dieticians, physical therapists) is astonishing.

Finally, humans employ various means to promote or prevent births (see, e.g., Stinchcombe, 1983:191–197), which makes somatic control all the more diverse and important.

Genetic Engineering. For millennia humans have altered the shape, size, weight, color, composition, and behavior of animate things through selective breeding. That kind of biotic control only narrows the gene pool of particular sets of organisms. Now, however, humanity has reached the penultimate biotic control—the direct alteration of genetic material, which could be a step toward innovative prolongations of life and its literal creation from inanimate substances.

Control is the only candidate for sociology's central notion that facilitates describing and thinking about modes of producing genetic change, which is all the more important because sociologists have a terrible record when it comes to anticipating change. They have no notion that facilitates describing and thinking about all logically possible future worlds; instead, many of them are preoccupied with such time-bound notions as bureaucracy and capitalism.

Basic Types: Control over Human Behavior: Self-Control

What must I do to eat less? If I find a new job, will I be less depressed? How can I stop smoking? Such questions pertain to attempted self-control, defined as: overt behavior by a human in the belief that (1) the behavior increases or decreases the probability of some particular kind of subsequent overt or internal behavior by the human and (2) the increase or decrease is desirable.

Some Issues

Those who equate reality with observable events or things will question the idea of self-control; but "observable" is no more the touchstone of reality than is "experienceable," and the latter justifies the notion of self-control. Humans strive to modify their behavior—to drink less, to act more decisively, etc.; but self-control is not just avoiding vices, overcoming fears, and the like, all of which illustrate the "challenge" view of self-control.[15] Much of human behavior is self-control primarily because of beliefs that acts are functionally interrelated, as when a particular act is perceived as necessary for a subsequent particular act. For example, an individual acts in the belief that dialing increases the probability that he/she will speak on the telephone. The example appears silly only because a particular act may be believed to follow another with absolute certainty, but such beliefs simply pertain to maximum probability (i.e., 1.0.).

Many humans never use the term *probability*, let alone calculate probabilities; but no sense of "self" would develop without beliefs as to behavioral consequences. Consider Blumer's statement about the term "self" (1969:12): "It means merely that a human being can be an object of his own action." To be an object of one's action is to engage in self-control, but self-control is not an exclusively mental phenomena. It entails overt behavior and perhaps even the use of material objects. After all, setting an alarm clock is overt behavior in the belief that it increases the probability of some subsequent behavior.

Some Alternative Conceptualizations. A definition of self-control that makes exclusive reference to *overt behavior* could reflect a concern with empirical applicability rather than an epistemological dogmatism, such as that displayed by Watson and Skinner in psychology.[16] Be that as it may, such overt-behavior-only definitions are vague or arbitrary, if not grotesque. Consider Thorsen and Mahoney's version (1974:12): "A person displays self-control when in the relative absence of immediate external constraints, he engages in behavior whose previous probability has been less than that of alternatively available behaviors." Subsequently (1974:14), they write: "Thus the individual who has usually smoked at parties is exhibiting self-control if—in the absence of externally controlled factors such as physical illness or the unavailability of cigarettes—he refrains from smoking at a party." The illustration clarifies the definition because withdrawal discomfort can be attributed to the ex-smoker. Nonetheless, the definition is astonishing in light of another illustration: after decades of unblemished conduct, a male professor molests a coed in his office.

Although "behavioristic" definitions of self-control are conducive to absurdities, the present definition is compatible with the behavioral view Blankstein and Polivy (1982:2) attribute to Skinner: "an individual engages in self-control when she or he arranges the environment so that only certain controlling stimuli are present." While Blankstein and Polivy recognize that "behavior is a function of the environment, but the environment itself is controlled by the organism," they ignore Skinner's failure to emphasize the need for conceptual recognition of internal behavior.[17] For that matter, the greatest sensitivity to self-control's importance has been displayed not by a psychologist or a sociologist but by an economist, Thomas C. Schelling (1984).

Avoiding Ambiguities

The present conceptualization would be incomplete without recognizing some ambiguities, two of which can best be introduced as major questions. First, what constitutes internal behavior? If only cognitive phenomena (e.g., perceiving) and affective phenomena (e.g., feeling) are designated, what is loosely called "physiological functioning" would be excluded. Such instances as heartbeat may appear beyond control, but research on biofeedback (see Yates, 1980) indicates that some individuals can alter certain physiological functions within a broad range. But granted that any biofeedback technique is *attempted* self-control, what of dieting to lose weight or exercising to alter body contours? Stated more generally, what is the distinction between self-control of internal behavior and somatic control of body structure? Since the weight, size, or shape of a body part is scarcely "behavior," an individual's attempt to alter those structural properties of his/her body is somatic control, a subtype of biotic control. Correlatively, an individual's effort to alter his/her physiological functioning is an attempt at self-control.

Second major question: are the means relevant in identifying self-control? A simple negative answer must suffice, but some implications warrant consideration. Psychopharmacology (see Pope, 1985) is largely the study of attempted control, including "chemical self-control." Only an incorrigible Durkheimian or Skinnerian would deny the potential significance of psychopharmacology for the behavioral and social sciences, especially on recognizing that drugs are not necessarily taken or administered to alter or maintain only *internal* behavior (see Gabe and Lipshitz-Phillips, 1984).

Although creating, preparing, transporting, or ingesting any chemical substance requires inanimate control, control behavior is commonly a series of acts, no two of which are the same type (or subtype or kind) of control. Hence, if what is taken as the final goal in a series identifies the control type, all preceding goals are instances of a subtype or a subsubtype. Thus, "chemical self-control" (e.g., ingesting a tranquilizer) signifies "inanimate control in attempted self-control," and using an alarm clock to wake up is an instance of "mechanical self-control." However, Skinnerian derision notwithstanding, the alternative to inanimate control in self-control is not just "willing it." Virtually any successful control of one's internal behavior requires some kind of overt behavior, even if only remaining immobile momentarily.

Basic Types: Control over Human Behavior: Proximate Control

Attempted proximate control is overt behavior by a human in the belief that (1) the behavior *directly* increases or decreases the probability of a change in the behavior of one or more other humans and (2) the increase or decrease is desirable. The "directly" signifies no intermediary (third party). Thus, should X order Y to order Z, X's action in relation to Z would not be proximate control. But proximate control is not necessarily dyadic. There are situations in which an individual attempts to control numerous individuals directly and simultaneously, as when an officer shouts an order to an infantry company.

The Ubiquity of Proximate Control

Although commands and requests are conspicuous instances, there are various other kinds of attempted proximate control, even though command, order, instruct, and direct are treated here as synonyms, as are request, plea, beg, and implore. Thus, an explicit offer of an exchange is hardly a command or a request, but it is attempted proximate control.

Coercion is a very distinctive kind of proximate control. It entails the use of purely physical forces or processes, as when: (1) holding or shoving someone, (2) using an inanimate object to restrain or move someone by purely mechanical principles, (3) injecting a substance (e.g., a chemical) to immobilize or kill a human, or (4) using some inanimate object (e.g., a knife) to terminate or limit someone's behavior. One implication warrants emphasis: coercive control is not realized through symbols or any kind of communication; it is strictly mechanical or chemical (hence, its distinctiveness). So, Weber (1978:34–35) notwithstanding, "psychological coercion" is a misnomer; and control through the threat of coercion is not coercive control (i.e., the *threat* of coercion is not actual coercion), but such a threat is an attempt at proximate control.

Some Issues

The variety of proximate control is so great that some kinds can be described by a phrase but not by one word or term. For example, no one is likely to identify extending a dinner invitation as a request, let alone a command; nonetheless, it is attempted proximate control, as are numerous other phrases, such as: hailing a cab, signaling for a turn, and saying hello. Although no dictionary definition justifies it, many sociologists do not think of those phrases as describing control attempts, because they have a narrow conception of control over human behavior, even to the point of thinking of control as an evil. Thus, sociologists are not inclined to regard a dinner invitation as attempted control; and many would bristle at Burns' statement (1958:137): "the way in which persons deal with others always consists in an attempt to control them..."

One rationale of the control-as-evil argument is that attempts at control over human behavior are commonly resisted. But even if all attempts are resisted, the rationale for making resistance a criterion is obscure; and there would be an astonishing implication. Because a control attempt can be resisted only if recognized, *secretive* control becomes a logical impossibility. So the conclusion: neither evil nor resistance to control is conceptually relevant. It may well be that of all human behavior, control attempts perhaps are *commonly* the most evil and/or dangerous; but that is another rationale for making control sociology's central notion.

Another Issue. Given the variety of proximate control, it may be objected that most of interaction qualifies. Precisely so, and that recognition is still another rationale for identifying control as sociology's central notion. But the argument is not really radical, if only because numerous theorists have described interaction in terms that identify it as control in light of the present conceptualization. Consider Parsons's observation on interaction (1951:5): "Part of ego's expectation...consists in the probable reaction of alter to ego's possible action, a reaction which comes to be anticipated in advance and thus to affect ego's own choices." Insofar as ego's choice is manifested in overt behavior, ego is attempting to control alter's behavior.

Despite what has been said, some sociologists will claim that much of interaction is not proximate control. As a case in point, because "saying hello" appears unreflective and habitual, critics will deny that it is a control attempt. The denial implies that control is always conscious and deliberate, terms alien to the present conceptualization. Moreover, if in saying hello we do not act in the belief that the behavior increases the probability of a response and that the increase is desirable, why are we surprised and perhaps miffed by no response?

Basic Types: Control over Human Behavior: Sequential Control

To appreciate the limits of effective proximate control, try to imagine an army in which all social relations are dyadic (i.e., no component exceeds two members). That arrangement would not preclude commands, but there would be no *chain of command.* Yet in all armies there is a chain of command; and it is sequential control, not proximate control.

Attempted sequential control is a command or request by one human to another in the belief that (1) it increases the probability of a subsequent command or request by the other human to still other humans and (2) the increase is desirable. For simplicity, the definition pertains to minimum conditions—at least three individuals and at least two commands or requests. Further discussion is limited to a *chain* of commands (or orders, directives, or instructions), by far the most common sequential control.

The Near Ubiquity of Sequential Control

Most control over another's behavior is of the proximate type; but the amount of sequential control is beyond reckoning, one reason being the limits of effective proximate control. The sheer number of prospective controlees is the most conspicuous consideration; but the relation between those numbers and the limits of effective proximate control is highly contingent, especially on the communication technology. Whatever the relation, why are there effective limits? One can shout a command to thousands of individuals, perhaps millions, depending on the communication technology; but that is the case only if there is one command that applies to everyone, such as: Retreat! If each of numerous commands applies only to some individuals, the commands cannot be given simultaneously by one individual. Yet success in a major battle requires that numerous and diverse commands be given more or less simultaneously; hence, sequential control is an essential feature of military organization and perhaps of any large organization regardless of kind.

A variety of simultaneous commands implies differentiation in the activities of the control targets (e.g., some fire guns, others repair equipment, still others transport ammunition) and on the synchronization or coordination of those activities (e.g., an aerial bombardment followed by a land attack). Because hundreds of different activities cannot be carried out simultaneously unless there are hundreds of individuals, proximate control tends to give way to sequential control as the number of controlees increases. Yet sequential control is conspicuous in military units not because of uncritical conformity to tradition, nor does it stem *directly* from some structural property; rather, sequential control stems from the human concern with effective control. Any doubts can be ended by attempting to command an army in battle or managing a major airline through proximate control alone.

Basic Types: Control over Human Behavior: Social Control

Whereas sociologists have devoted little attention to proximate or sequential control, they have used the term *social control* extensively throughout this century; but it is a major sociological term only in that sense. There is no well-known theory on the subject, and no major line of work on it in sociology's literature other than, possibly, deterrence research (Gibbs, 1986).[18] The sad history (see Cohen, 1985:2-9) is hardly puzzling; from the outset sociologists failed to realize a defensible conceptualization, one of many manifestations of widespread indifference in the field to conceptual problems.

Principal Conceptualizations

In 1901 E.A. Ross published the first book on social control. Consistent with the book's subtitle, *Survey of the Foundations of Order*, Ross wrote as though social control is anything and everything that maintains social order. After quoting Ross's definition of social control as "concerned with that domination which is intended and which fulfills a function in the life of society," Pitts commented (1968:382): "Yet when he [Ross] described social control in action, he fell back upon all the forms of the Durkheimian *conscience collective* that constrain the individual: public opinion, law, belief systems, education, custom, religion..." So, despite his definition, Ross treated social control as though internal behavior (perception, beliefs, etc.) is irrelevant.

Ross suggested that social control stems from institutions—education, religion, law, etc.—meaning that institutions maintain social order. Because the terms "social order" and "institution" denote vague notions, they scarcely clarify the meaning of social control. For that matter, given that institutions are components of social order, to say that the former contribute to the maintenance of the latter is to imply that social order maintains social order. And what of social control within and over institutions? Presume a demonstration that Catholicism's confessional somehow promotes conformity to putative norms. Even so, why do priests and the laity engage in the confessional? Surely it is not instinctual, and it does not tax credulity to suppose that social control is required to maintain that practice.

Enter Talcott Parsons. In the 1950s sociologists began defining social control by reference to deviant behavior (or deviance). The change can be traced largely to statements by Talcott Parsons, like these (1951:297, 321): "The theory of social control is the obverse of the theory of the genesis of deviant tendencies. It is the analysis of those processes in the social system which tend to counteract the deviant tendencies... ... Every social system has, in addition to the obvious rewards for conformative and punishments for deviant behavior, a complex system of *unplanned* and *largely unconscious* mechanisms which serve to counteract deviant tendencies." (Italics added.)

Although Parsons' counteraction-of-deviance conception of social control became conventional, it is a thicket of problems. The immediate problem stems from the common definition of deviance, something like: behavior that is contrary to the norms of some social unit. Because Parsons defined social control by reference to deviance and because the latter is in turn conventionally defined by reference to norms, then problems in conceptualizing norms (Gibbs, 1981:chp. 2) create problems with the counteraction-of-deviance conception of social control. Briefly, the conception refers to something (deviance) that cannot be identified confidently and so as to realize agreement between independent observers, and the problems are not solved by defining deviance as that which is subject to social control and then defining social control by reference to deviance (see Black, 1976:9, 105).

Apart from problems with the notions of norms and deviance, Parsons' definition precludes identifying some highly organized manipulations of human behavior on a massive scale as social control. Think of American advertising, an industry in which hundreds of thousands attempt to manipulate the behavior of hundreds of millions. Yet those attempts are not social control in light of the counteraction-of-deviance conception unless a failure to buy a particular product is deviant, and such an extension of the notion of deviance raises doubts about the notion itself. If buying a Ford is deviant from the viewpoint of Chevrolet advertisers and vice versa, then deviance becomes an all inclusive notion, for in a large social unit virtually any act is disapproved by someone.

Finally, think of Hitler's efforts to further electoral support of the Nazi party. If an attempt to sway the electorate is the "counteraction of deviance," then that notion is unmanageably broad. Should it be argued that Hitler perceived himself as counteracting deviance, the argument makes deviance so relative that virtually any behavior qualifies, meaning that someone disapproves of it. Thus, even if most citizens disapprove of terrorism, terrorists view themselves as counteracting deviance; but advocates of the counteraction-of-deviance conception of social control are prone to identify terrorists as objects rather than *agents* of social control. Yet if an organized attempt to bring down a government is not an attempt at social control, what is it?

Parsons' definition amounts to a denial that social control has any necessary connection with internal behavior (recall his use of the terms "unplanned" and "unconscious"). Thus, if the custom of wearing a wedding ring promotes marital fidelity and if adultery is deviant, then the custom is social control *regardless* of anyone's intention, perception, or beliefs. Likewise, the billions of dollars spent annually on U.S. prisons and jails is not social control without a demonstration that incarceration does in fact "counteract" crime.[19] Finally, like Ross' conception, Parsons' conception precludes a distinction between successful and unsuccessful social control; and it makes this question illogical: does social control counteract deviance?

Proposed Alternative

Attempted social control is overt behavior by a human, the first party, in the belief that (1) the behavior increases or decreases the probability of a change in the behavior of another human or humans, the second party in either case; (2) a third party is involved but not in the way of sequential control; and (3) the increase or decrease is desirable. The definition can be better understood by considering what are five hopefully *inclusive* types of attempted social control.

Referential Social Control. In attempted referential social control the first party makes reference to a third party in the belief that the reference is necessary for success. The first party need not make reference to what the third party will do, is doing, or has done to the second party (or anyone else). Instead, the reference may be to what will happen, is happening, or has happened to the third party; or what the third party will think or feel, is thinking or feeling, or has thought or felt.

One simple illustration is a little boy's statement to his older brother: "Give me back my candy or I'll tell mother." As in all social control, there are three parties; in this case, the boy is the first party (always the one attempting control), the brother the second party (always the target of the control attempt), and their mother the third party (always the instrument of the control attempt). The illustration erroneously suggests a narrow range of behavior; for one thing, that the reference to the third party must be explicit and verbal.[20] A nonverbal and implicit reference is well illustrated by the discovery of a European administrative officer in the former Congo (Hallet, 1965:15) that the lenses in the glasses of his black assistant were ordinary glass. When the officer asked "Do things really look different to you when you put them on?," the assistant replied astutely: "No, monsieur. I look different. Those *bashenzi*—those ignorant natives—this way they have more respect for me." So it appears that the glasses were worn to prompt other blacks to identify the assistant with Europeans and thereby make them more compliant; hence, in this "associational" subtype of referential control, the assistant was the first party, Europeans the third party, and other blacks in the region the second party.

Impersonation is an implicit and nonverbal means of referential control. Thus, when a robbery gang member dresses like a uniformed police officer to enter a bank before or after business hours, he or she is the first party, any bank guard is the second party, and "police" the third party. So the third party may be an indefinite category of individuals, not known by name to the first party and/or to the second party. However, both the second and third party may be an indefinite category, as in Hitler's statement (quoted in Waite, 1977:367)): "My enemy is Germany's enemy: always and only, the Jew!" Note that the first party (Hitler) expressed a negative evaluation of the third party (Jews); hence, the subtype of referential social control is "disassociational." In seeking the electoral and financial support of German gentiles (the second party), Hitler adopted this Machiavellian principle of referential control: to control someone, attack his/her enemies or praise his/her friends.

The third party need not be a living human being, the illustration being this statement: "Your mother would die again if she knew of your addiction." Then when the first party threatens the second party with "God's wrath," the third party is a supernatural being. Finally, the third party may be fabricated by the first party, as in Rock's description (1973:23) of a creditor's tactic when writing to debtors: "One mail order firm invented a debt-collector because the word 'debt collector' flourishes a threat." However, here or elsewhere, the suggestion is not that social control is always "manipulative" (i.e., an evil).

Referential social control is not an exclusively micro phenomenon. Law is surely a macro phenomenon, but it is a study in referential social control. In American courts an attorney may address a judge something like this: "Your Honor, my argument is consistent with a Supreme Court ruling." As for criminal statutes, they threaten a punishment for a designated kind of behavior (e.g., burglary), but it is judges, wardens, guards, and executioners who impose legal punishment. So in enacting a criminal statute, legislators make implicit reference to what a third party will do to a violator (second party).

Allegative Social Control. In attempted allegative social control, the first party communicates an allegation about the second party to the third party in the belief that (1) the allegation will increase or decrease the probability of the third party doing something to the second party and (2) the "something" will change or maintain the second party's behavior. The allegation may be any kind: what the second party has done or may do, who the second party is, what could happen to the second party, etc. In any case, the first party perceives the allegation as an appeal to the third party's normative standards or interests and as necessary to elicit some action by the third party toward the second party.

Suppose that a boy makes his statement to his mother about his brother: "Fred took my candy." As for interpretation, no one should apply the present social control terminology in any context (be it a family or country) without thorough knowledge of that context. If the mother has commanded Fred to do things in the boy's presence, an experienced observer would entertain this conclusion: the boy believes that his mother can make Fred return the candy. Finally, while the allegation may be false, credibility is essential for success in allegative control.[21] In the illustration, the boy's attempt at control will fail if the mother does not believe his allegation.

Lest the illustrative cases suggest that allegative control is limited to the nuclear family, consider actions in tort law. The plaintiff or the plaintiff's attorney, the first party in either instance, makes allegations about the defendant (second party) to a judge or jury (third party). For that matter, a criminal trial is a study in allegations, and the police often investigate in response to allegations that they identify as complaints (indeed, commonly require complaints).

Although both allegative and referential control entail judgments by the first party about authority, normative standards, and credibility, the two control types are distinct. Whereas in referential control the first party does not presume that the third party will become involved directly, that presumption is essential in allegative control. However, one and the same act can be both allegative and referential control. To illustrate, although Hitler baited Jews to gain the support of German gentiles (referential control, with Jews as the third party), he may have acted also in the belief that it would provoke violence against Jews that would drive some of them from Germany (allegative social control, with Jews as the second party).

Vicarious Social Control. In all instances of attempted vicarious social control the first party attempts to punish the third party, reward the third party, or somehow rectify the third party's behavior, always presuming that such action will influence the second party's behavior. Because the first party does not make reference to the third party, vicarious control differs from referential control. Likewise, because the first party does not presume that the third party will do something to the second party, vicarious control differs from allegative control.

Vicarious control is conspicuous in the administration of criminal law. In imposing a prison sentence on a convicted felon, a judge may believe that it is necessary to deter others; if so, the judge is the first party, the convicted felon the third party, and all potential offenders the second party. Vicarious control is the basis of the general deterrence doctrine, which enters into criminal justice policy throughout most of the world (see Morris, 1966:631).

After decades of research, the deterrence doctrine's validity remains disputable (see Gibbs, 1986); nonetheless, imposing a legal punishment on someone to deter others is attempted vicarious control. However, some critics argue that legal punishments ought to be retributive; criminals should be punished solely because they deserve it. The argument suggests that general deterrence may not be even one aim of the officials who prescribe or impose legal punishments; and Durkheim (1933:89 [1893]) asserts that those punishments simply express the "outrage to morality," meaning that they are expressive rather than instrumental.

Retributivists (including Durkheim) tend to ignore an instrumental quality of what *appears to be* purely retributive punishments. A punishment may be imposed in the belief that it will terminate complaints and/or prevent revenge; if so, the punished individual is the third party, as in the case of general deterrence; but those demanding punishment are the second party. Such *placative* vicarious control is illustrated by Dillon's statement (1980:659): "...Rosemary Harris...reports that in order to prevent a disturbance in trade relations with neighboring groups, precolonial trading towns such as Ikom, on the upper Cross River of Nigeria, sometimes executed their own citizens for killing outsiders." However, one and the same action may be both placative and deterrent, as in the case of Henry VIII's harsh response to the "Evil May Day" riot against foreigners in London (1517). "But Henry wished to show the foreign merchants that they could safely come to London and carry on their business there; and, even more important, he would not tolerate anarchy in his realm, or any defiance of his royal authority and laws." (Ridley, 1984:107)

Vicarious control is limited neither to the legal sphere nor to punishment. The first party may reward the third party in the hope that the second party will emulate the third party. Thus, an employer may award a very productive employee in the hope that other employees will work harder, and it is significant that awards commonly have a public and ceremonial character.

Modulative Social Control. Influence is an empirical association between the overt behavior of one or more individuals and the subsequent behavior of other individuals. So there is a conceptual connection between influence and *successful* human control; the latter is a subclass of the former. That connection is essential for an understanding of modulative social control. In all instances the first party attempts to use the third party's influence on the second party's behavior but not in the belief that making any allegation about or reference to either party is necessary for success.

Advertising executives commonly offer celebrities money to praise products in commercials. The offer itself is attempted proximate control, but it makes no sense unless the executive (first party) perceives the celebrity (third party) as having an influence over potential consumers (second party) that the first party does not have. Note that the executive need make no allegation about consumers to the celebrity; so his or her action is not allegative social control. Nor does the executive communicate with potential consumers directly, let alone make reference to the celebrity; so the action is not referential social control. Finally, in vicarious social control the first party assumes that "doing something to the third party" will have an influence on the second party's behavior, which is not the case in modulative social control (rather, the third party must do something).

The political sphere is a study in modulative control, although attempts are commonly made to conceal it.[22] Political leaders often contemplate this question: whom shall I appoint? One common answer: appoint an influential person. Thus, the President may appoint a black or a woman with a view to furthering electoral and congressional support, the assumption being that the appointee will, among other things, defend the administration. As a quite different example, during the Korean War, Chinese officers reportedly moved "natural" leaders from one group to another in prisoner camps, thereby diffusing and supposedly reducing leadership influence (see Schein, 1956:153). A much more common instance occurs when a judge orders lengthy detention of a juvenile offender on the presumption that the isolation will diminish the offender's "bad" influence on the offender's siblings and friends.

Modulative control may take the form of the first party attempting to increase the third party's influence, as when a political party subsidizes a popular journalist. Likewise, mill owners have been known to make financial contributions to the ministry of fundamentalist preachers, who admonish millhands to accept their lot passively and work diligently (Pope, 1942). As the last two examples suggest, co-optation is a common kind of modulative social control.

In modulative control the first party perceives the third party as having an influence that the first party lacks, and that feature clarifies the distinction between modulative social control and sequential control. As a chain of command, sequential control operates by this logic: if X can order Y to order Z, then X can order Z.[23] However, when X orders Y to order Z because X presumes that he or she cannot substitute himself or herself for Y, it is modulative social control.

The most frequent kind of modulative social control cannot be described without using the terms *agent* and *representative*. Owners and managers of American business firms must look beyond their employees to experts, such as lawyers, public relations consultants, and advertising agents. However, when anyone solicits the services of such experts, they are in effect saying: "By virtue of your expertise, you have an influence over others that I lack."

Prelusive Social Control. Success in attempting to control a large number of individuals is unlikely unless the first party considers alternative means, but a systematic assessment of relative efficacy may require substantial time and expertise. Indeed, limited resources may prompt the first party to confront this question: which social unit members should be controlled the most and which are susceptible to particular kinds of control? The task of preventing or promoting certain behaviors can require so much time and resources that the first party must exclude entire categories of individuals from the control context, be it a country, a jury, a building, or a potential market. Finally, regardless of the control type—inanimate, biotic, or human—there are situations in which success is improbable unless something is done to facilitate the control attempt.

All of the foregoing control actions may be so demanding that the first party cannot undertake them. If so, the first party often turns to a third party to do what the first party cannot do; when so doing, the first party engages in prelusive social control. In all instances the first party attempts to increase the probability that the third party will (1) assess the efficacy of alternative means of control, (2) through surveillance or monitoring identify influential individuals or those who appear inclined to act contrary to the desires of the first party or those who appear particularly susceptible to control, (3) act so as to exclude certain categories of individuals from participation in some social unit or restrict their spatial movement, and/or (4) take any other action that facilitates the first party's subsequent attempts at control.

Because the third party's activities are not necessarily actual control attempts, prelusive social control may appear to be a misnomer. However, like numerous other activities, control can be so highly organized that preliminaries are perceived by the participants as a part of the activity, just as recruiting players is a part of professional football, although preliminary to actual games.

Prelusive social control is illustrated dramatically in Orwell's *1984* and Huxley's *Brave New World*; and there are also all manner of actual instances, such as advertising executives using psychologists to conduct research on the effectiveness of advertisements, the use of market researchers to identify the most likely purchasers of some commodity or service, governmental agents planting informants to identify members of some organization as potential subversives, legislators enacting laws that bar designated categories of individuals (e.g., "communists") from entering the country, and reliance of companies or corporations on agencies for "credit checks" of prospective customers or clients.

Exclusion from organizations is an especially common form of prelusive social control. Personnel officers (third parties) are instructed by a first party to be selective in recruiting or admitting members (employees or otherwise), meaning to bar particular categories of individuals. True, exclusionary practices are not necessarily followed with a view to reducing the need for control; but the purpose is only rarely obscure even when not made explicit. In any case, Etzioni's observations identify the benefits (1968:399): "The role of selection should be especially emphasized because the liberal-humanist tradition, which prevails in the social sciences, tends to underplay its importance and to stress that of socialization. Actually, various studies indicate that a small increase in the selectivity of an organization often results in a disproportionately large decrease in the investments required for control... One reason is that in most organizations a high percentage of the deviant acts are committed by a small percentage of the participants: hence, if these are screened out, control needs decline sharply."

Control and Power

As the following definitions indicate, in the social sciences the notion of power is a conceptual swamp.

DAHL (1968:407, 410): "power terms...refer to *subsets of relations among social units such that the behaviors of one or more units...depend in some circumstances on the behavior or other units... ...* The closest equivalent to the power relation is the causal relation. For the assertion '*C* has power over R,' one can substitute the assertion, '*C*'s behavior causes R's behavior'."

EMERSON (1962:32): "Thus...the power to control or influence the other resides in control over the things he values... In short, *power resides implicitly in the other's dependency.* ... If the dependence of one party provides the basis for the power of the other, that power must be defined as a potential influence."

MCFARLAND (1969:13): "Power...may be taken to mean intended influence (i.e., intended social causation): *C*'s behavior exercises *power* over *R*'s behavior if and only if *C*'s behavior causes changes in *R*'s behavior *that C intends.*"

NAGEL (1975:29): "A power relation, actual or potential, is an actual or potential causal relation between the preferences of an actor regarding an outcome and the outcome itself. ... In social power relations, the *outcome* must be a variable indicating the state of another social entity—the behavior, beliefs, attitudes, or policies of a second actor."

OPPENHEIM (1961:100): "To have power is to be capable of exercising power, that is, to be able to subject others to one's control or to limit their freedom."

RUSSELL (1938:35): "Power may be defined as the production of intended effects."

WALTER (1969:35): "One has power over another with respect to a particular act if he can control (cause) the act or make it punishable to perform or to withhold it."

WEBER (1978:53): "'Power' (*Macht*) is the probability that one actor within a social relationship will be in a position to carry out his own will despite resistance, regardless of the basis on which this probability rests."

Major Conceptual Issues and Problems

Whereas some authors (e.g., McFarland and Russell) depict power as intentional, others (e.g., Emerson, Nagel, Oppenheim, Walter, and Weber) are ambiguous about it, and still others (e.g., Dahl) imply that intention is conceptually irrelevant. Although no definition is demonstrably true or false, the failure to grant or deny intention's relevance is an obfuscation. Of course, intentionality is only one facet of internal behavior; and while a power definition may refer to other facets, it should clearly indicate whether internal behavior is relevant at all.

With few exceptions (e.g., Sites, 1973:1), social scientists who use both the term *power* and the term *control* define the former by reference to the latter. However, in the foregoing definitions only Emerson, Oppenheim, and Walter use the term *control*; and none of them explicitly define it or stipulate the connection between power and control. There are at least four possibilities: (1) control is a subclass of power, (2) power is a subclass of control, (3) control and power are synonyms, or (4) there is no logical connection between the two. Treating the terms as synonyms only sanctions conceptual redundancy, and the fourth possibility is inconsistent with most conceptualizations.

Note again that Dahl's definition of power (one among several) suggests denial of the relevance of internal behavior. The idea seems to be that if one individual's behavior causes another's behavior, then the former has power over the latter regardless of either individual's intention, perception, or belief. Moreover, because Dahl did not use the term control, his definition leaves the logical connection between power and control obscure.

Nothing is gained by avoiding the term *control* in defining power, nor by saying that power is control. That syntax creates either a conceptual redundancy or an ambiguity. If it makes power a subclass of control, there is no suggestion how power differs from other subclasses; and to equate power with "resource control" contributes to conceptual obscurantism.

Toward a Solution

Power can be defined such that neither control nor power is a subclass of the other. Specifically, power can be taken as the *capacity or ability* for control. That conceptual strategy was explicitly employed in only one of the eight illustrative definitions, Oppenheim's (the strategy is more nearly implicit in Walter's definition); and even his definition leaves a crucial question unanswered: how much control must an individual exercise before he or she has the capacity to control? Any answer would be arbitrary. The problem takes on special significance in examining Weber's definition of power. He did not even suggest how "probability" is to be identified in particular cases, let alone stipulate the level of probability necessary for a power relation.

Wrong's Conceptualization. In a thoughtful conceptualization, Wrong (1979:2) defines power as "the capacity of some persons to produce intended and foreseen effects on others." So defined, power is not a strictly behavioral phenomenon; rather, it is a perceptual phenomenon. However, the definition does not speak to another version of a previous question: how much intended and foreseen effects must a person produce to have such capacity? So, despite the divergent terminology, Wrong's definition and Oppenheim's definitions are subject to the same objection.

Wrong's definition may appear to make control the behavioral side of power—the actual production of intended and foreseen effects; but he rarely used the term *control*, and his summary diagram suggests that the only place for the notion in his elaborate conceptual scheme is the category of unintended influence. That syntax is contrary to the way that the vast majority of English-speaking people use the term "control"; and in various ways Wrong makes it appear that power is intended influence, thereby suggesting that power is *actual* behavior rather than a capacity. In any case, Wrong and everyone else who has offered a similar definition ignored this question: if *Y* or someone else punishes *X* because of *X*'s previous attempt to control *Y*, in what sense did *X* have power over *Y*? Virtually any adult is capable of producing intended behavioral effects by violence or threatening violence (e.g., pointing a pistol at someone); but because of the vulnerability to retaliation, it would be questionable to identify that capacity as power.

Proposed Definition. The following brief definition is offered as an alternative to Wrong: power is the perceived capacity for effective control, including the capacity to avoid or preclude retaliation as a reaction to an attempt at control. The definition avoids conceptual redundancy; it does not equate power and control,[24] and the logical connection between power and control is such that one is not a subclass of the other.

The key term in the definition—*perceived capacity* could be construed as redundant, the argument being that any capacity (or ability) must be perceived. Far from rejecting the argument, the term *perceived capacity* has been used to underscore the perceptual character of power. In particular, unlike control, power is not a particular overt act, nor a series of overt acts. As such, a previous question—how much control must an individual exercise before he or she has the capacity to control?—need not be answered. As for the identity of the "perceiver," that question can be best confronted by allowing theorists and researchers to recognize types of power consistent with their interests. Unless qualified, the term *power* relates to what researchers themselves perceive as an actor's capacity (or incapacity) for control. Another type of power is "reflexive," meaning that it relates to the actor's perceptions of his or her capacity for control. Still another type is "respondent" power, in which case the perceptions are those of at least one actual target of the actor's previous control attempts. Finally, in the case of "reputational" power the perceptions are those of potential objects of the actor's control attempts. Similar distinctions can be introduced in connection with inanimate, biotic, or self-control, meaning that the perceived capacity to control is not limited to control over the behavior of others.

Whatever the type of control in question, the conceptualization forces recognition that power is not peculiar to individuals who occupy what can be characterized loosely as formal or official positions. Moreover, even in the case of those individuals some "powers" may be a liability because it is an implicit criterion of *responsibility*. To illustrate, in a study of the aftermath of a major urban flood, Blocker and Sherkat (1992) reached this conclusion (p. 153): "Those who attributed economic and psychological losses to human agency believed that natural disasters are controllable and that it is the responsibility of government to control nature through the use of technology and regulation."

Notes

1. Another and much broader alternative would be a definition that permits such expressions as the environment controls (or ideology controls or society controls or culture controls). It would be difficult to formulate a clear definition of control that sanctions such expressions; and unless one longs for terminological duplication and ensuing confusion, why speak of the environment (or society or culture) as controlling rather than determining or causing? For that matter, how can the environment *attempt* control?

2. The principle can be restated as something akin to the law of effect: the probability of an instance of some kind of control is direct function of the proportion of previous instances that were successful. In any case, throughout this book space limits preclude an elaborate treatment of general control principles. Such principles are not logically interrelated, and they are only steps toward an even more general theory about control than is set forth in Chapters 3–7.

3. In robbing the bank the perpetrator undoubtedly acted in the belief that the robbery increased the probability of being shot, but it would strain credulity (psychoanalytic theory notwithstanding) to argue that robbers typically or even commonly believe that being shot is desirable. Hence, absurdities abound when control is defined without reference to both facets of internal behavior, cognitive and affective.

4. "the question of what we can see a person doing raises the most awkward epistemological and ontological issues. To say that we can see a person crossing the street or waiting for a bus or signing a contract...is a quite different kind of claim from saying that we can see a metal ball rolling down an inclined plane. All that we can actually *see*...is the person's movements." (Maze, 1983:6)

5. For a rare manifestation of sensitivity on the part of sociologists to this awful fact of human existence, see Emerson and Messinger (1977).

6. The need to recognize the purposive quality of human behavior may not be the same in all social and behavior sciences, specialties, or investigations; but Gibbs and Martin's praise (1959:33–34) of Sumner's dismissal of purposes was misguided even in connection with human ecology.

7. The robotic image reflects an indifference to the human behavior's purposive quality, and it is widespread in both sociology and anthropology largely as the remnant of a once pervasive functionalism and the still pervasive structuralism (not "French" structuralism). Gluckman's debate with Paine (see Merry's commentary, 1984:274) over gossip illustrates the issue in anthropology.

8. What Skinner (1971:30) has labeled the "literature of freedom" is a vast instruction in countercontrol. Many of the observations made by Goffman on "proper management of personal appearance" are also relevant. More important, perhaps, Durkheim makes essentially the same point about dress as that made here, but he ignored the implications (1938:2): "if in my dress I do not conform to the customs observed in my country and in my class, the ridicule I provoke, the social isolation in which I am kept, produce, although in attenuated form, the same effects as a punishment in the strict sense of the word." Yet Durkheim evidently could not bring himself to recognize the possibility that he dressed one way rather than another in the belief that it decreased the probability of others ridiculing or ostracizing him, which is to say that his mode of dress was an attempt at control over the behavior of others.

9. As argued at length elsewhere (Gibbs, 1989:6–8), there are seemingly insoluble problems in defining and identifying norms, all of which most sociologists conveniently ignore.

10. Friedman and Lackey's book (1991) is one vast answer, largely in terms of motivation; but there is no necessary connection between the proposal to make control sociology's central notion and the belief that references to motivation are necessary to explain human behavior. All that need be said on that issue is that motivation can be described or thought about in terms of control.

11. The argument applies not just to isolated acts but also to an indefinite repetition of some type of act, as in putative role performance. Goffman's observation is especially relevant (1961:87): "in performing a role the individual must see to it that the impressions of him that are conveyed in the situation are compatible with role-appropriate personal qualities effectively imputed to him: a judge is supposed to be deliberate and sober; a pilot, in a cockpit, to be cool; a bookkeeper to be accurate and neat in doing his work." However, rather than analyze role performance in terms of control and countercontrol, Goffman writes of image and self-image; but contemplate the implications of his phrase "the individuals must see to it." Why must the individual see to it?

12. Sociologists have surprisingly little to say about the origins and perpetuation of putative norms, and they shun the point of view suggested by the biologist Lewontin. He (1977:284) quotes Dawkins as saying: "The idea of hell-fire is, quite simply, *self-perpetuating*, because of its own deep psychological impact." Lewontin then says: "He shrugs off without analysis the much more plausible and clearly causal hypothesis that hell-fire is not *self-perpetuating*, but is perpetuated by some people because it gives them power over other people."

13. Convention is not the only justification for excluding food. If food is technological by definition, a crucial question (see Oswalt, 1976) becomes confusing: how do humans use technology to obtain food?

14. For elaboration, see Bimber, 1990:340. If the trend in definitions of technology continues, the term will become virtually meaningless. Consider Winner's commentary (1977:8): "In the twentieth century... *Technology* has expanded rapidly in both its denotative and connotative meanings. It is now widely used in ordinary and academic

speech to talk about an unbelievable diverse collection of phenomena—tools, instruments, machines, organizations, methods, techniques, systems, and the totality of all these and similar things in our experience." Perhaps worse, entire books on technology have been written without the slightest recognition of conceptual problems or issues (see, e.g., Alcorn, 1986).

15. This view ignores even the distinction between capacity for denial and management of stress. Yet so many types of self-control can be recognized that there is no immediate prospect of an all-purpose typology (see Klausner, 1965, especially 9–48). Accordingly even though the "challenge" view of self-control has generated virtually a publishing industry in self-help manuals (see the survey in Blankstein and Polivy, 1982:183–199), it pertains to only one of many kinds of self-control.

16. In what is now a hoary philosophical debate, some protagonists suggest a close connection between the notions of self-control and free will. The present conceptualization has no bearing on the debate, nor does it reflect acceptance of Parsons' voluntarism (see Scott's critique, 1971). Just as the experience of making a choice can be thought of as determined, so can the experience of controlling one's behavior. Likewise, the proposed definition of self-control has no *necessary* bearing on philosophical subtleties, such as Mele's question (1985:169): "Do we exhibit self-control *whenever* we act as we judge best?" The last two words are so ambiguous as to preclude a defensible answer.

17. Nonetheless, Skinner used the term "self-control" frequently (e.g., 1971,1974, 1978, 1983), and he apparently regarded control notions as important. There are even instances where he alludes to internal behavior in connection with control, one being (1974:190): "No mystic or ascetic has ever ceased to control the world around him; he controls it in order to control himself. We cannot choose a way of life in which there is no control. We can only change the controlling conditions."

18. Of the few possible exceptions, the most immediate doubts pertain to the theorist's conception of control. For example, Hirschi's "control" theory of delinquency (1969) reduces to the claim that the probability of a juvenile engaging in delinquency varies inversely with the juvenile's attachment to persons, commitment to conformity, involvement in conventional activities, and belief in the moral validity of societal norms. The claim may be valid; but even granting that the four conditions make a juvenile *vulnerable to control*, they are not control in the sense defined here. Indeed, Hirschi does not offer a conceptualization of control, and he appears to use the term as the loose equivalent of *influence*, a very common practice in sociology.

19. Requiring such a demonstration is more defensible than merely assuming that imprisonment can be identified as social control without any definition.

20. Although Goffman rarely used the term control in his publications, his books (e.g., 1961, 1963, 1974) provide numerous illustrations of referential social control, especially the implicit and/or nonverbal kinds. See particularly the chapters (4 and 6) on "fabrications" in Goffman's *Frame Analysis* (1974).

21. The seriousness of an allegation may be as important as its credibility. As Black (1984c:18) observed: "Reports of violence occasionally may even be fabricated in order to ensure that the police will handle cases that the callers fear—possibly with justification—would otherwise be dismissed as trivial..." Curiously, however, Black (1984b:6, 1976:7) denies any concern with the "subjective aspect" (e.g., intention, belief) of social control or law.

22. An attempt to conceal anything is an attempt to control human behavior.

23. This formula applies to control in bureaucracies despite Dunsire's argument about the discontinuous transmission of orders from the top of a hierarchy (1978:7): "it is well-nigh impossible, and will usually be unwise, for chief executives to give direct instructions to operating personnel." Dunsire simply identified a perennial tension in bureaucracies.

24. The definition makes the intention issue moot. As the perceived capacity to control, power is neither intentional nor unintentional. Lest the distinction between control and power appear to be logomachy, note that it makes the following phrase meaningless: "to use power effectively" (Ridgeway and Berger, 1986:604). Ridgeway and Berger do not indicate what constitutes "use of power," but it is difficult to imagine an instance that would not be an attempt at control.

PART TWO

The Intrinsic Part of the Theory

Whereas a theory may not comprise any definitions, it is difficult to imagine one with no constituent empirical generalizations. So it is meaningful to characterize the constituent empirical generalizations (testable or not) as making up the theory's "intrinsic" part and label each generalization as an intrinsic statement.

The theory about control in Chapters 3–7 comprises 43 intrinsic statements: fifteen axioms, seven postulates, six transformational statements, and fifteen theorems. As those labels indicate, the theory is stated in accordance with a particular formal mode of theory construction. A detailed version of that mode is set forth in the Appendix, but it need not be read to understand the theory. Nevertheless, the use of any formal mode is controversial because it implies rejection of the discursive mode, which has prevailed in sociology from the very outset. The discursive mode consists of nothing more than the conventions of some natural language (e.g., English, German); hence, the *form* of a discursively stated theory does not differ from that of a novel or a letter. By contrast, a formal mode is a set of rules for stating a theory, some or all of which transcend the conventions of a natural language, meaning that they were designed exclusively to state theories.

The primary rationale for a formal mode has to do with defects of the alternative, the discursive mode. First and foremost, the conventions of a natural language are such that the logical structure of a discursively stated theory is virtually certain to be obscure. In turn, an obscure logical structure precludes defensible deductions of conclusions from premises; were it otherwise, logicians would have never invented technical languages, such as that used to explicate the classical syllogism. Defensible deductions of conclusions are essential if the theory's premises are such that they cannot be tested directly, as is commonly the case for sociological theories. However, that consideration is a defect of the discursive mode of theory construction only if one grants that a scientific theory should be assessed in terms of its predictive power *relative* to that of contending theories. A formal mode is especially needed to promote testability, and the theory about control in Chapters 3–7 has been stated particularly with a view to realizing tests. Yet testability is only one of seven dimensions of predictive power (recall Chapter 1), and a formal mode of theory construction facilitates assessments of theories in terms of all of those dimensions, including parsimony.

Even those sociologists who grant the defects of the discursive mode are likely to cling to it and have grave misgivings about any formal mode. They will do so not just because the discursive mode is more familiar and flexible; no less important, the discursive mode does not tax the audience's patience. A discursively stated theory may run for hundreds of pages, but it is by no means essential for the reader to be aware of the logical interrelations among the theory's components. For that matter, the theorist may not and need not be fully aware of the logical interrelations (or the lack of them).

Even when it appears possible to comprehend a discursively stated theory with ease, the comprehension is commonly an illusion. Nonetheless, by comparison a formally stated theory is likely to appear complex, perhaps inordinately so; and the audience's irritation will escalate on recognition that the theory cannot be reduced to one central idea or argument, certainly not as readily as can the typical discursively stated theory. Described otherwise, it is much more difficult to summarize a formally stated theory, largely because all of intrinsic statements (axioms, postulates, etc.) are essential.

The only way that the theory in Chapters 3–7 can be summarized is to describe it as identifying several purported effects at the international level of two reciprocally related *construct* variables: (1) the extent and efficacy of control attempts (all basic types combined) and (2) perceived control capacity. That summary is not informative without a list of the asserted effects, as follows in the form of constructs or concepts: the extent and efficacy of inanimate control attempts, the extent and efficacy of attempts to control human behavior, the extent and efficacy of biotic control attempts, the amount of supernaturalism, the amount of scientific activity, concentration of biotic control, degree of division of labor, technological complexity, technological efficiency, variation in death ages (*intranational*), the level of educational attainment, predominance of animate industries, degree of industry differentiation, degree of occupational differentiation, and amount of inanimate energy use.

Even if each construct or concept in the list were defined at this point, it would still not be feasible to reduce the theory to one central idea or argument (e.g., something comparable to Marx's famous reduction of human history to class struggle). Again, though, such reduction is simply not feasible because the theory comprises numerous intrinsic statements (premises and theorems), none of which should be ignored. Should such "atomization" of a theory be construed as a defect, observe that it permits an unlimited expansion of the theory.

The foregoing notwithstanding, both the discursive mode and a formal mode can be used in stating a theory. Such a "mixture" can be realized by introducing each constituent generalization in a natural language, but at some point the generalization must be identified (e.g., axiom, postulate) and stated in accordance with some formal mode. It is further necessary to bring all of the formally stated generalizations together, if only to deduce conclusions through the application of explicit rules. Because the discursive mode has some advantages over a formal mode (a natural language is more conventional and more flexible), the strategy of mixing the two modes has been adopted in stating the theory about control.

3

Control, Supernaturalism, Science, and Education

Control can be analyzed from a functionalist perspective if only because human survival requires extensive inanimate, biotic, and behavioral control. Humans cannot survive without altering their environment, even if only extracting something from it; and both "altering" and "extracting" are two of numerous words that signify control. A no less conspicuous consequence is control's experiential impact. Both immediate (direct) experience and vicarious (indirect) experience are relevant, for either kind gives rise to some sense of control possibilities and limits. Very early in life humans come to have some fairly definite perceptions of control capacity, not just their own (i.e., perceived *personal* capacity) but also that of humans in general; and all goal-oriented behavior appears to require such perceptions.

Control and Perceived Control Capacity

Two correlates of perceived control capacity at the national level are depicted in Figure 3–1 (the diagram provides only an overview of the theory and need not be examined in any detail). Note, however, that the possible consequences are seemingly infinite, especially in light of Control Principle 3–1: what humans attempt to control and how often are governed by their perceptions of control capacity. Stated otherwise, the extent of attempted control is limited by beliefs as to what can and cannot be controlled effectively; and in some cases a belief can be described as determining (not just limiting) whether or not a control attempt will be made

Perceived control capacity has various consequences beyond its impact on the extent of control attempts. That point is illustrated by Axiom 2 in Figure 3–1; but the immediate consideration is Axiom 1, for it indicates that, despite the emphasis on perceived control capacity, neither the notion of control nor

70

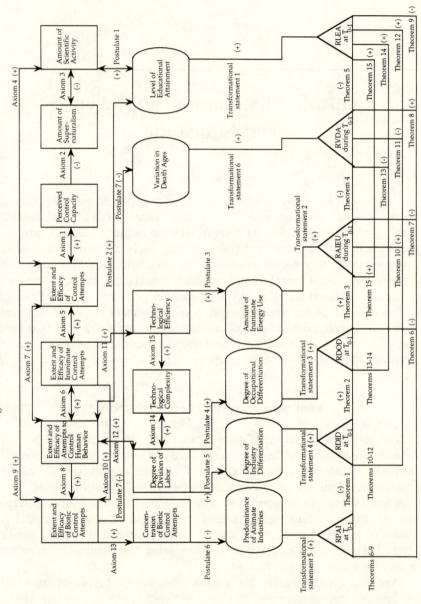

Figure 3-1: DIAGRAM OF A THEORY ABOUT PROPERTIES OF COUNTRIES

the theory is even predominantly phenomenological. For one thing, the term "control attempts" refers in part to *overt* behavior. For another, granted that perceived control capacity (internal behavior) limits what humans attempt to control and the frequency of attempts, those perceptions are shaped by immediate or vicarious experiences of attempted control. So, as indicated by Axiom 1, control attempts both determine *and* are determined by perceived control capacity. That generalization has a sobering implication for sociologists who point to social structure as the field's subject matter and are prone to dismiss a focus on control as reductionistic. If those sociologists ever realize a defensible definition of "social structure" (for elaboration, see Gibbs, 1989:232–241), they should entertain this argument: the reality of any structural variable lies in the rarity with which social unit members attempt to change or maintain the variable and related perceived control impotence.

The First Axiom

It is desirable to supplement Figure 3–1 with an explicit statement of each depicted relation, commencing with Axiom 1: *Among countries and for any country over time, the extent and efficacy of control attempts are the reciprocal, positive, bidirectional, and paramount determinants of perceived control capacity; and perceived control capacity is the reciprocal, positive, bidirectional, and partial determinant of the extent and efficacy of control attempts.* Lest such terminology appear arcane or pretentious, those who demand the use of a causal language in theory construction (e.g., Costner and Blalock, 1972) tend to ignore the ambiguity of assertions in the form of "X causes Y." Such an assertion does not reveal even whether an increase in X produces an increase *or* a decrease in Y. The point is that a simple causal language cannot be clear.

Although not shown in Figure 3–1 because of space limitations and the need to simplify, the causal relation between perceived control capacity and the extent-efficacy of control attempts is virtually the same for each of the three basic types of control (biotic, inanimate, and control over human behavior). So Axiom 1 is actually a composite of three independent sets of causal assertions, as follow:

Axiom 1a: Among countries and for any country over time, the extent and efficacy of inanimate control attempts are the symmetrical, positive, bidirectional, and partial determinants of perceived control capacity.

Axiom 1b: Among countries and for any country over time, the extent and efficacy of attempts to control human behavior are the symmetrical, positive, bidirectional, and partial determinants of perceived control capacity.

Axiom 1c: Among countries and for any country over time, the extent and efficacy of biotic control attempts are the symmetrical, positive, bidirectional, and partial determinants of perceived control capacity.

The terms "reciprocal" and "paramount" appear in Axiom 1 but not in 1a, 1b, or 1c because each of the three basic control types are only partial determinants of perceived control capacity, just as perceived control capacity is only a partial determinant of the extent and efficacy of each of the three basic types. Therefore, Axioms 1a, 1b, and 1c each imply (given the causal identification as "symmetrical") another set of causal assertions, one in which perceived control capacity is identified as the symmetrical, positive, bidirectional, and partial determinant of the extent and efficacy of the type of control attempts in question (inanimate, over human behavior, or biotic). Henceforth, unless indicated otherwise, observations on Axiom 1 also apply to Axioms 1a, 1b, and 1c. The notion of an axiom is analyzed at length in the Appendix (pp. 296–300); and here it will suffice to comment briefly on the types of causation asserted in Axiom 1, the two constituent property terms (or variables), the unit phrase, and some temporal considerations. However, the primary purpose is clarification and not to create the impression of offering systematic evidence in support of the axiom.

Types of Causation

Axiom 1 comprises two *sets* of causal assertions, with four types of causation identified in each set. The term "reciprocal," the first causal typification, signifies that at least one of the other three typifications (in this particular case, partial vs. paramount causation) is not the same in the two sets. If the four typifications were the same in each set, "symmetrical" would have been used rather than "reciprocal" to signify not only reciprocal causation but also formally *identical* types of causation. In either case, reciprocal or symmetrical, the form of the causal assertion is this: a change in X is a cause or the cause of a change in Y, and a change in Y is a cause or the cause of a change in X.

On the Causation of Perceived Control Capacity. The distinction between immediate and vicarious experience (or direct vs. indirect) is one reason why the relation between actual control attempts and perceived control capacity is much more problematical at the individual level than at the national level. At the national level, *complete* data on all actual control attempts in a country would make it more feasible to ignore vicarious control experiences; only the impact of foreign contacts would be a confounding factor. By contrast, it could be that for *some individuals* vicarious control experiences shape their perceptions of control capacity even more than do their actual control attempts, and to that extent the relation asserted by the axiom is especially problematical for individuals.

Even at the international level the relation is problematical, but measurement difficulties are irrelevant. Those difficulties are circumvented by treating the variables as constructs, meaning not subject to measurement (for an extensive treatment, see Appendix, pp. 284–288); hence, Axiom 1 is not directly testable. Nonetheless, if only because of the possibility of foreign contacts, there are probably at least some exceptions to the relation between the extent and efficacy of control attempts (*actual*) in a country and the residents' perceptions of control capacity.

The foregoing is consistent with what should be a principle for the social and behavioral sciences: even if human behavior is absolutely determined, each empirical generalization in a theory should be taken as problematical and for reasons apart from measurement error. If that principle is accepted, then one invidious comparison between contending theories is the extent to which each theory identifies sources of *indeterminacy*. As for Axiom 1, another source (i.e., in addition to foreign contacts) is that in some countries the dominant belief system or ideology emphasizes human omnipotence (i.e., anthropocentrism) inordinately; and that emphasis could create a disjunction between perceived control capacity and the *current* extent and efficacy of actual control attempts.[1] However, the emphasis is probably of such negligible importance relative to the extent and efficacy of control attempts that the latter can be identified as the *paramount* but not exclusive cause of perceived control capacity.

Any individual's perception of control capacity will increase eventually if he/she consistently and continually experiences, immediately or vicariously, only successful (effective) control attempts.[2] So the causation asserted in the first part of Axiom 1 is *positive*, the form being: increases in X cause increases in Y. Then there is every reason to suppose that the obverse holds. An individual's perception of control capacity will diminish eventually if he/she consistently and continually experiences (again, immediately or vicariously) only failures in control attempts.[3] So the causation is positive and *bidirectional*, the form being: increases in X cause increases in Y *and* decreases in X cause decreases in Y.

Despite the foregoing, it is not claimed that all dimensions of the construct "extent and efficacy of control attempts" have a causal relation with perceived control capacity. Elaboration of that qualification is best delayed until subsequent explication of the construct.

On the Causation of Control Attempts. Observe again that Axiom 1 asserts reciprocal causation. Insofar as changes in perceived control capacity cause changes in the extent and efficacy of control attempts, the causation clearly appears *positive* and *bidirectional*. An increase in perceived control capacity is hardly conducive to a decrease in control attempts, nor is there any reason to presume unidirectionality (increases in X cause increases in Y, but decreases in X do not cause decreases in Y). However, both the causation and the mechanism are debatable.

It may appear that the asserted causal relation is entirely compatible with reinforcement theory, including something akin to the law of effect.[4] Although it would be a mistake to argue incompatibility rather than compatibility, the second set of causal assertions in Axiom 1 is fundamentally different from the classical version of reinforcement theory. That version scarcely treats internal behavior (perception or otherwise) as a variable, let alone recognizes it as a determinant of overt behavior; and no version goes far enough in the way of recognizing that much of human learning does not require repeated reinforcement. To be sure, Axiom 1 suggests that a successful control attempt increases the probability of repetition, and in that sense the axiom is consistent with reinforcement theory. But the theory's classical version does not use the term "success," much less make the organism's perception a component of the causal mechanism. Moreover, classical reinforcement theory notwithstanding, it is not so much the environmental response to a control attempt that increases or decreases the probability of repetition; rather, *anticipation* of the environmental response partially determines the probability of repetition, and the anticipation is a manifestation of the perceived capacity for control capacity (for elaboration in the language of conventional psychology, see Fiske and Taylor, 1991:198, especially their references to Bandura).

The argument is not a denial that perceptions are shaped by experiences of control failures and successes; indeed, such determinacy enters into the first set of causal typifications in Axiom 1. But both sets are truly consistent only with a greatly expanded version of reinforcement theory, one that grants the importance of vicarious experience and recognizes perception's place in the causation of overt behavior.

Whatever the relevance of reinforcement theory, it is not needed to defend two claims. First, if an individual has contemplated but refrained from a particular kind of control attempt because he/she perceived only a negligible chance of success, the probability of that individual attempting the kind of control in question will be furthered by an increase in his/her perceived chance of success. Second, if an individual perceives success in a particular kind of control attempt as a virtual certainty and has made the attempt at least once, a great decline in his/her perception of the chances of success will reduce the probability of repetition.[5] Those two claims are a sufficient basis for (1) asserting that changes in perceived control capacity cause changes in the extent and efficacy of control attempts and (2) characterizing the causation as *positive* and *bidirectional*.

Why is perceived control capacity identified as only a *partial* cause of the extent and efficacy of control attempts? There are two reasons. First, Axiom 4 (*infra*) identifies variation in "amount of scientific activity" as another cause of variation in the extent and efficacy of control attempts. Second, variation in perceived control capacity influences three dimensions of the extent of control attempts—frequency, range, and scope; but the variation may have a negligible influence, if any, on intensity (the fourth extent dimension) and none on any efficacy dimension. The second consideration cannot be fully understood without an examination of the two constructs in Axiom 1, including dimensions of the extent and efficacy of control attempts.

The Two Constructs

Unlike any concept, only partial definitions of "extent and efficacy of control attempts" and "perceived control capacity" can be formulated; and even those definitions are bound to be so vague or incomplete that they promise negligible empirical applicability. The immediate consequence is that should independent investigators make observations or present data on the same individual or population concerning either the extent and efficacy of control attempts or perceived control capacity, even appreciable agreement would be most improbable. Appreciable agreement would require a standard research procedure and perhaps certain kinds of instruments (e.g., schedules, recording forms), but procedures and instrumentation presuppose a clear and complete definition of the phenomenon in question. Moreover, even if the human research subjects would tolerate all of the possibly relevant observations (including, perhaps, responding to survey questions), the research would require resources that are prohibitive for the social and behavioral sciences at present funding levels.

The extent to which *feasibility* limits research in the social and behavioral sciences cannot be exaggerated. Think of, for example, the difficulties of counting by direct observation the frequency of interaction of just one adult throughout a day. Many such limits would not be eliminated by greater resources or technical advances (e.g., innovations in devices for recording observations); legal and ethical restraints, such as respect for privacy, may be the most formidable barriers.

Should the purely practical problems, including limited resources, ever be solved and the requisite data gathered, it would have to be recognized that extent-efficacy of control and perceived control capacity are quantitative notions. Hence, the data could not be converted into measures without a formula, but it is a remote prospect at best. Even if the elementary values could be computed, there is no basis for choosing among alternative summary or composite measures. So the ultimate consideration is that, unlike a concept, in the context of a quantitative theory a construct is not linked to an empirically applicable formula.

The Extent of Control Attempts. In virtually any social unit the typical adult member engages daily in thousands of control attempts. Hazen and Trefil unwittingly provided an illustration (1991:1): "Your life is filled with routine—you set your alarm clock at night, take a shower in the morning, brush your teeth after breakfast, and fasten your seat belt. With each of these actions and a hundred others every day you acknowledge the power of predictability. If you don't set the alarm you'll probably be late for work or school. If you don't fasten your seat belt and then get into a freeway accident you may die."

What one acknowledges with each of such actions is the virtually continual engagement in diverse control attempts, including self-control. Moreover, predictability is not a power but, rather, an indication of the cognitive facet of control, meaning that an individual's belief about the consequences of his/her action is a necessary condition for the action to be a control attempt. The other necessary condition is something that Hazen and Trefil only suggest—a belief as to the desirability of the anticipated consequences, which is the *affective* facet of control attempts.

Given the sheer frequency of control attempts—one dimension of extent—it is inconceivable that anything like all attempts can be observed directly for even one individual from his/her birth onward, let alone for a national sample. Observations from birth onward are not essential to assess the relation between control attempts and perceived control capacity? Whatever the timing of the observations, various kinds of attempted control can be ignored? An affirmative answer to either question would be sheer conjecture.

The suggestion is not that one's perceptions are shaped solely by direct experiences, but extent and efficacy pertain to actual control attempts and not to vicarious experiences of control attempts. Yet "total control attempts" in a country include all within the national boundary, not excluding those made by nonresidents. Even if the behavior of nonresidents could be somehow excluded from observations, one resident's control attempt *may be* the source of another resident's vicarious experience.

Although the frequency of control attempts is the most conspicuous dimension of extent, *range* and *scope* are also relevant, especially when contemplating the determinants of perceived control capacity. To illustrate, a young child's control attempts are commonly numerous, but their range is typically limited to parents, toys (inanimate control), and pets (biotic control). For that matter, the *scope* of the child's attempted control over parental behavior is very narrow. The scope notion is not limited to control over human behavior, in which case it is a matter of the variety of kinds of acts that are subject to attempted control. When attempting inanimate control, a child often alters only an object's location, whereas adults commonly alter shape, size, composition, and/or color. Similarly, whereas a child may only hold a pet (thereby restraining its movement), an adult may train the animal or attempt to alter some of its anatomical characteristics (biotic control in either case).

Both dimensions of the extent of attempted control—range and scope—apply to populations as well as to individuals. Thus, in the former case, range pertains to the number and variety of things (humans, nonhuman organisms, objects, or substances) that at least one population member has attempted to control at least once during some stipulated period. By contrast, scope pertains to the variety of characteristics of those things that the would-be controller attempts to maintain or alter, including kinds of behavior (human or nonhuman).

Although beyond calculation, control range and scope appear much greater in the U.S. than in a foraging band (e.g., as among the Kalahari nomads). The difference is probably far less if the referents are the average for U.S. residents and the average for band members, but the construct encompasses such averages as well as *total* range and scope. Should it be argued that such distinctions are irrelevant when contemplating the determinants of perceived control capacity, the argument is purely speculative. In any case, the introduction of range and scope makes the construct all the more difficult to define, and the prospects of measurement become dimmer.

Various kinds of control attempts require only seconds and virtually no energy expenditure. Dialing a telephone or requesting directions is an example. The immediate implication is that two individuals or populations may have identical control attempt frequencies and yet differ sharply as to *intensity*, meaning the amount of time and/or energy invested.

The Efficacy of Control Attempts. Any control attempt may fail, and the success-failure distinction is the basis for speaking of control effectiveness. Briefly, whatever the units of comparison—individuals or social units—and whatever the time interval, control effectiveness is simply the proportion of control attempts that were successful (partially or wholly, depending on the purpose at hand) from the perspective of those making the attempt. The notion's quantitative character is realistic because only rarely do humans perceive themselves as incapable of control solely because of one failure.

Effectiveness is one of three dimensions of control efficacy, the other two being indispensability and efficiency. A particular kind of attempted control is indispensable if and only if perceived by those who engage in it as the *singular* effective means to the goal in question. Because the notion is predominantly relevant only in connection with the use of technological items in control attempts, its examination is delayed until the treatment of inanimate control.

Whether or not a control attempt is perceived as successful (i.e., effective), control efficiency is another matter. Control efficiency is reckoned in terms of the amount of time (temporal efficiency) and/or energy (energetic efficiency) *conserved*.[6] Briefly, the kind of control attempt is always assessed relative to some other kind in realizing the same goal, but the presumption is that both are effective (i.e., efficiency presupposes effectiveness). Thus, there is likely to be a difference in the amount of time and energy required to fell a tree with a power saw and felling it with an ax, though both are effective means for that particular kind of biotic control.

Efficiency can be conceptualized much more broadly, such that it refers not just to conservation of time and energy alone but to the conservation of "valued things" in general. That expansion makes the notion vague, but the suggestion is not that temporal or energetic efficiency can be measured readily; to the contrary, the difficulties are so great as to constitute still another reason for identifying "extent and efficacy of control attempts" as a construct.

Of the various dimensions just introduced, effectiveness may well be the pivotal determinant of perceived control capacity. As for the extent dimensions, great frequency, range, and scope promote perceived capacity only to the degree that the control attempts are effective; and intensity is especially problematical in connection with Axiom 1. Assuming that the feeling of effortless mastery promotes confidence in control attempts (a particular capacity perception), even effective intense control attempts may reduce perceived capacity somewhat. Still another possibility is that perceived control capacity promotes intensity, for the prospect of success may encourage the investment of time and energy. So of the four extent dimensions, there are more doubts about intensity in connection with Axiom 1. By contrast, efficient control attempts—those that *conserve* considerable amounts of human energy and time—promote a feeling of effortless mastery.

Perceived Control Capacity. Unlike actual control attempts, perceived control capacity is entirely *internal* (covert) behavior; hence, it is not even partially subject to direct observation. Nonetheless, the following question illustrates the kind of survey question that could be posed when attempting to measure perceived control capacity in a contemporary English-speaking social unit: "Can you fly a jet aircraft?" Consider just five of numerous problems. First, even if the survey could be limited to inanimate control, in some social units a jet aircraft is only one of millions of *kinds* of objects or substances that at least one member attempts to control frequently. Second, piloting an aircraft involves the coordination of numerous specific kinds of acts; hence, a separate capacity question could be posed about each kind. Third, the subject is *effective* control, but the illustrative question leaves that consideration implicit. Fourth, the question pertains to perceived *personal* capacity and ignores perceptions about *pan-human* control capacity (i.e., that of all humans). Fifth, doubts about the appropriate form of a capacity question are accentuated in the case of impersonal capacity. Such problems make a defensible measure of perceived control capacity a remote prospect at best.

There is at least one reason for assuming that the relation asserted by Axiom 1 is far from uniform internationally or over time for any country. Foreign contacts are likely to have had some impact on the beliefs of residents as to what humans can or cannot control, which alone is conducive to a problematical relation between actual control attempts by population members and their perception of human control capacity. For instance, Captain Cook's ship and all things aboard were products of inanimate control that took place far from Hawaii; but Cook's visits may have expanded the Hawaiians' perceptions of control capacity enormously. If so, the second part of Axiom 1 implies that during or shortly after Cook's first visit there was an increase in the average extent and efficacy of control attempts by Hawaiians (perhaps to Cook's misfortune). Yet it would not follow that all extent dimensions increased. After all, humans do not automatically commence more control attempts merely because they perceive a greater prospect of success.

The Axiom's Unit Phrase and Temporal Considerations

Although the unit phrase in all of the theory's constituent generalizations is "Among countries and for any country over time," the rationale is not the same for each generalization. In the case of Axiom 1 the primary concern is the source of experiences (immediate or vicarious, direct or indirect) that shape perceptions of control capacity. Some of those sources may be external to the country in question (e.g., as when a resident travels abroad), and such cases are conducive to a problematical relation between the extent and efficacy of control attempts *in the territory* and the residents' perceptions of control capacity. Hence, the unit terms in Axiom 1 are "countries" and "country" because they are thought to *minimize* exogenous experiences of control attempts (those that are external to the territorial unit in question, be it a city or country) and thereby reduce the association between the two variables.

The limitation of a theory to one type of unit (in this case, "countries") reduces its *explicit* range to the minimum, but its *implicit* range is not reduced if the theorist is willing, as here, to make an auxiliary generalization. For this particular theory the generalization is: the association between the variables is greater for countries than for any other type of social unit (e.g., cities). In a sense, that generalization extends the theory's range to all types of social units.

Temporal Considerations. Construe Axiom 1 as implying an auxiliary generalization about *temporality*, one that is consistent with a common conception of causation: for a country over time, changes in the extent and efficacy of control are more closely related to changes in perceived control capacity when there is some time lag between the variables than when there is no time lag. Although the generalization expands the axiom's *intensity*, it would be untestable even if the constituent variables were not constructs. The amount of lag time between the two variables that maximizes the association between them is unknown, but that ignorance need not halt theory construction.

The temporal specifications can be delayed up to the a point that concepts are linked to referentials (see Figure 3–1); and even then the decision may be, as it is here, that the available data are such that only a synchronic association (no lag) between referents should be considered when testing the theory. However, if the data situation improves, it may prove possible to increase the association's magnitude through exploratory research, wherein the time lag between referents is varied systematically.

Perceived Control Capacity and Supernaturalism

The general idea underlying Axiom 2 (Figure 3–1) is suggested by Skinner's argument (1971:7): "Man's first experience with causes probably came from his own behavior: things moved because he moved them. If other things moved, it was because someone else was moving them, and if the mover could not be seen, it was because he was invisible." When introducing an invisible mover Skinner came close to the notion of supernaturalism, and there are four related questions. First, is it defensible to expand Skinner's argument beyond movement to control, meaning that an attempt to move something is an attempt to control it? Second, when humans postulate an invisible being, are they inclined to attribute power (control capacity) to it? Third, are failures in control attempts conducive to the postulation of invisible beings or incomprehensible causal processes? Fourth, when humans postulate such a thing, are they inclined to attempt at least partial control of it? The control argument about supernaturalism consists of affirmative answers to the four questions; and the basic generalization is expressed by Axiom 2: *Among countries and for any country over time, perceived control capacity is the asymmetrical, negative, bidirectional, and partial determinant of the amount of supernaturalism.*

Amount of Supernaturalism

The term "amount of supernaturalism" cannot be linked to an empirically applicable formula, but it is a construct for a more immediate reason. There is no prospect of a complete and a clear definition of supernaturalism; and without such a definition the pursuit of an empirically applicable formula is virtually doomed to fail, even ignoring practical problems in acquiring requisite data.

Major Conceptual Difficulties. In defining the term "supernaturalism" several serious problems are not conspicuous because scholars often use the term when conceptualizing religion or magic but leave it undefined (see Guthrie's commentary, 1980:185). Treating the term as a primitive will not do, but dictionary definitions merely offer synonyms (e.g., miraculous) and uninformative phrases (e.g., above and beyond nature). As for the common suggestion that the term refers to a belief in the nonempirical or unobservable, the suggestion ignores the vocabularies of the advanced sciences. Those vocabularies bristle with terms that denote postulated entities or forces (e.g., photons, gravity), none of which are empirical or observable in the ordinary sense.

When scholars use the term "supernaturalism" in defining religion, it appears to denote a very broad class of phenomena. That broadness creates doubts not only about the empirical applicability of the term's definition but also as to how religion differs from supernatural beliefs and practices in general.[7] In particular, various problems arise when attempting to distinguish religion from (*inter alia*) magic and superstition (see, especially, *Current Anthropology*, Vol. 21, pp. 181–203, and Vol. 23, pp. 37–66). The general point, however, is that Axiom 2 should not be thought of in terms of religion or religiosity rather than supernaturalism.

Proposed Definition. Supernaturalism is a belief in the current, future, or previous existence of a supernatural being and/or a supernatural causal process. The definition promises negligible empirical applicability without an auxiliary definition of two key phrases.[8] First, "belief in the existence of a supernatural being": a conviction of the existence of an entity which (1) is unobservable to some if not all humans; (2) can communicate in some sense or another with some if not all humans; (3) may respond to some kinds of human behavior, though the kinds and the response are not necessarily predictable by anyone; and (4) can control at least one kind of condition that no human can control independently of the being, not even with any known technological item.[9] Second, "belief in the existence of supernatural causation": (1) a conviction that some or all instances of at least one class of events or things are caused by a process which can be initiated or prevented by at least one human being, who is unable or unwilling to communicate the technique of initiation or prevention publicly, such that some or all humans who do not share the conviction can learn to terminate or prevent the process and/or (2) a conviction of the existence of some causal process or condition, one held by someone who is unable or unwilling to stipulate what failures in predictions pertaining to the process or condition would prompt them to abandon the conviction.

In the case of the second kind of belief about supernatural causation (which may or may not be held simultaneously along with a corresponding belief of the first kind about the same causal process), one and the same belief may be supernatural for some individuals who hold it but not for others. It is entirely a matter of willingness and ability to stipulate what would prompt abandonment of the belief, which is an epistemological consideration and one less vague than reference to "faith."

The definitions make no reference to science if only because in recent decades numerous scholars have come to deny that science has any distinctive unity (see, especially, Feyerabend, 1975); hence, they have promoted doubts about any definition of supernaturalism that employs the term "science" or "scientific" and precluded consensus as to the term's meaning. The same may be said of empirical evidence or testability or truth.

The extent of the definition's empirical applicability is admittedly debatable, and for that reason alone the term "amount of supernaturalism" should be identified as a construct.[10] The likely fate of an attempt to devise a measure of supernaturalism is indicated by the multitude of purported measures or scales of religiosity (see Wulff's survey, 1991:chp. 5), all of which have been criticized for myriad reasons; and scores of historical or ethnographic studies (e.g., Eliade's history of religious ideas [1978, 1982, 1985] and Devlin's account [1987] of the supernatural in 19th-century France) create even more doubts.

However, the definition of supernatural should not be equated with any well-known definition of religion or magic (for some references, see Lehmann and Myers, 1985:1–5, 191–194, and Guthrie, 1980); and while separate generalizations about the two kinds of supernaturalism—beings vs. causation—are not presently feasible, that consideration does not invalidate Axiom 2. To be sure, the theory would be enriched by separate generalizations, possibly something like this: beliefs in supernatural beings are generated more by perceptions of total impotence in certain control spheres (e.g., earthquake prevention) than by perceptions of the problematical quality of effective control (as in hunting and gambling), which are more likely to be manifested in beliefs in the existence of supernatural causation (commonly identified as magic). But, obviously, to enrich a theory is not to invalidate it.

On the Causation of Amount of Supernaturalism

The theory is stated in the hope that some sociologists will test it, or at least judge it in light of tests. The hope is naive given the apparent inclination of many sociologists to judge theories in terms of preconceptions or presuppositions.[11] That inclination makes personal opinion sacrosanct, and it works against the statement of theories in accordance with a formal mode. Because they recognize the disinclination of sociologists to judge theories in light of tests, sociological theorists virtually specialize in rhetoric; and the discursive mode of theory construction permits polemics. Nonetheless, additional arguments are made in defense of Axiom 2 and other parts of the theory in the hope of furthering tests by promoting plausibility, something quite different from the promotion of plausibility as a substitute for tests.

A Few Observations on Hominid Evolution. Certain features of hominid evolution make Axiom 2 more plausible. Hominid evolution can be summarized in one generalization: over the past four million years (perhaps commencing with *Australopethicus*) hominids increasingly realized a greater range and scope of all basic types of control. Illustrating briefly (for a vast elaboration, see Gibbs, 1989:chp. 5, and Beniger, 1986:61–118), upright bipedalism enormously expanded the range of biotic control. Unprecedented dexterity made it possible for hominids to carry and share food more than do other primates. The eventual larger brain facilitated the invention of tools (e.g., the carrying bag, wooden instruments), perhaps long before the Stone Age, and expanded control over human behavior through new modes of communication.

Anything like a uniform increase in perceived control capacity throughout hominid evolution is not presumed. Assuming a high initial failure rate for various kinds of control attempts, very early on hominids may have become acutely aware of their control impotence in conditions threatening survival, such as large predators, storms, earthquakes, and droughts.[12] As hominids came to exercise more effective control, they probably grew aware of control possibilities; but it is likely that initially the range and scope of their effective control were very limited.

So supernaturalism grew out of two things that distinguished hominids from other animals—a sense of capacity for effective control but an equal appreciation of control failures and impotence. However, the claim differs somewhat from that suggested by Festinger (1981:313): "in the same way that we recognize the discovery of how to make, use, and control fire as a highly important technological event, we must also recognize that the invention of a god who controlled rain, together with the invention of ways to influence that god, was an equally or, perhaps, more important technological innovation." Because the word "invention" suggests conscious and deliberate, it is not used here in connection with the origin of the supernaturalism. Otherwise, Festinger's statement is fully consistent with Axiom 2.

In all populations—ancient or contemporary—perceived control capacity probably varies considerably from one sphere of life or kind of activity to another; and some of those contrasts lend support to Axiom 2. Contemplate Malinowski's observation on the Trobriand Islands (1954:31) "in the lagoon fishing, where man can rely completely upon his knowledge and skill, magic does not exist, while in the open-sea fishing, full of danger and uncertainty, there is extensive magic ritual to secure safety and good results." As for systematic research findings, Felson and Gmelch (1979) report two positive associations among types of activities (e.g., gambling, sports, taking examinations): first, the greater the uncertainty entailed in an activity, the great the proportion of individuals who report using magic in that activity; and, second, the greater the reported anxiety about an activity, the greater the proportion reporting use of magic in that activity.[13] Assuming an inverse relation between feelings of uncertainty or anxiety and perceived control capacity, then the latter is associated negatively with the use of magic.

Contemporary Affluence and Control. The very idea of an affluent society suggests extensive effective control, and international comparisons of standard of living are consistent with that suggestion. The U.S. has most of the characteristics conventionally taken as indicative of a relatively high standard of living (e.g., percentage of houses having indoor plumbing), and there is evidence that the extent and efficacy of control in the U.S. are much greater than in most countries. Some examples are: the country's enormous per capita consumption of inanimate energy indicates extensive inanimate control, the low percentage of the economically active in agriculture suggests very efficient biotic control, and America's large organizations require extensive human control.

What has been said of the U.S. can be said of numerous other countries (e.g., Australia, Canada, Japan, New Zealand, and most European countries), but critics are more likely to regard the U.S. as a glaring exception to Axiom 2. Various statistics can be cited as evidence that Americans exceed many nationalities when it comes to professing a belief in a god, affiliation with organized religion, and church-synagogue attendance.[14] Stating the matter more generally, critics will argue that Americans are known for "religiosity" despite the extent and efficacy of control in the U.S.

The counterargument goes beyond the most obvious consideration—religiosity is only one dimension or kind of supernaturalism. Even if it were the only dimension or kind, there is little agreement in definitions of religiosity, nor one that promises substantial empirical applicability. Moreover, there is no prospect whatever of a feasible and acceptable measure of religiosity (again, see Wulff, 1991:chp. 5), and it is pointless to rely on such "indicators" as the percent who ostensibly believe in a god or attend church-synagogue regularly (see, e.g., observations by Gallup and Castelli, 1987:21, on "gaps" in the U.S. between expression of religious belief and other features of religious life, such as professions of faith but no basic knowledge about that faith).

There is a special danger that the validity of Axioms 1 and 2 will be confused, and again the U.S. is a strategic case. While there is all manner of evidence indicating that the extent of control in the U.S. is much greater than in the typical country, there is really no systematic evidence concerning perceived control capacity; but the amount of insecurity stemming from rampant criminality, unemployment, recessions, and problematical access to expensive health care are alone reason for doubts about America's relative standing. Indeed, regardless of the affluence level, the continuing reality of lethal diseases (AIDS being the latest), the possibility of natural disasters (e.g., earthquakes), and the inevitability of death all lessen perceived control capacity.[15] The general point is that no social unit ever has come even remotely close to total effective control, and few humans are unaware of control failures and control impotence (see Garner and Garner's research [1991] on insecurity in two European cities). Indeed, the most pervasive source of perceived control impotence may be the sheer vastness of the universe.

The suggestion is not that the U.S. contradicts either Axiom 1 or Axiom 2 (i.e., that both cannot be valid in the American case). Rather, while general observations do suggest that the extent and efficacy of control in the U.S. are greater than in many other countries (perhaps all), any conclusion about international differences as regards perceived control capacity would be conjecture. If the general observations on international contrasts in the extent and efficacy of control are valid and if Axiom 1 is valid, then perceived control capacity should be greater in the U.S. than in most countries. Again, though, crime and economic insecurity are alone sufficient to anticipate considerable American supernaturalism, including what is commonly interpreted as a manifestation of religiosity.

Types of Causation in Axiom 2. Previous arguments imply that increases in perceived control capacity cause decreases in supernaturalism (hence, "negative" causation), but there are doubts and controversy. Although supernaturalism has been defined as a belief, any supernatural belief system—all beliefs pertaining to the same being or force—is associated with some kind of overt behavior. Such behavior is conventionally identified as a "practice," some of which take the form of attempted control of secular events or things through attempted control of the supernatural being or force in question. Illustrative support comes in this interpretation of the prayers of avowed Christians (though not peculiar to that religion): at least some of the prayers explicitly or implicitly solicit a supernatural being's intervention in secular situations.

Observe that such solicitations are in themselves indicative of some perceived control capacity; hence, they are contrary to Axiom 2. However, the argument is that such control attempts (i.e., through the supernatural) are quantitatively negligible in comparison to purely secular attempts; hence, the latter are the primary determinants of perceived control capacity.

Nothing has been said to suggest that changes in the amount of supernaturalism cause changes in perceived control capacity; instead, Axiom 2 asserts that the amount of supernaturalism is determined by perceived control capacity, and the causation is identified as asymmetrical (i.e., nonreciprocal). The rationale is introduced by this question: assuming that increases in perceived control capacity do lead to a decreases in supernaturalism, why would those decreases in turn lead to further increases in perceived control capacity? After all, abandonment of a supernatural belief or practice does not somehow automatically elevate perceived control capacity.

Supernatural control attempts are commonly ineffective even from the viewpoint of the participants; and failures are especially likely in the case of secondary supernatural control attempts, meaning attempts to control secular events or things through the control (primary) of supernatural beings or forces. So even if a change in the amount of supernaturalism does cause a change in perceived control capacity, it is likely to be a negligible partial cause and negative but unidirectional (i.e., increases in supernaturalism causes decreases in perceived control capacity but decreases in supernaturalism do not cause increases in perceived control capacity). Nevertheless, the possibility of some kind of reciprocal causation should be contemplated when revising the theory.

Another specific argument in support of Axiom 2: perceived control capacity is a human need in that (1) humans survive through control attempts and (2) for all practical purposes control attempts require perception of some prospect of success. Accordingly, when perceived control capacity declines to a very low level, the only alternative to catatonic immobility is the postulation of a supernatural being or force and attempted control of secular events or things indirectly—through the supernatural. The argument extends to the possibility of an evolutionary process wherein "supernatural credulity" was selected.[16] That possibility becomes less counterintuitive on recognition that the level of perceived control capacity is determined predominantly by purely secular control attempts (i.e., supernatural control attempts, primary or secondary, play a minor role). Hence, if perceived control capacity declines to a point approaching the absolute minimum, catatonic immobility can be avoided only by resort to the supernatural. Granted, if supernatural beliefs are not coordinated with secular attempts at control, they scarcely have environmental consequences and, therefore, do not promote human survival. But supernatural and secular control attempts are commonly coordinated; indeed, secondary supernatural control attempts are defined in terms of such coordination. Thus, among foraging peoples, hunters do not assume that a supernatural rite or ceremony, whether magical or religious, in itself provides game; rather, it is believed to enhance the chances of success in actual hunting.[17] Nevertheless, despite the coordination, increases in perceived control capacity eventually cause decreases in supernaturalism; and a corollary—a low level of perceived control capacity causes a high level of supernaturalism—takes on added significance when thinking of hominid history.

Again, perceived control capacity is predominantly determined by purely secular control attempts, and supernaturalism emerges only when control capacity is perceived over a long period as very limited.[18] Consequently, the causal relation has a quantum character, meaning that an enormous change in perceived control capacity (increase or decrease) is required for a discernible change in the amount of supernaturalism. Moreover, the effect of a change in perceived control capacity tends to depend on the original perceptual level, probably being most negligible when the original perceptual level was extremely high or extremely low. Even so, the typification of the causation as being bidirectional is debatable. As suggested earlier, secularism and supernaturalism appear to be fairly stable epistemological orientations rather than transitory mental states. Therefore, if an individual's perceived control capacity has remained near the maximum for several decades, not even a sudden and drastic decline would prompt him/her to abandon purely secular control attempts for supernatural control attempts. However, if the extent and efficacy of control in a country declines gradually but substantially and Axiom 1 is valid, then sooner or later subsequent generations will perceive themselves as having a very limited control capacity and will eschew a secular world view.

In the behavioral and social sciences assertions of monistic causation are likely to appear incredulous; therefore, the safest course is to assert only partial causation. Yet partial causation should not be equated with the mere recognition of other possible causes, some or all of which have only a negligible effect on the dependent variable. So one variable, X, should be identified as the partial cause of another, Y, if and only if in the theory at least one other variable, Z, is identified also as a partial cause of Y. In the present theory perceived control capacity is the X variable, amount of supernaturalism the Y variable, and amount of scientific activity the Z variable. The Z–Y causation is treated in observations on Axiom 3 (*infra*).

The Unit Phrase

Unless indicated otherwise subsequently, previous comments on the form of Axiom 1 apply to all other axioms. However, there is a particular need for additional comments on the unit phrase, and the comments illustrate how the unit phrase plays a crucial role in qualifying the theory (for a commentary on unit phrases in general, see Appendix, pp. 290–292).

The key unit terms in Axiom 2 are "countries" and "country" primarily because they are an essential qualification of Axiom 1 and some subsequent premises. By contrast, Axiom 2 may hold equally well for various other unit terms (i.e., metropolitan areas, age groups in a city), but there is a doubt about using "among individuals or for an individual over time" as the axiom's unit phrase. An individual's belief in the supernatural can be altered enormously by one dramatic event (e.g., accidental death of an intimate); hence, the relation asserted by Axiom 2 may be far more problematical for individuals than for countries, because an isolated dramatic event typically has a negligible impact on a large population. Stated otherwise, if the amount of supernaturalism could be measured, the values would be much more stable for countries than for individuals.

Supernaturalism and Scientific Activity

In myriad ways control notions facilitate anticipation of what otherwise would be puzzling empirical relations, but those notions must facilitate interpretation also of putatively obvious empirical relations. Such a relation is asserted in Axiom 3: *Among countries and for a country over time, the amount of supernaturalism is the symmetrical, negative, bidirectional, and partial determinant of the amount of scientific activity.* The axiom is consistent with what was at least once a conventional Western belief: science and supernaturalism are antithetical.[19] The argument is commonly expressed as though limited to science and religion (see, especially, Brooke, 1991); but there is no particular rationale for not extending the argument to science and supernaturalism in general, even though Brooke (1991:63) treats magic as playing a positive role in promoting the scientific revolution in the 16th century. For that matter, it is now fashionable to deny that science has any distinctive unity (the new "received view"), and that denial blurs the boundary between supernaturalism and science.[20] One manifestation is Winkelman's argument (1982) that anthropology should grant the existence of *psi* phenomena.

Beyond the Once Conventional Belief: Intrinsic Incompatibility

The belief itself does not answer this question: if the relation between science and supernaturalism is antithetical, why? The question does not signify endorsement of the demand for designations of ultimate causes, a most pernicious demand when assessing a theory. Nevertheless, there is every reason to doubt that a change in the amount of supernaturalism or a change in the amount of scientific activity somehow automatically causes a change in the other. Of course, pursuit of the "why" or "how" question presumes that the relation is one of incompatibility, but a recent scholarly work (Brooke, 1991) is a vast denial of that presumption as it applies to the relation between religion and science in Western history. Contemplate Brooke's summary denial (1991:6): "The popular antithesis between science...and religion...is assuredly simplistic."

Brooke has framed several important questions that no generalization like Axiom 3 would answer even if valid, one being (1991:1): "Did religious movements assist the emergence of the scientific movement, or was there a power struggle from the start?" However, it is one thing to recognize complexities but quite different to assert (Brooke, 1991:321) this: "There is no such thing as *the* relationship between science and religion. It is what different individuals and communities have made of it in a plethora of different contexts." The assertion borders on obscurantism because Brooke does not speak of a relationship with regard to particular dimensions, aspects, or properties of religion and science, such as the amount of activity, the proportion of beliefs, or a categorical preference of one over the other. Had he done so, the phrase "no such thing" would be unwarranted. Thus, suppose someone advances this generalization: since 1400 in Europe there has been a negative association between the annual amount of scientific activity and church-synagogue attendance. To be sure, it is inconceivable that the generalization can be tested in some defensible way, but testability is not the issue posed by Brooke's "no such thing."

There are two principal ways by which supernaturalism and science are incompatible. The intrinsic way is largely psychological; thinking in one mode, supernaturally or scientifically, is alien to thinking in the other mode. If the two were defined such that they are all inclusive but mutually exclusive (i.e., all behavior is either supernaturalism or scientific), the relation would be a logical necessity; but it would be grotesque to define the two such that they are all inclusive.[21] Indeed, by anything like conventional definitions, the bulk of human behavior is neither supernaturalism nor scientific. To illustrate, few if any definitions would justify identifying any of the following as supernaturalism or science: the belief that George Bush was not the first U.S. President; mowing grass, the belief that 4 is the square root of 16, driving a car, and on and on. Nor is it impossible for a human to believe in something clearly scientific but also believe in something else clearly supernatural. Thus, no one would be truly stunned if a physicist should express a belief in Christ's divinity or, for that matter, nurse a few superstitious beliefs. As Brooke (1991:5) succinctly makes the point: "many scientists of stature have professed a religious faith, even if their theology was sometimes suspect."

So there is a pressing need to describe the sense in which supernaturalism and science are intrinsically incompatible, at least to the point of justifying Axiom 3 beyond its consistency with convention. To that end it is imperative to think about the supernaturalism-science relation in terms of control.

Scientific activity commonly involves, is undertaken to realize, and/or results in secular control. As such, it is a quite different even from secondary supernatural control attempts (at secular control through supernatural beings or forces). Briefly, in science the justification for a belief in control effectiveness is some putatively demonstrable empirical regularity. Before dismissing that argument, critics should compare justifications of beliefs and practices given by avowed Christian fundamentalists or avid gamblers with those given by experimental physicists. Yet a belief in an empirical regularity need not be based on crude induction, as it may be, when lighting a Bunsen burner. Thus, the first atomic explosion was the product of inanimate control, but the related beliefs were not based on pure induction. Nonetheless, it would be obstinate to deny that some of those beliefs were based, at least in part, on previously demonstrated empirical regularities.

To justify Axiom 3 further, it is necessary to recognize two contending and incompatible epistemological orientations: (1) acceptance of demonstrated or anticipated empirical regularities as the ultimate justifications for beliefs or practices and (2) indifference if not hostility to such justification. The notion of intrinsic incompatibility anticipates an inverse relation among individuals between the two orientations. However, returning to the previous illustration, a physicist's belief in Christ's divinity would not invalidate the anticipation; but it would be invalidated by evidence that *in general* physicists and avowed fundamentalists (Christians or Muslims) do not differ as regards the two orientations.

Beyond the Conventional Belief: Extrinsic Incompatibility

Extrinsic incompatibility between the supernatural and the scientific is social rather than psychological. In many social units some members (e.g., government officials) encourage or discourage other members from believing and/or acting in accordance with one of the two orientations, the supernatural or the scientific. When the Church silenced Galileo, that action discouraged the scientific orientation; but the antireligious programs of Marxist regimes were designed to discourage supernaturalism, religion in particular. However, there is the well-known thesis (see Brooke, 1991:110–116, citing R.K. Merton) that Puritan values fueled British science.

Some Difficulties. It need not be assumed that extrinsic incompatibility prevails in all social units; rather, an inverse relation between science and supernaturalism requires only that in some social units one orientation is encouraged and/or the other discouraged. Tests of the theorems derived from Axiom 3 could support the axiom without identifying the types of social units (e.g., feudal) in which supernaturalism is encouraged and science discouraged or vice versa. That possibility is fortunate because formulating such a typology will be difficult. To illustrate, the Roman transition from paganism to Christianity was a major shift and involved much more than adoption of monotheism. Yet, according to Ferris (1988:42), science was not encouraged before or after the transition.

Then consider the traditional Marxist suggestion that capitalists support religion because of its conservative influence on the masses. Even if true, in Western Europe science continued to develop during the growth of capitalism.

On Types of Causation

The foregoing arguments justify the assertion of a casual relation between amount of supernaturalism and amount of scientific activity, but the arguments are all too general. Explications of the causation types are needed to identify relevant evidence and to justify deductions from Axiom 3 in conjunction with other premises.

On Causation of Amount of Scientific Activity. At this stage it is not feasible to assess the relative importance of intrinsic and extrinsic incompatibility. Fortunately, an assessment is not necessary to assert that changes in the amount of supernaturalism cause changes in the amount of scientific activity.

Whatever the type of incompatibility—intrinsic or extrinsic—the causation is *negative*. Specifically, increases in supernaturalism cause decreases in the amount of scientific activity. That particular causal direction may appear strange, for it is commonly believed that in Western history increases in scientific activity caused decreases in supernaturalism; but if the two are somehow incompatible, there is no obvious reason why an increase in supernaturalism would not cause a decrease in scientific activity. Nor is there any obvious reason why a decrease in supernaturalism could not cause an increase in the amount of scientific activity. So the causation is assumed to be *bidirectional*.

If a relation between variables is causal in the sense of mutual incompatibility, then one variable's magnitude somehow sets an upper limit on the other's magnitude. As such, an increase in one variable only reduces the upper possible limit of the other variable, which may or may not actually decrease. Similarly, a decrease in one variable only expands the upper possible limit of the other variable, which may or may not actually increase. Viewed that way, a change in supernaturalism is only a necessary condition for a change in scientific activity. But the necessary-sufficient distinction does not totally invalidate Axiom 3, because change in supernaturalism is asserted to be only a *partial* cause of change in scientific activity.[22] Axiom 4 (*infra*) asserts another partial cause of change in the amount of scientific activity.

On Causation of Amount of Supernaturalism. The rationale for asserting that change in scientific activity causes change in supernaturalism is not merely an ostensible association in Western history.[23] If viewed as a matter of incompatibility, there is no reason why a *decrease* in scientific activity would not further the probability of an *increase* in supernaturalism. That consequence might not be manifested for at least a generation, but the causation itself is so contrary to Western history that any estimate of the time lag would be wild conjecture. Nevertheless, whatever the lag, the type of causation is *negative* and *bidirectional*, though perhaps only of the limiting type described in previous observations on the incompatibility of science and supernaturalism. In light of those previous observations the causation is *symmetrical* (i.e., mutual incompatibility); but if only because of Western history, there are more doubts about increases in supernaturalism reducing the amount of scientific activity.

Symmetrical causation is not the only issue. Critics may grant that change in the amount of scientific activity is a *partial* cause of change in the amount of supernaturalism, but then argue that the additional causes are not limited to perceived control capacity (see Axiom 2, Figure 3–1). The only defense against the argument is to demand systematic evidence. Yet there are surely bases for reasonable doubts about Axiom 3, though some may stem from misinterpretations. In particular, although Axioms 2 and 3 taken together identify two causes of change in the amount of supernaturalism, no claim is made about their relative importance. Perceived control capacity may be a much greater determinant, and Axiom 3 does not claim that the amount of scientific activity is even a major determinant of the amount of supernaturalism.

The Symmetrical Relation Between Control and Science

Complexity in the social and behavioral sciences is exacerbated by the real possibility that many causal relations are reciprocal (or symmetrical). Such is the case for the relation between control extent-efficacy and amount of scientific activity, as expressed in Axiom 4: *Among countries and for any country over time, the extent and efficacy of control attempts are the reciprocal, positive, bidirectional, and partial determinants of the amount of scientific activity, and the amount of scientific activity is the reciprocal, positive, unidirectional, and partial determinant of the extent and efficacy of control attempts.* Note particularly that in the axiom's second part the causal relation is identified as *unidirectional*, meaning that an increase in scientific activity assertedly causes an increase in the extent and efficacy of control attempts; but it is not asserted that a decrease in the former causes a decrease in the latter. In this case the term "positive" comes before and qualifies unidirectional, thereby asserting that an increase in the causal variable (henceforth, "X") causes an increase in the effect variable (henceforth "Y"); and "negative" would be interpreted as asserting that a decrease in X causes a decrease in Y. If increases in X are asserted to cause decreases in Y unidirectionally, then the term "positive–negative" would qualify unidirectional; and if decreases in X assertedly cause increases in Y, then term "negative-positive" would be the qualification of unidirectional.

Although not shown in Figure 3–1 because of space limitations and the need to simplify, the causal relation between amount of scientific activity and the extent and efficacy of control attempts is the same for each basic type of control. So Axiom 4 is actually a composite of three independent sets of causal assertions, as follow.

Axiom 4a: Among countries and for any country over time, the extent and efficacy of inanimate control attempts are the reciprocal, positive, bidirectional, and partial determinants of the amount of scientific activity; and the amount of scientific activity is the reciprocal, positive, unidirectional, and partial determinant of the extent and efficacy of inanimate control attempts.

Axiom 4b: Among countries and for any country over time, the extent and efficacy of attempts to control human behavior are the reciprocal, positive, bidirectional, and partial determinants of the amount of scientific activity; and the amount of scientific activity is the reciprocal, positive, unidirectional, and partial determinant of the extent and efficacy of attempts to control human behavior.

Axiom 4c: Among countries and for any country over time, the extent and efficacy of biotic control attempts are the reciprocal, positive, bidirectional, and partial determinants of the amount of scientific activity; and the amount of scientific activity is the reciprocal, positive unidirectional, and partial determinant of the extent and efficacy of biotic control attempts.

Note that the *form* of the three axioms is identical with the form of Axiom 4. So, unless indicated otherwise, all subsequent observations on Axiom 4 apply to Axioms 4a, 4b, and 4c.

The Dependence of Science on Control

By virtually any definition, scientific activity is different from such sustenance activities as hunting, planting, and manufacturing. For one thing, scientific activity does not directly yield food or shelter. Indeed, science requires surplus time and energy, meaning beyond whatever is required to realize conditions absolutely essential for human survival. The requisite surplus largely depends on the efficacy of control attempts in sustenance activities, especially biotic and inanimate control.

The Immediate Complexity. The foregoing argument depicts science as dependent on control. That relation is especially conspicuous when scientific activity becomes a full-time occupation, a specialization that appears essential for extensive amounts of that activity. However, the problem is not just ascertaining the control *level* necessary for some particular amount of scientific activity. Even if that level could be ascertained, it is likely to be only a necessary condition for the amount of scientific activity in question.

The complexity is illustrated by the change in beliefs about hunting-gathering peoples (foragers). At one time those people were believed to struggle for existence, with little leisure time. Yet it now appears that some tribes or bands of foragers have (or had) more leisure time than do industrial workers, especially in the 19th century.[24] Nonetheless, by any conventional definition, there is little if any scientific activity among such peoples.

Science's Technological Character. A brief visit at a physics or chemistry laboratory would suffice to conclude that science's dependence on control is not just a matter of surplus time and energy. In those laboratories there are multitudes of machines, tools, and other diverse artifacts. Less conspicuous, there is an enormous daily use of water, electricity, and combustible substances (i.e., natural gas). Because all of those things are made or modified by humans, they are technological; and even scientists appear to underestimate the material basis of their activity.

There is no prospect for identifying the very first scientific activity, but it is difficult to imagine that it consisted merely of observations without technological items. Thus, huge stones arranged to mark celestial sightings are evidence of prehistoric astronomy, surely an early scientific activity (Hazen and Trefil, 1991:2–4). Whatever its origin, science's dependence on control has a long history, and general observations suggest an escalation in recent centuries. For instance, various kinds of experimental work in particle physics requires accelerators, the construction of which requires indescribable varieties of inanimate control.

Scientific Activity's Purposive Quality. Previous observations indicate that a certain level of control extent-efficacy is only *necessary* for a certain amount of scientific activity; and, if so, the causation asserted in Axiom 4 is unjustified. But both scientific activity and its promotion are purposive behavior.[25] So, contrary to those who belittle human behavior's purposive quality, substantial increases in scientific activity are not even largely crescive; rather, they are consciously produced primarily through control over human behavior, and the control is not just that of scientists over other personnel in organizations or facilities (e.g., laboratories). A large amount of scientific activity cannot be realized without such intramural control, but in recent centuries scientists or their agents increasingly have attempted to promote science by controlling those who control the requisite resources (see, e.g., *Science*, Vol. 248, pp. 803–804, and Bruce, 1987). However, the relation is commonly that of cooperation to further the interest of both parties, as in the case of the American Breeders' Association and geneticists in the early 1900s (Kimmelman, 1983).

Should the foregoing argument be doubted, the skeptic is encouraged to examine the activities of agents of (to mention only a few of many relevant organizations) the National Academy of Sciences, the Association for the Advancement of Science, the American Chemical Society, the American Institute of Physics, the National Science Foundation, and the American Psychological Association (see Fries, 1984). Those agents commonly attempt to control ("influence" is the euphemism) legislators, other government officials, and officers of foundations to obtain more resources for science. True, in any contemporary country such control attempts are only a minute fraction of the total, but it is assumed that promotional control attempts and total control attempts vary directly. The assumption is not limited to science. Durkheim and robotic sociology notwithstanding, substantial increases in some activity can be sustained only if the participants organize themselves to promote that mutual interest; and an interest cannot be promoted without control attempts (indeed, "promotion" is another euphemism), perhaps coercive control attempts.

The Dependence of Control on Science

Only a causal reading of the history of scientific discoveries (e.g., Harvey's of blood circulation, Mendel's of some principles of heredity, Roentgen's of X rays) is needed to appreciate the extent to which biotic control—medicine and plant-animal domestication in particular—came to depend on science. The same is increasingly true of inanimate control, especially the *creation* of technological items; but it is commonly difficult to trace a particular item or complex (e.g., computers, nuclear reactors) to any one particular scientific discovery.

The most conspicuous difficulty in attempting to demonstrate the dependence of control on science is the distinct possibility of an enormous time lag between scientific developments (pure science) and the practical use of those developments. Less obvious, the dependence is now so extensive that it may be impossible to identify all of the components of science that contribute to a particular kind of control, and that consideration takes on special significance in light of the argument (Collingridge and Reeve, 1986) that scientific research has little significance where policy decisions are concerned. Consider, for example, all of the scientific developments that furthered the inanimate control entailed in launching space vehicles. The only comfort in the face of such complexities is this: if control extent-efficacy and amount of scientific activity were both mensurable, the *synchronic* correlation between them internationally or for a country over time would be substantial despite time lags between *particular* scientific developments and *particular* kinds of control.

Science and Human Control. One of many complexities that haunts theorizing in the social sciences is a special kind of temporal relativity. Whatever the variables and whatever the empirical relation between them, a theory may prove inadequate because the theorist did not anticipate the emergence and/or end of a particular relation.

The emergence of a relation is especially relevant in contemplating the dependence of human control on science. Although there are obvious instances where a particular kind of human control was made possible or furthered by some scientific development, only in science fiction has that relation become, so to speak, the engine of social change (commonly depicted, as in Huxley's *Brave New World*, for the worse). However, there is every reason to assume that human control will increasingly rely on science; therefore, the importance of Axiom 4 and perhaps its full validity really lies in the future. Yet it is not just a matter of controllers "using" science; more important, scientific developments will create conditions that make possible or give rise to horrendous control practices (at least from the viewpoint of contemporary liberal democracies). One illustrative possibility must suffice: eventually, genetic engineering all but eliminates human deaths from degenerative diseases, and the world's population expands at an unprecedented rate. No imagination is required to appreciate how that demographic change could engender ranges and scopes of control over human behavior never known before.

On the Types of Causation

Previous arguments are sufficient to justify characterizing the causal relation between "extent and efficacy of control attempts" and "amount of scientific activity" as reciprocal. However, each of the two sets of causal assertions in Axiom 4 identifies three other types of causation, and more needs to be said in the way of justification.

On Causation of Amount of Scientific Activity. The argument that science depends on control is sufficient to identify the causal relation as *positive*, meaning that increases in control extent-efficacy cause increases in scientific activity.[26] But "dependency" suggests only *necessary* causation. Specifically, extensive and efficacious control attempts only create a condition in which science *could* develop; whether it will is another matter. Yet that argument reflects an insensitivity to scientific activity's purposive quality. Scientists need no special prompting to use the resources created by extensive and efficacious control attempts. As legislators would testify, scientists or their representatives never tire of demanding more support for science (see Fries, 1984, and *Science,*

Vol. 241, p. 141). To be sure, the argument may be much more valid for contemporary science, which is to admit that at one time an increase in the extent and efficacy of control attempts may have been only a necessary condition for expansion of scientific activity. The possibility of such historical relativity in causation should be contemplated in future restatements of the theory.

Historical relativity is not the only temporal complexity. Any stipulation of the lag (its length) between changes in control extent-efficacy and changes in amount of scientific activity would be sheer conjecture. There is even the awful prospect of the lag depending on the kind and amount of change in control. For example, both the harnessing of steam and the extensive use of electricity undoubtedly furthered scientific activity, but the lag may have been quite different for those two kinds of inanimate control. Some comfort can be taken in the possibility that changes in the amount of both scientific activity and control extent-efficacy are so aggregational and incremental that the correlation between them (if they were mensurable) internationally or for a country over time would not be markedly contingent on the time lag between the variables, at least not within broad limits (e.g., five vs. ten years).

Even so, the *bidirectional* quality of the causation creates another complexity. If science does depend on control, then decreases in the extent and efficacy of control attempts cause decreases in scientific activity. However, the time lag could be quite different for increases than for decreases. That differential is a possibility for all other bidirectional causal relations, but it is all the more real for Axiom 4 if only because scientists are so accustomed (dimly, albeit) to increases in control that the consequences of a *decrease* are especially conjectural.

The assertion that change in control extent-efficacy is only a partial cause of change in the amount of scientific activity creates still another complexity, even though the claim of partial causation is hardly unusual. However, when Axioms 1–4 are considered together, there is an inconspicuous implication—both variables in Axiom 4 are causally related in two ways—directly (Axiom 4) and indirectly (Axioms 1–3).

On the Causation of Control Attempts. If control does depend on science, the implication is the same as when contemplating the dependency of science on control—the causal relation clearly appears *positive*. There is also the same argument: the causation is necessary but not sufficient, meaning that increases in scientific activity only have the *potential* for furthering the extent and efficacy of control attempts. Although the impact of scientific activity is contingent on the nature of that activity, the "only potential" argument ignores the purposive quality of the behavior of those who use scientific discoveries, such as manufacturers, physicians, farmers, and advertisers.[27] They do not simply happen to stumble upon scientific discoveries and adapt them whimsically; rather, it is more accurate to say that multitudes monitor science with a view to increasing the extent or efficacy of control. What with the advent of corporate laboratories and industrial research (see Dennis, 1987), manufacturers become proactive users of science. The qualification is that only in recent centuries has science significantly furthered the extent and efficacy of control attempts, and its causal role is likely to expand even more in the future.

With one exception, the arguments made in connection with the two sets of causal typifications in Axiom 4 are essentially the same. The exception has to do with the causal direction. Whereas the dependence of science on control is bidirectional, dependence of control on science is *unidirectional*. It is difficult to see how even a major decline in scientific activity could cause a decrease in the extent and efficacy of control. A reduction in scientific activity might preclude further increases in control; but surely there would be no reason for abandoning *existing* effective and efficient means of control, whether derived from science or not.

The assertion of unidirectional causation may eventually create a serious difficulty when attempting to test the theory, though there is no immediate problem because general observations suggest that scientific activity has been increasing for decades throughout most of the world. However, even if scientific activity always increases, it is not claimed that those increases are more than partial causes of increases in control. For that matter, one other variable ("perceived control capacity" in Axiom 1) has been identified as determining the extent and efficacy of control attempts.

Science and Education

Even if research resources were unlimited, the term "amount of scientific activity" would remain a construct. The immediate problem is not quantification. A measurement procedure requires a definition of science, and extant definitions are extremely divergent.

Four Contending Notions

Taken together, extant definitions of science suggest that four notions are relevant, but each notion is emphasized in some definitions and slighted if not entirely ignored in others. Still another difficulty: each notion can be interpreted at least two ways.

Science as Knowledge. The most common difference between definitions of science is the relative emphasis on knowledge (or some other "product") and activity. When knowledge is emphasized, the definition clearly indicates that science is not just any body of knowledge; but there is considerable disagreement as to kind. Suppose that the requisite kind of knowledge is characterized as "defensible theories or accepted theories." Sciences necessarily evolve, and none of the putative sciences (i.e., physics, genetics) commenced with a theory. Moreover, if a putative science is not really a science unless it has given rise to at least one defensible theory, the status of some social and behavioral sciences (perhaps all) is disputable.

If scientific knowledge cannot be equated with defensible or accepted theories, what is the alternative? Surely it will not do to answer "scientific knowledge consists of facts." Virtually any extant definition of a fact is objectionable. If the definition emphasizes anything like "that which is known with certainty," then the notion becomes private and personal to the point of being alien to science's public character. Thus, the typical reader would be willing to state "I was not in Tibet last month" and regard that condition as a fact, but for the vast majority of humans the statement is an assertion.[28] In any case, a laundry list of facts (e.g., the U.S. is larger than Thailand, there is no record of snow in Miami during July) hardly constitutes scientific knowledge, but it is difficult to describe the sense in which facts must be organized so that they do qualify. For example, it could be argued that a mileage chart is not scientific even though its constituent "facts" are organized.

Science as a Method. A science-as-knowledge definition emphasizes the *product* of activity rather than the activity itself. By contrast, if science is defined in terms of some distinctive method for acquiring or generating knowledge, the emphasis is on the activity rather than the product.

There are at least two reasons why a science-as-method definition has a large following. First, it appeals to individuals in putative but insecure sciences, meaning those that do not have an impressive body of knowledge, accepted theories especially. Second, putative scientists obviously engage in activities, such as observing, recording, and experimenting, which are clearly methods of acquiring or generating knowledge.

Although perhaps the most common, a science-as-method definition is subject to a major criticism. Briefly, there is no effective consensus as to the essential scientific method; and when two definitions do agree, the meaning of the terms denoting the method are all too general or abstract.[29] Thus, the phrase "observing and recording" characterizes the activities of journalists just as much as it does the activities of putative scientists. The term "experimenting" may be an exception; but there are grave doubts about its present and/or past applicability to several putative sciences, not just anthropology, economics, political science, and sociology but also astronomy and geology.

The Purpose of Scientific Activity. Whereas a science-as-knowledge definition emphasizes a distinctive product of activity and a science-as-method definition emphasizes the nature of the activity itself, science-as-purpose emphasizes a particular human goal. Lest "goal" appear indistinguishable from "product," the former does not imply anything about realization. Hence, science-as-purpose definitions have a substantial following in putative but insecure sciences, and all the more because such a definition does not preclude the possibility of realizing a goal through any one of several methods, however that term be defined.

The problem is, of course, specifying the distinctive purpose of science. For one thing, it appears obvious that putative scientists engage in myriad activities, each with a different purpose. Thus, in one day a physicist may read journals in the morning, then repair a recording device, then complete some ongoing experiment, and then commence writing a paper. Diversity of purposes is even more conspicuous when comparing putative scientists as to activity, so much so that there must be doubts about the unity of science.

As for the idea of some ultimate goal of all scientific activity, there is little prospect of it ever being identified to the satisfaction of most interested parties, philosophers of science especially. The immediate problem is the seemingly idiosyncratic contrasts among putative scientists. Thus, it appears that Newton thought of his work as revealing God's plan of the universe. Then, even before Newton and up to the present, an army of putative scientists have ostensibly worked in the conviction that sooner or later the product of their activity will have applied value, meaning a contribution to the solution of some human problem, such as the eradication of diseases (see *Science*, Vol. 248, pp. 671–673). Such an applied orientation is consistent with the value-laden view of science; but advocates of that view seldom note the consistency, perhaps because they are commonly preoccupied with ideology. In any case, the major contending view—science is value-free—can be construed as an insistence that (1) science can or should be undertaken with no particular application in mind or (2) a scientific theory's validity is not contingent on its utility.

If there is a way to avoid the idiosyncratic, it must be the identification of some transcendent purpose, meaning some ultimate goal of all putative scientific activity; but any such identification is bound to be controversial. Thus, there is the argument that all scientists work with a view to satisfying a basic human quality—curiosity. Though common, that "pure science" argument is clearly contrary not just to the ostensible motivations of, say, Jonas Salk but also to the entire value-laden view of science.

There is an obvious alternative—the goal of scientific activity is knowledge acquisition. But like the science-as-knowledge definition, nothing is said about the distinctive feature of the knowledge; and any stipulation along that line will be difficult and controversial. Moreover, any quest-for-knowledge definition will not please those who argue that scientific activity contributes to the solution of human problems or that science is value-laden.

Numerous examples could be given to support the claim that scientific activity eventually contributes to the human capacity for effective control (all basic types). Hence, it is hardly surprising that the notion of control is stressed in some conceptions of science (e.g., Wallace, 1988:24–26); but that stress is alien to pure science, and it runs contrary to the argument that human curiosity is sufficient justification for scientific activity. For that matter, a concern with control appears far removed from many putative sciences, especially in their formative periods. Astronomy and geology are instances.

Science as an Epistemology. This definition combines some previous elements and adds others: science consists of activities that are believed by those who engage in or control them to be conducive to the formulation or assessment of theories, with the assessments governed primarily if not exclusively by a consideration of the predictive power of contending theories. The definition is not totally alien to a science-as-knowledge definition, even though various kinds of knowledge do not necessarily enter into the formulation or assessment of theories. For that matter, the activities in question are virtually certain to involve some distinct kind of method or procedure, but by no means the *same kind* in all instances. Even science's purposive quality is recognized, and yet *accepted* theories are not required for a field or discipline to qualify as a science.

The reference to theories permits an emphasis not just on the cognitive character of science (conceptualizations especially) but also on the argument that scientists both create and discover order. Moreover, because a theory is commonly regarded as explanatory in one sense or another, the definition comes closer to describing science as a quest for explanations than do the other three definitions (knowledge, method, and purpose).

The definition is virtually certain to encounter vociferous resistance in the social sciences and philosophy.[30] The reference to predictive power is likely to elicit characterizations of the definition as "positivistic," and all commentaries in Chapter 1 on antipositivism are again relevant.

The Bottom Line. In light of the foregoing, there is not a realistic prospect for a definition of science that even the majority of interested parties would accept.[31] There is even less prospect of an empirically applicable procedure for the measurement of the *amount* of scientific activity in any country, and the problem is by no means merely limited research resources. The most conspicuous problem is the sheer variety of what has come to be conventionally identified as "science indicators" (e.g., number of scientists, expenditures on science, volume of scientific publications). Virtually all of the rare attempts at international comparisons with regard to multiple indicators have been limited to a few highly developed countries (see, e.g., National Science Board, 1991, and OECD, 1984), and from the outset there have been informed doubts about the reliability, comparability, and/or coverage of the data (see, e.g., Carpenter and Narin, 1981). When the research has focused on one particular kind of indicator, such as scientific publications (e.g., Braun, *et al.*, 1985), the findings point to horrendous complexities.

So "amount of scientific activity" is identified as a construct. For that matter, it is an extreme construct, meaning one best left undefined (i.e., an attempt at a definition would serve no constructive purpose). However, that admission in no way lessens the importance of the notion; rather, the admission underscores the importance of the construct-concept distinction.

Scientific Activity and Educational Attainment

In light of the foregoing, it is hardly surprising that specialists in the sociology of science have never set forth purported measures of the amount of scientific activity at any level, international or otherwise. Yet those specialists are not likely to question the variable's importance; but as far as theory construction is concerned, there are only two alternatives—link "amount of scientific activity" to another construct or to a concept (see Appendix, pp. 288–289). The second linkage is made here in Postulate 1: *Among countries and for any country over time, the amount of scientific activity is the symmetrical, positive, bidirectional, and partial determinant of level of educational attainment.*

Because the form of Postulate 1 is identical with that of various previous premises, it need not be interpreted (see Appendix pp. 301–303, if needed). Nonetheless, its validity is debatable.[32] Most obvious, the rudimentary skills acquired in the early years of education—once largely limited to reading, writing, and arithmetic—may be used for all manner of purposes in addition to or rather than science. Yet those skills appear absolutely essential for one scientific activity or another, and it is unlikely that a large proportion of a country's population would acquire those skills without organized education.

If the relation asserted in Postulate 1 were just a matter of education being necessary for scientific activity, the deductive implications would be quite different. However, a high rate of engagement in any activity, scientific or otherwise, cannot be realized and sustained without organization; and in the case of science the organization takes the form of synchronized and coordinated instruction of novices by specialists. Such instruction commences before the university or college level, but that level is all the more important not just because it is commonly the gateway to "scientist" as an occupation but also because at that level the organization of science extends to recruitment, especially of graduate students. All of those considerations are important when anticipating the argument that science can be an avocational pursuit rather than an occupation. The history of science in several countries, Britain especially, is consistent with the argument; but scientific activity is bound to be extremely limited if not an occupational pursuit. More important, when numerous students enroll in scientific courses, education ceases to be merely necessary for scientific activity; the educational process generates more scientific activity in the same sense that the training of lawyers is believed to generate litigation.

Types of Causation

All of the foregoing arguments are limited to contemporary science and education, but Postulate 1 is not so limited; for that matter, assertions limited to the "here and the now" should not be taken as a theory regardless of their validity. Yet there are serious doubts about the postulate as it applies to the distant past, prior to the 16th century in the case of the West. It may well be that all relations pertaining to human behavior change historically, holding only in some periods. Hence, the admission of doubts about the past may be less damning than it appears; in any event, the postulate's validity cannot be assessed thoroughly without a more detailed explication of the two sets of causal assertions (only the first set is explicit because the two sets are identical).

On Causation of Level of Educational Attainment. For all practical purposes, in no country is the amount of scientific activity controlled by a particular individual, council, committee, or any other small group; but neither is it controlled by society or culture. Nevertheless, in all countries the amount is negligible unless the promotion of science is organized. One conspicuous feature of organized promotion is credentialism, meaning the establishment of performance requirements for participation.

The principal entry requirement for science is a certain amount and kind of training; and the criterion is certification by some organization engaged in higher education, known in English-speaking countries as colleges, universities, or institutes. That link is the foundation of the causal relation in question, but the link itself does not determine either the amount of scientific activity or the level of educational attainment. For that matter, credentialism *in itself* does not directly further the amount of scientific activity, but it does play a crucial role in the recruitment of prospective scientists. As control attempts come to depend more and more on science (*supra*), rewards for scientific activity increase. Credentialism tends to promote higher incomes by limiting the number of participants; but, appearances to the contrary, that limitation does more to generate scientific activity than to reduce it. Credentialism is a major factor in creating and sustaining "scientific" occupations; and like many other activities, science flourishes only if organized. The creation of occupations is a major component of that organization.

The foregoing observations on income notwithstanding, science promoters are concerned with advancing both the quantity and the quality of scientific activity (see, e.g., Golden, 1991). Credentialism ostensibly reflects a concern with quality; and it establishes the connection between scientific training and organized education, a connection that increases quantity. Promoters of science commonly attempt to control government officials, foundation agents, and philanthropists, such that more resources are invested in formal education—not just instructional salaries, buildings, and equipment but also fellowships or scholarships for students.

The amount of investment in organized education (not just higher education) varies substantially among countries, and that variation is the primary determinant of international and historical contrasts in educational attainment. Hence, much of variation in attainment stems indirectly from a greater concern in some countries than in others with promotion of science.[33] Evidence comes from several sources, one being Willink's study (1991) of science and education in the Netherlands. His conclusion after presenting various kinds of evidence is (1991:520): "Better training by the HBS, Polytechnische School and the universities, expansion of the number of professorships, decreasing numbers of students [but eventually an increase], and material investments seem to have been decisive factors in bringing about the new 'Dutch Golden Age of Science' between around 1860 and World War I."

The foregoing illustrates the complexities of social causation, especially when examining alleged causal links among institutional (or so-called structural variables), such as science or education.[34] Despite the complexities, if the causal relation in question does exist, it is *positive*, meaning that increases in the amount of scientific activity cause increases in the level of educational attainment. Moreover, if it does exist, the causal relation is *bidirectional*, meaning that (in addition to increases) decreases in the amount of scientific activity cause decreases in level of educational attainment. The "decrease" relation perhaps appears less credulous, but the appearance could be due to the historical rarity of decreases in scientific activity.

Neither type of causation makes sense if one thinks of certain amount of scientific activity as directly causing a certain level of educational attainment. Rather, the amount of scientific activity is linked through two paths with level of educational attainment. The most immediate path is the effort of science promoters to maintain or increase scientific activity by furthering the quality and quantity of education, which is to say that (like all other premises) the causal relation manifests control phenomena. The much less immediate path (i.e., longer lag) is through a positive association between scientific activity and technological complexity, and in any country the education-technology connection may be more of a rationale for promoting education than is the education-science connection (on the education-technology connection, see Rubinson and Ralph, 1984).

Change in amount of scientific activity is identified as a *partial* cause of change in level of education attainment; but, as elsewhere, the identification reflects a denial of exclusive or paramount causation in light of recognition of another partial cause—the extent and efficacy of attempts to control human behavior. That recognition is expressed by Postulate 2 (*infra*), and at this point it will suffice to say that promotion of science enters into causal arguments made in connection with both Postulate 1 and Postulate 2. Only the need to simplify prevents the introduction of "science promotion" as another variable in the theory's premises.

On Causation of Amount of Scientific Activity. Organized education provides essential skills for scientific activity; but even ignoring alternative kinds
of training (e.g., apprenticeships), a certain national level of educational attainment is at most only a necessary condition for a certain amount of scientific
activity. After all, the ability to read, write, and calculate does not automatically
convert students into scientists; and most tertiary students do not become
scientists. However, in addition to skills acquisition, it is imperative to consider
promotion of scientific training by *educators*, and not just by those who are also
scientists. Although the proper form and content of "science education" has
been a matter of public debate in some countries for over a century (see Atkinson, 1987), in virtually all countries scientific training has become the foremost
rationale for higher education.[35] Should that claim be doubted, presidents or
chancellors of universities should be asked: how would legislators, regents, or
trustees react on being informed that your university plans to discontinue
scientific training? Actually, educators face another reality—that enrollments
depend appreciably on offering scientific training and related degrees.

In responding to the need for scientists and "selling" science as a product of
university training, educators raise the national level of educational attainment.
True, many university courses have nothing to do with science, and many
students do not take a science degree. Yet virtually all students take science
courses; and various skills acquired in higher education are required for personnel to support scientific work, such as those skills used in manufacturing or
operating computers.

So, whatever the science component of education may be, increases in level
of education attainment are causes of increases in scientific activity. That
causal relation is therefore *positive*, and it is *symmetrical* in light of the first set
of causal assertions in Postulate 1.

The consequences of a decline in educational attainment are less obvious
and more disputable. However, if a particular level is even a *necessary* condition for a certain amount of scientific activity and that amount is being realized,
then a decrease in attainment will eventually reduce scientific activity. So the
causal relation is identified as *bidirectional*.

Control and Education

Of all premises, the possibility of misinterpretation is the greatest for Postulate 2: *Among countries or for a country over time, the extent and efficacy of
attempts to control human behavior are the symmetrical, positive, bidirectional, and partial determinants of level of educational attainment.* Only elementary level teachers fully understand that education is commonly not so much an
intellectual matter as a battle of wills, but the postulate could be misconstrued

as limited to attempts by teachers to control students.[36] For that matter, because sociologists are prone to equate control with "evil," they will grant that instruction and disciplinary measures are socialization but perhaps not fully recognize that those measures are also control attempts. Be that as it may, only school administrators, from university heads to elementary school principals, truly understand that control attempts in education transcend both instruction and discipline. The attempts extend, for example, to dealing with angry parents, irresponsible teachers, recruiting and supervising people in various staff positions (janitors, secretaries, etc.), and squeezing resources out of legislators, trustees, regents, foundations, and philanthropists.

The term "symmetrical" in Postulate 2 signifies a second set of causal assertions, exactly like the first set except the level of educational attainment is asserted to be the symmetrical, positive, bidirectional, and partial determinant of the extent and efficacy of behavioral control attempts. That set could be construed as partially tautological, being contaminated by the part-whole problem. Control attempts in the context of organized education (e.g., in the classroom) are a subclass of the effect variable—attempts to control human behavior—in the second set of causal assertions.[37] In recognition that level of educational attainment has no significance in itself (i.e., as simply a numerical value for a particular population), it is *not* treated here as reflecting a certain amount of particular kinds of attempts at behavior control, meaning those undertaken in connection with organized education. Rather, level of educational attainment is interpreted as being a correlate of the amount of particular kinds of knowledge and skills acquired by population members in connection with organized education; but it is not assumed that the character of the training is even approximately the same even for residents of a locality who report the same level of educational attainment, much less international contrasts.

Types of Causation

Given the various ways that Postulate 2 could be misinterpreted, an explication of the causation types is especially needed. But, again, rhetoric is not a substitute for systematic tests, and the explication's primary purpose is clarification.

Types of Causation of Educational Attainment. Postulate 2 is not restricted to attempted behavior control in connection with organized education; rather, the construct (first variable in the postulate) refers to all attempts at controlling human behavior. Nor is it assumed that there is even an approximate uniformity among the different kinds of control attempts. Thus, for example, it may be that in any country criminal justice (a vast control system) and parental control are not even approximately effective to the same degree. But it is assumed that the level of educational attainment for a population is markedly dependent on the extent and efficacy of myriad kinds of behavior control. Thus, when striving to motivate their children to perform well in school, parents are actually attempting behavior control; and its success could further the effectiveness of attempts by teachers to control pupils. While the teacher as disciplinarian is clearly a control agent, the motivation of pupils is much more subtle. Both discipline and motivation may be necessary for effective education, but their relative importance has been heatedly debated for decades.

Efforts of chief executive officers in educational organizations (university heads or superintendents of school districts) to wrest resources from legislators—federal, state, or local—are a study in control attempts. Less obvious, those resources are not even available unless legislators and/or other government officials exercise fairly effective control over the citizenry in matters pertaining to taxation.

Finally, the most distal causation has to do with surplus production, meaning production beyond and what the producers and their dependents consume themselves. Without enormous surpluses, there would be no organized education, especially at the secondary and tertiary levels. For all practical purposes, the amount of surplus production is a function of the extent and efficacy of control attempts, *all basic types.*

Although the foregoing causal arguments are supported only by general observations, the observations are sufficient for a conditional assertion. If the extent and efficacy of attempted behavior control is a cause of the level of educational attainment, the causation is *positive* (recall the form: an increase in X causes an increase in Y). However, the *bidirectional* character of the causation is more difficult to support through general observations, the principal reason being that historically (at least in the West) there have been no clear-cut instances of a decline in either variable over recent centuries. Nonetheless, the dependence of educational attainment on control is such that a decline in the latter would result eventually in a decline in the former. The real evidential problem is the possibility that the relation may hold *only if* the decline in control is substantial over several generations.

As Figure 3–1 indicates, level of educational attainment is asserted to be an effect of both extent and efficacy of attempts to control human behavior *and* amount of scientific activity. Hence, Postulate 2 asserts *partial* causation, but that identification does not mean that the empirical relation between the control variable and the educational variable is only moderately close. As suggested in explicating Postulates 1 and 2, the causal importance of the control variable (as a determinant of educational attainment level) far exceeds that of the amount of scientific activity. Even so, unless tests findings indicate that the causal relation between amount of scientific activity and level of educational attainment is truly negligible, the identification of the control variable as only a partial cause of the attainment level must stand.

On Types of Causation of Behavior Control. The implied set of causal assertions in Postulate 2 may appear counterintuitive. After all, it is commonly believed that formal education prompts students to question putative norms and thereby become more prone to resist control. That belief readily extends to a denial that level of education attainment is a determinant of the extent and efficacy of attempts to control human behavior (i.e., contrary to Postulate 2, the causal relation is asymmetrical or nonreciprocal). Then there is a more extreme denial. Whereas Postulate 2 asserts that an increase in the attainment level causes an increase in the control variable, the extreme denial would be that the causation is of the *negative* type.

The counterargument is not just that organized education undermines tradition far less than its conservative critics presume. Additionally, it would be difficult to exaggerate the extent to which even the most elementary skills—reading and writing—enter into attempts to control human behavior. One of them, the ability to read, makes humans vulnerable to control on a massive scale; and the other, the ability to write, promotes both the extent and the efficacy of attempted control.[38] The impact of the invention of writing on the *range* of attempted control over human behavior probably was considerable within a few centuries, and that impact has grown over the millennia along with the spread of literacy.[39] Thus, without writing, no charismatic leader, Christ included, would come to have a large following; and writing appears to be an essential feature of control over and within large organizations (see, especially, Yates, 1989). True, with the advent of electronic communication, the telephone in particular, human control through inanimate control went far beyond writing (Beniger, 1986); but writing is an essential component of radio and television because in both the bulk of communication originates and is guided by scripts. For that matter, though seldom recognized as such, scripts are control attempts in themselves.

In light of the foregoing, it is reasonable to assume that, *ceteris paribus*, increases in the level of educational attainment cause increases in the extent and efficacy of behavioral control attempts. The outcome of a decrease in the level of educational attainment is more conjectural, for the large decreases (if any) that may have occurred in human history took place in circumstances where even general observation on the consequences are not possible. Nevertheless, it would be more difficult to defend the argument that the causation is positive but *unidirectional* than the argument that it is positive and *bidirectional*.

The most serious doubt has to do with the extent of the causation. As shown in Figure 3–1, Axioms 6 and 12 identify other determinants of the extent and efficacy of behavior control, and both appear far more important than level of educational attainment. So, although the causation in question is designated as partial, eventually it may be necessary to recognize that the causation is negligible at most, in which case Postulate 2 will be restated such that it asserts only asymmetrical (nonreciprocal) causation.

Transformational Statement 1

At least one variable in all previous premises is a construct; hence, none of the premises are subject to anything like a direct test. A construct cannot be defined such that theorists regard the definition as complete and clear, let alone linked with an empirically applicable formula. By contrast, a quantitative concept is linked in a transformational statement with a symbol that designates an empirically applicable formula. The first such linkage is Transformational Statement 1: *Among countries and for any country over time, the greater the level of educational attainment at any point in time, the greater the RLEA at T_{0-1}.*

The nature of a transformational statement is explicated at length in the Appendix (pp. 303–307); so five brief comments will suffice here. First, the formula designated by the referential—the acronym RLEA—is found in the extrinsic part of the theory (Chapter 7), along with definitions of all key terms, formulas pertaining to other referentials, and instructions for gathering or otherwise obtaining the kinds of data stipulated for each formula. Second, each formula is implicitly asserted to be sufficiently empirically applicable, not only because intelligible but also because the field's resources permit acquisition of the requisite data. Third, each transformational statement asserts covariation rather than causation, for it is scarcely conceivable that the phenomenon designated by a concept causes the referential, the formula, or its application. Fourth, in setting forth a transformational statement, the theorist does not necessarily identify the referential formula as the ideal measurement procedure; rather, the implicit claim is that if ideal measures were given for each of two or more social units of the requisite type (countries in this case), there would be a very substantial positive correlation between those ideal measures and the referents computed by correct application of the designated referential formula. And, fifth, whereas the concept has no temporal context, the temporal quantifier ("at T_{0-1}" in this case) denotes time periods as to length and "locates" them relative to each other in historical time, all as implicit instructions to those who test the theory. Thus, if T_{0-1} denotes any calendar year and in some particular test "at T_{0-1}" is interpreted as any point during 1990, then "during T_{0-1}" would pertain to all of calendar year 1990, "at T_{1-2}" would mean any time point in 1991, and "during T_{1-2}" would pertain to all of 1991.

Note particularly that the referentials and the formulas designated by them are very much a part of the theory; without them, tests of the theory are virtually certain to be idiosyncratic (for elaboration, see Appendix, pp. 289–290). However, the values used in a test are *referents;* and while each referent was supposedly computed by application of the designated formula to the stipulated kinds of data for the particular social units identified in reporting the test (e.g., all Canadian cities as of the census year 1991), the referents themselves are *not* components of the theory. Nonetheless, they are evidence of the empirical applicability of the referential formula in question, especially when referents reported by the independent investigators for the same individuals or populations (two or more in either case) are highly congruent.

Notes

1. Perceived omnipotence may be the product of extensive and efficacious control attempts, but the temporal character of the causation could be such as to create evidential complexities.

2. Unless qualified, perceived control capacity refers to two things considered together: first, *personal*, the individual's perception of his/her capacity for effective control; and, second, *pan-human*, the individual's perception of the capacity for effective control by humans in general. The distinction has some correspondence to what Bandura (1982) has designated as "self-efficacy" and "collective efficacy."

3. Lest the qualifications appear pedantic or the generalization appear to be a truism, see the literature (e.g., Madsen, 1987) on political self-efficacy, a kind of perceived control capacity.

4. The substantial literature in psychology on the relation between "life events" and "basic beliefs about self and world" (e.g., Catlin and Epstein, 1992) is also relevant. However, psychologists do not necessarily emphasize the connection between such events or beliefs and perceived control capacity.

5. Despite the difference in terminology, Bandura's survey (1982) and Gecas' survey (1989) of the literature on correlates of "self-efficacy" provide extensive support for both claims.

6. Whereas control efficiency is a matter of the *conservation* of time and/or energy, control intensity is a matter of the *amount* of time and/or energy invested. Hence, there is no necessary conceptual (logical) connection between the two dimensions.

7. Scholars appear increasingly prone to avoid even an explicit attempt at a definition of religion (see, e.g., Wulff, 1991:3; Bellah, 1968; and Geertz, 1968), even going so far as to deny the possibility of a definition (see *Current Anthropology*, Vol. 21, p. 194). Some recognize the difficulties (e.g., Wulff, 1991) but do not confront specific conceptual problems and issues, while others (e.g., Bellah, 1968, and Geertz, 1968) do not even analyze the difficulties.

8. Guthrie (1980:185) objects to the use of the term "supernaturalism" in defining religion, his claim being that the notion of the supernatural "often is not found in non-Western religions." He does not confront either of two questions. First, how were such religions identified? Second, what criteria were used in finding or not finding the notion?

9. Many of these elements are consistent with Guthrie's characterization of religion as including anthropomorphism; but contemplate the ambiguities inherent in his definition (1980:184) of religion: "the systematic application of human-like models to nonhuman in addition to human phenomena."

10. Whatever the definition's shortcomings, it is a product of considerable reflection. By contrast, in an edited book subtitled "an anthropological study of the 'supernatural'" the editors (Lehmann and Myers, 1985) do not even attempt an elaborate conceptualization of the term "supernatural." Rather, they are content with this in the glossary (1985:384): "Supernatural: A force or existence that transcends the natural." A literate bartender could have done as well.

11. A preconception or presupposition may be such as to require that a theory answer certain questions to the exclusion of others. In that connection, the present theory pertains only to variation in the amount of supernaturalism among countries. As such, the theory is narrow; but many theories about the supernatural or religion (e.g., Guthrie, 1980, and O'Keefe, 1982) are studies in the pursuit of obscure questions. Specifically, it is not clear whether the theories even pertain to variation, let alone what kind.

12. The suggestion is not that perceptions of limited control capacity gave rise to supernaturalism only in the earliest stages of hominid evolution. Contemplate Freuchen's observation (1961:25): "those Eskimos who came down to the sea to live came upon something that was quite unknown and strange to them, and in their primitive fear and insecurity it gave rise to intricate precautions in the form of taboo rules and more complicated religious ideas."

13. These findings are consistent with the report (1989) of Albas and Albas on the frequency with which Canadian university students admit to engaging in practices to ward off "bad luck" when taking examinations.

14. Those who cite such statistics are prone to ignore Norval Glenn's assessment (1987) of 110 public opinion surveys in the U.S. since the late 1950s, in which respondents were asked a question about religious affiliation so as to permit a "no religion" response. Over the years in question, there was a definite increase in the percentage of Americans so responding, from about 2 to 8 percentage points.

15. Such observations should not be construed as being consistent with the argument (one ably made by Stark, 1992:412–431, and Wuthnow, 1992) that religiosity is something like a constant among social units and over time. The counterargument is not just that religiosity is only a subclass of supernaturalism. Additionally, if the extent and efficacy of control have increased appreciably over several centuries in at least some countries, then in those countries the amount of supernaturalism is now less than it once was. Unfortunately, Axiom 2 can be tested only indirectly (i.e., through tests of theorems derived in part from the axiom); and even if longitudinal tests are ever conducted, they will not provide crucial evidence for the argument and counterargument in question.

16. This argument is one of several that may make Axiom 2 appear to be another version of the "confidence" theory of religion or magic, but the asserted connection between supernaturalism and selective survival makes the axiom something more than purely psychological.

17. Evidence is by no means limited to the hunting practices of nonliterates. Henslin (1967) reports that dedicated crapshooters ostensibly believe that various "magical" acts enhance *control* of the dice.

18. If perceived control capacity decreases over several generations throughout a social unit, the decline influences the character of socialization and thereby persists independently of the personal experiences—control failures especially—of the social unit members.

19. Indeed, at one time it was fashionable to presume that science will extinguish supernaturalism (for elaboration, see Rolston, 1987:298); but the extinction thesis no longer appears to have a large following, and even the belief that the two are antithetical or clearly distinct has become far less conventional in recent decades. Sperry (1988:607) goes so far as to claim that the "incompatibility of science even with liberal theology no longer holds for psychology's new mentalist (cognitive) paradigm..." Be that as it may, there are now a multitude of publications in which the authors strive for a reconciliation of science and religion (for a brief survey, see Kevles, 1991).

20. See especially, Rolston, 1987. Advocates of the "externalist" view of science appear unconcerned with maintaining the science-supernaturalism distinction. For that matter, it is not at all clear how the externalists would or could deny that creationism is a science, nor how they could reject such Nazi notions as "Jewish physics."

21. Even a grotesque definition is preferable to the now fashionable practice in scholarly circles of avoiding explicit definitions. A recent instance is Brooke's analysis (1991) of the relation between science and religion. He not only balks at explicit definitions of the two key terms but also suggests rejection of the very idea of explicit definitions (1991:7–8, 63–71). The advantage is obvious: in the absence of an explicit definition, one can interpret evidence licentiously.

22. For that matter, one doubt about the theory stems from uncertainty as to which type of incompatibility, intrinsic or extrinsic, is operating. If both are operative, then the causal relation is more nearly necessary *and* sufficient but only in the sense of "additive" with other causes. The general point is that, unless qualified, the assertion of partial causation simply means "additive" causation in conjunction with one or more other causes; and if the causation has any other quality pertaining to the necessary-sufficient distinction, that quality must be introduced when explicating the premise. Most important, as argued in the Appendix, the variety of kinds of causation relevant for the social and behavioral sciences transcends conventional relational terms (even those prescribed here); hence, there is no immediate *general* solution of the problem.

23. Granted, the timing of the association's commencement and its regularity over the centuries are debatable ever since the 15th century (see Brooke, 1991).

24. The nature and extent of affluence among foragers *in general* remains debatable (see, e.g., *Current Anthropology*, Vol. 33, pp. 24–34, and Vol. 21, pp. 279–298).

25. Consider Brooke's statement (1991:152) as an illustration of a mountain of evidence: "Between 1660 and 1793 the scientific world established itself with more than seventy official scientific societies (and almost as many private ones) in urban centers as far removed as St. Petersburg and Philadelphia."

26. By any definition scientific activities commonly take the form of attempts at control; but it is asserted that Axiom 3, Axiom 4, and Postulate 1 would be valid even if those activities were excluded from total control attempts, thereby avoiding the part-whole problem.

27. The suggestion is not that promoters of science are exclusively scientists, nor do they necessarily "use" science for economic purposes. The wealthy or powerful may promote science for reasons that ostensibly have little to do with economic or political self-interest. For extensive observations on the support of U.S. science in the 19th century by wealthy Americans, see Miller (1970).

28. Indeed, it could be argued that science deals with assertions, not "facts" (see Gibbs, 1972:286–289, 290–292, 305).

29. Brooke (1991:6–7) has stated the argument even more forcibly: "But, as the Cambridge philosopher William Whewell observed, almost a hundred and fifty years ago, the *history* of science already showed that each new branch of scientific inquiry had required its own distinctive methodology."

30. Advocates of extreme relativism are likely to balk at even the idea of defining science or anything else such that the definition purports to be universally applicable (not equivalent to asserting that science is universal). Such relativism is manifested in Chattopadhyaya's declaration (1990:195): "What is 'science' in one culture is 'magic' in another." Fashionable though such declarations are, they only give rise to questions, in this case two of them. First, without a universal definition how can one possibly determine what is science and what is magic in any culture, especially where English is not the language? Second, in light of universal definitions of the two terms, how could science in one culture be magic in another?

31. To illustrate, in writing a dictionary of concepts in the philosophy of science, Durbin (1988:269) defines science such as to recognize products (treated here as knowledge) and the creation of such products (treated here as activities) but does not emphasize method or epistemology.

32. Because there is no prospect of a measure of the amount of scientific at the national level, a direct test of Postulate 1 (any postulate for that matter) is not possible. Nevertheless, support for the postulate is not limited to general observations. Taken together, Axiom 3 and Postulate 1 imply a negative relation between amount of supernaturalism and level of educational attainment. That *implied* postulate is consistent with repeated findings of a negative association among individuals between acceptance of traditional religious beliefs and educational level (see, especially, Lesthaeghe and Surkyn, 1988:18, and Eckhardt, *et al.*, 1992).

33. It is not claimed that the promotion of science brought about any of the major historical developments, such as the first mass education systems in 19th-century Europe. However, it often happens that in research on such developments, as in the case of Soysal and Strong (1989), no "science" variables are considered. Moreover, to attribute some development to the state or some religious variable (e.g., the prevalence of Protestantism) may be acceptable for structural sociology, but it does not preclude the possibility that state officials and/or religious leaders (especially in the case of Protestants) were sensitive to the science-education connection.

34. Sociologists rarely attempt to explicate such a causal relation (i.e., identify the causal mechanisms or links). Sara Delamont (1987) has noted the failure of sociologists of science to conduct research on learning environments in science and on socialization into science, but she herself failed to emphasize that such socialization involves *recruitment* into science.

35. See, especially, Salam and Kidwai, 1991. One summary of a UNESCO global survey (Morris, 1990:33) is also particularly relevant: "Perhaps the most incontestable facts to emerge are that both mathematics and science are now firmly entrenched in school curricula worldwide."

36. Yet organized education is a vast system of control attempts, and those attempts are not limited to control over student behavior.

37. So interpreted, even the first set of casual assertions (explicit) in Postulate 2 would be partially tautological.

38. Even though humans are always the immediate targets, in large production organizations much of biotic or inanimate control is realized through writing, not just directives but also technical manuals.

39. Contemplate Carlson's comment (1990:86) on pre-Columbian astronomy in
Mesoamerica: "To observe and predict the recurrent paths of divine lights was to know
the fates of kings and empires, to discern the proper day for rituals, to forecast animal
migrations, the season of the life-giving rain, and the time for planting. The power to
foretell required that observers, probably specially trained shamans or priests, make accurate records and preserve them." The comment suggests a point not yet made. Whatever the origin of religion and magic, both came to be "used" extensively in attempts to
control human behavior. However, it is doubtful whether there is a justification for asserting as a generalization (an axiom) that changes in the amount of supernaturalism
cause changes in the extent and efficacy of attempted control.

4

Interrelations Among the Three
Basic Types of Control

The bulk of the previous chapter treats some asserted effects of the extent and efficacy of control attempts *in general*, meaning all three basic types combined. By contrast, this chapter pertains to the *interrelations* among the basic types, Axioms 5–10 in Figure 3–1 (Chapter 3, p. 70). Each interrelation is expressed as an empirical generalization; but it is an axiom and, hence, no more testable than axioms pertaining to control attempts in general.

Three Empirical and Logical Relations: Axioms 5, 7, and 9

Figure 3–1 could be simplified by eliminating Axioms 5, 7, and 9, because each pertains to an obvious relation, that between the extent and efficacy of some designated basic type of attempted control (inanimate, biotic, or over human behavior) and the extent and efficacy of attempted control in general—all three basic types combined. The relation is obvious because it is *in part* logical (analytic). However, despite the logical connection, if all of the variables in Axioms 5, 7, and 9 were mensurable, there would be no necessity of a positive correlation between a set of *component* values (one value for each of two or more countries) pertaining to any basic type of attempted control and a corresponding set of *composite* values (all three basic types combined). Indeed, while the logical connection would necessarily preclude a correlation coefficient of −1.0, other than that both the sign and magnitude of the coefficient would depend on the *empirical* (i.e., contingent) association between the extent and efficacy of the basic type of attempted control in question and the extent and efficacy of each of the *other two* basic types of attempted control. But if those coefficients could be computed, the theory anticipates that all three would be positive and substantial. The anticipation stems from this general assertion—the extent and efficacy of any basic type *depends* appreciably on the extent and efficacy of one or both of the other two.[1] That general assertion translates into the following statements of Axioms 5, 7, and 9.

Axiom 5: Among countries and for any country over time, the extent and efficacy of control attempts are the reciprocal, positive, bidirectional, and paramount determinants of the extent and efficacy of inanimate control attempts; and the extent and efficacy of inanimate control attempts are the reciprocal, positive, bidirectional, and partial determinants of the extent and efficacy of control attempts.

Axiom 7: Among countries and for any country over time, the extent and efficacy of control attempts are the symmetrical, positive, bidirectional, and partial determinants of the extent and efficacy of attempts to control human behavior.

Axiom 9: Among countries and for any country over time, the extent and efficacy of control attempts are the asymmetrical, positive, bidirectional, and paramount determinants of the extent and efficacy of biotic control attempts.

Nothing more need be said about Axioms 5, 7, and 9, because each is actually a combination of two more *less general* axioms. In effect, Axiom 5 subsumes Axioms 6, 8, and 10; Axiom 7 subsumes Axioms 6 and 8; and Axiom 9 subsumes Axioms 8 and 10. So from this point onward the focus is on the *component* axioms—6, 8, and 10.

Inanimate Control and Control over Human Behavior

No sociological theory can be truly general (i.e., impressive predictive scope) unless it has some bearing on what is currently a largely ignored thesis—that material things are the very foundation of human behavior and all derivatives, such as society or culture. That "materialist" thesis is far too vague for systematic tests, and no amount of clarification or qualification would blunt the myriad objections by an army of social and behavioral scientists. Nonetheless, the thesis enters into the theory primarily through Axiom 6: *Among countries and for any country over time, the extent and efficacy of inanimate control attempts are the symmetrical, positive, bidirectional, and partial determinants of the extent and efficacy of attempts to control human behavior.*

Inanimate Control as a Cause of Human Control

The first set of four explicit causal assertions in Axiom 6 will be more understandable if recognized as a version of technological determinism.[2] Such is the case because, as argued in Chapter 2, effective inanimate control is virtually identical with the creation, use, and maintenance of technological items.

Some Common Examples. Should the connection between inanimate control and technology not make Axiom 6 credible, a few examples of the causation in question are all the more needed. However, the following list is misleading if only because (1) the variety of such causation is beyond description and (2) the variables in Axiom 6 pertain to highly aggregated behavior rather than particular isolated acts.

First: Someone uses a telephone in his/her home to summon a taxi.

Second: A motorist stops his/her car at a traffic light.

Third: A woman brandishes a pistol when demanding money from a clerk.

Fourth: A man gives a woman an expensive bracelet to further her seduction.

Fifth: A professor uses a video when giving a lecture.

Sixth: A soldier fires a mortar toward enemy lines.

Seventh: A customer gives a store clerk money before leaving with the purchase in hand.

Eighth: A television announcer warns of an approaching hurricane.

All eight examples are instances of attempted control of human behavior, but each attempt is made *through* use of an inanimate object. To use an inanimate object is to control it; hence, insofar as that control alters or maintains someone's behavior, *even if not in the way intended*, it was that behavior's proximate cause. In some of the eight examples the causation is only sufficient (in the third example the woman could have brandished a knife), only necessary for some others (in the fourth example it is unlikely that the gift alone assures the seduction), and in still others perhaps both necessary and sufficient (in the first example there are scarcely alternative ways to summon a taxi in seconds from one's home). But those distinctions in no way invalidate Axiom 6; they only show its applicability to myriad situations.

The examples represent various kinds of control, and they were selected for precisely that reason. Thus, in the fifth example the goal of the attempted control is especially obscure, but one does not have to know the actor's goal to identify his/her action as attempted control. Then the identities of the would-be controller and the targets are unknown in the second example, but surely the traffic light was designed, manufactured, and/or installed (inanimate control in any case) by someone with a view to altering the behavior of motorists in general; and the "who" is irrelevant. Then only in the case of the soldier (sixth example) is an attempt made to control behavior by *ending it*. Finally, only the customer (seventh example) used an object—money—to promote *inaction*, paying in the belief that it reduces the probability of a punitive reaction. Despite the contrasts, the examples only suggest the sheer variety of control over human behavior through inanimate control.

Materialism. Although there are numerous versions of materialism, none suggests that objects or substances determine human behavior primarily through control attempts.[3] However, one major problem with materialism is revealed by this rendition: human behavior is determined by material conditions that originated and exist independently of human behavior. That rendition does make material conditions the ultimate cause, but it limits the material conditions to what are loosely designated as natural geographic or physiographic features (e.g., terrain, weather, mineral deposits). The problem is not just a narrow range of behavior determinants, nor that the features in question are increasingly altered by humans (e.g., various kinds of human activities directly or indirectly alter the weather). Even if geographic or physiographic features do determine rather than merely limit human behavior, they do so only through their influence on kinds and properties of control attempts.

Marvin Harris (1979:105) unwittingly supplied an illustration: "Rainfall agriculture leads to dispersed, multicentered forms of production. Hence it is doubtful that any pristine state ever developed on a rainfall base." There is no suggestion that the dispersion-concentration of agriculturalists stems from the awareness of *someone* (not necessarily the agriculturalists themselves) that the efficacy of various kinds of biotic control, whether plant or animal domestication, depends appreciably on the availability of water. Nor did Harris recognize the distinct possibility that many *potential* rulers perceive the difficulty of controlling a widely dispersed population, and that such perception is surely a major factor in reducing the probability of even an attempt to establish a state amidst a widely dispersed population (whatever the cause of that dispersion). However, the illustration should not be construed as suggesting that control is relevant only when contemplating the relation between rainfall and state formation. Any instance of a claim about environmental or geographic determinism is bound to be incomplete unless the relevance of control is recognized. Thus, meager rainfall is most likely to disperse a population if its members are engaged in biotic control as the primary means of subsistence.

A control version of materialism would promote reconsideration of environmental or geographic determinism, something that social and behavioral scientists abandoned prematurely, and enhance its credibility.[4] Contemplate the sudden disappearance of all highways, bridges, dams, railway tracks, utility lines, runways, and buildings. Surely that change would have an immediate and enormous impact on human behavior, and that recognition is nothing less than tacit support for materialism (i.e., that material things shape human behavior). True, all such material things (highways, etc.) are products of inanimate control; but many were produced by individuals now deceased, and they were produced for reasons that may have little to do with their current impact on behavior. Hence, a control version of materialism is not limited to particular attempts by particular individuals to control a particular act of a particular individual through inanimate control. Many products of inanimate control endure long after deaths of their creators, and they now influence the behavior of multitudes in ways perhaps never anticipated by those creators.

Finally, a control version of materialism could revive work on the infrastructure of Marx's theory. Contemporary Marxists are so obsessed with class and class conflict that Marx's technological determinism is all but forgotten or merely debated (see *Philosophy of Social Science*, Vol. 22, p. 151 and p. 124 for a recent wrangle). Yet inanimate control is the core of the means of production, which Marx often depicted as being the ultimate determinant of societal characteristics. Indeed, a control terminology can be used to restate Marx's theory so as to avoid the conceptual swamp created by such locutions as means of production, forces of production, factors of production, relations of production, and mode of production (for elaboration, see Gibbs, 1989:253-270).

Special Comments on the Types of Causation. The first set of causal assertions in Axiom 6 (note again that the other set is implicit) may appear to be an overly complex rendition of this simple generalization: humans often use technological items to control human behavior. Examine the following illustrative list of technological items (each a product of inanimate control): baby cradles, handcuffs, telephones, prison cells, automobile horns, radios, television sets, dollar bills, and printing presses. The list is only indicative of the astonishing variety of technological items that are used to control human behavior; and control of human behavior through inanimate control is not largely limited to the micro level, let alone to coercive proximate control (e.g., handcuffs). If anything, inanimate control in the mass media context (radio, printing presses, television) appears essential for behavior control on a massive scale, including various kinds of social control (e.g., records, files, or computer tapes in the case of prelusive social control).[5] However, even if it is truly understood that technological items are produced by inanimate control, the causal argument may be misconstrued. Technological items are not just "used" in attempts to control human behavior; rather, in a very real sense they determine the extent and efficacy of a wide variety of attempts to control human behavior, and in that sense the variety reflects the extent and efficacy of inanimate control.

Contemplate the innumerable control attempts in the U.S. that are loosely identified as advertising. The sheer extent of those control attempts would be reduced enormously if inanimate control were not such as to produce that vast number of material items used in mass communication—transmission towers, printing presses, etc. So the vast conglomeration of attempted control known as advertising would not exist without extensive and efficacious inanimate control. The point is not that advertisements are even commonly effective (whatever the criterion); rather, the sheer frequency of the *attempts* and their range—number of control targets—reflect the character of inanimate control in the U.S.

Now contemplate the size of the incarcerated population in the U.S., perhaps the greatest in the world absolutely and/or per capita. It does not tax credulity to argue that the sheer number of inmates somehow reflects the extent and efficacy of inanimate control. Without the material restraints (walls, cells, locks, etc.) and the technological items required to produce a food surplus, there might well be no prison population at all.

Given all of the foregoing, if there is a causal relation along the lines suggested, it must be *positive*, meaning that an increase in the extent and efficacy of inanimate control causes an increase in the extent and efficacy of human control. Yet there is an issue, one that makes the last two illustrations all the more relevant. Numerous countries have the technology required for levels of advertising and incarceration comparable to the U.S. (especially per capita), but they are far below both levels. So it could be argued that the causation is necessary but not sufficient. The argument has merit; but even if the causation is only necessary, sustained substantial *decreases* in the extent and efficacy of inanimate control will result in a decline of both advertising and the incarceration rate.[6] More important, to characterize the causation as "only necessary" is to ignore inanimate control's purposive quality. The facilities and other technological items used by advertisers and criminal justice officials were not created without some credible basis for anticipating their eventual use. Stated more abstractly, for all practical purposes technological items are produced with a view to their use by someone (even if described as "the market"); hence, the empirical relation between inanimate control attempts and behavior control attempts, extent and efficacy in both cases, is likely to appear as the manifestation of causation that is both necessary and sufficient.

The assertion that the extent and efficacy of inanimate control determine the extent and efficacy of attempts to control human behavior will appear incredulous unless three considerations are recognized. First, because both component variables, extent and efficacy, pertain to highly aggregated and diverse kinds of behavior, general observations are not a justifiable basis for rejecting the axiom. Second, given that Postulate 2 (Chapter 3) and Axiom 12 (*infra*) identify other determinants of the extent and efficacy of attempts to control human behavior, the causation asserted in the first part of Axiom 6 is rightly identified as *partial*. Third, throughout history there have been billions of attempts to control human behavior without using any material thing (an object or a substance); but international or temporal variation in the extent and efficacy of such attempts is another matter.

Human Control as the Cause of Inanimate Control

The term "symmetrical" in Axiom 6 implies that the extent and efficacy of attempts to control human behavior are the positive, bidirectional, and partial determinants of the extent and efficacy of inanimate control attempts. That implied assertion will confuse unless the reader recalls that the three basic types of control are distinguished not by the identity of the agent (the would-be controller), but, rather, by the identity of the *target* of the control attempt. Obviously, all control is "human" in that the agents are humans; but there are three types of targets: (1) human behavior, (2) organisms and their behavior in the case of nonhuman organisms, and (3) inanimate objects or substances.

Nonetheless, the idea of human control (always attempts to control human behavior) causing inanimate control requires clarification.

When someone brandishes a pistol and demands money from a store clerk, he/she can be described as attempting inanimate control (handling the gun) in an attempt to control human behavior; but the ultimate situational goal of the robber is inanimate control—to obtain money (i.e., relocation of particular kinds of *objects*). By contrast, if the clerk responds by ringing a concealed alarm bell, it would be a case of causation in the other direction (i.e., behavior control through inanimate control). So the causation in question can be defined thus: any attempt at inanimate control through an attempt at external human control (control over someone else's behavior, in contrast to self-control) as one or more of the previous sequences in the causal process.

Modes of Production. The causation in question can be illustrated readily by simple kinds of acts, as when a customer requests some object or substance from a store clerk; but such actions are minor components of the causation of inanimate control through behavior control, and the point is not merely that the inanimate control attempts of store clerks are largely restricted to the locational subtype. The other major subtype, the transformational, is conspicuous only in particular industries, notably manufacturing. Yet the really crucial consideration is the mode of organization that prevails in those industries, especially in highly industrialized countries.

Judging from the characteristics of sustenance activities among contemporary foragers (hunter-gatherers), the earliest predominant mode of production was "autonomous," meaning that much of what economists might identify as commodities, goods, services, or benefits were produced *and* consumed (ingested, used, enjoyed, etc.) by members of the same household. So in the *purely* autonomous mode of production there is no exchange *among* households, especially if the sharing of big game kills is identified as tacit and delayed reciprocity rather than exchange.

As just suggested, the autonomous mode is most conspicuous in foraging bands. Those social units may have as few as 20 members, but even that size would not permit a measure of the extent and efficacy of attempted inanimate control in an all-seasons time period. However, three general observation suggest that the value for such a measure would be lower for the autonomous mode of production than for either of the two alternative modes (*infra*). First, foragers must invest so much time in biotic control that more extensive inanimate control would eliminate their leisure time, considerable though it is. Second, when foragers do attempt what is technically the most difficult subtype of inanimate control, the transformational (e.g., making arrows, axes, etc.), the work is laborious and failures are fairly common, which is to say that the attempts do not conserve very much human energy or time and are often ineffective. To be sure, the products are impressive given the crude tools used to create them, but the crudity is itself indicative of ineffective inanimate control. Third, the extremely limited variety of items in a foraging band's technology indicates that the temporal and energetic efficiency of transformational control (especially *gross* efficiency) is far less than is realized in the factories of industrialized countries.

The negligible extent and efficacy of inanimate control is due in part to the *low* degree of division of labor, a characteristic of the autonomous production mode. Age and sex are usually the only conspicuous bases for the division of labor in a foraging band, and one consequence is very little variation from one household to the next as regards the character of sustenance activities. Indeed, the activities of the adult household members vary so much over time (hourly, daily, and seasonally) that the Western notion of an occupation scarcely applies; rather, an adult forager tends to be a jack-of-all-trades.

By definition, an occupation is indicative of appreciable specialization, which requires not just efficient production (such that an adult member produces more of some type of item or service than is consumed or used by his/her household) but also an exchange among households. When such exchange commences, the autonomous mode begins to give way to the *symbiotic* mode; and the latter may come to be so predominant that the bulk of things consumed or used in the typical household originated elsewhere. Specialization in the symbiotic mode of production may reach the point where there are distinct occupations, such as the medieval baker, blacksmith, and cobbler. However, companies and corporations are essentially alien to the symbiotic mode of production, though relations among companies and corporation are predominantly symbiotic.

Exchanges *among* households contribute to specialization and functional interdependence (i.e., a division of labor), but attempts of a household member to control the behavior of nonmembers are largely limited to proposing or rejecting terms of exchange. Hence, in the symbiotic mode what is produced, how, when, and where are ostensibly decided predominantly by household heads.[7] Should a particular household not participate in one kind of exchange or another, the members may suffer some loss; but the loss is self-imposed. Stated otherwise, in the symbiotic mode the use of sanctions in attempts to control production behavior are limited to members of the same household.

Once members of a household commence sanctioning members of other households in attempts to control production behavior, it marks the beginning of the organized mode of production. The large corporation in a capitalist country exemplifies that mode, but the constituent organization can be any kind of unit that transcends households.

An increase in the division of labor requires an increase in the coordination and synchronization of production activities, and the latter cannot be appreciable without the organized mode of production. Whereas coordination and synchronization in the symbiotic mode are largely limited to members of the same household, in the organized mode thousands of individuals may collaboratively engage in one vast production enterprise. By contrast, try to imagine the members of one particular household constructing a hydroelectric facility, manufacturing a jet airplane, or operating a transcontinental railroad. All such enterprises are vast conglomerations of diverse kinds of inanimate control; and the necessary coordination-synchronization of production activities is nothing less than highly organized attempts at controlling human behavior, commonly sequential control and social control in addition to proximate control. Were there no need to simplify, two axioms would be added. Together, the two would make "predominance of the organized mode of production" the causal link between the extent and efficacy of attempts to control human behavior and the extent and efficacy of inanimate control attempts. However, that term would have to be identified as a construct if only in recognition that the predominance of any of the three modes is a matter of degree and there is no empirically applicable formula.[8] For that matter, while it would be difficult to exaggerate how much the organized mode of production (a particular form of human control) furthers the extent and efficacy of inanimate control attempts, it is by no means the only link between behavior control and inanimate control. So explicitly "placing" the organized mode in the theory is best left to future work.

Special Comments on the Types of Causation. The notion of perceived control capacity is only one reason why attempted behavior control is not considered to be the exclusive or paramount determinant of inanimate control attempts. In any country innumerable attempts at behavior control have no necessary connection with inanimate control. A very short illustrative list must suffice: demanding an apology, inviting dinner guests, requesting a police investigation, and asking for directions. Nonetheless, it is difficult to think of any major kind of inanimate control that is not dependent on control over human behavior. Any factory vividly illustrates that dependence.

Granted justified doubts about the uniformity of the causation, there is no obvious basis for doubting that the causal relation is *positive*. In particular, the efficacy and perhaps even the extent of inanimate control attempts are far greater in the typical factory than they would be if each worker should try to manufacture the same product alone (i.e., no collaborative production). The comparison is relevant because the coordination and synchronization of production activities in factories indicate extensive and fairly effective attempts at behavior control. Similarly, should production organizations disappear entirely, the expectation would be a decline in both the coordination-synchronization of production activities and the volume of production. That expectation is the principal reason for characterizing the causal relation between the extent and efficacy of behavioral control and the extent and efficacy of inanimate control attempts as *bidirectional*.

Control over Human Behavior and Biotic Control

There are several reasons for doubting the validity of Axiom 8: *Among countries and for any country over time, the extent and efficacy of attempts to control human behavior are the asymmetrical, positive, bidirectional, and partial determinants of the extent and efficacy of biotic control attempts.* So the first step is to state the doubts and then allay them.

Human Control as a Cause of Biotic Control

Trends in American agricultural employment could be construed as evidence contrary to Axiom 8. Census data for the U. S. indicate that in 1900 nearly 50 percent of the labor force were employed in agriculture, and by 1990 that percentage had declined to less than 3.0. The enormous decline suggests a *reduction* in the extent of biotic control; and given numerous justifications for assuming that human control expanded over the 90 years, the two trends appear totally contrary to Axiom 8.

The counterargument cannot be limited to pointing out that various kinds of biotic control have nothing to do with farming. The percentage of the U.S. labor force in hunting, fishing, and forestry also declined in this century, and it may well be that today farmers and farm laborers are grossly outnumbered by those who work as veterinarians, animal trainers, gardeners, landscapers, physicians, dentists, physical therapists, geneticists, or genetic engineers. Yet employment trends in biotic control are not directly relevant. There may have been an increase in the extent of biotic control (all kinds combined), despite the enormous decline in farm employment; and anything like a perfect correlation between volume of employment and the two control properties in question, extent and efficacy, is not presumed.

The Biotic Control Variable in the Axiom. Although "extent and efficacy of biotic control attempts" is a construct and not subject to measurement, its meaning can be clarified. As for extent, the number employed in various "animate" industries (not just agriculture) is relevant only in that it indicates the amount of human time and energy invested, both of which pertain to the *intensity* of attempted biotic control. However, even if intensity has *decreased* in the U.S. and many other countries since 1900, there has been a proportionately greater *increase* in efficacy. There is not even a metric for its expression, but general observations and some statistics suggest an enormous increase in both the effectiveness and the temporal-energetic efficiency of American agriculture during this century. For one thing, if only because of irrigation, crop failures have declined; for another, immunizations alone have reduced the premarket mortality of livestock far below what it was in 1900. Change in the production *efficiency* of agriculture has been even more dramatic.[9] No matter what the production metric (e.g., caloric values, tons), the products per unit of time or number of workers has increased enormously in this century.

Less obvious, intensity is only one dimension of the extent of control, biotic or otherwise; and there is diverse evidence of an enormous increase in the *range* of biotic control. American farmers now grow a much greater variety of plants than they did in 1900, and aquatic agriculture alone has broadened the domestication of animals. Then in the medical and health care fields, transplants and prosthetics have introduced a quality of biotic control that cannot be expressed readily in terms of numbers. Finally, whereas the *scope* of biotic control in agriculture was once limited primarily to the alteration of a few features of animals and plants through selective breeding, today virtually all features are controlled one way or another; and genetic engineering promises to escalate biotic control's scope exponentially.

Modes of Production Again. In all countries the most conspicuous determinants of changes in biotic control are technological, but change in the mode of production warrants special recognition. The long-run course of change in the mode of biotic production has been similar to change in inanimate production: predominantly autonomous, then predominantly symbiotic, and currently becoming predominantly organized. However, the last transition took place later in the case of biotic production.

In many countries, one obvious manifestation of the trend in biotic production is the decline of family farms and their absorption by corporations, with a concomitant increase in the average size of "producing units" (isolated individuals, families, and corporations). Before that the mode of production in American agriculture was predominantly symbiotic, but for generations the trend has been toward the organized mode of production. One manifestation has been an increase in the coordination-synchronization of work on farms and ranches and the division of labor in that work, both of which require more extensive human control than does the autonomous or symbiotic mode. So, while the volume of employment in American agriculture has declined enormously in this century, increasingly biotic control has come to be realized through control over human behavior, the behavior of employees especially. Those employees virtually always use tools or machines; hence, their work exemplifies the causation of biotic control through inanimate control, which is consistent with Axiom 10 (*infra*). However, Axiom 8 does not preclude this sequence: control over human behavior→inanimate control→biotic control.

While the decline in the number of independent farmers (i.e., self-employed) largely reflects the substitution of technology (including inanimate energy) for human energy, the organized mode of production facilitated that substitution. For the typical production unit, the capital investment in agriculture technology has become so great that large-scale farming or ranching is now a virtual economic imperative.

Although the change in the character of agriculture has incalculable socio-political significance (e.g., a decline in the rural electorate), an increase of control over human behavior in connection with biotic control has taken place also in medicine, immunology, and genetics (plant or animal, experimental or applied). In the case of medicine, for example, try to imagine a surgeon performing a successful heart transplant without a surgical team and the concomitant intense behavior control. Some experimental work in genetics and immunology is still undertaken by isolated individuals, but that work is rapidly becoming virtually peculiar to employees of corporations or universities.

There is no defensible measure of the extent to which change in control over human behavior has made biotic control more effective and efficient, but general observations indicate an enormous increase. Nor is there doubt that increases in the extent and efficacy of behavior control were necessary for a great expansion of the range and scope of biotic control. Various kinds of biotic control (e.g., heart transplants, gene splicing) were impossible until fairly recently; and a change in the character of human control, including that in education and scientific training especially, may have been just as necessary as technological change (inanimate control). As a case in point, genetic engineering could become the greatest of all revolutions in biotic control, and it has been almost entirely within the organized mode of production from the outset.

Special Commentary on the Types of Causation

There are at least two bases for doubts about Axiom 8. Each pertains not so much to the possibility of a causal relation between the two variables but, rather, to one or more of the types of causation asserted in the axiom.

Asymmetrical Causation. Axiom 8 must be construed as implying that changes in the extent and efficacy of biotic control attempts are followed less regularly (whatever the time lag) by changes in the extent and efficacy of attempts to control human behavior than is the reverse sequence. However, that implied criterion of causation does not extend to a denial of instances where a change in biotic control ostensibly caused a change in control over human behavior.

The referent is not simply an isolated practice, as when dogs are trained to guard buildings, or when surgeons perform a lobotomy, or when farmers raise plants or animals in the anticipation of selling them.[10] There are even instances where biotic control enters into attempts to control human behavior on such a vast scale that it amounts to an epoch. Lynn White (1962) provided an example when describing feudalism as a social organization designed to create and maintain cavalry suited for mounted shock combat. Men on horseback were equipped to charge and scatter grouped militants, be the militants regular infantry, light cavalry, or rebellious peasants. The rider grasped a shield with his left hand, held a heavy lance at rest between the upper right arm and body, and smashed into his foes with the combined mass of man and horse. With nothing more than a saddle for lateral support, a mounted warrior maintains his seat with difficulty, even when swinging a heavy sword. The solution came with the adoption of the stirrup by European cavalry (possibly initially by the Franks under Charles Martel) in the 8th century, long after the saddle. Granted that the stirrup was an inanimate innovation, to control a horse by any means is biotic control.[11] Moreover, even if such heavy cavalry was far from the sole determinant of feudalism, military action is a very distinctive attempt to control human behavior coercively; and in the historical period described by White a very distinctive kind of biotic control was necessary for military success.

Despite the examples, instances where biotic control enters into attempts to control human behavior appear too rare and idiosyncratic to warrant recognition in the theory. Yet that judgment is debatable; and it is likely to become more so in the future, especially if genetic engineering becomes a major means for controlling human behavior *through biotic control*. Should that prospect occur, the theory must be altered; but one of its merits is that it prompts recognition of future possibilities.

Partial Causation. Without doubt, if changes in control over human behavior do cause changes in biotic control (extent and efficacy in both cases), the causation is *positive* and *bidirectional*. However, typification of the causation as *partial* gives rise to an issue.

To repeat a previous point, Axiom 8 is not invalidated by instances of this causal sequence: control over human behavior→inanimate control→biotic control. Stated otherwise, the "extent and efficacy of inanimate control" are not necessarily determinants of the "extent and efficacy of biotic control" (Axiom 10, *infra*) that operate *independently* of the extent and efficacy of attempts to control human behavior. That recognition gives rise to a question: why, then, is the behavior control variable not identified as the exclusive or at least paramount determinant of biotic control attempts rather than the *partial* determinant? There are two answers. First, even when the mode of agricultural production is *predominantly* organized, there are numerous self-employed, who work without direction or supervision. Second, geographic factors may influence biotic control attempts to the point that other determinants cannot be identified justifiably as paramount causation.

Inanimate Control and Biotic Control

Recall from Chapter 2 that any control attempt is at one and the same time cognitive and affective behavior (both internal) as well as overt behavior. The cognitive quality takes on special significance in the case of Axiom 10: *Among countries and for any country over time, the extent and efficacy of inanimate control are the asymmetrical, positive, bidirectional, and partial determinants of the extent and efficacy of biotic control attempts.* As in all other premises, the variables are aggregate in the extreme, referring as they do to billions of acts in a country over an all-seasons period. So the affective and cognitive qualities of those acts are made less conspicuous by the nature of the variables. Indeed, the very idea of inanimate control causing biotic control suggests neither desires nor judgments, but the phrase "using inanimate control to further biotic control" suggests both an affective and cognitive quality. One does not *use* one type of control (inanimate or otherwise) to further another type without some belief as to desirability and some belief as to the nature of causation. Cognition is all the more obvious in the case of inanimate control, for humans do not merely happen to use it to further other types of control. Humans often create inanimate things or substances (tools and machines in particular) for use in biotic control, and those creations demonstrate that humans are both teleological creatures and natural scientists.

A Few Examples

There is only one way to promote both understanding and the plausibility of Axiom 10—give examples of the causal relation; but the illustrations are not offered as a substitute for systematic tests of the conclusions (theorems) derived in part from the axiom. For that matter, here as elsewhere, any example is only suggestive.

Particular and Specific Actions. The first instance in hominid history of inanimate control to further biotic control could have been the throwing of a rock at a predator to drive it away. Bear in mind that the mere alteration of an inanimate object's spatial position is a kind of inanimate control, the locational; and surely the hominid acted in the belief (1) that his/her behavior reduced the probability of the predator moving closer and (2) that such reduction is desirable. To be sure, any such *inference* might be incorrect in a few isolated cases, but observers need not "get into the mind" of those observed to apply the control terminology.

There is no fundamental difference between the early hominid example just given and contemporary instances of inanimate control to further biotic control. Think of a rider moving the harness reins so as to alter the horse's movement, of an animal trainer closing the door of a cage, of a farmer using a plow to dig a furrow for planting seeds, of a cowboy stringing barbed wire, of a girl lowering a hook in water, or of a dentist opening a tooth with a drill. Those examples do not remotely convey the sheer variety of biotic control through inanimate control; but the examples do suggest what all instances share in common—the use of some modified inanimate object or substance in biotic control.

The Creation of Control Objects and Substances. All of the objects in the foregoing examples (e.g., the hook) were *designed* as a means for biotic control (granting isolated unanticipated uses). So another way to illustrate the causal relation is to list other such types of object or substance: nets, lariats, vaccines, condoms, scalpels, pesticides, fertilizers, plows, and irrigation conduits. Needless to say, the list could go on for pages.

One implication is that the creation of a kind of inanimate thing for use in biotic control can become so highly organized as to constitute a manufacturing subindustry. Those subindustries are much more developed in some countries than in others, and in any country much more in this century than ever before; but such contrasts are only evidence of the variation presumed by Axiom 10.

Extent and Efficacy as Pivotal Considerations. In all countries, biotic control attempts *independently of inanimate control* are so uncommon as to be unimportant. Hence, the frequency, intensity, range, scope, effectiveness, and efficiency of biotic control cannot increase appreciably *without* a change in inanimate control. Specifically, an appreciable increase in those properties of biotic control are realized primarily through increases in properties of inanimate control. However, the inanimate control increases are not limited to technological items used in biotic control attempts. For example, fabricated metals are often used in biotic control (e.g., in plowing), but the kinds and amounts of available metals depend on the character of inanimate control in general and not just those kinds closely linked with biotic control.

The point of the foregoing is clearly illustrated by genetic engineering and transplants. Obviously, such biotic control could not succeed without the use of various technological items, many of which are metallic. The availability of metals depends not just on the extent and efficacy of inanimate control in mining and metal processing but also in various other industries as well (e.g., hydroelectricity). The dependence in genetic engineering and transplants is so great that they illustrate a seldom recognized dimension of efficacy—indispensability. The idea is not that certain types of control make others more effective; rather, they are absolutely necessary for any effectiveness at all, and the notion of necessity bears on the control dimension designated as "indispensability."

Special Comments on the Types of Causation

The reference to indispensability indicates only one of many reasons why Axiom 10 may appear more plausible than Axioms 6 or 8. Nonetheless, while the causation asserted in Axiom 10 appears clearly *positive* and *bidirectional*, there are grounds for doubting the other two causal typifications (asymmetrical and partial).

Asymmetrical Causation. Although Marvin Harris did not use the present control terminology, one of his observations (1977:29) is especially relevant: "In the New World the wheel was invented by the American Indians, perhaps for making pottery and certainly as a toy, but its further development was halted by the lack of animals suitable for hauling heavy loads." The statement suggests that American Indians did not engage in a certain kind of inanimate control because they had not gone very far in a particular line of biotic control. True, without some inanimate control, even if only the creation of a harness, animal use cannot be extensive; hence, inanimate control is the distal (indirect) cause of all *consequences* of biotic control. Even so, proximate as well as distal causation enter into the relations asserted by Axiom 10.

So it is the aggregate character of Axiom 10 that justifies the typification of the causation as asymmetrical (nonreciprocal). Specifically, instances where causation runs the other way are presumably so rare that they scarcely influence the axiom's validity. Yet those instances could become so common that the causal relation is truly symmetrical (reciprocal), and the genetic engineers' creation of an organism that consumes polluting petroleum may be a harbinger.

Another Reconsideration of Partial Causation. As suggested in connection with Axiom 8, even when humans attempt biotic control through behavior control (as when a farm manager directs a subordinate to plant a particular field), the use of some tool or machine (e.g., tractors, plows) is virtually inevitable. So, at least in the proximate sense, biotic control is predominantly realized through inanimate control. That recognition leads to this question: why not identify the extent and efficacy of inanimate control as the exclusive or paramount determinant of the extent and efficacy of biotic control attempts rather than *partial*?

Granted the possible need to reidentify along the lines suggested by the question, two considerations caution against it. First, in the case of foraging bands some gathering activities (e.g., picking fruits or nuts) may be carried out by social subordinates without tools or machines but under the direction or supervision of a social superordinate (parent or elder); and the same is true of certain sustenance activities (e.g., harvesting a crop) in simple horticulture. Second, the extent and efficacy of biotic control may be influenced *somewhat* by geographic factors and independently of the extent and efficacy of inanimate control attempts.

Notes

1. The argument is very much like that set forth in Chapter 1. Just as the extent and efficacy of attempted control in any social unit is taken as a given because it defies explanation, so is it that the primacy of any basic type of attempted control cannot be ascertained, let alone explained. The "inexplicables" stem from the sheer unestimable number and variety of instances of attempted control.

2. The term "symmetrical" means that each of the four types of causation also describes the extent and efficacy of attempts to control human behavior as determinants of inanimate control.

3. The point is not just that humans commonly attempt to control human behavior through inanimate control, as when advertisers use radio, television, or the press. Additionally, the extraction, transportation, manufacturing (creating, fabricating, etc.),

and maintenance of all manner of material things entail far more than inanimate control. Extensive synchronization and coordination of production activities—which is to say control over human behavior—appear essential. So material things determine human behavior in that various kinds of inanimate control are possible only through extensive control over human behavior, a kind of causal connection that is teleological.

4. On the whole, behavioral and social scientists either reject geographic determinism categorically or content themselves with the uninformative conclusion that geographic factors limit human behavior.

5. But note that humans often use technological items to control their own behavior, meaning self-control, as when an individual ingests a tranquilizing substance.

6. How much decrease in inanimate control would be required and the length of the time lag are questions that cannot be answered at this juncture.

7. Of course, sumptuary law, guilds, church intervention, and perhaps even criminal law are idiosyncratic factors.

8. In a previous work (Gibbs, 1989:172) the construct was linked to a concept—ratio of the members of employees and unpaid family workers to the number of self-employed and employers. That ratio was construed as indicative of the size and participation in production organizations (i.e., the greater the size and participation, the greater the organized mode of production). Census data can be used to compute the ratio, but the international empirical association between the ratios and measures of occupational differentiation (a presumed manifestation of the division of labor) proved to be less than the association between occupational differentiation and a techno- logical variable.

9. The increase would be substantially less if top-soil erosion were taken into account. Recall, however, that efficiency is defined exclusively in terms of short-run conservation of time and energy.

10. Lest the last example be confusing, observe that to sell or buy or exchange is to control someone's behavior.

11. This passage illustrates how a control terminology, though abstract, can be used to describe not just particular acts but also entire episodes. Such descriptions indicate the sense in which control notions have definite empirical referents.

5

The Remaining Premises

Ideally, constructs are linked with representations of "real" things or events through concepts (in postulates) and through referentials (in transformational statements). However, the constructs pertaining to control are so abstract that such linkage is not feasible in all cases; rather, some of them are linked to a concept through another construct (i.e., one or more axioms, then a postulate). Such linkage makes it impossible to identify the false axiom or axioms in the series when evidence indicates that *some* of them are false. That problem haunts most of the remaining premises (see Figure 3–1 in Chapter 3, p. 70); but those premises enrich the theory enormously if only because some of them pertain to the division of labor and/or technology.

Inanimate Control and Technological Efficiency

There is nothing unusual about the form of Axiom 11: *Among countries and for any country over time, the extent and efficacy of inanimate control attempts are the asymmetrical, positive, bidirectional, and paramount determinants of technological efficiency.* The types of causation need not be explicated, but there is a special need to clarify the meaning of both constructs.

A More Detailed Commentary on Inanimate Control

Some comments on inanimate control attempts have been made previously in connection with Axioms 5, 6, and 10. A more detailed treatment is required to distinguish various dimensions of inanimate control and to clarify the meaning of technological efficiency (the second construct in Axiom 11).

Extent of Inanimate Control vs. Efficacy. All control variables in the theory are constructs, in part because there is no feasible way to count instances of any basic type of control, not even for an individual over a few days, let alone a population over an all-seasons period. Thus, it is not feasible to count the number of times that residents of a country attempt to alter or maintain some characteristic of an inanimate thing (an object or substance), meaning the *frequency* of attempted inanimate control; and even if a count could be made, there is no defensible basis for distinguishing the kinds of things, which would be essential to measure the *range* of attempted inanimate control (i.e., the greater the variety of things, the greater the range). Similarly, there is no defensible basis for reckoning *scope*, meaning the variety of characteristics of things that population members attempt to alter or maintain; and intensity (the amount of human energy and/or time invested in control attempts) may be the least mensurable of all dimensions of control extent.

The problem is not that the four extent dimensions of inanimate control—frequency, range, and scope, and intensity—are vague notions; rather, there is not the remotest prospect of computing corresponding measures, not even for small populations. Yet there is a definite distinction between *efficacy* and the four *extent* dimensions.

Effectiveness vs. Efficiency as Dimensions of Efficacy. Amateur automobile mechanics would readily grasp the meaning of failure in attempted inanimate control. Hence, they would understand a measure of effectiveness; it is simply the proportion of any set of inanimate control attempts that were perceived by those making the attempts as successful. But one need not wonder about "partial success vs. total success" or other distinctions, because there is no prospect of computing effectiveness measures for large social units.

Again, attempted inanimate control commonly involves the use of technological items, and virtually always that use appears to further both the effectiveness and the efficiency of control attempts. However, in many attempts the *technique* (the behavior itself as distinct from any technological items used) is crucial, as golf novices quickly discover. So for some purposes a distinction should be drawn between technique effectiveness and technological effectiveness in inanimate control. Both refer to the proportion of control attempts that succeeded, and both may be considered in some absolute sense or relatively. In the latter case (relatively), it is a matter of the success proportion of one kind of technique vs. another when the *same* technological items, if any, are used *or* one kind of technological item vs. another with the same technique. Whatever distinctions are recognized, the relation between inanimate control effectiveness and efficiency is an *empirical* association. Such is the case because there is no *logically necessary* connection between the success or failure of a control attempt and the amount of energy or time invested, much less the amount conserved; and conservation is the key idea in the subsequent treatment of technological efficiency.

Indispensability vs. Efficiency. Regardless of how effective any particular kind of control attempt may be, commonly there is at least one effective alternative. Yet there are kinds of inanimate control that appear absolutely essential for anything like even partial success. Many have to do with the *technique* of inanimate control attempts. Thus, one obvious illustration is the positioning of the body when driving an automobile (an attempt at locational inanimate control), for some positions would result in erratic movements of the vehicle and collisions (i.e., failures in attempted inanimate control).

Whatever the importance of technique, the most conspicuous examples of indispensable kinds of inanimate control involve technological items. Consider the attempted placement of an inanimate object in orbit around the earth. Because the object itself has been fabricated, it is technological; and the attempt to place it in orbit is attempted locational inanimate control. However, the attempt involves the use of a fabricated substance—some kind of rocket fuel—and that use alone appears indispensable for success (effectiveness). Try to imagine human coordinating or synchronizing their behavior such that the object reaches orbital speed through human energy alone. By contrast, automobiles conserve time and human energy, but they are not indispensable.

There may be a positive empirical association between the efficiency and indispensability of a particular kind of inanimate control, especially when the control entails the use of technological items. That use commonly results in enormous conservation of time and/or human energy, and conservation alone is indicative of indispensability. Nonetheless, whatever the association may be, there is no logically necessary connection between the efficiency and the indispensability of a given kind of inanimate control. Stated otherwise, those two dimensions of *efficacy* are conceptually distinct.

Kinds and Dimensions of Technological Efficiency

Two kinds of inanimate control, X and Y, may be both equally effective in realizing some kind of inanimate goal, G; and yet the time and human energy required to realize G through X is far less than through Y. If so, the X kind of inanimate control is more *efficient* than Y. The comparison implies that X requires *both* less time and less human energy than does the Y; but such contrasts are not always congruent, meaning that one kind of inanimate control may require less energy but more time (or vice versa) than another. Hence, a distinction between *temporal* efficiency and *energetic* efficiency should be recognized and maintained.

Still another warranted distinction is that between *technique* efficiency and *technological* efficiency. In the former case it is a matter of the amount of time and/or human energy required to realize some inanimate goal through a particular kind of behavior relative to the amount required to realize the same goal through some other particular kind of behavior. One dramatic demonstration of such efficiency took place when a time–motion expert (as described by Taylor,

1911:77–81) nearly tripled the number of bricks laid per hour by reducing the conventional movement of brick layers from eighteen motions per brick to five. The illustration pertains to the technique's temporal efficiency rather than its energetic efficiency, but it was not a change in *technological* efficiency because the same technological items were used with the new technique.

Dimensions of Technological Efficiency

Time–motion experts and "Taylorism" notwithstanding, it is assumed that the greatest amount of human energy and time is conserved in inanimate control by the use of technological items and selectivity in that use (one kind rather than another). More specifically, even though technological efficiency is a subclass of inanimate control efficiency, it is argued that differences among human populations with regard to inanimate control efficiency largely reflect variation in technological efficiency. Hence, a special conceptual treatment of technological efficiency is warranted.

Absolute vs. Relative Technological Efficiency. The conservation of time and human energy through the use of technological items is commonly so great that technological efficiency can be easily confused with technological indispensability. As a case in point, various kinds of objects (e.g., pieces of wood, rocks, and certain kinds of metal) can be shaped by rubbing it against some part of the human body; but any shaping of even a small piece would be so laborious that some kind of tool appears essential. The appearance is incorrect, but the contrast illustrates the notion of *absolute* technological efficiency. The difference between the amount of time to shape an object by rubbing it against some part of the body (which part would be a matter of technique) and realizing the same shape with a technological item (e.g., a file or sandpaper) is the absolute *temporal* efficiency of that item, while the difference as regards human energy invested in each of the two alternatives is absolute *energetic* efficiency.

Even if the absolute efficiency (energetic and temporal) of all technological items in all human populations were mensurable, the notion itself has been of little significance since the very early stages of hominid history. Hominids commenced making stone technological items some 2,000,000 BN, and it is possible that even before then *Australopithecus* created bone and wood items, possibly including the carrying bag. Whatever the earliest use of technological items in inanimate control, their use has become so pervasive that the major difference between human populations is *relative* technological efficiency, meaning the amount of time (temporal efficiency) and/or human energy (energetic efficiency) required to realize some inanimate goal by the use of a kind of technological item vs. the use of some other kind. To appreciate the distinction, consider the movement of a large pile of rocks a distance of some 200 meters along a smooth and level path by the use of a wicker basket and then by the use of a wheelbarrow. The exact difference might vary considerably (the individual engaged in the two tasks, the nature of the basket, the quality of the wheelbarrow, etc.); but there is every reason to suppose that the time and human energy required would be much less for the use of the wheelbarrow, and the difference would be indicative of the relative efficiency of those two items.

Gross vs. Net Technological Efficiency. The last illustration pertains to *gross* technological efficiency because the amount of time and energy (human or inanimate, such as hydroelectricity) invested in the creation, distribution, and maintenance of the two technological items, the basket and the wheelbarrow, were ignored. If those investments were somehow taken into account, the comparison would pertain to *net* technological efficiency, temporal or energetic.

The distinction and the previous one (absolute vs. relative) are not mutually exclusive. Hence, one can speak of absolute-gross, absolute-net, relative-gross, or relative-net efficiency.

The Question of Measurement. The foregoing conceptualizations of types of technological efficiency is very brief for a particular reason. Even though all of the types are clearly quantitative, anything like measurement is far from feasible. Even if a formula and a related procedure could be articulated, the practical problems of application to the technology of even one population are prohibitive. Indeed, any estimate of the absolute, relative, gross, or net efficiency (temporal or energetic) of just one kind of technological item is difficult.

The immediate implication is that technological efficiency must be designated as a construct. That designation is all the more imperative because there is no prospect whatever of sociology acquiring the resources necessary to surmount the measurement problems. However, lest the notion of technological efficiency be dismissed as metaphysical, there have been a few instances of the measurement of at least one aspect of technological efficiency. As one instance, Hurtado and Hill (1989) report that Machiguenga women spend two to three times as many minutes when harvesting manioc with wooden tools than metal tools (see, also, Hames, 1979).

Commentary on Axiom 11

Despite the foregoing, it may appear that a tautology is entailed in Axiom 11 (i.e., the extent and efficacy of inanimate control attempts are the asymmetrical, positive, bidirectional, and paramount determinants of technological efficiency). A tautology is suggested all the more on recognition that in the case of "inanimate control techniques" there is no counterpart of absolute efficiency, nor does the gross-net distinction apply. Hence, for all practical purposes, to speak of the efficiency of inanimate control is to speak of technological efficiency and vice versa. Yet Axiom 11 should be construed as asserting a causal relation between technological efficiency (as the effect) and all dimensions of the extent and efficacy of inanimate control attempts, and there

138

is no conceptual (logically necessary) connection between technological efficiency and any dimension of inanimate control *other than* efficiency (i.e., extent, effectiveness, and indispensability). The point is that if both variables in Axiom 11 denoted a mensurable phenomenon, there would be no mathematical necessity for even a positive correlation between them.

The Empirical Character of Axiom 11. A thorough defense of the axiom would require a detailed estimate of the level of efficiency of numerous technological items and an elaborate argument in each case as to why that level could not have been realized without extensive and efficacious inanimate control. Space limitations permit nothing more than an incomplete illustrative instance of such a defense of the axiom.

Consider a hydroelectricity station as a technological item (more aptly labeled a "technological complex"). If the station's efficiency could be measured, regardless of the type considered (absolute vs. relative, gross vs. net), the numerical value would be enormous. Now think about the components of that station (down to the last nut and bolt, so to speak) and contemplate this argument: the variety of those components alone are indicative of the frequency, intensity, effectiveness, indispensability, range, and scope of the inanimate control attempts made in producing the station's equipment (e.g., the installed machines) and in the constructing the structure itself.

Axiom 11 illustrates why it is difficult to use the term "causation" in describing the relation between kinds of behavior, or between a kind of behavior and its product, or between behavioral products. In this case the causal relation obtains because of the purposive quality of human behavior. Specifically, humans invest vast amounts and varieties of inanimate control in technological items with a view to making those items efficient, and they have a very limited choice when it comes to the amount and variety required for a high level of efficiency. Think of the matter in light of this question: how could the extent and indispensability of inanimate control embodied in a hydroelectricity station (all component equipment and machines as well as the building) be reduced substantially and yet have a station that operates efficiently? To be sure, a series of technological innovations could eventually result in an enormous reduction, but those innovations themselves would require inanimate control.

Special Comments on the Types of Causation

Although asymmetrical or nonreciprocal causation is simpler than the symmetrical or reciprocal, the types of causation asserted in Axiom 11 are not beyond question. Indeed, two are especially debatable.

An Argument for Reciprocal or Symmetrical Causation. Inanimate control is technologically driven in that virtually all instances involve the creation, use, or maintenance of a technological item; and, as suggested earlier, the items commonly are indispensable for control effectiveness. Moreover, technological efficiency appears to determine certain dimensions of inanimate control. Illustrating briefly, if the fabrication of objects essential for survival (e.g., clothing and buildings in certain climates) require enormous amounts of time and human energy because of an inefficient technology, the range and scope, perhaps even the frequency, of inanimate control must be very limited.

The argument is correct as far as it goes; but contemplate this question: where, when, and how were the current technological items produced? The vast majority originated in the country of present location, at least several months previously and through extensive and efficacious inanimate control. So the issue of causal direction in the case of Axiom 11 hinges largely on temporal considerations. Viewed synchronically, the direction of causation may appear the reverse of that asserted by Axiom 11; but one obvious consideration suffices to justify the antecedence suggested by Axiom 11. If only because of technique, the efficiency of inanimate control is not entirely a matter of technology, and the very idea of technological efficiency presumes the existence of technological items.

Nothing has been said that totally precludes the possibility of symmetrical (reciprocal) causation. In light of that possibility Axiom 11 may prove to be an oversimplification; and, if feasible, tests of the theorems should be interpreted with a view to (*inter alia*) detecting some evidence of reciprocal causation. Such evidence would mandate revision of Axiom 11, altering the first causal typification from "asymmetrical" to "symmetrical" or "reciprocal." However, whatever the causation, asymmetrical or symmetrical, there is no reason to question the identification of it as *positive* and *bidirectional*.

In Defense of Paramount Causation. Consistent with Axiom 11, no other cause of variation in technological efficiency is shown in Figure 3–1 (Chapter 3, p. 70). However, to assert paramount causation is not to deny other causes, trivial though they may be; and in the case of Axiom 11 there are at least two possibilities.

One of the two has to do with the origination of the technological items presently in use. For an *intranational* territorial unit (e.g., a city), most of the items probably originated elsewhere; if so, in a strictly proximate sense "importation" was the cause of the presence of those technological items. True, large volume of importation ordinarily requires extensive and efficacious control by the importing population, but the control need not be inanimate. If the unit is an agricultural community, the extent and efficacy of biotic control is the primary determinant of imports (technological or otherwise). But that consideration justifies the use of the unit term "countries." Specifically, at the national level the causation of technological efficiency is predominantly endogenous, meaning determined largely by the extent and efficacy of inanimate control in each country. So if international trade continues to increase, eventually it may be necessary to alter the identification of the causal type from paramount to partial; but recognition of such historical relativity does not eliminate the possibility of defensible theories in the social sciences. After all, the prediction of "no association" is a prediction; hence, a change in a relation does not invalidate the theory if it is anticipated in light of some explicit rationale.

It is difficult to imagine the efficiency of technological items completely uninfluenced by purely geographic factors (e.g., terrain, weather), but geographic factors are not recognized as causal variables in the theory, Axiom 11 or otherwise. Their exclusion reflects something more than difficulties, horrendous though they are. Far more important, it is assumed that international variation in geographic factors has a negligible influence on variation in technological efficiency. That assumption would be far more questionable if tests of the theory were based on data prior to this century, but such tests are not real prospects.

Technological Efficiency and Inanimate Energy Use

The terms "extent and efficacy of inanimate control attempts" and "technological efficiency" illustrate why the construct-concept distinction is not just a matter of abstractness. Even though the latter term designates a subclass of the former, both are constructs. Yet the contrast in abstractness does make a difference; it is easier to link technological efficiency with a concept.

Postulate 3

The link is made in Postulate 3: *Among countries and for any country over time, technological efficiency is the asymmetrical, positive, bidirectional, and paramount determinant of the amount of inanimate energy use.* Given that the postulate makes no reference to behavior, it may appear that the asserted relation has nothing to do with control. To the contrary, the causation emanates from the purposive character of control.

Inanimate Energy. The subject can be defined best residually and by reference to sources of energy. Inanimate energy is energy from any source other than *living* humans, animals, or plants. For all practical purposes, living plants are only logically possible sources of *animate* energy, which is to say that humans have yet to make anything like extensive use of them as direct energy sources (i.e., not as food), though wood at one time was the principal *inanimate* energy source. Similarly, the use of humans and animals as energy sources has been limited to the muscular (ectodermic movement of bodily parts), but electrical or chemical uses would be construed also as "animate."

Inanimate energy sources can be defined another way—identification of all major kinds, past and present. This list is virtually exhaustive: coal, petroleum, natural gas, peat, wood or other dead plants, wind, moving water, solar, geothermal, and nuclear fission. However, such a list is likely to prove far from complete in the future. Nuclear fusion may be only a few years off, and gravitational force is only one of several distant possibilities.

On the Rationality Issue. Although space limitations preclude an extensive treatment of the subject, the theory is a continuous rejection of robotic sociology, as exemplified by Durkheim's work. That brand of sociology depicts humans as slavishly conforming to norms created by society. Hence, insofar as the internal behavior of humans is recognized at all, it is affective behavior (e.g., sentiments) that predominate to the exclusion of cognition. Yet it should be obvious to even the most robotic sociologist that virtually any technological item reduces the amount of human energy and/or time of *someone* in their pursuit of a goal.[1] The phrase "pursuit of a goal" is simply one of numerous ways of describing attempted control. The attempted control may be any of the three basic types; but when it comes to the use of technological items in attempted control, human action is predominantly in accordance with Control Principle 5–1: if two kinds of technological items are perceived by potential users as equally effective facilitators of some particular kind of control, the kind of item that reduces the amount of time and/or human energy the most tends to predominate.

The principle should not be construed as suggesting that technological items are simply "there" awaiting selection or rejection. All technological items are products of inanimate control; and if created to be used in control attempts (inanimate or otherwise), such utilitarian items are commonly devised so as to conserve human energy and/or time in the pursuit of physical goals. One obvious means of reduction is to devise a technological item such that it is powered in part or in whole by inanimate energy (e.g., energy from combustible substances or in the form of electricity).

Observe particularly that nothing has been said to suggest any generalization, such as: all human behavior is rational. Instead, there is a more immediate justification for avoiding the notion of rationality: no extant definition of it will bear scrutiny. Moreover, whatever the definition, anything like the illustrative generalization has no bearing on the validity of Postulate 3. The immediate point is that whatever one means by "rational," it would not follow that any human is rational in all of his/her activities. For that matter, Postulate 3 does not imply that humans *always* act so as to reduce their expenditures of human energy and/or time when attempting control. Rather, the assumption is this: the energy-time reduction is sufficiently common and of such a magnitude as to result in what would be a very close positive association between the two variables in Postulate 3, *were both mensurable*. Should critics read more than that assumption into the postulate, it is their own creation.

Comments on the Types of Causation

Unlike previous commentaries, those that follow are not limited to some of the types of causation identified in Postulate 3. There are justifiable doubts about all four types.

Asymmetrical Causation. If the arguments made in connection with Postulate 3 had to be summarized, there would be no alternative to this: the efficiency of any set of technological items depends largely on the related amount of inanimate energy use. That summary statement clearly suggests that inanimate energy use is the determinant of technological efficiency, the exact opposite to what Postulate 3 asserts.

The counterargument is that for all practical purposes inanimate energy sources are never used without some intervening technological item (e.g., moving water does not somehow generate electricity without dams, turbines, etc.) and in virtually all instances the inanimate energy source has been created, modified, and/or relocated through the use of a technological item, in which case the source itself qualifies as technological. So the illustrative but crucial question: how could hydroelectricity increase technological efficiency if producing and transmitting it requires more human energy and time than are conserved through its use? The same question applies to all other inanimate energy sources.

Positive Causation. It could be that international variation in proportionate energy *loss* during conversions (e.g., from coal to steam to electricity) has reached or shortly will reach the point where the major contrast is not the amount of energy used but the efficiency of its conversion (see *Scientific American*, Vol. 263 [September, 1990], pp. 54–163). Conceivably, the contrast could reach the point where there is a *negative* association between total (gross) use of inanimate energy per capita and the amount effectively used per capita (net, meaning the total minus conversion loss). Should that happen and there is a *positive* association between technological efficiency and the ratio of effective inanimate energy use (Ei) to total use (Tu), then the causal direction will be completely wrong (i.e., it should be *negative* rather than *positive*).

There is no basis for doubting that the association between the Ei/Tu ratio and technological efficiency is positive. Moreover, general observations and isolated data on both Tu and Ei clearly indicate that the association between these two variables is positive and substantial. So at least for some time there is no reason to abandon the identification of the causal relation asserted by Postulate 3 as *positive*.

Bidirectional or Unidirectional? Recall that symmetrical bidirectional causation takes one of two forms. In the case of positive bidirectional causation, an increase in X causes an increase in Y, and a decrease in X causes a decrease in Y; while in the case of negative bidirectional causation, an increase in X causes a decrease in Y, and a decrease in X causes an increase in Y. Postulate 3 asserts positive bidirectional causation, and the only immediate doubt stems from the historical rarity of decreases in technological efficiency. However, it will not do to deny the possibility of a change in the type of causation; and in that connection the prospect of depletion of inanimate energy sources take on special significance, for depletion could be such that increases in the extent of attempted inanimate control do not result in greater inanimate energy use. The reference is not just to a reduction in *accessible* deposits of coal, peat, petroleum, and natural gas, but also the reduction in potential sites for the production of electricity from moving water, wind, or thermal vents. For that matter, the notion of depletion extends to a consideration of safe and clean sources of inanimate energy; hence, fossil fuels and nuclear energy must be discounted (for extensive general observations, see Holdren, 1990).

Even if inanimate energy use declines, a *decrease* in the conservation of human energy or time in the pursuit of physical goals would not be inevitable. There are at least four possibilities, all of which taken together could invalidate Postulate 3. First, as suggested earlier, the efficiency of energy converters could increase to the point that more human energy and time is conserved despite a decline in total (gross) inanimate energy use (see Reddy and Goldemberg, 1990). Second, energy-intensive activities (e.g., long-distance travel, commuting or otherwise) could decline. Third, the perfection of human-powered machines, such as bicycles, could compensate for a decline in inanimate energy use. Fourth, there could be a renaissance of the human use of nonhuman animals as energy sources.

Paramount Causation. The prospective depletion of inanimate energy sources lends credence to the identification of the causal type as *paramount* rather than exclusive. The location of pristine inanimate energy sources is a matter of geography, not technology. But there is an argument against identifying the causation as partial, thereby tacitly admitting that geographic (physiographic) factors have an appreciable influence on the amount of inanimate energy used in a country. Both accessibility and convertibility of inanimate energy sources are virtually totally dependent on a wide variety of technological items, and the utilization of gravitational force as a regular energy.source will not be the first corroboration. Throughout human history various potential inanimate energy sources (e.g., petroleum deposits) have gone *unused* for technological reasons. Despite what has been said, there is a need to consider the eventual alteration of the causal identification from "paramount" to "partial." Geographical determinism may never become totally irrelevant; and if systematic tests of the theory were based on data as late as the 19th century, the relation between technological efficiency and amount of use of inanimate energy might well be appreciably contingent on geographic factors. So why not incorporate geographic factors as a variable in the theory to avoid the temporal relativity in question (i.e., less predictive accuracy in the past than in the future)?

It is not entirely a matter of assuming that geographic factors can be excluded without seriously lessening the theory's predictive accuracy, especially in tests based on contemporary data. Geographic factors would have to enter into the theory as a construct; but the proper terminology is debatable, for such diverse phenomena as rainfall, terrain, and mineral deposits cannot be subsumed readily under one notion. Whatever the appropriate construct, there is no obvious link with other constructs, let alone a concept. The "linkage" difficulty stems from the possibility that geographic factors have no direct causal relation with either technological efficiency or amount of inanimate energy use; rather, the association between those two variables may be *contingent* on geographic factors. If so, geographic factors must be introduced in an extension of the theory from second-order to third-order. All of the component generalizations in a second-order theory are bivariate, whereas in a third-order theory at least one generalization is in this form: the relation between X and Y is contingent on Z (its magnitude and/or variance).

The other doubt about asserting paramount rather than partial causation stems from recognition that efficiency is only one major dimension of technology or inanimate control in general, and it surely appears that both access to and conversion of some inanimate energy sources depends on the effectiveness and indispensability of specific kinds of technological items. For example, try to imagine hydroelectricity without a metal technology. However, there are two justifications for not linking "amount of inanimate energy use" directly with "extent and efficacy of inanimate control attempts," rather than through "technological efficiency," as in Axiom 11 and Postulate 3. First, as asserted by Axiom 11, technological efficiency is presumed to vary directly with all other dimensions of inanimate control attempts, including effectiveness and indispensability. Second, humans are unlikely to use an inanimate energy source if its use requires more human energy and time than is conserved; hence, technological efficiency is the pivotal variable.

The Policy Implications of Postulate 3

Despite previous disclaimers concerning rationality, the relation asserted in Postulate 3 may appear to be an implied depiction of human technology as entirely beneficial for humanity. After all, the substitution of inanimate energy for human energy reduces drudgery and may well be essential for a high standard of living. Even if the latter is really a function of the division of labor, two subsequent components of the theory, Axioms 14 and 15, assert a connection between the division of labor and technology.

Granted diverse benefits of technology, most of earth's fundamental environmental problems stem from the extensive use of inanimate energy. The immediate problem is not just the real prospect of a crisis brought on by the exhaustion of readily accessible inanimate energy sources. Because of the use of huge amounts of inanimate energy over numerous generations, further extensive use could damage the environment irreparably, one possibility being a catastrophic diminution of the ozone layer.

Now contemplate the argument that inanimate energy use can be substantially reduced once it becomes an unquestioned environmental threat. It is merely a comforting belief. In many countries no government agency exercises effective control over inanimate energy use, and currently no international organization can compel such control. Worse, insofar as the standard of living and related conditions (e.g., level of employment) depend on extensive use of inanimate energy, it is an illusion to suppose that the kind and degree of control in question can be realized without enormous conflict and perhaps even widescale coercive control. Although the relation asserted by Postulate 3 may have held throughout recorded human history, humanity's fate hinges appreciably on the possibility that the relation will not continue indefinitely.

Transformational Statement 2

No introduction is needed for Transformational Statement 2: *Among countries and for any country over time, the greater the amount of inanimate energy use, the greater RAIEU during T_{0-1}.* An introduction is not needed because such a generalization's form, its position in a theory, and even the principal issues have been discussed at length in connection with Transformational Statement 1 (see, also, Appendix, pp. 303–307). As to the meaning of RAIEU, it will suffice to say that it denotes a formula that expresses the estimated amount of inanimate energy used in a country during a year (hence, "during T_{0-1}"), with the amount of each type of energy (e.g., number of barrels of oil) translated into a particular metric (e.g., kilograms of coal equivalent). The sum of those transformed numerical values is divided by the estimated number of residents of that country at some point during the year.

The formula and instructions as to requisite data are set forth in a section of Chapter 7, but that section need not be read to understand the relation between the concept (amount of inanimate energy use) and the formula. To that end the concept is defined partially as: the sum of all energy from sources other than living organisms that were used by one or more members of some designated population during some designated period in an attempt at inanimate control.

The definition need not be examined with regard to empirical applicability. Because the concept pertains to a quantitative phenomenon, its empirical applicability is solely a matter of the referential formula to which it is linked through Transformational Statement 2. However, if a definition is not clear in the *theorist's own thinking*, he/she is less able and less willing to stipulate what would be construed as an empirically applicable formula. Yet there may be no strictly *logical* connection between a concept's definition and the referential formula, such that there are rules by which two individuals could independently derive the same formula (much less the same data instructions) from the definition.

The foregoing should not be construed as suggesting that an abstract definition is necessarily vague or incomplete. Thus, the reference to "some designated period" translates as *any* temporal interval, be it a minute, an hour, a day, 365 days, or any other definite duration. Why, then, in the case of the referential formula is a calendar year stipulated? Because the research resources of those who will attempt to test the theory are so limited that they must rely on published information, and in those publications data are reported on an annual basis. But there are other than practical considerations. If the variables denoted by the construct (technological efficiency) and the concept (amount of inanimate energy use) could be measured, the association between them would depend on the length of the time period, with the magnitude of the association being greater *up to a point* for longer time periods (e.g., measures based on a one-day period might prove highly unstable). However, the temporal quantifier of the referential pertains only to the association between the concept and the referential; and it may be little more than a guess by the theorist as to what is the most appropriate period, even ignoring the feasibility of the formula's application.

An application of the referential formula yields a per capita value, because the amount of inanimate energy used in a country is undoubtedly an appreciable function of population size, something that may have no connection with technological efficiency. So division of the amount by population size is warranted, but it could be that the number of technological items should be controlled in addition to or rather than population size (i.e., to maximize the association between technological efficiency and the energy variable). Finally, even if the theorist knows with absolute certainty what the referential formula should be, in light of limited research resources and other feasibility considerations he/she may refrain from stipulating that ideal.

If applied correctly to reliable data, an *ideal* referential formula would maximize the association between computed referents and technological efficiency, were the latter mensurable. So in advancing a referential formula the theorist commonly makes a tacit assertion something like this: even if I knew the ideal referential formula, its application would not be feasible; but the ideal referents (those computed by application of the ideal formula) and the referents computed by the correct application of the stipulated formula would be highly correlated. Although the assertion is untestable, tests of the theorems derived *in part* from the transformational statement will reflect the assertion's validity. If that claim is doubted, imagine someone saying: the outcome of tests of this generalization will in no way depend on the formula selected for the numerical expression of the variables or on stipulations as to requisite kinds of data.

Attempted Control of Human Behavior
and the Division of Labor

The explication of Axioms 6 and 8 emphasized the increase in effective control over human behavior concomitant with transitions from the autonomous to the symbiotic to the organized mode of production. Each mode is present to some degree in all countries, and the amount of coordination or synchronization of sustenance activities is more important than the predominance of any particular mode.[2] Extensive coordination and synchronization are essential for a high degree of division of labor, and even at the household level (i.e., within households) there is likely to be some coordination and synchronization of sustenance activities. Nonetheless, within a household differences in sustenance activities tend to be associated with age-sex distinctions (i.e., age and sex are *bases* of the division of labor), and for that reason alone the degree of division of labor is negligible in the autonomous mode of production (no exchange among households).In that mode the division of labor tends to be duplicated *across* households, which drastically limits the amount of it for the larger social unit.

An increase in sustenance activity specialization commences with an exchange (goods, services, benefits, or commodities) among households, the beginning of the symbiotic mode of production.[3] However, in the symbiotic mode there is a definite limit on specialization in sustenance activities and, hence, the degree of division of labor. The limit is overcome in the organized mode of production, where production behavior is controlled in some organizational context (corporations or companies in capitalist countries) through the persistent threat of sanctions. Only in that condition does the coordination-synchronization of sustenance activities reach the point where specialization takes the form of particular *positions* in collaborative production (e.g., supervisors, operatives, and secretaries as employees of a corporation that manufactures automobiles). From that point onward there is usually an exponential increase in occupational distinctions (socially recognized by titles) within the territorial unit as a whole, be it a community or a country; and those distinctions are indicative of a conspicuous division of labor. But the organized mode does not become suddenly predominant, and the division of labor may continue to increase long after its predominance. Such is the case because the mode's predominance is a direct function of the proportion of sustenance activities that take place in production organizations *and* the average size of those organizations.

The foregoing references to coordination and synchronization have not introduced something alien to the notion of control, for prolonged and intense coordination or synchronization require effective control attempts. Hence, the entire argument is expressed by Axiom 12: *Among countries and for any country over time, the extent and efficacy of attempts to control human behavior are the symmetrical, positive, bidirectional, and partial determinants of the degree of division of labor.*

Conceptualization of the Degree of the Division of Labor

Although the degree of division of labor is treated as a construct, a conceptualization is needed to link that term with a concept; and all the more because of the notion's history. Adam Smith and Emile Durkheim both had a keen interest in the division of labor, as did Karl Marx and Max Weber. Unfortunately, none of them offered a genuine conceptualization of the notion, much less one that comes to grips with issues and problems. For that matter, Smith's conception and Durkheim's conception are starkly divergent. Whereas Smith was preoccupied with the coordination and synchronization of activities in the collaborative production of a particular commodity (as in his famous pin factory), Durkheim was preoccupied with consumption and functional interdependence at the societal level.

A Definition. The following definition is compatible with both Smith's conception and Durkheim's conception.[4] The degree of division of labor is the amount of differentiation among members of a population as regards their sustenance activities and the related amount of functional interdependence.

The definition applies to any population, but the phenomenon is most meaningful when analyzing the division of labor in a social unit. Contrary to both Durkheim and Smith, the social units could be of any type—a tribe, a band, an organization (e.g., a company or corporation), a city, a country, etc.—provided that the members are necessarily functionally interdependent (either through exchange or collaborative production) to some degree. Lest the definition appear alien to Smith's conception, the very idea of a position in a production process implies differentiation in activities; and the notion of functional interdependence extends to collaborative production, such as two workers at different position on an assembly line. As for Durkheim (1933), he wrote as though there could be no division of labor without occupations or industries; but that requirement would preclude the phenomenon among some if not all foragers. In those social units an individual's sustenance activities vary so much over time (perhaps even hourly) that he/she cannot be said to have an occupation; rather, adult foragers tend to be a jack-of-all-trades. However, members of a foraging band do differ in their sustenance activities qualitatively (e.g., only some members hunt large game) and quantitatively (e.g., some members fish more than others). Such differences are not socially recognized if the criterion is the presence of occupational or industry titles; but the differences are commonly correlates of age and sex, meaning that age and sex are possible *bases* of the division of labor. Any basis of the division of labor implies some degree of it; but otherwise the two are distinct notions, and the present theory has no necessary bearing on bases of the division of labor.

Brief Commentaries on Causation

One issue transcends the types of causation asserted in Axiom 12. If the division of labor were mensurable, each country would have a particular value. Regardless of the country or its value, many sociologists would make this argument: no resident of that country may know of that value, much less planned it; and even if the country is English-speaking, it could be that many residents never heard of the division of labor. The suggested conclusion is that Axiom 12 must be invalid, for the division of labor (like all other macro or aggregate variables) is uncontrolled. On the whole, the argument is accepted, but the suggested conclusion is unwarranted.

On Causation of the Division of Labor. Neither Axiom 12 nor any comment on it suggests that the degree of division of labor is controlled in any country, not even that attempts are made to control it.[5] However, no logic of causation would be violated by this *form* of an assertion: such-and-such extent and efficacy of attempts to control human behavior constitutes a necessary and sufficient cause of such-and-such degree of division of labor. To be sure, a precise statement in that form may never prove feasible, but there is no ontological basis for declaring that variation in features of human control cannot be a cause or the cause of variation in the degree of division of labor.

General observations suggest that a sharp increase in the division of labor was a major feature of the Industrial Revolution, the most conspicuous flowering of capitalism. However, less obvious, capitalism did not truly flourish until the feudal laws regulating production and consumption were abandoned in a move toward *laissez-faire* or free-market economics. So if it is recognized (rightly) that regulatory law is an attempt to control human behavior, the suggestion is this: the causation identified in Axiom 12 as *positive* is really *negative*.

That suggestion ignores evidence of a great increase in the division of labor in many countries, European and Anglo-American in particular, long *after* a turn to much more regulatory law, especially during the Great Depression. Nonetheless, the argument against positive causation does have one merit. It prompts recognition that the "extent and efficacy of attempts to control human behavior" encompasses much more than regulatory law, even more than the control that employers exert over their employees. As one of numerous examples, political campaigns are attempts to control human behavior on a massive scale; and yet they have little to do with the coordination or synchronization of sustenance activities, the crucial factor in the division of labor. One solution would be to relabel the construct such that it pertains only to the attempts to control sustenance activities or, more conventionally, economic behavior. However, that change would alter the theory drastically (perhaps revision or abandonment of some axioms considered up to this point) and reduce the theory's scope. The alternative is simply to grant a point: if the variables in Axiom 12 were mensurable, the association between them would be far from maximum.

Doubts about the strength of the association grow in light of Axiom 14 (*infra*). It is the reason for identifying the causation in question as *partial* rather than paramount or exclusive. However, that identification does not speak to this question: what is the relative importance of the extent and efficacy of the control (Axiom 12) and technological complexity (Axiom 14) as determinants of the division of labor? There is no satisfactory answer, but the subsequent explication of Axiom 14 indicates that technological complexity is of enormous importance.

On Causation of Behavior Control. The first of the four implied causal typifications in Axiom 12—that changes in the degree of division of labor cause changes in the extent and efficacy of attempts to control human behavior—cannot be understood without some appreciation of the purposive quality of the organized mode of production. The coordination and synchronization of collaborative production activities is more effective if those involved are somehow differentiated as to "position," be it designated a status, an occupation, or a job. That point is not lost on those who create production organizations, and they do more than allocate members (e.g., employees) to positions. To realize coordination and synchronization, they must direct the members' activities. Their directions are attempts at human control; but in a particular sense the division of labor has created what the organizers perceive to be a need for more human control, the very need that they created. Indeed, the concern for control effectiveness promotes the creation of "control" positions in the organizations—supervisors, directors, etc.—that in turn results in more attempts at human control. Most important, the appearance of such positions as police officers, judges, teachers, and priest represent an increase in the differentiation dimension of the division of labor, and they in turn increase the extent of attempts at behavioral control.

Accepting what has been said, the causation of the extent and efficacy of attempts to control human behavior is *positive* and *bidirectional*. The latter typification is best understood by contemplating the consequences of the total disappearance of the division of labor. According to the argument, there would be (*inter alia*) a drastic decline in the extent of attempts at behavior control. Conversely, assuming that the division of labor continues to increase, the argument anticipates an increase in the extent of behavior control attempts.

As Figure 3-1 (Chapter 3, p. 70) indicates, the division of labor is only a partial cause of the extent and efficacy of attempts to control human behavior. In light of Axiom 6, the extent and efficacy of inanimate control attempts constitute another partial cause. Lest it be presumed that the division of labor is of little significance in comparison to inanimate control attempts, recall that the extent of inanimate control (perhaps even its efficacy) is dependent on the coordination and synchronization of production activities, notions implicit in any conception of the division of labor.

The Division of Labor and Occupational Differentiation

Whatever the social unit, be it a tribe or a country, it is doubtful that an empirically applicable measure of the division of labor can be devised. The solution is to link the notion with a concept, as done in Postulate 4: *Among countries and for any country over time, the degree of the division of labor is the asymmetrical, positive, bidirectional, and paramount determinant of the degree of occupational differentiation.*

Occupational Differentiation

The term is identified as a concept because (as a necessary condition) it can be defined such that the definition is regarded as clear and complete. Degree of occupational differentiation is defined as the number of occupations in some designated population at some designated time point and the uniformity or evenness of the distribution of population members among those occupations at that time, excluding those members who cannot be described as working or seeking work in a particular occupation. The definition recognizes two dimensions of occupational differentiation—the categorical (number of categories) and the distributional (uniformity of distribution among the categories); hence, it can be thought of as the *improbability* of any two population members having the same occupation.

Postulate 4 is not a tautology. The division of labor is defined as pertaining *in part* to the amount of functional interdependence and *in part* to differentiation in sustenance activities, but there is no conceptual connection between functional interdependence and occupational differentiation. Indeed, the postulate expresses an assumption—that of a close positive *empirical* association between those two variables. One may or may not regard the assumption as tenable; in any case, it is not true by definition.

Postulate 4 is still another reason why the theory's unit term is "country." As indicated earlier, in some bands or tribes, foragers especially, the notion of an occupation does not apply readily, if at all.[6] The suggestion is not that all tribal or band members engage even approximately in the same sustenance activities; some differences along age and sex lines are a virtual certainty. However, the sustenance activities of adult members are likely to vary so much over time (even within the same day) that a common feature of an occupation—appreciable uniformity over time—is rare. The most conspicuous manifestation is the absence of occupational titles, meaning no terms in the population's natural

152

language that denote categories of people distinguished by kinds of and amounts of sustenance activities.[7] Such labels are found in all countries, and many of them are so old that they cannot be dated with confidence (e.g., in the case of English-speaking countries, "baker" and "blacksmith").

The Question of Causation

The basic causal argument has been suggested previously. As differences among population members increase, sooner or later those differences come to be socially recognized to the point that labels come to be used in the population to identify categories of members. The causal argument need not extend to a consideration of either of two questions. First, what determines one occupational label rather than another? Second, how much differentiation in sustenance activities is necessary before any labels are used? With one qualification, it need only be said that increases in differentiation eventually cause the use of occupational labels (or "titles").

The qualification pertains to the possibility that functional interdependence is relevant. It could be that a certain level or intensity of interdependence is necessary for the related occupational differentiation to be recognized in the population's natural language. However, the reference to "population" is not a denial that in recent centuries much of the differentiation in sustenance activities has taken place in production organizations, where differentiation is both created and *labeled* to further the coordination and synchronization of collaborative production.

Brief Commentaries on Some of the Causation Types. Research findings may eventually lead to the revision of Postulate 4, such that it asserts symmetrical (reciprocal) causation. That possibility is suggested by these terms: supervisor, director, and superintendent. They are only a few of many titles in the English language that denote a special type of occupation, one in which the incumbents are primarily responsible for controlling activities (commonly in production organizations). The point is that occupational differentiation may reach the point where it encourages or makes possible still more differentiation, and in that sense it becomes a cause of an increase in the division of labor. Yet such "occupational generation" of the division of labor appears so negligible that it does not warrant recognition even as partial causation. What the future holds is another question, of course.

Population members who engage in what they perceive as the same sustenance activities may presume that an occupational title would be to their advantage, perhaps to justify demands for higher wages. As a consequence, they grossly exaggerate the distinctive character of those activities, thereby promoting social recognition of them as constituting an occupation. That possibility is not denied, but the extent to which there are major international differences as regards such "interest group promotion" is another question. Hence, it remains to be seen whether the causation type should be reduced from paramount to partial. Similarly, the quantity and quality of a country's international trade may have some influence on the amount of differentiation in sustenance activities and on occupational composition, but it is assumed that the influence is not substantial. So there are two reasons why the causation is identified as paramount rather than exclusive, and eventually the outcome of tests could force a change from paramount to partial causation.

Transformational Statement 3

No particular issue is posed by the wording: *Among countries and for any country over time, the greater the degree of occupational differentiation, the greater RDOD at T_{0-1}*. Rather, issues surface when examining the formula and related statements pertaining to data, all of which appear in the extrinsic part of the theory (Chapter 7). One issue is especially likely when the formula appears incongruent with the concept's definition. That appearance introduces the idea of "rules of correspondence." Although different arguments about that idea are made subsequently in connection with particular transformational statements, all of the arguments are relevant regardless of the transformational statement in question.

Even the "correspondence" between the temporal quantifier (T_{0-1} in this case) and the concept's definition is misleading. The definition is to be construed as pertaining to the degree of occupational differentiation at any point in time. Similarly, "at T_{0-1}" means any point during any calendar year. However, the referential's temporal quantifier is not necessarily "given" by the concept's definition (i.e., deducible from it).

To illustrate another "lack of correspondence," the suicide rate may be defined as the number of members of a designated population who committed suicide during a designated period as a ratio to the *average* daily number of members during the period, excluding from both the numerator and denominator those individuals (if any) who became a member or terminated membership but not from suicide during the period. Yet the referential for the suicide rate (RSR) could be stipulated as: $RSR=([Ns/3]/P)100,000$, when Ns is the number of *officially* reported suicides of members of the population in question during a three year period, and P is the total number of population members at any point during the period's second year. Observe that the definition of the suicide rate (i.e., the concept) does not refer to "officially reported" or to a three-year period. That particular lack of correspondence and all of the others could stem from the theorist's concern with the stability of the rate (hence "three years" rather than a shorter period) and the availability of official published data on the incidence of suicide. Indeed, the data stipulations reflect a stance on a very controversial matter—the reliability of official statistics on the incidence of suicide. None of these subjects are in any sense given by or deducible from the concept's definition.

Alternative RDOD Formulas. The issue at hand is especially relevant in the case of Transformational Statement 3 because the referential formula stipulated in Chapter 7 does not appear to correspond with the concept.[8] That formula is:

$$RDOD_1=(1-[\Sigma X^2/(\Sigma X)^2])/[1-(1/Nc)],$$

where X is the number of individuals reported as being in one of the country's occupations or occupational categories, and Nc is the number of occupations or occupational categories. The numerator's value is a direct function of the number of occupational categories (Nc) *and* the uniformity of the distribution of individuals among the categories. So the numerator appears fully congruent with the definition of occupational differentiation; but because the denominator is the *maximum* numerator value given the number of occupations or occupational categories, the formula eliminates the influence of variation among units (countries or otherwise) in that number, meaning that a RDOD value reflects *only* distributional uniformity. Why? International variation in the number of occupations or occupational categories in published census data is artificial; specifically, there is no basis for assuming any association between the number of census occupational categories and the *true* number of occupations in the country. So while sociology's limited research resources make it necessary to stipulate the use of census data, it is imperative that the referential formula eliminate the influence of international variation in the number of occupations or occupational categories. Such a formula is not even suggested by the definition of the concept. The general point is that the nature of accessible data may force the theorist to stipulate a formula that does not appear to correspond to the definition in one or more respects. However, there are alternative formulas for circumventing defects in the stipulated kind of data, one being:

$$RDOD_2=1-[(\Sigma \mid X-M \mid /2)/(\Sigma X-M)],$$

where X and Nc are as previously defined and $M=\Sigma X/Nc$. Unlike the denominator of the first formula, an $RDOD_2$ value is not influenced by the number of occupations or categories.

Now assume that international variation in the number of census occupations is not an artifact (i.e., in each country the number of census occupations corresponds very closely to the true number). Even so, there may be at least two formulas and both appear to correspond to the definition of the concept. Two illustrations follow:

$$RDOD_3=1-[\Sigma X^2/(\Sigma X)^2] \text{ and } RDOD_4=Nc(1-[(\Sigma \mid X-M \mid /2)/(\Sigma X-M)]),$$

where X, Nc, and M are as previously defined. Both formulas reflect the number of categories and uniformity of distribution simultaneously, but they are not mathematical equivalents. They are highly correlated, though perhaps not to such an extent that the choice between them is inconsequential. So which of the two should the theorist choose and on what basis? It may be that a defensible choice between alternative formulas cannot be made; if so, the theorist should stipulate more than one referential formula, and when feasible all formulas should be used in tests. Yet a large number of alternatives is impractical, and it has the effect of making at least some components of the theory unfalsifiable.

Given the artificiality of variation in the number of census occupations, the choice must be made between $RDOD_1$ and $RDOD_2$. Because a defensible choice cannot be made, both are stipulated in the extrinsic part of the theory (Chapter 7); but the strategy is not an implicit denial of the possibility of still other alternatives, some of which may increase the theory's predictive accuracy. The only mitigation is that the same can be said for any theory.

The Division of Labor and Industry Differentiation

Because virtually all comments on Postulate 4 and Transformational Statement 3 extend to Postulate 5 and Transformational Statement 4, the latter two components of the theory can be set forth without extensive commentary.
Postulate 5: Among countries or for a county over time, the degree of division of labor is the asymmetrical, positive, bidirectional, and paramount determinant of the degree of industry differentiation.
Transformational Statement 4: Among countries or for a country over time, the greater the degree of industry differentiation, the greater RDID at T_{0-1}.

The Occupation-Industry Distinction

The concept "degree of industry differentiation" refers to the number of industries in some designated population at some designated time point and the uniformity or evenness of the distribution of population members among those industries at that time, excluding those members who cannot be described as working or seeking work in a particular industry. Given that the definition is virtually identical with the previous definition of degree of occupational differentiation, it may appear that the referential formulas for the two concepts measure the same thing.[9] Such is not the case because there is a fairly clear-cut distinction between occupations and industries.

An occupation is a distinctive set of sustenance activities performed so frequently and regularly by some members of a population that there is a term in the population's language that denotes those members. To illustrate, no one is likely to question that "secretaries" and "mechanics" are occupational titles in English-speaking populations, nor that the sustenance activities of the individuals so identified are distinctive in several respects. However, the suggestion is not that the empirical applicability of any occupational term (i.e., label or title) is even near the maximum in any population, English-speaking or otherwise. Rather, it is assumed that the degree of empirical applicability permits the use of census data on occupations without reducing the theory's predictive accuracy to an unacceptable level (i.e., relative to whatever is taken to be a contending theory about the correlates of occupational differentiation).

The same assumption applies to census data on industries, even though an industry is different from an occupation. An industry is a particular kind of *product* (what an economist would identify as a good, commodity, service, or benefit) *and* a distinctive set of related sustenance activities engaged in by some members of a population. As such, the term "industry" refers, simultaneously, to a kind of product, the related production activities, and the participating population members. As for the occupation-industry distinction, observe (as examples) that a secretary, a mechanic, a supervisor, and an executive are in different occupations; but they may be in the same industry (automobile manufacturing) or in different industries (e.g., agriculture, airline transportation, retail, and manufacturing).

Similarities of Referential Formulas

The distinction between occupations and industries is all the more important because the referential formulas, RDOD and RDID, are identical except one refers to occupations or occupational categories and the other refers to industries or industry categories. Indeed, the issues concerning the connection between concepts and referential formulas are exactly the same; and because it is feasible to apply the two formulas only to census data, the related problems are the same. Hence, whatever the rationale for selecting one version of RDOD rather than another, it extends to the choice among versions of RDID.

Given that both occupational differentiation and industry differentiation are asserted (Postulates 4 and 5) to be effects of the division of labor, it follows that, accepting the two transformational statements (3 and 4), there should be a substantial correlation among countries between RDOD referents and RDID referents. That correlation is anticipated in the subsequent deduction of a theorem but it could be argued that a substantial correlation is somehow a mathematical necessity. Thus, if occupational composition is exactly the same from one industry to another (the same occupations in each industry and the same proportionate distribution among those occupations), then the degree of occupational differentiation for the country as a whole cannot be different from the degree in any industry. The suggestion is, of course, that the degree of occupational differentiation within industries sets limits on the degree for all industries combined. But differences or similarities among industries as regards occupational composition has no mathematical connection whatever with the number of industries or the distribution of individuals among the inustries. The only real problem is that in actual practice a few occupations are assigned to a particular industry (e.g., farmers to agriculture and miners to the extraction industry), but that connection determines the correlation between RDOD referents and RDID referents only within exremely broad limits.

Biotic Control and Control Concentration

Whatever the kind of control, one can speak of a demand, market, or need for it; and that is the case regardless of the type of economy—capitalist, socialist, command, etc. But economists have yet to describe how the demand, market, or need for anything can be and should be judged independently of *actual* exchanges, purchases, consumption, etc. Hence, statements about the demand or the market or need tend to be tautologies, as when a jump in actual car sales is interpreted described as signifying an increase in demand. No tautology is entailed in Control Principle 5–2: for any kind of control in any social unit, if the goals realized through that kind of control are realized or exceeded, an increase in the efficacy of that control is followed by a decrease in the proportion of the unit members regularly engaged in it.

The principle is illustrated by trends in U.S. agriculture over the past two centuries. All available statistics indicate substantial changes in three things: first, productivity per agricultural worker increased; second, gross energetic and temporal efficiency of agricultural production increased; and, third, the percentage of the labor force in agriculture decreased. The three changes cannot be explained adequately, nor can the principle they exemplify be made a component of the theory without an elaborate conceptualization of a free market, competition, and occupations in terms of control. Space limitations and the need to simplify preclude that conceptualization.[10] So what is actually a theory in itself must be reduced to one generalization, Axiom 13: *Among countries and for any country over time, the extent and efficacy of biotic control are the asymmetrical, positive, bidirectional, and paramount determinants of the concentration of biotic control attempts.*

Concentration should not be confused with centralization. The former refers to nothing more than the extent to which control attempts of some designated type or kind are limited to particular members of the population in question. Two kinds of somatic control in the U.S. illustrate the extremes. With the exception of the incapacitated and the very young, all Americans engage in something akin to personal hygiene; hence, the concentration of that kind of control is near the absolute *minimum*. By contrast, only a minute proportion of Americans perform neurosurgery; so the concentration of that kind of somatic control approaches the *maximum*.

The examples serve also to indicate the difference between concentration and centralization. The latter always refers to attempts at control over human behavior; and the question is this: of those who engage in the kind of control in question, to what extent is an attempt made to control their behavior (while so engaged) by other particular members of the population? Observe that both personal hygiene and neurosurgery are highly decentralized kinds of biotic control, even though they differ sharply as to concentration.[11] Still another illustrative contrast is agriculture in the U.S. versus the People's Republic of China (PRC). That kind of biotic control is highly concentrated in the U.S., highly deconcentrated in the PCR, highly decentralized in the U.S., and highly centralized in the PRC (though evidently far less now than in the 1960s).

On the Causation of Concentration

Axiom 13 is a special case of a generalization about any basic type of control or all types considered together. The generalization's rationale is essentially the same regardless of the control type, and it reduces to two interrelated considerations. First, by definition, as the gross energetic and temporal efficiency of some kind of control increases, the less human energy and time are required to realize the goals of that kind of control; and, in accordance with Control Principle 5–2, the outcome is a reduction in the proportion of population members regularly engaged in that kind of control. Second, whatever the country, there are innumerable kinds of control that cannot be effective without considerable expertise; and because both training resources and talent are always limited, participation in those kinds of control tends to be very selective and, hence, limited to particular population members.

Axiom 13 is questionable because "extent and efficacy of biotic control attempts" is a compound construct ("extent" and "efficacy"), but the relation asserted in Axiom 13 holds primarily through two dimensions of efficacy, efficiency and effectiveness, rather than through extent. The problem could be avoided by restricting the construct to "efficacy of biotic control attempts," but that restriction might force the abandonment of many premises in which the compound character of the construct is essential (i.e., instances where both extent and efficacy are relevant).

Brief and Selective Comments on the Types of Causation. Despite the problem created by the compound character of the first construct in Axiom 13, there is no real basis to doubt that the causation is *positive* and *bidirectional*. Yet it may appear that the causation should be identified as symmetrical (reciprocal) rather than asymmetrical (nonreciprocal). If the kind of control in question cannot be efficacious without expertise, then its concentration reduces the problem of scarce training resources and talent. Even so, it is assumed that the expertise requirement results in a concentration of control attempts with or without the deliberate promotion of that concentration.

If Axiom 13 were intended to apply only to countries in which the economy is based on a totally and absolutely free market, the causation might be characterized as exclusive rather than *paramount*. However, it may well be that there is not and never will be such an economy, and political considerations prompt attempts to control certain facets of the economy. Thus, for one reason or another, a regime may attempt to prevent a decline in agricultural workers even though the mechanization makes the present number unnecessary to maintain the production level. Such practices do not appear so common as to invalidate Axiom 13, but even their recognition as a possibility cautions against identifying the causation as exclusive.

Control Concentration and the Predominance
of Animate Industries

"Concentration of biotic control attempts" refers to the extent that the frequency of biotic control attempts varies among members of some designated population during some designated period. Even if various key words in that definition had a clear meaning, it would be difficult to formulate a measurement procedure. The principal difficulty is that extent refers to frequency, range, scope, and intensity; and in any case perhaps it would be necessary to give special weight to the proportion of population members who do not engage in any biotic control attempts. Whatever the measure, the resources required for its application at any level are prohibitive; so "concentration of biotic control attempts" is treated as a construct.

Postulate 6

The immediate problem when linking the construct with a concept is that the construct pertains to biotic control in general—hunting, fishing, other foraging, forestry, domestication of plants, domestication of animals, somatic control, and genetic engineering. Nonetheless, in countries throughout the world the bulk of biotic control attempts occur in the context of animate industries, those in which the principal product is either a living thing or processed from living things—animals (meat, milk, etc.) or plants (grains, lumber, etc.). That observation is the basis for Postulate 6: *Among countries and for any country over time, the concentration of biotic control attempts is the asymmetrical, negative, bidirectional, and paramount determinant of the predominance of animate industries.*

The last term in the postulate, "predominance of animate industries," is defined as the proportion of all sustenance activities in some designated population that take place in the context of industries identified as agriculture (including farming, ranching, gardening, and marine domestication), hunting, fishing, and forestry at some designated time point. Should the assertion of causation appear esoteric, recall the interpretation of Axiom 13—that a great concentration of biotic control attempts is indicative of their efficacy. Hence, if the biotic control attempts are so efficacious that they yield a vast quantity of biotic products (grains, meat, milk, wood, etc.), they will represent only a small proportion of the country's sustenance activities. Stated conversely, if a large proportion of national sustenance activities take the form of biotic control attempts, that condition is indicative of three things: first, the predominance of animate industries; second, inefficacious biotic control attempts; and, third, a low degree of concentration of those attempts.

Selective and Brief Comments on the Types of Causation. One obvious consideration cautions against identifying the causation as exclusive rather than paramount. A country's animate industries could be markedly predominant not because of any considerations introduced by Axiom 3 or Postulate 6 but because of international trade. Independent of properties of biotic control, exports of biotic products may contribute to the predominance of the country's animate industries. Similarly, imports of biotic products tend to lessen that predominance.

Rather than further complicate an already complicated theory, it is assumed that international trade does not reduce the asserted relations to the point that the theory's predictive accuracy will be less than that of contenders. However, that assumption will become increasingly untenable if international trade continues to increase. In any case, the eventual goal is the conversion of the theory from second-order (all synthetic statements are bivariate) to third-order. So Postulate 6 may eventually be the basis for a third-order postulate, something like this: among *sets* of countries, the greater the average international trade per capita for a set, the less the negative relation in that set between the concentration of biotic control attempts and the predominance of animate industries. That generalization by itself would not be testable, but it would lead to the deduction of testable third-order theorems—versions of Theorems 1, 6, 7, 8, and 9 in Figure 3–1 (Chapter 3, p. 70).

Transformational Statement 5

Here is a rare instance where the concept and the referential formula may appear to correspond exactly—Transformational Statement 5: *Among countries and for any country over time, the greater the predominance of animate industries, the greater the RPAI at T_{0-1}.* As explained at length in Chapter 7, RPAI is a simple ratio: $RPAI=(A+H+Fg+Fy)/T$, where A is the number of residents reported by an official agency (e.g., the U.S. Bureau of the Census, the United Nations Statistical Office) as engaged in the industry of agriculture; H, the number in hunting; Fg, the number in fishing; and Fy, the number in forestry; and T is the total number in the labor force or economically active but excluding those with industry unknown or undesignated.

The appearance of exact correspondence stems from the equivalence of the list of industries in the definition of the concept and the list in the explication of the referential formula. The appearance is misleading and apart from recognition that only the referential formula (*not* the concept) makes reference to data sources. Observe especially that the concept alludes to the proportion of *sustenance activities,* whereas the explication of the referential formula refers to *number of individuals.* To be sure, one can assume, as here, a very close positive relation among a country's industries between the number of individuals in an industry and the proportion of sustenance activities in that industry; but it is an assumption, and its validity is not somehow assured by any real or imagined rule of correspondence between concepts and formulas.

Biotic Control and Variation in Death Ages

Whatever the human population, virtually any member's death can be described (without logomachy) as a consequence of a control failure. Even a criminal homicide would not be an exception, because the threat of legal punishment did not deter.[12] If accidental deaths appear inconsistent with the generalization about control failures, the reply would depend on the kind of accident. Thus, deaths from automobile accidents are certain to be describable as resulting from failures in inanimate control.

Although the previous observations suggest that inanimate control and control over human behavior are relevant, the extent and efficacy of biotic control are presumed to be the paramount determinants of mortality prevention. The immediate consideration is something that residents of affluent countries tend to ignore—an abundance of food is a testimonial to the efficacy of two major types of biotic control, plant domestication and animal domestication. However, throughout human history diseases may have caused far more human deaths than has starvation, and a marked increase in the extent and efficacy of somatic control, another major type of biotic control, brought about an unprecedented decline in human mortality. Physicians can take little credit for that enormous decline, for it was primarily realized through public health measures, a very broad kind of somatic control. Indeed, although medical care does prevent innumerable illnesses and injuries from becoming fatal, revolutionary developments in transplants and prosthetics are the only immediate prospect of still another quantum decline in human mortality. A more distant prospect is commonly known as genetic engineering, the latest and potentially the most revolutionary major type of biotic control. Only genetic engineering holds forth the promise of substantially reducing the most intractable cause of human mortality—a wide range of degenerative diseases among the elderly.

Postulate 7

All observations up to this point suggest a simple generalization: the greater the extent and efficacy of biotic control in a population, the less that population's mortality rate. The generalization's validity depends appreciably on the kind of mortality rate considered. If the extent and efficacy of biotic control could be measured, the generalization might be false when the crude death rate is the mortality measure. That rate does not take the population's age composition into account, and age is of special significance in contemplating the control-mortality relation. Whatever the country, deaths of the elderly appear inevitable, which is to say *beyond contemporary control in any country*. Hence, only when deaths are common *at all ages* is mortality truly indicative of limited and inefficacious biotic control, a condition that is especially conspicuous among nonliterate peoples. There death is not just common; it is typically perceived by those people as mysterious. The mystery is not just that people commonly die from causes, diseases especially, that the survivors cannot identify, or misidentify when attributing a death to sorcery (as they often do). Perhaps equally important, death appears to strike the young, the middle-aged, and the old indiscriminately.

In light of the foregoing, as far as the control argument is concerned, the most relevant feature of mortality in a population is variation in death ages *within* that population. If a population is so large (as in the case of a country) that numerous members are certain to die annually, how much do those members differ as regards age at death during any year? So the final expression of the generalization is Postulate 7: *Among countries and for any country over time, the extent and efficacy of biotic control are the asymmetrical, negative, bidirectional, and paramount determinants of variation in death ages.*[13] Observe particularly that the concept "variation in death ages" refers to variation among individuals within a country (intranational variation) and not to *international* variation in the mean, median, or modal age at death.

What has been said about variation in death ages (always variation *within* a population, *not* variation among populations) extends to all mortality rates that take age composition into account, meaning for all practical purposes any mortality rate other than the crude death rate. The arguments do not extend to the crude death rate because extensive and efficacious control *eventually* results in an age composition so elderly that the social unit may have a crude death rate greater than that of a social unit where control is substantially less extensive and efficacious. However, a qualification and a special claim should be noted. The qualification is that, unlike variation in death ages (VDA), no conventional mortality rate (CMR) is a *distributional* measure; hence, an empirical relation between VDA and any CMR reflects their mutual dependence on the extent and efficacy of control, whether through age composition or otherwise, and not some strictly mathematical necessity. The related claim is this: because VDA is more sensitive than any CMR to the extent and efficacy of control, tests of the present theory as it pertains to mortality will yield more support when VDA is the mortality variable.

A Major Doubt About the Causal Relation. Postulate 7 is somewhat unusual in that doubts have to do more with the extent of causation than with the identification of types. Those doubts stem from recognition that causation of *intranational* variation in death ages may have been misidentified in a particular way. It could be that the extent and efficacy of *all* types of control attempts are the paramount determinants and not just the extent and efficacy of biotic control attempts. That alternative identification has been avoided in the belief not only that biotic control attempts are paramount but also that multitudinous kinds of inanimate control attempts and attempts to control human behavior are scarcely relevant. Nonetheless, the possibility of reidentifying the causation should be entertained, especially in light of tests of the theorems.

However causation is eventually identified (i.e., whatever types of control are considered relevant), doubts will continue about identifying it as paramount rather than partial. The primary reason is that a population's age composition influences the amount of variation in death ages independently of the *immediate* extent and efficacy of control.[14] Thus, if the age-specific death rates are the same for two populations but one is much more "elderly," then variation in death ages is likely to be *less* for the older population. However, because extensive and efficacious control attempts reduce age-specific mortality rates, the control variable is a major determinant of age composition; but the time lag is probably much greater than it is in the case of the causal relation between the control variable and mortality (including variation in death ages). So the extent and efficacy of control attempts determine variation in death ages both directly and indirectly, in the latter case through age composition. Yet age composition is also influenced by the fertility rate over many previous decades (especially by substantial changes in that rate), and the relation between fertility and the control variable is much more problematical than is the control-mortality relation. Accordingly, there is a need to consider somehow taking age composition into account when stipulating a formula for expressing the amount of variation in death ages.

Transformational Statement 6

Defined explicitly, "variation in death ages" refers to the amount of difference in age at death of members of some designated population (e.g., residents of a particular country) who died during some designated period. Appearances to the contrary, that definition does not eliminate the need for Transformational Statement 6: *Among countries and for any country over time, the greater the amount of variation in death ages within a country, the greater the RVDA during T_{0-1}.* For that matter, the definition may appear to make the stipulation of a referential formula superfluous, the argument being that it must be the standard deviation formula. However, only rarely are there no alternatives in the way of conventional statistics, and in this case the coefficient of variation is a strategic alternative because it more nearly takes age composition into account (i.e., the more elderly the population, the greater the mean death age).

The immediate point is that the concept's definition does not imply any particular way (conventional or otherwise) of expressing the amount of variation. Nor does the definition imply anything about the length of the period and the source of the requisite data. As stipulated in Chapter 7, the period is a calendar year for each country, and national or international agencies are to be the data source. Reliance on those sources is dictated by limited research resources; and, as indicated in Chapter 7, that reliance makes it necessary to express the amount of death age variation in an unconventional way.

Two Special Possibilities

For the sake of lessening complexity, two possible correlates, one antecedent and one postcedent, of variation in death ages are not recognized as components of the theory. Far from being a flaw, such possibilities are indicative of the ease with which the theory can be expanded by the formulation of additional premises.

Another Possible Direct Determinant. As indicated by Axiom 10 (Chapter 4, p. 128), the extent and efficacy of inanimate control attempts are positive determinants of the extent and efficacy of biotic control attempts. Therefore, if the latter is a negative determinant of variation in death ages within a country (as asserted by Postulate 7), then the extent and efficacy of inanimate control attempts are *indirect* negative determinants of that variation. However, the causation may be *both* indirect and direct. The most relevant consideration is that effective inanimate control attempts prevent numerous lethal vehicular accidents and thereby reduces variation in death ages because of the age composition of those who use vehicles frequently and age selectivity in vehicular mortality.

At this point there is no basis to so much as estimate the contrast between the direct and indirect effects of inanimate control on variation in death ages, but the possibility of the two kinds of effects need not remain only speculative. Should tests of Theorem 4 (see Figure 3-1 in Chapter 3, p. 70) indicate a much more substantial association between the RAIEU referents and the RVDA referents than would be anticipated if the extent and efficacy of inanimate control attempts have *only* an indirect effect on variation in death ages, then the theory should be expanded by adding a postulate that connects the two variables (a construct and a concept).

An Unrecognized Possible Consequence. Two major names in the early anthropology of religion emphasized the importance of human mortality (see commentary by Palgi and Abramovitch, 1984:387). According to Tylor, religion originated from a collective response to death, and Frazer attributed the idea of a soul and afterlife to that response. Neither argument now receives much attention, perhaps because neither identifies a mechanism that links the collective response to death and religion or supernaturalism in general. The present theory suggests such an identification. Deaths reduce the survivors' perceived capacity for control, especially in cases of unpredicted deaths, which are common if there is enormous variation in death ages. The suggestion is not that humans can control whatever they regard as predictable, but for all practical purposes unpredictable phenomena are uncontrolled phenomena. Described otherwise, death is feared not just because it is generally perceived as undesirable and unavoidable but also because it is unpredictable, and observe again that predictability is reduced by variation in death ages.

The impact of death age variation on perceived control capacity need not remain purely speculative. Should tests of Theorem 5 indicate a much more substantial association between the RVDA referents and the RLEA referents than is suggested by the causal circuits in Figure 3-1 (Chapter 3, p. 70), that outcome would justify the addition of another causal circuit, one in which a postulate connects variation in death ages and perceived control capacity.

Technological Complexity and the Division of Labor

Although the coordination and synchronization of sustenance activities in the organized mode of production are essential for a high degree of division of labor, a question remains. What is the impetus for the division of labor?

Three Theories

Adam Smith (1952) answered by postulating a human propensity to trade and barter, without recognizing that such a constant hardly explains variation. Moreover, his answer scarcely applies to the very kind of division of labor—within organizations (his famous pin factory)—that was central in his thinking.

Karl Marx devoted an enormous amount of attention to the division of labor (for some citations, see Gibbs, 1989:137 and 177), but he scarcely offered a theory on the subject. For that matter, Marx often wrote as though the division of labor was created by capitalists, although at various places he does recognize that it existed prior to capitalism (his "social" division of labor). However, to attribute the division of labor to modes, forces, or means of production is worse than uninformative; it tends to blur the distinction between empirical associations and conceptual connections.

Durkheim's "functional" answer is something like this—increases in population (material) density eventually *would* lead to lethal competition were it not for the division of labor (e.g., farmers, blacksmiths, bakers, etc., do not compete with each other). But comparisons of Australia, China, India, and the U.S. (to mention only four countries) suggest a *negative* relation between population density and the division of labor. As for Durkheim's vacillation between material density and social or moral density, invoking the latter makes Durkheim's argument untestable. For that matter, if social or moral density is taken as the causal variable, Durkheim's functional argument becomes obscure (i.e., it is not clear how increases in that kind of density would lead to lethal competition were it not for the division of labor). Finally, given Durkheim's assertion (1933:257) of a positive relation between the two kinds of density, the general observation on Australia, China, India, and the U.S. again indicates that something is fundamentally wrong with that theory.

So the predictive power of each of the three theories appears negligible (for a more elaborate commentary, see Gibbs, 1989:136–137). Adam Smith's theory is not merely untestable; even if the "propensity to truck and barter" were mensurable, Smith alluded to it as though it is a constant. The sense in which Marx's theory (if it is such) could have any predictive power is debatable. Finally, insofar as Durkheim's theory is testable, its predictive accuracy appears worse than negligible.

Axiom 14

Even gifted humans have a very limited capacity for mastering the creation and use of technological items. Thus, as a wild guess, it is doubtful if any human can make effective use (not to mention creation and maintenance) of more than one percent of all *types* of technological items in the U.S. Accordingly, were it not for the division of labor, the complexity of any social unit's technology could not exceed the variety of technological items that the most capable member can create, use, and maintain.

With a division of labor, there is virtually no limit on technological complexity; and all the more so given that no country ever remotely approaches maximum occupational differentiation (no more than one individual in any occupation). However, the argument is not some vague functionalism. Rather, the relation between the division of labor and technological complexity stems from the human concern with effective control.[15] Many persons recognize a limit on the variety of technological items that a human can create, use effectively, and maintain properly; hence, at least in literate populations, specialization in sustenance activities is the rule rather than the exception. Most occupations can be described in terms of distinctive kinds of inanimate control, and resort to specialization in coping with the problem of technological complexity is conspicuous in production organizations (corporations or otherwise).

Despite the foregoing, technological complexity is not the cause and the division of labor the effect. The division of labor promotes technological complexity, and that causal relation also stems from human perception. No prospective creator of a technological item is likely to be discouraged by the possibility that its use will require the mastery of new skills. They may even envision the appearance of a new occupation in which the incumbents specialize in the use and/or maintenance of the kind of technological item in question. So the relation is as asserted in Axiom 14: *Among countries and for any country over time, technological complexity is the symmetrical, positive, bidirectional, and partial determinant of the degree of division of labor.*

The Meaning of Technological Complexity. The generalization is identified as an axiom because both property terms are constructs. The rationale for so identifying the degree of division of labor has been given previously, but none has been given for technological complexity.

The possibilities in the way of defining technological complexity appear beyond counting, which alone indicates the difficulty of realizing a complete definition. One possibility is simple: technological complexity refers to the variety of technological items used by members of some particular population. The principal objection is that the notion of variety is abstract to the point of bordering on the meaningless. Hence, technological complexity is defined this way: a set of technological items is complex to the extent that a proportion of the items cannot be created, used effectively, or maintained properly by the typical adult human.[16] Although that definition is comprehensible, the reference to the "typical adult human" alone creates grave doubts about the definition's empirical applicability—feasibility of application as well as congruence when applied by independent observers. Accordingly, technological complexity is treated as a construct.

Technological complexity is not linked to a concept in the theory. That consideration does not make the construct indefensible, and its exclusion would lessen the theory's scope more than merely numerically. With the possible exception of environmental dangers, few aspects of technology promote more fears or concern than does its complexity.[17] Nor is there any puzzle. Humans are becoming increasingly dependent on something that they do not understand, let alone control as individuals. In brief, technological complexity is perceived as a major threat to human autonomy.

Selective and Brief Comments on the Types of Causation. The term "symmetrical" or "reciprocal" is misleading if interpreted as suggesting the possibility of an eventual demonstration of definite sequences, in which a change in one variable, X, is followed by an obvious and proportionate change in the other variable, Y, which in turn is followed by another obvious and proportionate change in X, and so forth. In the case of Axiom 14, whatever the country, both variables pertain to billions of events each year. Hence, there may be no obvious change (increase or decrease) in either variable over several years, much less so conspicuous that there is even an impression of uniform temporal interval between a change in one variable and a subsequent change in the other. Accordingly, even if the two variables were mensurable, there would be little prospect of examining the validity of Axiom 14 through application of conventional space-time criteria of causal evidence to data derived from longitudinal or synchronic comparisons at the national level.

The foregoing problem is exacerbated by two assertions: first, that technological efficiency is another cause of technological complexity (Axiom 15, *infra*); and, second, that taken together the extent and efficacy of attempts to control human behavior is another cause of the division of labor (Axiom 12, *supra*). However, it is one thing to grant the gravity of the evidential problems but a quite different thing to argue that those premises are divorced from human experience. That argument does apply to social science theories that reify society and/or culture, but the sense in which the present premises relate to human experience can be illustrated readily. Ask the personnel manager of a large corporation why advertisements of employment opportunities use such terms as "mechanic," "secretary," "electrician," and "accountant." In the case of Axiom 14, visit a large hospital and take note of all tools, machines, other objects or substances made or modified by humans; then ask yourself: how many of those items could I use effectively?

Technological Efficiency and Technological Complexity

Even though the rankings would have to be based on general observations and extensive use of the anthropological and historical literature, there is reason to presume substantial agreement in the following ranking of social units as to per capita use of inanimate energy: U.S., 1990 (greatest), U.S., 1890; Aztecs, 1490; and any Comanche band, 1850 (least). Some social scientist would reject the implied criterion, but in the present context that ranking would order the social units *also* as to level of technological efficiency. Still other general observations would suggest the same order of technological complexity, however defined. There is nothing special about the four social units in question. Others could be ranked along the same lines, and the rankings would suggest a substantial positive correlation among social units and over time between technological efficiency and technological complexity.

More than correlation is presumed. Variation in technological efficiency is a major cause of variation in technological complexity. The argument is simple. A wide variety of technological items is indicative of a complex technology, but a wide variety cannot be produced without extensive modification and combinations of raw materials (wood, stone, metallic substances, etc.); and those material changes would be very limited if they could be realized only through human energy alone. In that connection, recall that technological efficiency is defined in terms of the conservation of time and human energy. Viewed that way, it is difficult to imagine a technology that is complex but inefficient as regards the conservation of time and human energy.

Axiom 15

The foregoing argument is sufficient to justify Axiom 15: *Among countries and for any country over time, technological efficiency is the asymmetrical, positive, bidirectional, and partial cause of technological complexity.* The genesis of the axiom does not mean it is divorced from control notions. *Anything* pertaining to technology has something to do with control, because the creation, use, or maintenance of any technological item is by definition inanimate control. Moreover, while in no country does any set of individuals control the amount of technological complexity (indeed the amount is unknown in any country), the relation asserted by Axiom 15 holds only because of the purposive quality of human behavior, especially in attempted control. Stated otherwise, a complex technology reflects a perennial human concern with efficiency; but should that claim be translated as an "assumption of rationality," the translation would only extend a sterile controversy.

Selective and Brief Comments on Types of Causation. The causal relation asserted in Axiom 15 may prove more symmetrical (reciprocal) than the supporting argument suggests. Granted that inanimate energy use makes possible a great variety of technological items, some of those items are necessary for exploiting new kinds of inanimate energy sources and perhaps increasing inanimate energy use even more. Witness, for example, the key role played by railroads in the exploitation of coal deposits and, subsequently, petroleum deposits.

The eventual termination of the causal relation asserted in Axiom 15 is a possibility, and it cannot be dismissed if only because the relation stems from the purposive quality of human behavior. Specifically, the human concern with environmental problems, depletion of natural resources, and even the increasing diminution of individual autonomy may eventually promote efforts to *simplify* technology—reduce its complexity—*without sacrificing efficiency.* Various human goals cannot be pursued without the use of technological items and perhaps the creation of new items, as the moon landing illustrates; but the indispensability of technological items, even new ones, depends on the goals pursued. Thus, when humans commenced exploring the solar system, technology became more indispensable; but there are numerous "environmental" goals that scarcely require any new technology. So despite the arguments made in support of Axiom 15, the character of the causal relation between technological efficiency and technological complexity could change in the distant future, though perhaps never entirely disappear. Indeed, even if it were assumed that human choices are never determined, it would not follow that there are no limits on the choices; and the relation between technological complexity and technological efficiency may be one of numerous constraints.

Notes

1. Technology has been defined such that the time-energy reduction is *not* true by definition. Hence, the generalization is not a tautology.

2. Defined again, a sustenance activity is the production of what economists would identify as a good, commodity, service, or benefit, one which may or may not be exchanged.

3. Some collaborative production is symbiotic. What anthropologists loosely describe as organized hunting does take place among foragers without anyone attempting to control all of the participants, much less through a persistent sanction threat.

4. It is also compatible with Marx's conception, which realistically recognizes a "social" division of labor (akin to Durkheim's conception) and a "capitalist" division of labor (akin to Smith's conception). But Marx erred in writing as though the two are mutually exclusive; and his reduction of the division of labor to "mental vs. manual" is grotesque, a point commonly overlooked by his interpreters (e.g., Rattansi, 1982).

5. Yet it does not follow that attempts are never made to control any macro or aggregate variable. As a case in point, in countries throughout the world legislators and/or other government officials often take action in the belief that it will reduce or check increases in the country's human mortality rate. To be sure, they are not likely to have any idea as to how much, but their actions are nonetheless attempts to control a macro variable.

6. It would be a mistake to say that the term "occupation" is not empirically applicable in those cases. The empirical applicability of a term has nothing to do with the presence or absence of instances of what the term denotes in a particular context. Rather, the empirical applicability of a term hinges on this question: to what extent can independent observers agree that instances of what the term denotes are absent or present in particular contexts. Needless to say, unless a term is left undefined, its empirical applicability hinges on its definition. So suppose someone offers a definition of a law. The definition may imply nothing whatever about the universality of law, but its empirical applicability would be contingent on the amount of agreement between independent observers as to the presence or absence of law (so defined) in any given social unit.

7. Such considerations were ignored by Watson (1929) in his survey of the division of labor in "preliterate" social units, predominantly tribes or bands.

8. The admission that a formula may or may not appear congruent with the concept is not a tacit acceptance of the idea of rules of correspondence It is one thing to say that a formula *appears* to correspond with the concept's definition, but quite another to say that the formula was deduced from the definition.

9. There are two reasons why the referential terminology should not be translated into measurement terminology. First, that terminology suggests a degree of precision

and correspondence with a concept that theorists may disavow in using a referential terminology. Second, whereas the phrase "a measure" means either a measurement procedure or a particular numerical value, there is no ambiguity in the referential terminology; a referential denotes a formula, and a referent is a numerical value ostensibly computed by application of the formula.

10. Nonetheless, it must be said that the conceptualization and related argument would indicate why the principle applies even in a command or socialist economy.

11. If only because of the character of the socialization of children in the U.S. and medical boards or other regulatory bodies, neither kind of somatic control can be described as decentralized to the maximum degree; but centralization would be much greater if there were only one "socializer of children" and one "regulator of neurosurgeons" in the U.S.

12. Should anyone argue that criminal law is commonly not based on the deterrence doctrine, they should reconsider in light of Morris' global survey (1966:631).

13. Here the theory does what any theory should do—anticipate novel empirical relations. For that matter, in their survey of the "anthropology of death" Palgi and Abramovitch (1984) make no reference to variation in age at death, and it is not a conventional variable in demography.

14. But doubts are admitted as regards the need to exclude deaths caused by or in the form of genocide, executions, and military action. Even though not emphasized in observations on the phenomenon (see, especially, Fein, 1990), genocide is a form of successful control attempts. Yet at the same time it also reflects failures in attempted control or countercontrol by the victim or their associates (e.g., parents), and the impact of genocide on variation in death ages is problematical. Executions may be more indicative of extensive and effective control than of control failures, and they probably contribute to variation in death ages; but their rarity makes that contribution negligible. By contrast, if only because military actions can cause an enormous increase in a mortality rate for (approximately) ages 17–49 and thereby greatly inflate variation in death ages, any test of the theory that bears on Postulate 7 should exclude countries that were engaged in warfare (international or civil) for the time period in question.

15. Festinger (1981:318–319) expressed the argument this way: "I suspect that what ultimately produced specialization of function in human societies (apart from possible male-female differentiations) was not skill differential but the eventual proliferation of so many technologies that one person, in his short life span, could not adequately learn them all, or even a large proportion of them." However, Festinger did not recognize that the relation will not hold unless humans are concerned with the *effectiveness* of control. The only alternative is to assume some kind of selective survival.

16. Note that the definition is implicitly a *control* version of technological complexity, meaning that it is expressed in terms of control notions.

17. The fears and concern are commonly manifested in ghastly reifications of technology, often anthropomorphic reification in which conceptual problems are totally ignored.

6

Recapitulation and Derivation
of Theorems

Both the discursive mode and a formal mode of theory construction may be used when stating a theory. All intrinsic statements can be introduced and defended in an ordinary (natural) language; but at some point each one must be articulated in accordance with some formal mode, and eventually they must be brought together as the theory's formal version, if only to display the theory's logical structure. That strategy was followed throughout Chapters 3–5, and the foremost advantage for any theory is the possible promotion of the audience's understanding. Despite the advantage, a theory's logical structure is not fully clarified until the premises are brought together, as here in this chapter. Most important, that recapitulation facilitates the systematic derivation of theorems.

The recapitulation also points to the most conspicuous difference between a theory's discursive version and its formal version. Whereas a discursive version of the typical sociological theory runs for hundreds of pages, the formal version may take up less than ten pages. So adoption of a formal mode would enable sociologists to publish more theories and reports of tests without an increase in publication costs for the field. But space conservation is not the primary consideration. Given any communication that runs for hundreds of pages, its logical structure is likely to be so obscure that theorems cannot be deduced systematically by the rules of any conventional logic.

The Premises

The formal version of the theory comprises 34 premises: 21 axioms, 7 postulates, and 6 transformational statements. However, only 16 axioms are shown in Figure 6–1, which was designed to expedite explication of the theorems, the derivational procedure in particular. That diagram differs from Figure 3–1 (the initial diagram, Chapter 3, p. 70) in that the most inclusive independent variable—the extent and efficacy of control attempts (all basic types combined)—has been deleted. Hence, Axiom 1 in Figure 3–1 is replaced in Figure 6–1 by Axioms 1a, 1b, and 1c, each of which pertains to the relation between perceived control capacity and the extent-efficacy of a particular basic type of control. Then Axiom 4 in Figure 3–1 is replaced by Axioms 4a, 4b, and 4c, each of which pertains to the relation between amount of scientific activity and the extent-efficacy of one of the basic types of control. Note, however, that the theorems are the same in both diagrams, Figures 3–1 and 6–1.

The deletion of the inclusive variable (the extent-efficacy of *all* types of control attempts combined) eliminates what are Axiom 1, 4, 5, 7, and 9 in Figure 3–1. Although not shown in Figure 6–1, those five axioms appear in the subsequent list of axioms, so as to be consistent with Chapters 3–5. Bear in mind, though, that the inclusive control variable does not actually enter into the derivation of theorems; consequently, as far as those derivations are concerned, there are only 16 axioms: 1a, 1b, 1c, 2, 3, 4a, 4b, 4c, 6, 8, 10, 11, 12, 13, 14, and 15.

Axioms

Like all other premises (postulates and transformational statements), the axioms are numbered as in Chapters 3–5. Numbered designations facilitate identification of the premises that entered into the derivation of each theorem.

Axiom 1: Among countries and for any country over time, the extent and efficacy of control attempts are the reciprocal, positive, bidirectional, and paramount determinants of perceived control capacity; and perceived control capacity is the reciprocal, positive, bidirectional, and partial determinant of the extent and efficacy of control attempts.

Axiom 1a: Among countries and for any country over time, the extent and efficacy of inanimate control attempts are the symmetrical, positive, bidirectional, and partial determinants of perceived control capacity.

Axiom 1b: Among countries and for any country over time, the extent and efficacy of attempts to control human behavior are the symmetrical, positive, bidirectional, and partial determinants of perceived control capacity.

Axiom 1c: Among countries and for any country over time, the extent and efficacy of biotic control attempts are the symmetrical, positive, bidirectional, and partial determinants of perceived control capacity.

Axiom 2: Among countries and for any country over time, perceived control capacity is the asymmetrical, negative, bidirectional, and partial determinant of the amount of supernaturalism.

Axiom 3: Among countries and for any country over time, the amount of supernaturalism is the symmetrical, negative, bidirectional, and partial determinant of the amount of scientific activity.

175

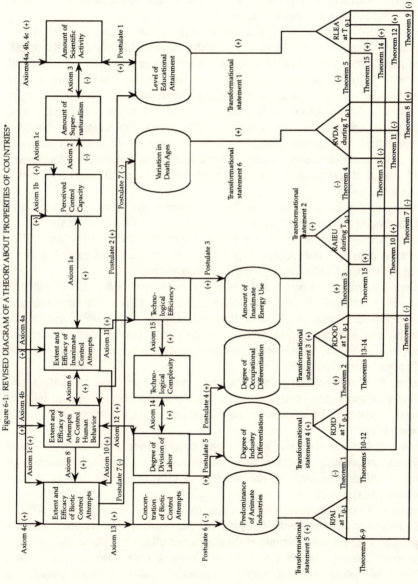

Figure 6-1: REVISED DIAGRAM OF A THEORY ABOUT PROPERTIES OF COUNTRIES*

*Axioms 1, 4, 5, 7, and 9 in Figure 3-1 are not repeated in this diagram.

Axiom 4: Among countries and for any country over time, the extent and efficacy of control are the reciprocal, positive, bidirectional, and partial determinants of the amount of scientific activity; and the amount of scientific activity is the reciprocal, positive, *unidirectional*, and partial determinant of the extent and efficacy of control attempts.

Axiom 4a: Among countries and for any country over time, the extent and efficacy of inanimate control attempts are the reciprocal, positive, bidirectional, and partial determinants of the amount of scientific activity; and the amount of scientific activity is the reciprocal, positive, *unidirectional*, and partial determinant of the extent and efficacy of inanimate control attempts.

Axiom 4b: Among countries and for any country over time, the extent and efficacy of attempts to control human behavior are the reciprocal, positive, bidirectional, and partial determinants of the amount of scientific activity; and the amount of scientific activity is the reciprocal, positive, *unidirectional*, and partial determinant of the extent and efficacy of attempts to control human behavior.

Axiom 4c: Among countries and for any country over time, the extent and efficacy of biotic control attempts are the reciprocal, positive, bidirectional, and partial determinants of the amount of scientific activity; and the amount of scientific activity is the reciprocal, positive, *unidirectional*, and partial determinant of the extent and efficacy of biotic control attempts.

Axiom 5: Among countries and for any country over time, the extent and efficacy of control attempts are the reciprocal, positive, bidirectional, and paramount determinants of the extent and efficacy of inanimate control attempts; and the extent and efficacy of inanimate control attempts are the reciprocal, positive, bidirectional, and partial determinants of the extent and efficacy of control attempts.

Axiom 6: Among countries and for any country over time, the extent and efficacy of inanimate control attempts are the symmetrical, positive, bidirectional, and partial determinants of the extent and efficacy of attempts to control human behavior.

Axiom 7: Among countries and for any country over time, the extent and efficacy of control attempts are the symmetrical, positive, bidirectional and partial determinants of the extent and efficacy of attempts to control human behavior.

Axiom 8: Among countries and for a country over time, the extent and efficacy of attempts to control human behavior are the asymmetrical, positive, bidirectional, and partial determinants of the extent and efficacy of biotic control.

Axiom 9: Among countries and for any country over time, the extent and efficacy of control attempts are the asymmetrical, positive, bidirectional, and paramount determinants of the extent and efficacy of biotic control attempts.

Axiom 10: Among countries and for any country over time, the extent and efficacy of inanimate control are the asymmetrical, positive, bidirectional, and partial determinants of the extent and efficacy of biotic control attempts.

Axiom 11: Among countries and for any country over time, the extent and efficacy of inanimate control attempts are the asymmetrical, positive, bidirectional, and paramount determinants of technological efficiency.

Axiom 12: Among countries and for any country over time, the extent and efficacy of attempts to control human behavior are the symmetrical, positive, bidirectional, and partial determinants of the degree of division of labor.

Axiom 13: Among countries and for any country over time, the extent and efficacy of biotic control are the asymmetrical, positive, bidirectional, and paramount determinants of the concentration of biotic control attempts.

Axiom 14: Among countries and for any country over time, technological complexity is the symmetrical, positive, bidirectional, and partial determinant of the degree of division of labor.

Axiom 15: Among countries and for any country over time, technological efficiency is the asymmetrical, positive, bidirectional, and partial determinant of technological complexity.

Postulates

Granted the need for a formal mode that applies to qualitative properties of units, the present mode is appropriate only when the theorist asserts relations between *quantitative* properties but is not prepared to express those assertions as equations.[1] The immediate implication is that the derivation of theorems (*infra*) is not based on anything like a logic of classes or algebra. Specifically, in no postulate does the concept pertain to a subclass of the phenomenon denoted by the construct, and there are no mathematical derivations.

Postulate 1: Among countries and for any country over time, the amount of scientific activity is the symmetrical, positive, bidirectional, and partial determinant of level of education attainment.

Postulate 2: Among countries and for any country over time, the extent and efficacy of attempts to control human behavior are the symmetrical, positive, bidirectional, and partial determinants of level of educational attainment.

Postulate 3: Among countries and for any country over time, technological efficiency is the asymmetrical, positive, bidirectional, and paramount determinant of the amount of inanimate energy use.

Postulate 4: Among countries and for any country over time, the degree of the division of labor is the asymmetrical, positive, bidirectional, and exclusive determinant of the degree of occupational differentiation.

Postulate 5: Among countries and for any county over time, the degree of division of labor is the asymmetrical, positive, bidirectional, and exclusive cause of the degree of industry differentiation.

Postulate 6: Among countries and for any country over time, the concentration of biotic control attempts is the asymmetrical, negative, bidirectional, and paramount determinant of the predominance of animate industries.

Postulate 7: Among countries and for any country over time, the extent and efficacy of biotic control are the asymmetrical, negative, bidirectional, and paramount determinants of variation in death ages.

Transformational Statements

Traditionally, in the social and behavioral sciences, sociology especially, theorists do not set forth a procedure for testing a theory, including methods, measures, and stipulations as to kinds of data. Again, a better way to insure idiosyncratic tests, if any at all, would be difficult to imagine.[2] Because it would be extremely cumbersome to mix a test procedure and intrinsic statements, the procedure's essential elements are set forth in the theory's extrinsic part; and transformational statements link the two parts. However, transformational statements are not just necessary for defensible tests; they are components of the theory no less than are the axioms, postulates, and theorems.

Transformational Statement 1: Among countries and for any country over time, the greater the level of educational attainment at any point in time, the greater the RLEA at T_{0-1}.

Transformational Statement 2: Among countries and for any country over time, the greater the amount of inanimate energy use, the greater RAIEU during T_{0-1}.

Transformational Statement 3: Among countries and for any country over time, the greater the degree of occupational differentiation, the greater RDOD at T_{0-1}.

Transformational Statement 4: Among countries and for any country over time, the greater the degree of industry differentiation, the greater RDID at T_{0-1}.

Transformational Statement 5: Among countries and for any country over time, the greater the predominance of animate industries, the greater the RPAI at T_{0-1}.

Transformational Statement 6: Among countries and for any country over time, the greater the amount of variation in death ages within a country, the greater the RVDA during T_{0-1}.

Derivation of Theorems

When the property terms (variables) in the premises are quantitative and the relational terms are causal or a mixture of causal and covariational, deductions are indefensible unless made in accordance with several complex rules, some of which are general in that they apply to all theories and others are special in that their relevance depends on the particular premises (their nature and/or assumptions about them) in question. For reasons indicated in the Appendix (pp. 312–328) the deduction of empirical generalizations, whether designated as theorems or not, is a study in issues and problems. Fortunately, the issues and problems need not be introduced to explicate the deduction of the 15 theorems shown in Figure 6–1 (earlier in Figure 3–1), nor is it necessary to set forth all of the rules, general or special. At this point it will suffice to define the key term, "causal circuit," and state four deductions rules, three general and one special (for a much more elaborate explication, see the Appendix, pp. 317–325).

The Notion of a Causal Circuit

The initial and incomplete definition of a causal circuit is: a link of two causal paths. Obviously, that definition creates the need to clarify the meaning of a causal path.

A causal path is a series of two or more variables linked by causal assertions (axioms, postulates, and/or propositions) such that (1) only one of the variables, the terminal variable, is the asserted effect or an asserted effect—direct or indirect, symmetrical or asymmetrical, reciprocal or nonreciprocal—of all of the other variables and (2) only one of the variables is the asserted cause or an asserted cause—direct or indirect, symmetrical or asymmetrical, reciprocal or nonreciprocal—of all of the other variables. Henceforth, the last type of variable is referred to as the *distal* variable.

Given the foregoing, the final and complete definition of a causal circuit is: two causal paths having the same distal variable or having distal variables that are asserted to be connected through symmetrical or reciprocal causation, but excluding distal variables (if any) that are not necessary for the two paths to be so connected. So defined, all of the causal circuits in Figure 6–1 end with concepts, and the deduction of relation between two concepts (an implied proposition) can be thought of as "closing" what would otherwise be an incomplete circuit. However, each causal path is to be construed as extending to the referentials that are connected with the concepts in the two transformational statements. That extension makes it possible to deduce statements (theorems) that connect referentials. In that sense a causal circuit is actually "closed" with a theorem, and the circuit is incomplete until so closed.

Deduction Procedure

Each of the 15 theorems is subsequently deduced from one or more incomplete causal circuits as that notion applies to all of the premises—axioms, postulates, and transformational statements. It so happens that any two of the six referentials are connected through at least one causal circuit, and the relevant causal circuits are shown for each theorem (i.e., each pair of referentials) in Table 6–1. That all but one theorem (the second) is deducible from more than one causal circuit should not be confusing; and there is a related principle: other things being equal, the greater the number of causal circuits from which a theorem was deduced, the greater the magnitude of the association between the two sets of referents in tests of that theorem.

Both the identification of the causal circuits and the deduction of the theorems can be understood by examining Figure 6–1, but the deductions themselves are based on three general rules and a special rule.

General Rule 1: Preliminary to the deduction of theorems from premises (causal and/or covariational statements), each premise that asserts positive causation or a positive association (the relational term is "greater...greater" or "varies directly with") is to be characterized by a plus (+) sign, and each causal premise that asserts negative causation or a negative association (the relational term is "greater...less" or "varies inversely with") is to be characterized by a negative (–) sign.

General Rule 2: The sign and the corresponding covariational relational term (greater...greater, greater...less, varies directly with, or varies inversely with) of a theorem is negative if and only if there is an odd number of negative premises (causal and/or covariational) in the circuit closed by the theorem.

General Rule 3: A relation between two referentials cannot be deduced unless all of the variables, concepts or constructs, that are an asserted cause—direct or indirect—of the corresponding concepts (those linked with the two referentials in question) appear in at least one of the causal circuits connecting the referentials.

Special Rule: No construct is considered as being in a causal circuit if more than two constructs removed from a concept in at least one causal path in that causal circuit.

A detailed explication of all rules is provided in the Appendix, pp. 312–328.[3] Here a few brief comments will suffice. General Rule 2 is designed to preclude deductions when one or both of the variables in what would otherwise be an implied proposition or a theorem is asserted (in the theory) to be partially determined by an isolated cause, meaning a variable that does not enter into any causal circuit that is closed by the implied proposition or theorem. When there is such an isolated cause (or causes), the wording of the implied proposition or the theorem must stipulate that the relation holds only when the isolated cause is somehow controlled or taken into account.

The Special Rule could not be justified if it were possible to derive some of the theorems *only* from causal circuits in which at least one construct is more than twice removed from a concept. If such a causal circuit is not ignored, then the validity of at least three of the constituent axioms cannot be distinguished in light of test findings (i.e., if test findings indicate that some of the axioms are false, there would be no basis to identify the most likely).

Table 6-1: CAUSAL CIRCUITS CONNECTING REFERENTIALS IN FIGURE 3-1 AND FIGURE 6-1.

Variables and Premises

Referentials, ⏢ ; Concepts, (*); Constructs, [**]; Transformational Statements, *T*; Postulates, *P*; Axioms, *A*

THEOREMS	CIRCUITS	Variables and Premises																
1	1A	RPAI	T5	PAI	P6	CBCA	A13	EEBCA			A8			EEACHB	A12	DDL	P5	DID	T4	RDID
	1B	RPAI	T5	PAI	P6	CBCA	A13	EEBCA	A4c	ASA	A4b	EEACHB	A12	DDL	P5	DID	T4	RDID
	1C	RPAI	T5	PAI	P6	CBCA	A13	EEBCA	A1c	PCC	A1b	EEACHB	A12	DDL	P5	DID	T4	RDID
	1D	RPAI	T5	PAI	P6	CBCA	A13	EEBCA	A10	EEICA	A6	EEACHB	A12	DDL	P5	DID	T4	RDID
2	2A	RDID	T4	DID	P5	DDL	P4	DOD	T3	RDOD								
3	3A	RDOD	T3	DOD	P4	DDL		A14		TC		A15		TE	P3	AIEU	T2	RAIEU
	3B	RDOD	T3	DOD	P4	DDL	A12	EEACHB		A6		EEICA	A11	TE	P3	AIEU	T2	RAIEU
	3C	RDOD	T3	DOD	P4	DDL	A12	EEACHB	A4b	ASA	A4a	EEICA	A11	TE	P3	AIEU	T2	RAIEU
	3D	RDOD	T3	DOD	P4	DDL	A12	EEACHB	A1b	PCC	A1a	EEICA	A11	TE	P3	AIEU	T2	RAIEU
4	4A	RAIEU	T2	AIEU	P3	TE	A11	EEICA			A10			EEBCA	P7	VDA	T6	RVDA
	4B	RAIEU	T2	AIEU	P3	TE	A11	EEICA		A6		EEACHB	A8	EEBCA	P7	VDA	T6	RVDA
	4C	RAIEU	T2	AIEU	P3	TE	A11	EEICA	A1a	PCC		A1c		EEBCA	P7	VDA	T6	RVDA
	4D	RAIEU	T2	AIEU	P3	TE	A11	EEICA	A4a	ASA		A4c		EEBCA	P7	VDA	T6	RVDA
	4E	RAIEU	T2	AIEU	P3	TE	A11	EEICA	A4a	ASA	A4b	EEACHB	A8	EEBCA	P7	VDA	T6	RVDA

Table 6-1 (*continued*)

Variables and Premises

Referentials, ⬠ ; Concepts, (*) ; Constructs, ▭ ; **▮** ; Transformational Statements, *T*; Postulates, *P*; Axioms, *A*

CIRCUITS / THEOREMS

Circuit	Chain (left → right)
4F	RAIEU — T2 — AIEU — P3 — TE — A11 — EEICA — A1a — PCC — A1b — EEACHB — A8 — EEBCA — P7 — VDA — T6 — RVDA
5	
5A	RVDA — T6 — VDA — P7 — EEBCA — A4c — ASA — P1 — LEA — T1 — RLEA
5B	RVDA — T6 — VDA — P7 — EEBCA — A10 — EEICA — A4a — ASA — P1 — LEA — T1 — RLEA
5C	RVDA — T6 — VDA — P7 — EEBCA — A8 — A1c — EEICA — A4b — ASA — P1 — LEA — T1 — RLEA
5D	RVDA — T6 — VDA — P7 — EEBCA — A1c — EEACHB — A3 — AS — A2 — PCC — ASA — P1 — LEA — T1 — RLEA
5E	RVDA — T6 — VDA — P7 — EEBCA — A1a — EEICA — A3 — AS — A2 — PCC — ASA — P1 — LEA — T1 — RLEA
5F	RVDA — T6 — VDA — P7 — EEBCA — A1b — EEACHB — A3 — AS — A2 — PCC — ASA — P1 — LEA — T1 — RLEA
6	
6A	RPAI — T5 — PAI — P6 — CBCA — A13 — EEBCA — A8 — EEACHB — A12 — DDL — P4 — DOD — T3 — RDOD
6B	RPAI — T5 — PAI — P6 — CBCA — A13 — EEBCA — A4c — ASA — A4b — EEACHB — A12 — DDL — P4 — DOD — T3 — RDOD
6C	RPAI — T5 — PAI — P6 — CBCA — A13 — EEBCA — A1c — PCC — A1b — EEACHB — A12 — DDL — P4 — DOD — T3 — RDOD
6D	RPAI — T5 — PAI — P6 — CBCA — A13 — EEBCA — A10 — EEICA — A6 — EEACHB — A12 — DDL — P4 — DOD — T3 — RDOD
7	
7A	RPAI — T5 — PAI — P6 — CBCA — A13 — EEBCA — A10 — EEICA — A11 — TE — P3 — AIEU — T2 — RAIEU
7B	RPAI — T5 — PAI — P6 — CBCA — A13 — EEBCA — A4c — ASA — A4a — EEICA — A11 — TE — P3 — AIEU — T2 — RAIEU
7C	RPAI — T5 — PAI — P6 — CBCA — A13 — EEBCA — A1c — PCC — A1a — EEICA — A11 — TE — P3 — AIEU — T2 — RAIEU

Table 6-1 (*continued*)

Variables and Premises

Referentials, ⬡ ; Concepts, ⬭ * ; Constructs, ▭ ** ; Transformational Statements, *T*; Postulates, *P*; Axioms, *A*

THEOREMS	Chain
7D	RPAI — T5 — PAI — P6 — CBCA — A13 — EEBCA — A8 — EEACHB — A6 — EEICA — A11 — TE — P3 — AIEU — T2 — RAIEU
8 / 8A	RPAI — T5 — PAI — P6 — CBCA — A13 — EEBCA — P7 — VDA — T6 — RVDA
9 / 9A	RPAI — T5 — PAI — P6 — CBCA — A13 — EEBCA — A8 — EEACHB — P2 — LEA — T1 — RLEA
9B	RPAI — T5 — PAI — P6 — CBCA — A13 — EEBCA — A4c — ASA — P1 — LEA — T1 — RLEA
9C	RPAI — T5 — PAI — P6 — CBCA — A13 — EEBCA — A1c — PCC — A2 — AS — A3 — ASA — P1 — LEA — T1 — RLEA
10 / 10A	RDID — T4 — DID — P5 — DDL — A14 — TC — A15 — TE — P3 — AIEU — T2 — RAIEU
10B	RDID — T4 — DID — P5 — DDL — A12 — EEACHB — A6 — EEICA — A11 — TE — P3 — AIEU — T2 — RAIEU
10C	RDID — T4 — DID — P5 — DDL — A12 — EEACHB — A4b — ASA — A4a — EEICA — A11 — TE — P3 — AIEU — T2 — RAIEU
10D	RDID — T4 — DID — P5 — DDL — A12 — EEACHB — A1b — PCC — A1a — EEICA — A11 — TE — P3 — AIEU — T2 — RAIEU
11 / 11A	RDID — T4 — DID — P5 — DDL — A12 — EEACHB — A8 — EEBCA — P7 — VDA — T6 — RVDA
11B	RDID — T4 — DID — P5 — DDL — A12 — EEACHB — A4b — ASA — A4c — EEBCA — P7 — VDA — T6 — RVDA
11C	RDID — T4 — DID — P5 — DDL — A12 — EEACHB — A1b — PCC — A1c — EEBCA — P7 — VDA — T6 — RVDA
11D	RDID — T4 — DID — P5 — DDL — A12 — EEACHB — A6 — EEICA — A10 — EEBCA — P7 — VDA — T6 — RVDA
11E	RDID — T4 — DID — P5 — DDL — A12 — EEACHB — A1a — EEICA — A10 — EEBCA — P7 — VDA — T6 — RVDA

184

Table 6-1 (*continued*)

Variables and Premises

Referentials, ⬱ ; Concepts, ⬭ * ; Constructs, ▭ ** ; Transformational Statements, *T*; Postulates, *P*; Axioms, *A*

THEOREMS — CHIRODTS

11F: RDID —T4— DID —P5— A12 —EEACHB— A4b —ASA— EEICA —A10— EEBCA —P7— VDA —T6— RVDA

12
12A: RDID —T4— DID —P5— A12 —EEACHB— P2 —LEA— T1 — RLEA
12B: RDID —T4— DID —P5— A12 —EEACHB— A4b —ASA— P1 —LEA— T1 — RLEA
12C: RDID —T4— DID —P5— A12 —EEACHB— A6 —EEICA— A4a —ASA— P1 —LEA— T1 — RLEA
12D: RDID —T4— DID —P5— A12 —EEACHB— A1b —PCC— A2 —AS— A3 —ASA— P1 —LEA— T1 — RLEA
12E: RDID —T4— DID —P5— A12 —EEACHB— A6 —EEICA— A1a —PCC— A2 —AS— A3 —ASA— P1 —LEA— T1 — RLEA

13
13A: RDOD —T3— DOD —P4— A12 —EEACHB— A8 —EEBCA— P7 —VDA— T6 — RVDA
13B: RDOD —T3— DOD —P4— A12 —EEACHB— A6 —EEICA— A10 —EEBCA— P7 —VDA— T6 — RVDA
13C: RDOD —T3— DOD —P4— A12 —EEACHB— A1b —PCC— A1c —EEBCA— P7 —VDA— T6 — RVDA
13D: RDOD —T3— DOD —P4— A12 —EEACHB— A1b —PCC— A1a —EEICA— A10 —EEBCA— P7 —VDA— T6 — RVDA
13E: RDOD —T3— DOD —P4— A12 —EEACHB— A4b —ASA— A4a —EEICA— A10 —EEBCA— P7 —VDA— T6 — RVDA

14
14A: RDOD —T3— DOD —P4— A12 —EEACHB— P2 —LEA— T1 — RLEA
14B: RDOD —T3— DOD —P4— A12 —EEACHB— A4b —ASA— P1 —LEA— T1 — RLEA
14C: RDOD —T3— DOD —P4— A12 —EEACHB— A6 —EEICA— A4a —ASA— P1 —LEA— T1 — RLEA

Table 6-1 (*continued*)

T H E O R E M S

Variables and Premises

Referentials, ◻ ; Concepts, ◯* ; Constructs, ▢** ; : Transformational Statements, *T*; Postulates, *P*; Axioms, *A*

14D: RDOD — T3 — DOD — P4 — DDL — A12 — EEACHB — A1b — PCC — A2 — AS — A3 — ASA — P1 — LEA — T1 — RLEA

14E: RDOD — T3 — DOD — P4 — DDL — A12 — EEACHB — A6 — EEICA — A1a — PCC — A2 — AS — A3 — ASA — P1 — LEA — T1 — RLEA

15

15A: RAIEU — T2 — AIEU — P3 — TE — A11 — EEICA — A4a — ASA — P1 — LEA — T1 — RLEA

15B: RAIEU — T2 — AIEU — P3 — TE — A11 — EEICA — A6 — EEACHB — A4b — ASA — P1 — LEA — T1 — RLEA

15C: RAIEU — T2 — AIEU — P3 — TE — A11 — EEICA — A1a — PCC — A2 — AS — A3 — ASA — P1 — LEA — T1 — RLEA

*Concepts: AIEU=amount of inanimate energy use; DID=degree of industry differentiation; DOD=degree of occupational differentiation; LEA=level of educational attainment; PAI=predominance of animate industries; VDA=variation in death ages.

**Constructs: ASA=amount of scientific activity; AS=amount of supernaturalism; CBCA=concentration of biotic control attempts; DDL=degree of division of labor; EEACHB=extent and efficacy of attempts to control human behavior; EEBCA=extent and efficacy of biotic control attempts; EEICA=extent and efficacy of inanimate control attempts; PCC=perceived control capacity; TC=technological complexity; TE=technological efficiency.

An even more stringent special rule would require that each construct be linked to one or more concepts, but that requirement would eliminate Axioms 1, 2, 3, 14, and 15 from any causal circuit.

In accordance with the four rules as they apply to the theory's premises and the casual circuits shown in Table 6–1, 15 theorems have been deduced (*infra*). They are identified by numbers so as to be consistent with Figure 3–1 (Chapter 3, p. 70) and Figure 6–1.

Theorem 1: Among countries and for any country over time, the greater RPAI at T_{0-1}, the less RDID at T_{0-1}.

Theorem 2: Among countries or for any country over time, the greater RDID at T_{0-1}, the greater RDOD at T_{0-1}.

Theorem 3: Among countries and for any country over time, the greater RDOD at T_{0-1}, the greater RAIEU during T_{0-1}.

Theorem 4: Among countries and for any country over time, the greater RAIEU during T_{0-1}, the less RVDA during T_{0-1}.

Theorem 5: Among countries and for any country over time, the greater RVDA during T_{0-1}, the less RLEA at T_{0-1}.

Theorem 6: Among countries and for any country over time, the greater RPAI at T_{0-1}, the less RDOD at T_{0-1}.

Theorem 7: Among countries and for any country over time, the greater RPAI at T_{0-1}, the less RAIEU during T_{0-1}.

Theorem 8: Among countries and for any country over time, the greater RPAI at T_{0-1}, the greater RVDA during T_{0-1}.

Theorem 9: Among countries and for any country over time, the greater RPAI at T_{0-1}, the less RLEA at T_{0-1}.

Theorem 10: Among countries and for any country over time, the greater RDID at T_{0-1}, the greater RAIEU during T_{0-1}.

Theorem 11: Among countries and for any country over time, the greater RDID at T_{0-1}, the less RVDA during T_{0-1}.

Theorem 12: Among countries and for any country over time, the greater RDID at T_{0-1}, the greater RLEA at T_{0-1}.

Theorem 13: Among countries and for any country over time, the greater RDOD at T_{0-1}, the less RVDA during T_{0-1}.

Theorem 14: Among countries and for any country over time, the greater RDOD at T_{0-1}, the greater RLEA at T_{0-1}.

Theorem 15: Among countries and for any country over time, the greater RAIEU during T_{0-1}, the greater RLEA at T_{0-1}.

Although temporal quantifiers become crucial only when contemplating tests of the theory, note that each pair in the 15 theorems signifies a synchronic association. Because the appropriate time lags in the premises (i.e., the interval between cause and effect) are not known and cannot be deduced, one temporal quantifier signifies either any calendar year or any time point in that year; and the other temporal quantifier (same theorem) signifies either the same year or any point in that year. Lest the stipulation of temporal quantifiers appear pedantic, observe that their exclusion from an empirical generalization makes the generalization ambiguous or vacuously true, as when it is asserted that a change in X is followed by a change in Y with no indication as to when the change in Y will take place. For all practical purposes, whatever X and Y may be, a change in X is certain to be followed by a change in Y *sooner or later*. Observe also that any generalization is ambiguous or vacuously true unless some spatial limit on the relation is stipulated; but that stipulation is implied by the unit phrase in the generalization, which underscores the need for the consistent inclusion of explicit unit phrases in a theory.

Notes

1. Eventually, the theorist may restate some or all of the constituent synthetic statements (the intrinsic part of the theory), the theorems particularly, as equations; but that modification or extension of the theory is likely to require extensive tests and secondary use of the data to identify the constants that enter into the equations.

2. Imagine someone making this declaration in connection with any particular theory: the outcome of the tests will not be contingent in any way or extent on the method, measures, or kinds of data. Yet one generation of sociologists after another has balked at demanding that the theorist stipulate a test procedure as part of his/her theory.

3. Some of the rules and their explications are stated differently in recognition of the need to make the formal mode of theory construction more general than is illustrated by this particular theory.

PART THREE

The Theory's Extrinsic Part and One Series of Tests

A field's conventions could be such that a theory is systematically testable even though it comprises no definitions; but that condition is largely alien to the social and behavioral sciences, perhaps sociology more than the others. However, granted that definitions of at least some of a sociological theory's constituent terms are essential for defensible tests, it is no less essential that the definitions be clearly separated from the intrinsic statements (the empirical generalizations). To that end the formal mode calls for a theorist to distinguish and label two major parts of his/her theory, the intrinsic and the extrinsic, with the latter part comprising (1) definitions; (2) formulas in the case of a theory that pertains to quantitative variables; and (3) instructions as to requisite kinds of data, including how the prescribed data are to be gathered or otherwise obtained.

Chapter 7 is the extrinsic part of the control theory, the intrinsic part having been set forth in Chapters 3–6. The extrinsic part calls for the use of published data in testing the theory. That stipulation would not be feasible for some theories in the social and behavioral sciences; but it is imperative for the control theory because it pertains to countries, in which case the resources required to gather the requisite data through surveys are prohibitive. Yet reliance on published data will not severely limit the tests, such that there can be no tests in the distant future. In principle at least, the theory can be tested indefinitely, because the stipulated requisite kinds of data are likely to continue to be published.

Although Chapter 8 reports a series of tests (one of each of the 15 theorems), it scarcely provides a sufficient basis for a confident assessment of the theory's predictive accuracy. Additionally, though, the chapter illustrates a particular test procedure, one designed to complement the formal mode of theory construction. The argument is not just that any formal mode is incomplete unless coupled with a test procedure. Whatever the theory and its mode of construction, defensible tests of it are most improbable unless conducted in accordance with a procedure stipulated by the theorist or one signified by the use of a mode of theory construction that is coupled with a particular a test procedure.

The commentary on test procedure is contrary to a pernicious belief in sociology—that a theorist need not and perhaps should not stipulate or signify a test procedure. The belief is pernicious in that it virtually insures idiosyncratic tests (if any at all) and related sterile debates as to the correct test procedure. The point is best appreciated (and it warrants repeating time and again) by trying to imagine someone seriously defending this declaration: the outcome of a test will not depend on the procedure employed, including the kinds of data. Of course, the point is irrelevant if one is determined to accept or reject theories on the basis of preconceptions or presuppositions (including ideological predilections) rather than predictive accuracy in tests and other dimensions of predictive power. But a sociologist who accepts the belief (i.e., that a theorist should not stipulate or signify a test procedure) and yet stresses the need for tests of theories must subscribe to an assumption—that researchers, though working independently, will agree as to the appropriate procedure for testing the theory in question. That assumption is quite contrary to sociology's history, one replete with failures by theorists to stipulate or signify a test procedure; and the assumption insures that personal opinion will remain sacrosanct in assessments of sociological theories. But insuring the supremacy of personal opinion is consistent with the trend in sociology over the past quarter of a century, a period in which sociologists became increasingly disinclined to test theories. Instead, more and more they appear determined to interpret theories, restate them, or debate them, which is to say anything other than test theories and simply report the outcomes.

7

The Theory's Extrinsic Part

In accordance with the mode of construction in the Appendix, the theory is divided into two major parts. The first one, the intrinsic part, comprises the empirical generalizations—all of the axioms, postulates, transformational statements, and theorems in Chapters 3–6. The second part, the extrinsic, comprises definitions of the key terms in the empirical generalizations, the referential formulas, stipulations of requisite kinds of data, and some procedural matters pertaining to tests of the theory. The "extrinsic" label should not be interpreted as meaning unessential. It is conceivable that in some scientific fields the conventions are such that definitions of terms, formulas, data instructions, and procedural matters need not be stipulated to realize systematic tests of the theory. Be that as it may, the condition is so alien to the social or behavioral sciences that a theory without an extrinsic part is grossly incomplete, which is to say that in any of those fields the extrinsic part is essential for systematic tests of the theory.

Throughout sociology's history, only rarely have sociological theories included anything like an extrinsic part. Nonetheless, if the test procedure is left to the discretion of those who conduct the tests, the outcome is likely to be idiosyncratic, meaning contingent on the investigators rather than the populations considered in the tests. Stated another way, when the tests pertain to the same populations (particular sets of individuals, cities, organizations, etc.) but were conducted by different investigators, divergent outcomes are virtually inevitable unless the investigators employed similar procedures. Indeed, an astonishing belief in sociology is that investigators will somehow agree as to the appropriate procedure when testing a theory, even though the procedure is not stipulated as a part of the theory or in the mode used to state the theory.

The stipulation of a test procedure is surely different from particular tests of a theory, because each test always pertains to particular populations at particular times (e.g., a sample of Canadian residents at some time in 1991, all Japanese metropolitan areas at the end of 1990). By contrast, the articulation of a test procedure need make no reference whatever to a particular population.

Similarly, the other principal component of the extrinsic part—definitions of key terms—has nothing to do with particular events or things.

Virtually everything in a sociological theory's extrinsic part is likely to entail a problem or give rise to an issue; but rhetoric is alien to that part, and the constituent commentaries should be made solely with a view to clarification. If only because of the ambiguities inherent in any language and the difficulty of anticipating the circumstances in which the theory may be tested, a concern with clarification should be manifested throughout the extrinsic part. Especially over recent decades, the inevitability of ambiguity has been emphasized in the social sciences and humanities by avowed antipositivists; but a curious argument is suggested: given the inevitably of ambiguity, concern with clarity or empirical applicability is pointless.

If all of the property terms pertain to qualitative characteristics of units, the theory's extrinsic part focuses on terminology and data instructions; but if the property terms pertain to quantitative characteristics, the extrinsic part must extend to referential formulas and data instructions. In either case, no effort need be made to clarify a construct, beyond possibly noting at least one reason why its definition is neither complete nor clear, or why it has been left undefined. As for general issues and problems, they are treated in the Appendix. However, once a mode is in the literature, in using it to state a particular theory the theorist need not confront general issues and problems.

Definitions of Unit Terms and Phrases, Constructs, and Concepts

There are five sets of key terms in the theory's intrinsic part: a particular unit term, eleven constructs, six concepts, six referentials, and various combinations of four kinds of relational terms. The relational terms are not defined here because they are treated in the mode used to state the theory (see Appendix, pp. 292–295).

The Unit Term and Phrase

A country is a politically sovereign, autonomous, and unified territorial unit—though not necessarily continuous or contiguous—in that a particular set of inhabitants and only that set make decisions as to (1) military actions by the inhabitants and (2) coercive control attempts concerning who and what may cross the unit's boundary. If there are divisions of a territorial unit (as in the case of, e.g., Latin America) and such decisions are made by different sets of inhabitants, that territorial unit is not a country.

Although the requisite data for tests of the theory are to be obtained from published sources (e.g., a *Demographic Yearbook*), the tables in such sources are not to be the basis for identifying countries, for those tables commonly list—in addition to countries—colonies, possessions, or mandated territories. If any criterion other than the definition (*supra*) is used, it must be the specific identification of territorial units as countries in the publications of international organizations (e.g., the Organization of American States) or in a series of publications commonly recognized as pertaining to political features of or events in territorial entities (e.g., *The Statesman's Yearbook*). No territorial unit is to be identified as a country if any such publication explicitly contradicts that identification.

The unit phrase "among countries" denotes two or more countries. Similarly, the unit phrase "for any country over time" refers to a particular country at two or more time points or periods.

Constructs

Each construct pertains to a quantitative property of a country. Some repetition of definitions is unavoidable because Chapters 3–5 were stated in accordance with both the formal mode in the Appendix *and* the discursive mode (recall that the latter mode mixes empirical generalizations and definitions). Recognize, however, that had the theory been stated solely in accordance with the formal mode, Chapters 3, 4, and 5 would have been excluded entirely; and there would be no need for repetition of definitions.

The construct "amount of scientific activity" refers to the total human energy and time invested by members of some designated population in any kind of scientific activity over some designated period, relative to the opportunities or possibilities for such investment.[1] Even if auxiliary definitions could clarify the meaning of the term "scientific activity" and even if the amount could be computed for any given country, there is no defensible basis for stipulating what is the appropriate denominator of that amount (i.e., opportunities or possibilities for scientific activity). If only contemporary countries were considered, there might be a substantial correlation between the amount of scientific activity and population size; but it would be dubious to argue that only population size is relevant.[2] As the commentary indicates, perhaps it would be more appropriate to speak of "relative amount of scientific activity," but that rewording would not convert the term from a construct to a concept.

The construct "amount of supernaturalism" is the relative prevalence of supernatural beliefs and practices in some designated population over some designated period.[3] The key term, "supernaturalism," defies anything like a clear and complete definition; and it would be difficult to defend any particular basis for expressing the amount in relative terms (e.g., per capita, as a ratio to all practices, proportion of all beliefs).

The construct "concentration of biotic control attempts" refers to the extent that the frequency of biotic control attempts varies among members of some designated population during some designated period. Even if the measure of variance (e.g., the standard deviation or the coefficient of variation) and the length of the period could be stipulated with absolute confidence, limits on research resources would make the measure empirically inapplicable.

The construct "degree of division of labor" refers to the amount of differences among members of some designated population as regards their sustenance activities at some designated time point and the related amount of functional interdependence among the members at that time. Although "some designated time point" cannot be equated with "any time point" (after all, in most populations neither the amount of differentiation nor the amount of functional dependence is uniform throughout the day), there is no basis to further clarify the temporal context. Moreover, differentiation in sustenance activities cannot be linked with a concept such that the relation holds regardless of the type of social unit; and, whatever the type of social unit, it is doubtful whether functional interdependence can be linked with any concept (but see Ervin, 1987).

The construct "extent and efficacy of control attempts" refers to the frequency, range, scope, intensity, effectiveness, efficiency, and indispensability of all control attempts made by members of some designated population during some designated period. Even ignoring questions about the period's length and how population size should be treated, there is not the slightest possibility of computing any of the seven component values for any country, nor is there any obvious formula for combining the component values into one composite value.

The construct "extent and efficacy of biotic control attempts" need not be defined. The generic definition of the extent and efficacy of control attempts (*supra*) and the comment on it apply to all three basic types of control. However, note particularly that in the case of biotic control the efficiency dimension is bound to reflect the technology employed and the character of whatever control over human behavior is involved in the biotic control.

When the generic definition is applied to the construct "extent and efficacy of attempts to control human behavior," it is important to recognize that efficiency reflects both the technology and the techniques of control attempts, no less than in the case for the two other basic types of control. That consideration in no way alters the definition of this basic type of control set forth in Chapter 2.

In the case of the construct "extent and efficacy of inanimate control attempts," efficiency is not determined solely by the kind of technological items employed; technique is also relevant. All such commentaries may promote understanding of the construct (whatever it is), but they do not make it empirically applicable.

The construct "technological complexity" refers to that proportion of the items in some designated population's technology that cannot be created, maintained, and used effectively by the typical member of that population at any time point during some designated period. Quite apart from the imponderables (e.g., the criteria of a typical member), the research resources required to apply the definition would be prohibitive.

The construct "technological efficiency" is the amount of human energy and time conserved through the use of technological items by members of some designated population over some stipulated period. Even if the various ambiguities of the definition (see pp. 38–41 of Chapter 2 and pp. 133–141 of Chapter 5) could be eliminated, limited research resources alone would preclude application of the definition to even one country.

Concepts

Although each of the six concepts is linked in a postulate to at least one of the constructs, in no sense is the definition of any of those concepts implied by the definition of the construct to which the concept is linked. Rather, in each case the link is extralogical, meaning an empirical generalization, though not testable in anything like the direct sense.

The concept "amount of inanimate energy use" refers to the sum of all energy from sources other than living organisms that were used by one or more members of some designated population in a control attempt during some designated period. Although a lengthy list of "inanimate energy sources" (e.g., coal, wind) would promote understanding of the definition, it could be only illustrative and might be misleading.

The concept "degree of industry differentiation" refers to the number of industries in some designated population at some designated time point and the uniformity or evenness of the distribution of population members among those industries at that time, excluding those members who cannot be described as working or seeking work in a particular industry. The *excluded* population members are individuals who have yet to engage in any particular industry on a regular basis and those who are retired, but the unemployed (those seeking work) are not excluded if their prospective industries are identified.

The previous definition and subsequent comment apply to the concept "degree of occupational differentiation," with two modifications. "Occupation" is substituted for "industry," and "occupations" is substituted for "industries."

The concept "level of educational attainment" is the amount of time as of some designated date that members of some designated population have participated in organized education as a student or pupil, with that amount expressed as some measure of central tendency, a proportion, or a percentage. The proficiency achieved and the character of the education are not recognized in defining the concept because it is not possible to describe them defensibly.

The concept "predominance of animate industries" is the proportion of all sustenance activities in some designated population that take place in the context of industries identified as agriculture (including farming, ranching, gardening, and marine domestication), fishing, forestry, or hunting at some designated time point. Previous comments on the exclusion of population members in connection with industry affiliation apply in this case also.

The concept "variation in death ages" refers to the amount of difference in age at death of those members of some designated population (e.g., residents of a particular country) who died during some designated period. Stillbirths are not considered as "deaths."

Referentials and Referential Formulas

Each referential (an acronym in a transformational statement or a theorem) is to be construed as denoting nothing more than a particular formula or a particular version of it and related data instructions in either case. When two or more versions of a formula are denoted, only one is to be used in a particular test of the theorem in question. Similarly, for one and the same formula there may be two or more kinds of requisite data and/or two or more kinds of sources of the data. Unless stipulated otherwise, a particular test of a particular theorem is to be based on the same kinds of data for all countries and the same kinds of sources. All of the requisite data are to be obtained from designated kinds of publications.

It would be possible to stipulate data-gathering procedures (e.g., surveys) as an alternative; but because limited research resources would prohibit application of the procedure to even a few countries, the stipulation would serve no purpose. However, if and when there is an enormous expansion of those resources, the theory can and should be extended to a stipulation of data-gathering procedures.

RAIEU: The Referential of Inanimate Energy Use

The referential formula is:

RAIEU$=\sum[k(E_1\text{-}E_2)]/P,$

where E_1 is the total amount of some type of inanimate energy source (e.g., barrels of petroleum) produced in or imported by the country in question during a particular calendar year, E_2 is the total amount of the same type of inanimate energy source exported or unused (e.g., stored) during the same year, k is a constant that expresses $E_1\text{-}E_2$ as the equivalent of some standard amount of a particular type of inanimate energy source, and P is the country's total population at some point during that year. In publications of data pertaining to inanimate energy use in countries, k is commonly "kilograms of coal equivalent"; but there are conventional alternatives, and the choice is irrelevant as long as k is the same for all countries considered in a test of the theory. The basic criterion for reckoning P can be either the *de facto* population or the *de jure* population, and it need not be the same for all countries in a particular test.

Requisite Data and Some Observations on Test Procedure. Limited research resources dictate the use of published data in computing RAIEU referents. Hence, all of the data required by the formula (the values of k, E_1, E_2, and P) are to be acquired from publications of national government agencies or from the publications of international organizations (e.g., the United Nations Statistical Office). In either case, the data can be used even if identified in the publication as "estimates."

Fortunately, there are publications (e.g., the United Nations' *Statistical Yearbooks*) in which a table reports ostensible RAIEU referents for each of several countries. Even though the values in those tables are not labeled as "RAIEU referents," they can be used in a test (i.e., the formula need not be actually applied in those cases). The calendar year of those published referents depends on the date of the publication; and while those years are generally the same for all of the countries listed in the table, the year need not be the same for each country considered in a test. Each test is to be based exclusively on either RAIEU referents published in the same source series (e.g., all in one or more of the *Statistical Yearbooks*) or on RAIEU referents computed by application of the formula.

No country is to enter into any particular cross-sectional test of a theorem (any of the 15) more than once, not even with different calendar years for the same kind of referents, RAIEU or otherwise. To illustrate, in a test of Theorem 3 it would be possible to obtain RAIEU and RDOD referents for Canada as of 1971 and 1981, but in any test there must be only one pair of referents for Canada. The justification for that procedural rule pertains to the substantial stability of instances of a particular kind of referent (not just RAIEU) for a country from one time point or period to the next. That stability can be such as to inflate the measure of association between sets of referents (e.g., RAIEU and RDOD) if any country enters into the test more than once (especially if the time interval between the referents is a decade or less). So the rule applies to all kinds of referents, not just to RAIEU.

RDID: The Referential of Degree of Industry Differentiation

The first formula is:
$$RDID_1 = (1 - [\Sigma X/(\Sigma X)^2])/(1 - [1/Nc]),$$
where X is the number of members of the country's population in a *specific* industry (e.g., railroads) or industry *category* (e.g., transportation), and Nc is the number of such specific industries or industry categories in the country. Unemployed persons may be included in the total—ΣX—if and only if they

have been allocated to particular industries or industry categories (along with the employed); otherwise, if the unemployed are reported as a separate category, they must be excluded from the total. Should the categories of "students" and "retired" be shown in the source table, they are to be excluded from the total, meaning they are not to be treated as an industry or industry category. Finally, those individuals identified in the source table as "industry unknown" or a similar designation are to be excluded from the total.

The second formula is:

$RDID_2 = 1 - ([\sum |X-M|/2]/[\sum X-M])$,

where $M = \sum X/Nc$, and X and Nc are as defined previously in connection with $RDID_1$. All observations made on the unemployed, the retired, students, and "industry unknown" in connection with $RDID_1$ apply to $RDID_2$.

Any test of a RDID theorem can be based on referents computed by application of either $RDID_1$ or $RDID_2$, but all of the RDID referents in a particular test must be based on only one of the two formulas. The suggestion is not that the theorem will be supported only by one or the other formula; instead, the claim is that *both* formulas will support the theorem. Should research eventually demonstrate that one of the two provides substantially more support than does the other, the theory must be reformulated so as to stipulate only one RDID formula.

Requisite Data and Observations on Test Procedure. Because there is no possibility of gathering data on the industry composition of even a few countries, the stipulation of a data-gathering procedure (e.g., through surveys) would serve no constructive purpose. Hence, the formula ($RDID_1$ or $RDID_2$) is to be applied to industry data from one of two kinds of sources (1) official census reports of countries or (2) publications of international organizations, such as the International Labour Office's *Yearbook of Labour Statistics* or the United Nations Statistical Office's *Demographic Yearbooks*. In each test the RDID referents are to be based on one of those two *kinds* of data sources (official census reports *or* publications of international organizations) and not a mixture of the two.

In publications of international organizations industry data for countries are reported only in terms of broad industry categories (e.g., manufacturing, services), commonly no more than ten. However, the number is less for a few countries because two or more categories have been combined, and no country should enter into a test of a RDID theorem unless the data source reports the number of individuals in each of at least five industry categories.

In the case of official census reports, the most detailed list of industries or industry categories (the table with the greatest number of industries or industry categories) is to be used in computing $RDID_1$ or $RDID_2$ referents. Yet the number of such "detailed" industries varies considerably from one country to the next, and such variation is clearly an artifact. The number reported for any country is far less than the true number, and the discrepancy is probably substantially greater for some countries than others. Hence, there is a need to eliminate the influence of variation in the number of industries or industry categories. Both $RDID_1$ and $RDID_2$ were so designed.

RDOD: The Referential of Degree of Occupational Differentiation

With three exceptions, everything said in connection with RDID (the referential of degree of industry differentiation) applies to the RDOD formula. The exceptions are the substitution of occupation for industry, occupational category for industry category, and occupational categories for industry categories. Given those substitutions, just as there are two versions of RDID (i.e., $RDID_1$ and $RDID_2$), so are there two corresponding versions of RDOD.

One particular kind of table in published census reports should be avoided in applying either version of RDOD or either version of RDID. Some of the tables report a cross-classification of industries (or industry categories) and occupations (or occupational categories), and such data are not suited for a test of RDOD or RDID theorems. The data would be suitable only if the two concepts (occupational differentiation and industry differentiation) are combined and the two referential formulas are combined; but even ignoring the comparability problem, the composite formula's empirical applicability is likely to remain negligible for decades.

RLEA: Referential of Level of Educational Attainment

Even ignoring the character and quality of the educational experience, there are various ways to compute level of educational attainment for a particular population; but the possibilities are reduced substantially because any referential formula must be taken as empirically applicable. The suggestion is not that the formula must be applicable to all countries at all times in the future; but it must be applicable to several countries, with some assurances that the formula will remain applicable in the indefinite future.[4] Because of the limited research resources of prospective investigators, the requisite data must be obtainable from published sources; and that consideration alone enormously reduces the range of alternative formulas.

The observations just made extend to all of the theory's six referential formulas, but there is an additional restraint on the choice of a RLEA formula. Because Postulate 1 asserts a causal relation between amount of scientific activity and level of educational attainment, the RLEA formula should be limited to those kinds of education that further scientific activity. Consequently, for reasons suggested in Chapter 3, the most relevant published data on countries pertain to education at the tertiary level (college or university).

The first version of the formula is:

$$RLEA_1 = (T/P)100,000,$$

where T is the number of members of a country's population reported as having been a third-level student (not necessarily full-time and possibly enrolled for only one course or other unit) at any point during a designated period (e.g., the year of the survey), and P is the total number of members of the population regardless of age or educational attainment level. It might be desirable to limit T to those who have completed a first degree at a third-level educational organization (college, university, or institute) at some point during a designated period, but that limitation would sharply reduce the number of countries to which the formula can be applied (i.e., on the basis of published data).

The second version is:

$$RLEA_2 = Ct/Pa,$$

where Ct is the number of members of a country's population over 24 years of age who at some point during a designated period were reported as *ever having been* a student (full-time or part-time and possibly enrolled for only one course or other training unit) at some third-level educational organization, and Pa is the total population members who at that point were over 24 years of age. Again, for some purposes it might be desirable to limit the numerator to those population members who have completed a first degree at the third-level, but that limitation would reduce the range of the formula's applicability as far as published data are concerned.

Requisite Data and Some Observations on Test Procedure. Various international organizations (e.g., UNESCO) conduct surveys in which the relevant government ministry, department, or agency are asked to report data on educational attainment in the country, including the data required by $RLEA_1$ and $RLEA_2$. Such data are reported also in official publications (e.g., census reports, statistical abstracts, yearbooks) of various countries. Either kind of source can be used to test a RLEA theorem, but the data used to compute the referents must be obtained exclusively from one kind of source or the other and not a mixture of the two kinds. Moreover, each test is to be based exclusively on $RLEA_1$ or on $RLEA_2$ referents rather than a mixture of the two.

In many instances a published data source reports what are described here as RLEA referents. Those data can be used directly in tests of a RLEA theorem, meaning without actual application of the formula (either version). However, such usage is permissible if and only if the explication of the data in the publication clearly indicates that the formula in question ($RLEA_1$ or $RLEA_2$) has been applied to arrive at the reported values.

RPAI: Referential of Predominance of Animate Industries

The one and only formula is:

$$RPAI = ([A+Fy+Fg+H]/Ti)100,$$

where A is the number of members of a country's population who are in the industry of agriculture (regardless of type—cultivation, ranching, horticulture, etc.), Fy those in the forestry industry, Fg those in the fishing industry, H those in the hunting industry, and Ti all of those who have been identified as to industry. Population members who are economically active (in the labor force) but not identified as to industry (i.e., "unknown" or "inadequately described") are to be excluded from the Ti category, as are the retired, full-time students, and unemployed persons unless identified as to industry.

In some publications of international organizations or particular government agencies (e.g., a census bureau or registrar's office) there are percentages that have been computed in accordance with the RPAI formula. Such percentages can be used directly in a test of a RPAI theorem, even though it may not be truly explicit and clear as to the population members that have been excluded from or included in the Ti category.

Requisite Data. All of the observations made on data sources in connection with RDID apply in this case. More specifically, any source for data on a particular country's industry composition can be used to obtain the data required for computing the RPAI referent for that country.

Here and in the case of RDID, RDOD, and RLEA, the most common original data sources will be censuses; and that is true even for relevant publications by international organizations. However, data from surveys not described as censuses can be used, as can data that are described as estimates, provided that (in either case) the data appear in the publication of an international organization.

RVDA: Referential of Variation in Death Ages

The ideal referential formula cannot be stipulated because the requisite data would be available without prohibitively costly surveys for only a few countries. The ideal formula is the coefficient of variation, in this case Sx/Mx, where x is the age at which a particular member of a country's population died during a designated calendar year, Sx is the standard deviation of all such x values (i.e., all death ages during that year), and Mx is the mean of all such x values.

The formula cannot be applied unless individual death ages are published or on accessible tapes for the country being considered. Anticipating the argument that Sx and Mx can be computed when death ages are tabulated by age groups (e.g., <1, 1–4, 5–9...>84), the argument ignores the point that in published reports such age groups are not uniform from one country to the next. Above age four there are five-year intervals for some countries, ten-year intervals for others, fifteen-year intervals for still others, and for some countries there is even a mixture of interval lengths (e.g., <1, 1–4, 5–9, 10–14, 15–24 25–34...>74). Worse, the oldest age group for any country is "open-ended" (e.g., >84, >74, >59), and the lower limit of that age group is not the same for all countries. The upshot is that the mean and standard deviation of ages at death cannot be computed for grouped data (not even if the age groups are the same for all countries) without making some arbitrary and, hence, questionable interpolations. The same may be said for anything akin to the interquartile range as a measure of variation.

Given the nature of published international data pertaining to death ages, the referential formulas cannot be construed as anything like a conventional measure of variance. The first formula is:

RDVA$_1$=1-[($\sum$Pr-1)/(Na-1)],

where *Pr* is the proportion of all deaths in an age group and all older age groups during some designated calendar year, and *Na* is the number of age groups.[5] The lower limit of the oldest age groups should be at least 50; and the age groups must be the same for all of the countries being compared, because the RVDA$_1$ value is determined appreciably by the number of age groups and their limits.

To appreciate the rationale for RVDA$_1$, variation in death ages is reduced if population members die only *after* their reproductive and productive years. Such a mortality pattern would indicate that control, biotic control particularly, is especially extensive and efficacious in the population.[6] No kind of attempted control can prevent all deaths in a population, but the extent and efficacy of control determine the proportion of members who survive to elderly age.

The second version of the formula is:

RVDA$_2$=100–Md,

where *Md* is the median age at death of those members of a country's population who died during a designated calendar year. The connection between the formula and the notion of "variation" is not obvious and can rightly be regarded as disputable.[7] Nevertheless, the formula becomes more understandable in light of demonstrable patterns in the association between age and mortality. In many national populations the median death age is so great (e.g., above 70) that variation in death ages is substantially reduced by the very existence of some apparent *general* upper limit on human longevity. Anticipating the argument that a high median makes possible enormous variation in lesser death ages (i.e., those less than the median), the argument ignores the marked tendency for deaths of the young to become numerically unimportant as the median increases. Finally, the formula is much more empirically applicable than are alternatives, the reason being that for most countries the median death age is well below the open-ended age group (e.g., >74) in mortality tabulations; hence, disputable inferences about the distribution of death ages in that group are not necessary for an interpolation. Unlike the requirement for RVDA$_1$ that age groups need be the same for all countries, it is necessary only that the median death age for each country be less than the lower limit of the open-ended age group.

In recognition that $RVDA_2$ is a far cry from the conventional notion of variance, several observations are needed to allay doubts about it. Using data sources subsequently described in Chapter 8, for 53 countries (*circa* 1980) the rank-order coefficient of correlation (*rho*) between $RVDA_1$ referents and $RVDA_2$ referents is .980. Note that $RVDA_1$, though applicable to fewer countries, is more in keeping with the conventional variance notion. Then official 1980 U.S. mortality tapes make it possible to compute the coefficient of variation (CV) in individual death ages for each state during 1980, and *rho* (N=50) between those variation measures and $RVDA_2$ referents is .802.

Lest it be presumed that *rho* is inappropriate, the two corresponding *r*'s are .954 ($RVDA_1$ and $RVDA_2$ for the 53 countries) and .832 (CV and $RVDA_2$ for the 50 states). Finally, whereas *rho* between $RVDA_1$ and $RVDA_2$ approaches unity (.980) for the 53 countries, it is only slightly less (.973) for the 50 states. So even if it were feasible to use the coefficient of variation formula or the $RVDA_1$ formula for the 66 countries considered in tests of the 15 theorems (Chapter 8), the consequence of the choice among the three alternatives would not be appreciable, at least as far as outcomes of tests of RVDA theorems are concerned.

Requisite Data. Either version of the RVDA formula is to be applied to one of two kinds of sources of data on individual countries. The first kind is any series of publications by an international organization, such as the World Health Organization or the United Nations Statistical Office. The second source is any relevant series of publications by a national government agency, such as a registrar's office, a bureau of vital statistics, or a health department.

Any test of a RVDA theorem is to be based exclusively on one of the two kinds of sources rather than a mixture of the two. In either case, however, should a source report the median of death ages, that value cannot be used. To further comparability, the median value must be computed from deaths tabulated by age groups, but the age groupings need not be the same internationally. It is necessary only that (1) the groupings be such that the median of any country is not in the open-ended group and (2) the interpolation procedure (whatever it may be) is the same for all countries.

Temporal Quantifiers and Final Observations on Test Procedures

If a particular formal mode of theory construction is complete and published, in using the mode to state a theory the theorist need not set forth a test procedure. A truly complete mode of theory construction offers a procedure for testing any theory stated in accordance with the mode. Yet it may be necessary for the theorist to modify that procedure, and in this case the principal modification of the test procedure in the Appendix (i.e., the one set forth in conjunction with the mode itself) has to do with temporal quantifiers, selection of countries for tests, and requisite statistical techniques.

The Temporal Quantifiers

The temporal quantifier of each referential is T_{0-1}, and the subscripts are to be translated as "any calendar year." So, when feasible, each of the two referents for any country that enters into a test of a particular theorem (e.g., the RPAI referential and the RDID referential in the case of Theorem 1) would pertain to the same calendar year; but that calendar year need not be the same for all countries. To illustrate, in testing Theorem 1 the year for both referents could be 1990 for one country, 1991 for another country, and 1981 for still another country. Even so, because of the reliance on published data, requiring that the year be the same for each of a country's two referents would considerably reduce the number of countries in each test; and it is not essential. Regardless of the referential (RPAI, RDID, RAIEU, etc.), it appears that annual changes in the magnitude of the referents are not substantial; hence, the outcome of a test does not depend appreciably on the choice of the referent year for a particular country over, say, a ten-year interval. Accordingly, the special rule is this: in testing a theorem both referents for any country (two referents for each) are to be within a ten-year period. So if in testing Theorem 7 the RPAI referent for a particular country must be 1980 (i.e., the reliance on published data permits no recent alternative to that year), then the RAIEU referent for that country could be any year over 1970-1990.

The ten-year rule applies only in the case of cross-sectional tests of a theorem, meaning a comparison of two or more countries. Moreover, as indicated by the temporal quantifiers, each such test is to be at least approximately synchronic, meaning that the referents are to be for more or less the same time (given the special rule, both within a ten-year period). But the unit phrase indicates that each theorem can be tested also through longitudinal comparisons (any country over time), and in that case the special rule is not appropriate if only because it might create confusion. In a longitudinal test of a theorem each pair of referents must pertain to the same calendar year, and there is a need for another special rule. The reliability of the ordinal difference between two referents of the same kind over time (e.g., Canada's RAIEU referent for 1990 and for 1991) is disputable if the absolute difference is relatively small, and a small difference is likely if the time interval is short. Consequently, in testing a theorem through longitudinal comparisons (any country over time), the interval between each pair of referents must be at least ten years. Thus, if for a particular country there is a RPAI referent and a RAIEU referent for 1971 (i.e., both for that year), for 1981, and for 1994, that series would be sufficient for a test of Theorem 7.

Nothing in the foregoing contradicts the previous misgiving about the lack of any basis for stipulating temporal quantifiers such that they reflect the presumption of a temporal lag in the causal relations asserted in the premises. Given that presumption, there is no basis to expect anything remotely approaching maximum association (e.g., a correlation coefficient of +1.0 or −1.0) when testing theorems with the synchronic temporal quantifiers.

The most realistic expectation in those tests is a measure of association in each test that is significant by one standard or another.[8] Such a finding would set the scene for and justify exploratory research in which the temporal quantifiers are altered systematically to determine if a particular kind of lag (e.g., for each country the RAIEU referent precedes the RDOD referent by ten years) increases or decreases the measure of association substantially. If so, the finding would lend much more support to the theorem than do the synchronic temporal quantifiers, and the findings might provide a basis for reasonable inferences about the temporal lag in the causal relations asserted by the premises.

A Few Additional Observations on Test Procedure

As suggested earlier, when stating a theory in accordance with a particular mode, the test procedure is part of the mode itself if the mode is truly complete. In that case, as it is here because of the Appendix, the theorist need only stipulate what modifications of that procedure are needed for tests of the particular theory in question; but the theorist is free to repeat certain features of the general procedure, those that are of special importance for one reason or another in testing the theory.

Selection of Countries. Because of the reliance on published data, there can be only one general rule for selecting countries to test any of the theorems: include all countries for which the requisite data are available. However, because of constraints on research resources (including time), it may be necessary to limit the countries to those for which the requisite published data are available for some particular period, such as 1985-1995. Even that kind of limitation may result in an excessive number of countries. If so, the investigator is free to select a random sample of those countries, using any conventional method to that end.

There are only two rules concerning the selection of countries or the selection of years for a longitudinal test of a theorem. First, at least three countries must enter into each cross-sectional test, and at least three time points or periods separated by at least ten-year intervals must enter into a longitudinal test (i.e., any country over time).[9] Second, no country or year is to be selected with a view to influencing the test outcome one way or another.

The principal qualification of the foregoing pertains to instances where the investigator plans to compare the test findings for two or more theorems. Such comparisons are necessary to assess the theory's discriminatory power—the extent to which variation in the measures of association *among theorems* is predictable. There is every reason to anticipate that the magnitude of the measure of association in any test of a theorem depends somewhat on the countries or years that entered into the test; consequently, when the test outcomes of two or more theorems are to be compared, the same countries or years (in the case of longitudinal comparisons) must enter into the test of each theorem. Accordingly, given the special ten-year rule (*supra*), if the test outcomes of all of the 15 theorems are to be compared, any two of the six referents (RPAI, RDID, etc.) for each country must be no more removed than ten years from each other.

Measures of Association. Either of two kinds of measures of association must be used to test any of the six theorems. The first measure, the rank-order coefficient of correlation (*rho*), is prescribed for a reason beyond its conventionality and ease of computation. A monotonic but nonlinear association between some of the sets of referents is a distinct possibility, especially in the case of occupational differentiation, industry differentiation, and inanimate energy use.

Rho values are to be used only as the initial answer to this question: is the direction of the association as predicted by the theorem and is the magnitude of the association significant by some conventional standard? Kendall's *tau* must be used in all cases when the predictive accuracy of the theory is to be compared with that of other theories (i.e., only *tau* values are to be used in the comparison).

There is still another rationale for prescribing *rho* or Kendall's *tau*. The use of published data in a test of the theory (whatever the theorem) is alone sufficient for expecting only substantial *ordinal* predictive accuracy. Doubts about the reliability of the data (the congruence of values computed by investigators for the same country and time) are not the only consideration. Those data are extremely crude and far from ideal (meaning the kind of data that would be gathered if there were no constraints on research resources). Accordingly, there are far more reasons for doubting the *magnitude* of the difference between any two referents of the same kind (e.g., Canada's RDID referent, 1991, and the U.S.'s RDID referent, 1990, or Canada's two RDID referents, one for 1981 and the other for 1991) than there are for doubting the *direction of the difference*. Consequently, to judge a theory's predictive accuracy by some criterion other than *ordinal* accuracy is to risk rejecting the theory prematurely, meaning before the nature of the data used in the tests justify the rejection.

Notes

1. Although not essential, a brief commentary should be made to indicate why the definition is not considered as clear or complete. However, in this case and in defining

all other constructs, the commentary is not to be construed as exhaustive. Nor is the omission of a reference to a particular term or phrase in the definition to be construed as suggesting that its meaning is sufficiently clear. What all of the definitions of a quantitative construct share in common is this: the definition is such that the construct cannot be linked with an empirically applicable formula.

2. The constructs and concepts in the theory's premises are not defined with explicit reference to countries, because each of them refers to a property of a population. In that connection, "a country" does refer in part to a population; and just as a social unit's population is a subclass or a subtype of a population, so is a country's population a subclass or a subtype of a social unit's population.

3. Although "period" denotes any time interval—an hour, a day, a calendar year, etc.—it could be that the correlates of a variable (amount of supernaturalism or otherwise) is contingent on the length of the period. But it is unlikely that the theorist has a basis for stipulating any particular length, which makes the definition all the less clear and incomplete.

4. This observation applies to all referential formulas; and it illustrates the need to treat empirical applicability as a matter of degree, especially in connection with the feasibility of a formula's application.

5. Whatever the formula, no claim is made that the theory applies to all types of conventional mortality rates as well as it does to variation in death ages. In particular, the theory does not apply to crude death rates, because those rates may reflect changes in age composition (especially over, say, two generations). Because extensive and efficacious control attempts eventually result in an older population, variation in death ages and mortality rates are positively associated only if the rates are age-adjusted. However, because no mortality rate is a *distributional* measure, the positive association is *empirical* as opposed to a logical or mathematical necessity.

6. The $RVDA_1$ formula and the rationale suggests that it might be desirable to change the corresponding concept from "variation in death ages" to "coefficient of geriatric mortality," meaning by the latter term the extent to which deaths in a population are limited to the elderly. But that very limitation reduces variation in death ages.

7. The formula illustrates why referentials are not and should not be described as "measures." Still another argument: the connection between a concept and a referential is extralogical, and in no sense is a referential formula (even ignoring the data stipulations) implied in any strict logical sense by the definition of the concept to which it is linked in a transformational statement. See comments in the Appendix on "rules of correspondence" (pp. 304–307).

8. For reasons set forth in Chapter 8, there is no basis for expecting that synchronic temporal quantifiers reduce the measure of association more or less the same for all theorems. It will suffice to say here that short causal lags in the causal circuit reduce the influence of synchronic temporal quantifiers on the measure of association, meaning that the measure of association is reduced less by synchronic temporal quantifiers when the actual causal lags in the causal circuit closed by the theorem are all very short.

9. Needless to say, many measures of association require only two units (in those cases, countries or years), but that number makes the outcome appear totally consistent with or completely contrary to the theory; and for that reason alone it is unrealistic, especially for sociology. For that matter, tests based on only three units leave much to be desired.

8

A Series of Tests

Given the theory's scope, the following report of tests may appear inordinately brief, and all the more so because the chapter extends to comments on methodological considerations that transcend the theory. The brevity is due to the use of a formal mode of theory construction. In particular, the theory's extrinsic part identifies the kinds of data needed to test the theorems, and the test procedure is given by the formal mode that was used to state the theory (see Appendix, pp. 333–343).

Principal Steps in the Test Procedure

Six steps were taken in the tests. At this point a list will suffice: (1) the selection of countries; (2) application of referential formulas to the requisite kind of data, so as to compute four referents for each country and acquire two more from an appropriate source; (3) linking sets of referents to particular theorems through epistemic statements; (4) deducing hypotheses (predictions) from theorems and epistemic statements, each hypothesis about the association between two particular sets of referents; (5) computing instances of the prescribed measure of association and reporting it in a descriptive statement, as the basis for accepting or rejecting the corresponding hypothesis; and (6) assessing the congruence of hypotheses and descriptive statements.

Selection of Countries

Given the stipulations in the theory's extrinsic part of requisite kinds of data and the prescribed temporal relations of the referents (any two referents for a country must be within a ten-year interval), there are these alternative approximate periods for tests: 1945-1955, 1955-1965, 1965-1975, 1975-1985,and 1985-1995. Those are the most relevant periods because international organizations (e.g., the International Labour Office) rely indirectly but extensively on national censuses, most of which are taken the first or second year of each decade (e.g., 1990 or 1991). So the 1975-1985 period is the most recent for which census data have been compiled such that they can be reported by national agencies (e.g., the U.S. Bureau of the Census) to international organizations. Examination of various possibly relevant publications by international organizations revealed that the requisite six referents (1975-1985) can be computed or otherwise acquired directly from a source for 66 countries.[1] Those countries are shown in Table 8–1. Unless indicated otherwise in a table note, a country's six referents pertain to the calendar year shown in the second of the unnumbered columns.

Application of the Referential Formulas

Each referent was computed or otherwise obtained exactly as prescribed in the theory's extrinsic part.[2] Although data published by national agencies (census reports especially) could have been used for many countries, limited resources made it necessary to rely exclusively on publications of the United Nations, the International Labour Office, and UNESCO.

The RPAI Formula. The formula pertaining to the predominance of animate industries (see Chapter 7) can be applied readily to data on the industry composition of individual countries as reported in various annual issues of the *Year Book of Labour Statistics* (International Labour Office, 1980, 1981, 1982, 1983, 1984, 1985, 1990) or the *Demographic Yearbook* (United Nations, 1982a, 1984, 1985a, 1986a, 1987, 1990).[3] Fortunately, both organizations use the same International Standard Industrial Classification of All Economic Activities, and one of the major (gross) industry categories in that scheme is "agriculture, forestry, hunting, and fishing." So the application of the formula is a matter of the dividing the number in that major category by the total number economically active (i.e., all industries combined but excluding, if any, individuals reported as "activities not adequately defined") and expressing the quotient as a one-decimal place percentage. All such percentages are designated as "referents."

The RPAI symbol denotes a variable in five of the 15 theorems (numbers 1-5, Chapter 6); and in each instance the variable (i.e., the referential) is connected with the 66 referents through Epistemic Statement 1: *Among the countries shown in Table 8–1, the greater the RPAI, the greater the value in Column 1 of that table.* That statement is not part of the theory; and lest it appear that the connection could not be other than what the statement asserts, recognize that the RPAI symbol in each of the five theorems refers to the value that would be computed if the formula were applied *correctly* to *reliable* data of the kind in question. Even assuming that (1) the data qualify as instances of the prescribed kind, (2) such data are reliable, and (3) incorrect values were not

Table 8-1: SIX REFERENTS FOR EACH OF 66 COUNTRIES, *CIRCA* 1980*

Countries	Years	RPAI: Predomin- ance of Animate Industries Col. 1	RDID[1]: Industry Differen- tiation Col. 2	RDOD[1]: Occupational Differen- tiation Col. 3	RAIEU: Inanimate Energy Use Col. 4	RVDA[2]: Variation in Death Ages Col. 5	RLEA[1]: Educational Attainment Col. 6
Afghanistan	1979	61.3	.655	.638	65	96.14	143
Algeria	1977	31.2	.911	.883	1582[c]	96.11[e]	261[a]
Argentina	1980	13.0	.924	.804	1746	32.28	1741
Australia	1981	7.0	.941	.908	6205	27.45	2203[e]
Austria	1981	8.5	.912	.890	3856	24.06	1811[e]
Bahrain	1981	2.7	.891	.858	11865	50.00[e]	551[e]
Bangladesh	1981	79.0	.406	.418	44	94.85	272[e]
Barbados	1980	11.4	.909	.911	1165	27.11	1621
Belgium	1981	3.3	.911	.894	5542	24.36	2111[e]
Bolivia	1976	48.1	.797	.797	337[a]	77.01	971[a]
Brazil	1980	31.5	.943	.921	761	51.27	1162
Bulgaria	1975	23.6	.888	.867	4488	28.17	1474
Canada	1981	5.3	.919	.960	10159	27.60	4057[e]
Chile	1982	15.1	.891	.925	916	34.24	1305[e]
Colombia	1980	31.0	.884	.902	923	61.02[a]	1053
Costa Rica	1984	35.0	.870	.927	452	34.36[h]	2414[i]
Denmark	1981	7.0	.893	.930	5618	24.72	2074[e]
Dominican Republic	1981	30.9	.880	.908	450	52.94[g]	1929[j]
Ecuador	1982	35.4	.870	.877	741	76.46[f]	3321[e]
Egypt	1976	48.6	.788	.846	248	78.41	1323[a]
El Salvador	1980	40.7	.847	.856	199	67.64	692[a]
Fiji	1976	47.0	.811	.816	476[a]	47.36	287[a]
Finland	1980	11.6	.943	.926	5516	27.29	2577
France	1982	8.3	.925	.909	3995	23.16	1998[e]
Germany, West	1981	5.8	.887	.905	5827	24.33	1987[e]
Greece	1981	28.8	.922	.905	2020	24.24	1256[e]
Guatemala	1981	56.5	.719	.733	224	83.68	736[e]
Guyana	1980	27.1	.884	.884	872	43.47[b]	285
Hungary	1980	18.5	.924	.805	3787	27.51	944
Iraq	1977	31.5	.865	.862	682[c]	42.94	781[a]
Ireland	1981	15.9	.941	.930	3198	25.25	1610[e]
Israel	1983	5.5	.900	.933	2470	26.72	2742[j]
Italy	1981	11.9	.934	.985	3002	25.22	1981[e]
Jamaica	1982	30.2	.882	.955	1524	29.50	644[e]
Japan	1980	10.9	.928	.922	3669	26.57	2065

Table 8-1 (*continued*)

Countries	Years	RPAI	$RDID_1$	$RDOD_1$	RAIEU	$RVDA_2$	$RLEA_1$
Jordan	1979	11.3	.840	.778	527	56.73	1607[e]
Korea, South	1980	37.8	.860	.873	1373	39.02	1698
Kuwait	1980	1.9	.816	.878	5019	59.91	992
Malawi	1977	86.2	.284	.319	51[c]	97.22	57[d]
Malaysia	1980	41.4	.838	.874	1017	39.38	419
Mali	1976	93.1	.149	.269	25	96.56	47[a]
Mexico	1980	37.0	.885	.913	1665	56.91	1321
Netherlands	1981	5.5	.901	.930[d]	5716	24.45	2544[e]
New Zealand	1981	11.2	.930	.911	3213	27.67	2463[e]
Norway	1980	8.1	.912	.929	6530	23.89	1937
Pakistan	1981	55.3	.732	.751	196	95.80[d]	182[d]
Panama	1980	29.9	.897	.947	948	41.81	2065
Paraguay	1982	47.5	.799	.814	238	42.61	855[e]
Peru	1981	39.6	.854	.889	698	72.23	1771[e]
Philippines	1980	52.1	.764	.795	346	65.82	2641
Poland	1978	30.2	.902	.860	4709	29.20	1656[e]
Portugal	1981	19.2	.918	.881	1274	27.30	944[e]
Singapore	1980	1.6	.897	.873	3716	33.69	963
Spain	1981	16.3	.951	.891	2287	25.58	1859[e]
Sri Lanka	1981	49.9	.782	.815	128	41.89	288[e]
Sweden	1980	5.6	.887	.901	5472	23.56	2062
Switzerland	1980	6.3	.906	.898	3636	24.16	1346
Syria	1981	26.1	.917	.788	1167	51.38[h]	1593[e]
Thailand	1980	70.8	.546	.399	372	49.89[d]	1284
Trinidad	1980	10.2	.956	.854	6992	34.71	516
Tunisia	1980	36.3	.906	.810[a]	671[i]	59.98[b]	499
Turkey	1980	60.5	.673	.684	752	55.05[c]	554
United States	1980	3.0	.901	.934	10415	27.39	5311
Uruguay	1975	17.6	.898	.926	931	31.27	1153
Venezuela	1981	14.4	.933	.891	3109	49.00[e]	2044[e]
Yugoslavia	1981	31.0	.917	.885	2266	28.49	1848[e]

*See text for explication of the six referential formulas used to compute the referents and identification of data sources. Qualification of years: [a]1975, [b]1976, [c]1978, [d]1979, [e]1980, [f]1981, [g]1982, [h]1983, [i]1984, [j]1985.

deliberately reported (i.e., no misrepresentations), it is nonetheless possible that undetected errors were made when applying the formula. Repeated applications by independent investigators to the same data and countries might result in the same values, and such agreement would inspire confidence in the formula's empirical applicability; but there is no way that any referent can be identified as correct with *absolute* certainty. However, epistemic statements do not assert *agreement* between the reported referents and the "true" referents (those that would be entirely free of error); rather, an epistemic statement asserts at least a substantial positive ordinal *correlation* between the reported referents and the true referents.

The RDID Formula. Fortunately, the formula can be applied to data from the same published sources that were used to compute the RPAI referents; hence, the publications need not be cited. Yet it must be stressed that the data pertain to nine very gross (broad) industry categories, as the following titles indicate: (1) agriculture, hunting, forestry, and fishing; (2) mining and quarrying; (3) manufacturing; (4) electricity, gas, and water; (5) construction; (6) wholesale trade, retail trade, restaurants, and hotels; (7) transport, storage, and communication; (8) financing, insurance, real estate, and business services; and (9) community, social, and personal services. The grossness of the categories is exacerbated when, as for some countries, two or more categories are combined; but in no case was the formula applied to less than seven industries categories, and the number designated as "activities not adequately defined" was excluded entirely.

Both $RDID_1$ and $RDID_2$ are such as to eliminate the influence of the number of categories on the value yielded by the formula. $RDID_1$ was chosen for this set of tests simply because it is more conventional.

The connection between the computed referents and the $RDID_1$ referential (i.e., as a variable in five of the theorems) is made in Epistemic Statement 2: *Among countries shown in Table 8–1, the greater the $RDID_1$, the greater the value in Column 2 of that table.* The comments made on Epistemic Statement 1 (which pertains to RPAI) apply in this and all other subsequent cases. However, the gross character of the industry categories should not be construed as necessarily invalidating (falsifying) Epistemic Statement 2.

Again, doubts about the validity of epistemic statements always pertain to (1) the possibility of misrepresentation, (2) undetected errors in application, or (3) the reliability of the data, all considerations that have nothing to do with the grossness of the categories.[4] But the gross categories do create doubts about the relation between the referents and true amount of industry differentiation (i.e., the concept variable). There is no way to know the true amount for any country, the immediate reason being that compositional data for a truly detailed list of specific industries have never been gathered. Nevertheless, there could be a substantial positive association among countries between measure of "detailed" industry differentiation and the referents shown in Column 2 of Table 8–1, even though the latter are based on extremely gross categories.

The RDOD Formula. Reporting the referents of occupational differentiation is simple because the data are from the same published sources (different tables but the same publications) used in computing RPAI and RDID referents. However, whereas there are nine major industry categories, there are only seven occupational categories, excluding "workers not classifiable": (1) professional, technical, and related workers; (2) administrative and management workers; (3) clerical and related workers; (4) service workers; (5) agricultural and animal husbandry workers, forestry workers, fishermen, and hunters; (6) production and related workers, transport equipment operators, and laborers; and (7) members of the armed forces. Worse, some of those categories are combined for many of the countries, and the formula was applied in a few instances (three of the 66) to data on only five categories. Given the grossness of the occupational categories and arbitrary variation in the number of categories, previous observations on bases for doubting the relation between the referents and differentiation (as the concept variable) apply all the more here. Yet, as in previous instances, only misrepresentation, computational errors, and data reliability are bases for doubting the validity of Epistemic Statement 3: *Among the countries shown in Table 8–1, the greater the $RDOD_1$, the greater the value in Column 3 of that table.* $RDOD_1$ was chosen over $RDOD_2$ only because it has been used more in previous research.

Although both series of published data sources include commentaries on the quality of the data (especially the *Demographic Yearbooks*), very little is known about the data's reliability. Unfortunately, regardless of the referential formula in question, the observation on reliability applies to all of the published data.

The RAIEU Formula. Were it not for a particular practice of the United Nations Statistical Office, far less inanimate energy referents would be shown in Table 8–1 (Column 4) and there would be much more doubt about international comparability. The practice is to report a RAIEU referent (designated here as such) for each of various countries in annual issues of the *Statistical Yearbook* (for the relevant references, see United Nations, 1983a, 1985b, 1986b, 1988) and the 1981 *Yearbook of World Energy Statistics* (United Nations, 1983b).

Despite the origin of the energy referents in Table 8–1, from an evidential point of view they are not really different from the other referents—those that were computed especially for the tests reported here. Hence, there is no less a need to link the energy referents and RAIEU, as follows in Epistemic Statement 4: *Among countries shown in Table 8–1, the greater the RAIEU, the greater the value in Column 4 of that table.*

Quite apart from reliability or comparability, the RAIEU referents pertain only to the per capita amount of inanimate energy used (or "consumed") and have no necessary connection with the efficiency of energy conversion, transmission, or distribution. Thus, although two countries may have quite different RAIEU referents, it is possible that because of contrast in the efficiency of energy conversions or transmissions the two scarcely differ as regards the per capita amount of inanimate energy used *effectively*. Should the energy concept and the RAIEU formula be altered such that only the efficiency of energy transformation is relevant or such that both transformational efficiency and gross use per capita are relevant? That question warrants attention in further work on the theory, but more than purely theoretical considerations are at stake. If the referential formula were changed along any such line, the feasibility of its application would be reduced enormously, because international data are published annually only on *gross* energy use.

The RVDA Formula. As suggested in Chapter 7, it is questionable to use any conventional measure (e.g., the standard deviation) to express the amount of variation in death ages *if* those ages are reported in published mortality data. Such data are virtually always tabulated by age groups (e.g., <1, 1–4, 5–9...), the oldest of which is always open-ended, but not uniform internationally (e.g., >84 for some countries, >74 for others, and >59 for still others). For that matter, the number of years for lesser age groups is not uniform, being 5 years beyond age four (i.e., 5–9, 10–14...) for some countries, 10 for others (some of the age groups) and 15 for still others (again, some of the age groups).

The foregoing problems characterize the mortality data in the most relevant series of publications, that being various issues of the *Demographic Yearbook*.[5] International divergence in the age groups made it inadvisable to apply the first of the two alternative referential formulas (RVDA$_1$, based on the cumulative proportion of deaths over all age groups; see Chapter 7, pp. 201–203) to several of the countries in Table 8–1. By contrast, the second alternative referential formula (RVDA$_2$, 100 minus the median death age) can be applied to all countries for which there are published data on mortality by age, because the median is always less than the lower limit of the upper (open-ended) age group and because international contrasts in the age group intervals is not a serious problem in computing the median of death ages.

Given the nature of the referential formula, it is all the more necessary to interpret Epistemic Statement 5: *Among the countries shown in Table 8–1, the greater the RVDA$_2$, the greater the value in Column 5 of that table.* Because of the possibility of unreliable data, misrepresentation, or computational errors, absolute agreement between the values in Column 5 of Table 8–1 and the *true* values cannot be assumed; but even if there were absolute agreement, those values are in no sense *measures* of variation in death ages (i.e., of the concept variable). Instead, the only assertion, one implied by the transformational statement and the epistemic statement, is that of a substantial positive ordinal correlation between the referents and the unknowable values of the concept variable. That observation applies to all sets of referents in Table 8–1; but it should be the most understandable in the case of $RVDA_2$, for "100 minus the median death age" is scarcely a *measure* of anything.

The RLEA Formula. The *Statistical Yearbook, 1990* (UNESCO, 1990), proved especially strategic for present purposes. It reports several kinds of data on educational attainment in various countries throughout the world (*circa,* 1975-1985). Although both of the alternative RLEA formulas could be applied to those data, $RLEA_1$ (number of third-level or tertiary students per 100,000 population) was selected because it can be applied to a greater number of countries.[6] Described more abstractly, the feasibility dimension of $RLEA_1$ is greater than that of $RLEA_2$; but if only because that may not be the case for other sets of tests (i.e., some other data source and/or some period other than 1975-1985), the latter formula must be retained as an alternative. For that matter, future exploratory research may justify still other alternatives, and the same is true of RPAI, RDID, RDOD, RAIEU, and RVDA.

The nature of the relation between a concept and a referential is of special significance in contemplating Epistemic Statement 6: *Among the countries shown in Table 8–1, the greater the RLEA $_1$, the greater the value in Column 6 of that table.* Although the values are not *measures* of educational attainment levels (i.e., the concept variable), there is at least one doubt concerning both the concept and the referential formula. Both ignore the *quality* and in a sense even the "character" of the education received.[7] The possibility of altering the concept and its definition so as to recognize quality should be entertained, but that alteration will exacerbate the difficulty of linking the concept with a referential.

Hypotheses and Descriptive Statements

No theory is testable unless demonstrably true or false predictions can be derived from the theory or some component of it (in this case, a theorem). Yet it is seldom recognized, particularly in sociology, that purported tests are defensible only if there is every reason to assume that independent investigators can agree as to: (1) the kinds of events or things that are relevant for a test, including kinds of data, (2) what predictions about those events or things are implied by the theory, and (3) whether each prediction is true or false. The assumption is sheer conjecture for virtually all sociological theories; and it perpetuates the use of the discursive mode of theory construction, for that mode obscures the requirements for defensible tests.

Clarification of Two Key Terms. The mode of theory construction in the Appendix stipulates a specific procedure for deriving predictions about the association between two sets of referents, with each prediction designated as a hypothesis. In a sense every theory makes predictions about the future, but a hypothesis does not pertain (indeed, cannot pertain) to *future* referents. Instead, a hypothesis is a *derived* prediction about something taken as unknown, and in actuality may be unknown at the time of the derivation.

Whether a hypothesis is identified as true or as false by the investigators conducting the test depends on its *congruence* with a descriptive statement, meaning a statement that purportedly describes the association between two sets of referents, the same association to which the hypothesis pertains. Although a descriptive statement is as close to a fact in the sense of "that known with certainty" as sociologists ever come, it is nonetheless an assertion and not beyond question.

Even ignoring the possibility of misrepresentation, investigators may make a mistake when applying a measure of association, in which case the descriptive statement itself is false. A mistake is less likely if the association measure is conventional, and the theorist should take that consideration into account. In any case, the theorist jeopardizes the theory unless he/she prescribes a formula that promises a high degree of empirical applicability, meaning not only that investigators will understand the measure but also report the same values—coefficients or what have you—when independently reporting application of the measure to the same sets of referents. However, not even a series of agreements would constitute absolutely conclusive evidence that any of the reported association measures are correct. Viewed in that light, science deals with assertions rather than facts in the sense of "that known with absolute certainty"; and those who seek or demand absolute certainty should eschew science.

Particular Hypotheses and Descriptive Statements. Because each theorem enters directly into the derivation of a hypothesis, a test of the hypothesis is also a test of the theorem; and tests of theorems are the only truly defensible evidence concerning the validity of the premises from which the theorems were derived. However, no hypothesis can be derived systematically without epistemic statements (or call them what you will); hence, each subsequent derivation identifies a theorem and two epistemic statements as the bases. As explained in the Appendix (pp. 325–328), all derivations were made in accordance with the "sign rule" (also used in Chapter 6 to derive the theorems). The form of a test is illustrated by Figure 8–1. It pertains to Theorem 1, Epistemic Statement 1, Epistemic Statement 2, Hypothesis 1, and Descriptive Statement 1, but all of the 15 tests have the same form.

A descriptive statement follows each hypothesis, and a comment on their congruence in each case is not needed. It so happens that congruence can be summarized after the listing of all hypotheses and descriptive statements.

Hypothesis 1 (from Theorem 1, Epistemic Statement 1, and Epistemic Statement 2): Among the countries shown in Table 8–1, the greater the value in Column 1, the less the value in Column 2. *Descriptive Statement 1:* For Table 8–1, the rank-order coefficient of correlation (*rho*) between Column 1 and Column 2 is −.652.

Figure 8-1: THE FORM OF A TEST OF THE FIRST THEOREM

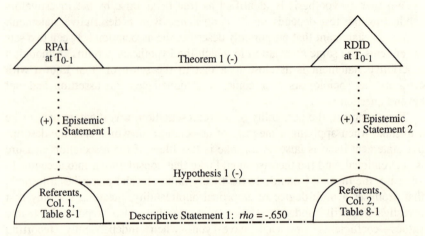

Hypothesis 2 (from Theorem 2, Epistemic Statement 2, and Epistemic Statement 3): Among the countries shown in Table 8–1, the greater the value in Column 2, the greater the value in Column 3. *Descriptive Statement 2:* For Table 8–1, *rho* between Column 2 and Column 3 is +.576.

Hypothesis 3 (from Theorem 3, Epistemic Statement 3, and Epistemic Statement 4): Among the countries shown in Table 8–1, the greater the values in Column 3, the greater the value in Column 4. *Descriptive Statement 3:* For Table 8–1, *rho* between Column 3 and Column 4 is +.570.

Hypothesis 4 (from Theorem 4, Epistemic Statement 4, and Epistemic Statement 5): Among the countries shown in Table 8–1, the greater the value in Column 4, the less the value in Column 5. *Descriptive Statement 4:* For Table 8–1, *rho* between Column 4 and Column 5 is −.742.

Hypothesis 5 (from Theorem 5, Epistemic Statement 5, and Epistemic Statement 6): Among the countries shown in Table 8–1, the greater the value in Column 5, the less the value in Column 6. *Descriptive Statement 5:* For Table 8–1, *rho* between Column 5 and Column 6 is −.564.

Hypothesis 6 (from Theorem 6, Epistemic Statement 1, and Epistemic Statement 3): Among the countries shown in Table 8–1, the greater the value in Column 1, the less the value in Column 3. *Descriptive Statement 6:* For Table 8–1, *rho* between Column 1 and Column 3 is −.607.

Hypothesis 7 (from Theorem 7, Epistemic Statement 1, and Epistemic Statement 4): Among the countries shown in Table 8–1, the greater the value in Column 1, the less the value in Column 4. *Descriptive Statement 7:* For Table 8–1, *rho* between Column 1 and Column 4 is −.878.

Hypothesis 8 (from Theorem 8, Epistemic Statement 1. and Epistemic Statement 5): Among the countries shown in Table 8–1, the greater the value in

Column 1, the greater the value in Column 5. *Descriptive Statement 8:* For Table 8–1, *rho* between Column 1 and Column 5 is +.725.

Hypothesis 9 (from Theorem 9, Epistemic Statement 1, and Epistemic Statement 6): Among the countries shown in Table 8–1, the greater the value in Column 1, the less the value in Column 6. *Descriptive Statement 9:* For Table 8–1, *rho* between Column 1 and Column 6 is –.555.

Hypothesis 10 (from Theorem 10, Epistemic Statement 2, and Epistemic Statement 4): Among the countries shown in Table 8–1, the greater the value in Column 2, the greater the value in Column 4. *Descriptive Statement 10:* For Table 8–1, *rho* between Column 2 and Column 4 is +.702.

Hypothesis 11 (from Theorem 11, Epistemic Statement 2, and Epistemic Statement 5): Among the countries shown in Table 8–1, the greater the value in Column 2, the less the value in Column 5. *Descriptive Statement 11:* For Table 8–1, *rho* between Column 2 and Column 5 is –.658.

Hypothesis 12 (from Theorem 12, Epistemic Statement 2, and Epistemic Statement 6): Among the countries shown in Table 8–1, the greater the value in Column 2, the greater the value in Column 6. *Descriptive Statement 12:* For Table 8–1, *rho* between Column 2 and Column 6 is +.468.

Hypothesis 13 (from Theorem 13, Epistemic Statement 3, and Epistemic Statement 5): Among the countries shown in Table 8–1, the greater the value in Column 3, the less the value in Column 5. *Descriptive Statement 13:* For Table 8–1, *rho* between Column 3 and Column 5 is –.644.

Hypothesis 14 (from Theorem 14, Epistemic Statement 3, and Epistemic Statement 6): Among the countries show in Table 8–1, the greater the value in Column 3, the greater the value in Column 6. *Descriptive Statement 14:* For Table 8–1, *rho* between Column 3 and Column 6 is +.634.

Hypothesis 15 (from Theorem 15, Epistemic Statement 4, and Epistemic Statement 6): Among the countries shown in Table 8–1, the greater the value in Column 4, the greater the value in Column 6. *Descriptive Statement 15:* For Table 8–1, *rho* between Column 4 and Column 6 is +.534.

Interpretation of Test Outcomes

Two kinds of test interpretations should be distinguished. The first is concerned with at least two series of tests, and it is a formidable undertaking if only because the outcome could be rejection or modification of the theory. The second kind of interpretation is concerned, as here, only with one particular series of tests.[8] If there have been previous tests, there must be very special rationale for limiting the interpretation to the latest tests; and incomparability is a questionable rationale. Indeed, comparable tests are essential for a constructive interpretation, and that need is still another justification of formally stated theories (i.e., a formal mode promotes test comparability).

An interpretation pertaining to only one series of tests is necessarily very limited, because it is extremely unlikely that one series is sufficient for rejecting or even modifying a theory.[9] The present interpretation is all the more simplified because of a particular uniformity of outcomes from one hypothesis to the next, but there is considerable variation in the magnitude of the correlation coefficients. Hence, a distinction between two major concerns in test interpretations is especially relevant.

Directional Congruence

Again, whether a hypothesis is judged as true or false depends on its congruence with a corresponding descriptive statement. However, there are two dimensions or kinds of congruence—direction and magnitude. Recognition of that distinction facilitates the interpretation of tests.

The Directional Rule. In the case of directional congruence the question for each test is simple: is the sign of the association measure in the descriptive statement consistent with the corresponding hypothesis? The answering rule: the hypothesis and the descriptive statement are directionally congruent if (1) the relational term in the hypothesis is "greater...greater" and the sign of the correlation coefficient in the descriptive statement is plus (+) *or* (2) the relational term in the hypothesis is "greater...less" and the correlation coefficient's sign is negative (–).

The directional rule is not as narrow as the terminology suggests. It can be modified to fit association measures other than correlation coefficients, and the relational terms in the hypothesis could be "varies directly with" and "varies inversely with" rather than "greater...greater" and "greater...less."

Application of the Rule. The outcome of applying the directional rule to the tests of the 15 hypotheses can be summarized readily: directional congruence is at the *maximum*, meaning that in each of the 15 instances the hypothesis and the descriptive statement are congruent. The summary takes on special significance on recognition that if congruence and incongruence were equally likely for each hypothesis, maximum congruence for a set of 15 tests would be expected in only one of 37,768 sets or .00003 of the sets (i.e., $1/2^{15}$).

Directional congruence is the weakest criterion that can be used in assessing a theory's predictive accuracy, and the primary rationale for the criterion is suggested by a question. If the theory does not correctly anticipate even the sign of the association among at least some of its constituent variables, why retain it? As the question suggests, directional congruence is the only facet of predictive accuracy that may be judged *absolutely*, meaning without reference to contending theories (if any). The decision to reject, modify, or retain the theory does become complicated (see the Appendix, pp. 345–349) when directional congruence is realized in only some tests; but in this case it is one basis for retaining the theory unmodified.

Magnitude

The prescribed form of the hypotheses is ambiguous as to the expected magnitude of the correlation coefficient; but whether one series of tests or more than one, there can be no obvious or simple criterion concerning magnitude. For any theory in the social sciences, a unity correlation coefficient (i.e., +1.0 or −1.0) is not even a reasonable hope; hence, the foremost question should be: does the theory equal or exceed the predictive accuracy of contenders? When there are no contending theories or, as in the present case, none has been tested defensibly, some absolute criterion could be such that test outcomes justify the theory's modification or rejection.[10] However, the criterion for rejection should not be rigorous when there are no contending testable theories. After all, a theory with some predictive accuracy is better than no theory at all. Moreover, if there has been only one set of tests and there is no directional incongruence, the most realistic goal is to identify lines of work that might increase the theory's associational magnitude.

Levels of Significance. It is virtually a convention in the social and behavioral sciences to report a level of statistical significance for a measure of association (or independence), even when the units of comparison are not described as a random or representative sample. Needless to say, that practice is debatable, but it is likely to be continued because it at least provides a standard for interpreting tests. Hence, it should be said that with a N of 66 countries, all 15 correlations coefficients (*supra*) are significant at the .01 level in a one-tail test.

Because of the one-tail test, the significance level actually bears on both magnitude and directional congruence of each correlation coefficient; but the level does not take into account the uniformity of test outcomes as regards both directional congruence and magnitude. As suggested previously, by any reckoning the probability of maximum congruence in 15 tests is extremely low; and the odds against all 15 correlation coefficients being significant at the .01 level by chance alone are astronomical.

The Theory's Discriminatory Power. By any reasonable absolute standard, the magnitude of some of the correlation coefficients in the descriptive statements is only moderate; and there is substantial variation in those coefficients, from .468 to .878 (ignoring the signs, though all in the direction predicted). However, the import of such an outcome depends on the theory's discriminatory power, meaning a generalization about variation *among theorems* as regards the magnitudes of the association measures in the related descriptive statements (assuming directional congruence). Such generalization should be based on a principle of discriminatory power that transcends particular theories; and one possibility is especially relevant when the theorems assert synchronic associations (i.e., the temporal quantifiers are such that they do not signify any time lag between the variables), as is the case for all of the 15 theorems.

The principle is this: the greater the length of the causal circuit or circuits in the premises from which a *synchronic* theorem was deduced, the less the measures of association reported in tests of the theorem.[11] The "length" of a causal circuit is simply the number of its constituent premises; but to understand the principle it is necessary to recognize that the theorist may have no basis to stipulate the appropriate lag between the variables in each premise, meaning the time interval that maximizes the association between change in one variable and subsequent change in the other variable. When that is the case, as here, the theorist has no real alternative to synchronic temporal quantifiers of the referentials (i.e., in the theorems), hoping that the causal lags in the premises are not so long as to preclude at least an appreciable synchronic association among the referents in tests.

If the principle is accepted and if the lengths of the causal circuits in question differ appreciably, the magnitude of the association measure should vary inversely among the theorems with the length of the causal circuit or circuits from which the theorems were derived. To the extent the variation is consistent with that generalization, the theory has discriminatory power.[12] Yet the suggestion is not that the principle is valid for all casual circuits and all theories, let alone valid to the same extent. There is no truly necessary relation between the number of premises in a causal circuit and the interval of the lag between change in the two *terminal* variables, those at the end of the circuit (i.e., the amount of time between change in one and change in the other that maximizes the association between the two terminal variables—the referentials).

Unfortunately, as even casual inspection of Table 8–2 will reveal, application of the principle did not demonstrate that the theory has any discriminatory power, at least not for this particular series of tests.[13] The application was complicated because some of the theorems can be deduced from more than one causal circuit (see Figure 3–1 in Chapter 3, p. 70, or Figure 6–1 in Chapter 6, p. 175). However, regardless of the reckoning of causal circuit lengths—the number of premises in all of the casual circuits, premises as a ratio to circuits, the number of premises in the shortest circuit, or the number in the longest circuit—there is a *negligible* association *among the theorems* (N=15) between casual circuit lengths and coefficients of predictive accuracy (CPA). For each theorem, CPA is the correlation coefficient in the descriptive statement multiplied by +1.0 if the relational term in the hypothesis is "greater...greater" or by –1.0 if "greater...less."

Still another principle is relevant when at least some of the theorems can be deduced from more than one causal circuit. In such a situation there is an obvious basis for this argument: the greater the number of causal circuits from which a theorem can be deduced, the greater the CPA for that theorem. Again, the association among the theorems is negligible (examine Columns 1 and 6 in Table 8–2).

Table 8-2: SOME STRUCTURAL FEATURES OF THE THEORY

Theorems	Number of Causal Circuits from Which the Theorem Can Be Derived Col. 1	Number of Premises in all Causal Circuits* Col. 2	Number of Premises as a Ratio to the Number of Causal Circuits Col. 3	Number of Premises in Shortest Causal Circuit Col. 4	Number of Premises in Longest Causal Circuit Col. 5	Coefficient of Predictive Accuracy** Col. 6
1	4	13	3.25	7	8	.650
2	1	4	4.00	4	4	.578
3	4	13	3.25	6	8	.570
4	6	14	2.33	6	8	.742
5	6	14	2.33	5	8	.545
6	4	13	3.25	7	8	.610
7	4	13	3.25	7	8	.878
8	1	5	5.00	5	5	.725
9	3	11	3.67	6	8	.555
10	4	13	3.25	6	8	.702
11	6	14	2.33	5	9	.647
12	5	13	2.60	5	9	.454
13	5	13	2.60	6	8	.644
14	5	13	2.60	5	9	.629
15	3	11	3.67	6	8	.536

* No premise is counted more than once.
** Each coefficient of predictive accuracy (CPA) is positive, meaning that the sign of the correlation coefficient (*rho*) is as anticipated by the theorem. See text for a more elaborate definition of a CPA.

The failure to demonstrate discriminatory power does not negate the directional congruence and levels of statistical significance realized in the tests; but it could prove to be a serious shortcoming, especially once there are testable contending theories (but note that a contending theory may or may not have appreciable discriminatory power). Again, though, there is no necessary connection between the length of causal circuits (number of premises) and the total of the temporal intervals in the constituent causal lags (the sum of the lags). When and if the appropriate diachronic temporal quantifiers are identified, the theory may prove to have maximum discriminatory power, because the generalization would be: no substantial difference between the CPA's of any two theorems. An assessment of that generalization is only a distant prospect. Hence, a distinction between "potential" and "test" discriminatory power must be recognized; and, here or elsewhere, unless indicated otherwise the reference is to potential discriminatory power.

Particular Premises

Given evidence that some of the theorems are false, the theory as a whole need not be rejected. In such a case the trick, so to speak, is to reformulate the theory; and the simplest possibility is to eliminate or modify only one premise (altering a referential formula, possibly only the data instructions, in effect modifies the corresponding transformational statement). However, that strategy requires test evidence indicating that (1) one particular premise enters into the derivation of *only* false theorems and (2) each of the other premises enters into the derivation of at least one theorem *not* falsified by the tests.

The General Procedure. Even when tests clearly indicate that some theorems are true and others false, the identification of a false or dubious premises is complicated; and it may be impossible if the theory was stated discursively.

Because one set of tests is hardly sufficient for a conclusive identification of particular theorems as true or false, only the general features of the procedure need be considered. Moreover, the goal is nothing more than identification of questionable premises, something needed to guide future work on the theory.

In Table 8–3 each premise is identified by a column heading, and each theorem is identified by a row heading. Within each row the entry of the theorem's coefficient of predictive accuracy (CPA) in a particular cell signifies that the premise in the column heading entered into the theorem's derivation; hence, the CPA value may be repeated in several cells within the same row.[14] The CPA values should express the outcomes of two or more series of tests; but even if there has been only one series, a single negative CPA in a column makes the premise dubious and a prime candidate for rejection if all of the CPAs *in the column* are negative. The same is true of CPA values that are positive but of insufficient magnitude, presuming some criterion for systematic judgments.

Given such a table, a premise is automatically suspect if all of the CPA values in the respective column are either negative or positive but of insufficient magnitude. Yet even one positive CPA value of sufficient magnitude would caution against rejection of the premise, especially if the premise is a link in the *only* circuit that entered into the derivation of an unfalsified theorem. Caution is necessary because it is difficult to see how a false premise could enter into the derivation of even one true theorem; and even when a premise entered into what has become (in light of tests) a false theorem, the premise need not be rejected if the false theorem can be attributed to some other premise.

Five Dubious Premises. Because the one series of tests indicates *unexceptional* directional congruence, only associational magnitude is relevant. Given that the synchronic temporal quantifiers make it impossible for the theorems to

Table 8-3: COEFFICIENTS OF PREDICTIVE ACCURACY FOR COMPONENTS OF THE THEORY*

Theorems	Axioms																Postulates							Tranformational Statements					
	1a	1b	1c	2	3	4a	4b	4c	6	8	10	11	12	13	14	15	1	2	3	4	5	6	7	1	2	3	4	5	6
1		.650	.650				.650	.650	.650	.650	.650		.650	.650							.650	.650						.650	.650
2															.578	.578				.578	.578					.578	.578		
3	.570	.570				.570	.570		.570			.570			.570	.570			.570	.570					.570	.570			
4	.742	.742	.742			.742	.742	.742	.742	.742	.742	.742	.742						.742				.742	.742					.742
5	.545	.545	.545	.545	.545	.545	.545	.545	.545	.545	.545						.545						.545	.545					.545
6			.610				.610	.610	.610	.610	.610		.610	.610						.610		.610				.610		.610	
7	.878	.878	.878			.878		.878	.878	.878	.878	.878	.878	.878					.878			.878			.878			.878	
8														.725									.725					.725	.725
9		.555	.555	.555	.555			.555		.555				.555			.555	.555				.555		.555				.555	.555
10	.702	.702				.702	.702		.702			.702	.702		.702	.702			.702		.702						.702		
11	.647	.647	.647			.647		.647	.647	.647	.647	.647	.647								.647		.647				.647		.647
12	.454	.454		.454	.454	.454	.454		.454				.454				.454	.454			.454						.454		
13	.644	.644	.644			.644	.644	.644	.644	.644	.644		.644							.644	.644		.644			.644			.644
14	.629	.629		.629	.629	.629	.629		.629				.629				.629	.629		.629		.629				.629			
15	.536	.536		.536	.536	.536	.536	.536	.536		.536	.536					.536		.536					.536	.536				

*All coefficients are positive, meaning the sign of the correlation coefficient (*rho*) is as anticipated by the theorem and the related hypothesis. See text for a more elaborate definition of a coefficient of predictive accuracy (CPA).

manifest whatever causal lags are operative among the premises, a correlation coefficient greater than .50 (either positive or negative) is substantial by any reasonable standard. Only one of the 15 theorems, Theorem 12, does not meet the minimal standard.

As inspection of Table 8–3 will reveal, in one causal circuit or another a total of 13 premises entered into the derivation of Theorem 12. However, eight of the 13 also entered into the derivation of at least one theorem that has a CPA value greater than .700; hence, they are much less dubious than are Axiom 2, Axiom 3, Postulate 1, Postulate 2, and Transformational Statement 1, none of which entered into the derivation of a theorem that has a CPA greater than .634.

Although any one of the five premises could account for the less-than-sufficient CPA of Theorem 12, for reasons explained at length in the Appendix (pp. 345–349) it is most unlikely that an axiom or a postulate can be modified readily (without altering a constituent construct and/or concept) so as to improve the CPA of any related theorem.[15] By contrast, an alteration of a referential formula—the formula itself and/or data stipulations—can enhance the CPA of the corresponding theorems substantially. So Transformational Statement 1 heads the list of dubious premises, especially when contemplating modification of the theory. Specifically, there is a ample justification for contemplating the alteration of the RLEA referential formula, and assigning that work a high priority. The only qualification is the distinct possibility that the problem with Transformational Statement 1 is not the referential formula but, rather, the use of synchronic temporal quantifiers. It is hardly implausible to assume that the impact of synchronic quantifiers is by no means the same for all 15 theorems, nor to assume that the lag between the causes or consequences of a change in the concept variables is longer for level of educational attainment than for the other variables.

Discriminatory Power Reconsidered

As indicated previously, *contrasts* in the coefficients of predictive accuracy (CPA's) are not as anticipated by a principle that is relevant when and only when (as in the present case) all temporal quantifiers are synchronic. However, the principle will not correctly anticipate those contrasts if some of the premises are much more valid than the others. Stated otherwise, if even one premise (axiom, postulate, proposition, or transformational statement) is false, that condition alone could generate contrasts in the CPA's of several theorems.

Table 8–4 offers evidence of the possibility in question. Observe that Transformational Statement 1 entered into the derivation of five theorems, and not one of the five has a CPA in the upper third. So one particular premise accounts for much of the variation that must be explained for the theory to have discriminatory power. However, a defect in a theory, in this case a dubious premise, is not a suitable basis for discriminatory power. The constructive argument has to do with the modification of Transformational Statement 1, the related referential formula in particular. Should that modification enhance the CPA's of the theorems, it could be asserted that the contrast in the CPA's will not prove to be consistently substantial in future tests. If such an assertion proves defensible, the theory does have discriminatory power. After all, "no substantial and consistent differences in associational magnitudes" is a generalization about all theorems.

Table 8-4: A CLASSIFICATION AND RELATED COUNT OF THE 15 THEOREMS

		Coefficient of Predictive Accuracy in the Descriptive Statement Corresponding to the Theorem*			
		<.578	.578-.649	>.649	
Transformational Statement 1 Is One of the Premises from Which the Theorem Was Derived	Yes	4	1	0	5
	No	1	4	5	10
		5	5	5	

*All of the coefficients are positive, signifying that the descriptive statement and the corresponding hypothesis are congruent.

Notes

1. Observe that a particular country may have been excluded even though as many as five of the six referents could be computed or otherwise acquired for that country.

2. The point is made because in some tests a difficulty may arise that makes it necessary to modify a referential formula, and all such modifications should be noted in reporting the tests. For that matter, ambiguities and their resolution should be noted, because ambiguities raise doubts about empirical applicability. Tests may extend to experimental work in which the investigators use referential formulas and/or kinds of data not prescribed by the theory. That work could expand the theory, especially the prescription of alternative formulas and/or kinds of data; but negative findings are truly pivotal only if the test procedure was as prescribed in the theory's extrinsic part.

3. Here and elsewhere, the years in a reference is the publication date, not necessarily the year in the volume's title, which in the case of the *Demographic Yearbook* is commonly two years earlier than the publication date.

4. As for reliability, in stipulating requisite kinds of data for a particular referential formula, the theorist asserts (expressly or not) that such data are sufficiently reliable. More specifically, the assertion has to do with the congruence dimension of empirical applicability: should independent investigators gather the same kind of data for the same entities (individuals or populations) and at the same time, the data gathered by any two of the investigators will not differ substantially. If the assertion is incorrect, the theory's predictive accuracy (at least that of some of the theorems) is likely to suffer. Nevertheless, as a variable in a theorem, the referential itself is interpreted as denoting the referents that would be computed if the formula were applied correctly to absolutely reliable data of the stipulated kind. Hence, doubts about the validity of an epistemic statement go beyond the possibility of misrepresentation or computational errors.

5. Two issues were used almost exclusively in the present research, one having *1980* in the title and the other *1985* (United Nations, 1982 and 1987).

6. Both of the two kinds of referents are reported in the source, which is to say that the formula need not be actually applied. However, neither formula was stipulated in Chapter 7 solely with a view to the publication in question. If that were so, then prospects for tests other than those reported here would be drastically diminished. The point is that the two referential formulas in question and all of the others (RPAI, $RDID_1$, etc.) were stipulated with a view to the requisite kind of data *continuing* to be published, meaning that there is no definite temporal limits on testability. Nevertheless, as so ably demonstrated by Talcott Parsons, ignorance or indifference on the part of theorists as to what researchers have done and the availability of data is one reason why sociology is a warehouse of untested and seemingly untestable theories.

7. Nevertheless, should it appear that such referents could not possibly be associated with the amount of scientific activity (as implied by Postulate 1, Transformational Statement 1, and Epistemic Statement 6), consider the National Science Board's report (1991:300–301) of the number of scientists and engineers engaged in R and D per 10,000 labor force participants in each of seven countries. Of the seven, six are in Table 801501; and the rank-order coefficient of correlation (*rho*) between those R and D rates and the $RLEA_1$ referents is .77. The coefficient's magnitude is all the more impressive because the six countries are commonly regarded as "developed"; hence, there is not appreciable variance among them as regards educational attainment level and the R and D rates. Then consider Salam and Kidwai's (1991: Table 1) compilation of data that make it possible to compute per capita expenditures in U. S. dollars for science and technology in 87 countries, *circa* 1985. Of those 87 countries, a $RLEA_1$ referent can be computed for 86, *circa* 1980 (data from UNESCO, 1990, Table 3.10). *Rho* between the per capita expenditures and the $RLEA_1$ referents is .70. There are serious doubts about both the reliability and international comparability of numbers pertaining to science-technology expenditures, and even the inclusion of technology is debatable. For that matter, currently such data are not compiled by international organizations with such regularity as to insure availability for future tests. Nonetheless, there is a prospect for adding a postulate to the theory, one that asserts a positive association between the amount of scientific activity (a construct variable) and science expenditures (a concept variable).

8. The tests reported here constitute a series because each theorem entered into the derivation of a hypothesis, and tests of the hypotheses are based on the same units (countries) and time period. Had some of the theorems not entered into the tests, the tests would be a set but not a series.

9. As indicated in the Appendix, rules governing the rejection, modification, or retention of a theory (unmodified) cannot be both simple and defensible. Decisions should depend not just on the number of tests, the completeness of each set of tests, and the tests outcomes but also and principally on the contending theories and outcomes of their tests, if any.

10. There are contending theories in that both Adam Smith and Emile Durkheim formulated theories about the division of labor, but neither theory is subject to anything like systematic tests (for references and further commentary, see Gibbs, 1989, 1993a).

11. Here and elsewhere, the phrase "tests of a theorem" should be translated as "tests of hypotheses derived from the theorem."

12. A theory may have discriminatory power without acceptance of the principle in question, and the magnitude of the measure of association may vary substantially from one theorem to the next even though none of them assert synchronic association. For elaboration, see the Appendix, p. 343.

13. Even if it had been possible to use diachronic (lagged) temporal quantifiers in stating the theorems, access to the requisite data might have been limited to a few countries, perhaps precluded altogether. Nonetheless, although synchronic temporal quantifiers enhance testability, critics may be inclined to think of their use as somehow being a dodge. Should that be the case, they are reminded that the synchronic temporal quantifiers may have reduced predictive accuracy substantially, and discriminatory power has been sacrificed. The general point is that the emphasis on *all* dimensions of predictive power makes anything akin to dodges costly.

14. In an interpretation concerning two or more series of tests each CPA would be an average value.

15. A postulate or an axiom can be modified so as to change a CPA from negative to positive (i.e., make the theorem directionally congruent); but, again for reasons set forth in the Appendix, pp. 345–349, even that kind of modification is rarely feasible.

PART FOUR

Final Considerations

It is unlikely that any novel sociological theory will impress a large number of sociologists. The vast majority of sociologists take the notion of explanation seriously; but a sociological theory, especially one formulated with a view to systematic tests, is not likely to be regarded as providing a truly adequate explanation of variation in its dependent variables. Rather, the most that a novel theory can do initially is to set the scene for explanation by promoting the demonstration of some uniformities, and the initial tests are certain to indicate far less than maximum predictive accuracy. So from the outset a sociological theory is virtually certain to give rise to this question: how can its predictive power be enhanced? Chapter 9 focuses on that question.

Some of the subjects in Chapter 9, such as prospective work on modification of the temporal quantifiers in the theorems or altering the test procedure, pertain exclusively to enhancement of predictive accuracy. Again, though, predictive accuracy is only one dimension of predictive power, and some parts of Chapter 9 are concerned with ways to enhance other dimensions, especially scope and intensity.

No matter how clearly a theory's domain is demarcated, the theory bears on or exemplifies something broader, such as the theorist's perspective or some kind of explanatory mechanism that transcends particular theories. In the present case one such broader consideration is obvious. The theory clearly bears on the argument that control could be sociology's central notion; indeed, it is the product of thinking about diverse phenomena in terms of control. That quality is all to the good, even granting the danger of judging the merits of a central notion candidate on the basis of only one theory. The danger is real; nevertheless, the theory should throw light on some advantages and problems with control notions. Chapter 10 (the last) examines that subject at length.

The first part of Chapter 10 identifies some problems in formulating control theories, although a single theory does not provide a sufficient basis for a complete treatment of the subject. Because one major problem is the highly abstract and inclusive character of the properties and dimensions of control in the present theory, some attention is devoted to the possibility of theories about less abstract and less inclusive properties or dimensions. Finally, despite the theory's scope (eleven constructs and six concepts), there are some conspicuous gaps, meaning phenomena clearly within sociology's subject matter but outside the theory's domain (range and scope). The last part of Chapter 10 examines prospects for treating some of those phenomena in other (subsequent) theories about control.

9

Future Work on the Theory

The test outcomes justify retaining the theory, but its predictive power, predictive accuracy in particular, leaves much desired (as do all testable social science theories). Consequently, even though there are no genuinely testable contenders, there is a real need to enhance the theory's predictive accuracy. Because of limited research resources, it must suffice to illustrate what would be especially strategic lines of work.

Possible Directions for Exploratory Work
on the Temporal Quantifiers

As indicated by the temporal quantifiers in the theorems, there is no appreciable time lag between any two of the six sets of referents used in the tests. Therefore, whatever casual lags were operative in the relations asserted by the premises, those lags could not be reflected in the associations among the referents. For that reason alone, it is hardly surprising that the tests indicate only moderate predictive accuracy. The argument is not contradicted by the differences in the predictive accuracy of the theorems in the test (CPAs ranging from .468 to .878), as there is no basis to assume that the total lag length is even approximately constant from one causal circuit to another. The most relevant consideration is *not* the number of links (premises) in a causal circuit, or the length of the causal lag in each link, or even variation in those lengths. Consider three hypothetical but simple causal circuits, with the length of the causal lag (whatever the temporal metric—hours, days, years, etc.) shown in brackets:

A←[2]—B←[6]—C←[4]—D—[12]→E
F←[1]—G←[2]—H←[1]—I—[1]→J—[1]→K—[2]→L
M←[3]—N←[3]—O—[5]→P—[8]→Q

The first and second circuit differ as to number of links, average lag length of the links, and total length of each of the two constituent causal paths; but they are identical in one crucial respect. In both circuits the lags are such that the *synchronic* association between the terminal variables (A and E in the first circuit, F and L in the second) could be substantial. Such is the case because in the first circuit the total length of the causal lag is twelve *for both causal paths* (D to A and D to E), and in the second causal circuit it is four *for both paths* (I to F and I to L). By contrast, in the third causal circuit, the total length of the lag from O to M (one of the two causal paths) is six temporal units but thirteen from O to Q (the other causal path). Therefore, a substantial synchronic association between M and Q would be most unlikely.[1] Described differently, a substantial M–Q association is unlikely unless it is diachronic—M at T_0 and Q at T_7.[2] So, if the terminal variables were referentials, synchronic temporal quantifiers would be justified in testing the theorem that closes the first causal circuit (A–E) and the theorem that closes the second causal circuits (F–L); but synchronic quantifiers would be entirely inappropriate in tests of the third causal circuit (M–Q). Observe that, common sense notwithstanding, synchronic temporal quantifiers may be appropriate even when there are long lags in the causal circuit.

One criterion for establishing the lag length is suggested by this question: given that X is the cause of Y, what is the interval between each conspicuous *reversal* in the direction of changes in X (a series of increases followed by a series of decreases, or vice versa) and the subsequent reversal in the direction of Y changes? Unfortunately, the relation between sociological variables over time is not such that change in one is clearly the cause of change in the other; and when the longitudinal relation between two variables is plotted on a graph, it is commonly difficult to detect any *uniform* interval separating change reversals in one variable and reversals in the other.

The only realistic procedure is to experiment with temporal quantifiers and compute a measure of association for each of the various alternatives. Suppose, for example, that for each of several countries it is possible to compute a RVDA referent (variation in death ages) and a RAIEU referent (inanimate energy use) *for each year* over the 1950-1990 period. Then suppose that measures of association show that the cross-sectional (international) RAIEU-RVDA relation is by far the closest when the RVDA referents are lagged, say, 22 years. Even if replicated, that finding would not justify an inference about length of the causal lag in any of the premises that imply Theorem 4 (which connects RAIEU and RVDA); but it would provide an alternative to the present synchronic temporal quantifiers, and greatly enhance the theorem's predictive magnitude.[3] The method for identifying appropriate temporal quantifiers is inductive rather than deductive; but in formulating a theory resort to exploratory research may be necessary for any of several purposes, and there is nothing about formal theory construction that precludes it.

The foregoing use of RAIEU and RVDA as examples is appropriate because they denote the only referential formulas that can be applied to regular *annual* published data for numerous countries, an essential condition for exploratory research on temporal quantifiers. Even in the case of RVDA no international organization publishes a truly regular annual series of data on mortality by age for a global range of countries; hence, it will be necessary to use the publications (or mortality tapes) of national agencies that report annual vital statistics. Whatever the difficulties, there is an acute need for an answer to this question: when diachronic temporal quantifiers (those that signify time lags) are used, what impact do varying lags between the two sets of referents (RAIEU and RVDA) have on the CPA of the RAIEU-RVDA theorem?

Special Significance for Educational Attainment

The problem introduced by synchronic temporal quantifiers appears to be the greatest for RLEA theorems (those in which RLEA is one of the two referentials). The average coefficient of predictive accuracy (CPA) for the five RLEA theorems, .550, is less than each CPA for the other 10 theorems, which range from .570 to .878; and various observations can be made in support of this assumption: the appropriate time lag (that which maximizes the association) is longer for changes in level of educational attainment than for changes in any of the other five conceptual variables in the theory. Accordingly, synchronic temporal quantifiers are the least realistic for RLEA theorems (perhaps any version of the RLEA formula), and the relatively low average CPA's for those theorems is not surprising.

The most obvious observation in support of the assertion about differential time lags has to do with educational attainment and occupational or industry composition (hence, the amount of differentiation). While the exact nature of the causal connection is disputable, no one is likely to deny that the full impact of a change in level of educational attainment on occupational or industry composition is not realized for as much as a generation, perhaps a far greater lag than for any other of the other five variables in the theory. That possibility alone makes experimental research on the "temporal problem" imperative.

The Bearing on Discriminatory Power

Although exploratory work on the temporal quantifiers may enhance the theory's predictive magnitude (recall that predictive congruence is not a problem), there is a more distant goal. With or without modification of referential formulas, lagged temporal quantifiers could result in fairly uniform CPAs for the theorems. If so, the discriminatory power problem would be eliminated.

Discriminatory power is needed only when the CPAs of at least two theorems differ substantially and consistently. In the absence of such contrasts, there is nothing to explain; but "no substantial and consistent contrasts" is a generalization that bears on discriminatory power.

Prospective Modifications of Referential Formulas

Even if exploratory work on the temporal quantifiers enhances the theory's predictive accuracy, some doubts about particular referential formulas are likely to linger, either about the formulas themselves or the data (the kind and/or source). Interpretation of the tests reported in Chapter 8 focused on doubts about RLEA (level of educational attainment); but exploratory work is needed on all of the referentials, though not the same kind for each one.

RPAI

The RPAI formula is unusual in that, unlike all of the other formulas, there is no obvious alternative as regards the formula itself, the kind of data, or data acquisition. However, whatever the theory, there are bound to be doubts about the reliability of the kind of data prescribed by the referential formula; and those doubts are especially justified when it comes to published data.

Exploratory research should examine at least two doubts about the reliability of the prescribed kind of RPAI data, one of which is usually expressed in terms of international comparability.[4] Specifically, several commentators have alleged that the percentage of a nations' population reported as "in agriculture" depends appreciably on the way that census officials classify women and children as to labor force status (i.e., whether identified as economically active). One practice in some countries is particularly relevant: wives and co-resident children of farmers tend to be identified as economically active and in agriculture regardless of their actual activity. Inferences about the extent to which that practice reduced the predictive accuracy of the RPAI theorems can be made through exploratory research.

It is possible to compute two special RPAI values for countries, one that excludes women and one that excludes all individuals (both sexes) who are less than, say, 20 years of age at the time of the census.[5] The question then becomes: for those countries, what is the correlation between each of those two *special* sets of RPAI referents and the corresponding set in Table 8–1? If both correlations approach unity, the choice among the alternative in testing the theory would be inconsequential. Otherwise, the choice should depend on which set of referents results in the greatest CPAs for the five RPAI theorems. If either special set of RPAI referents results in a greater CPAs than do the referents computed in accordance with instructions in the theory's extrinsic part, then those instructions would be modified. To be sure, such a modification can never be made with absolute confidence, but it would be grossly unrealistic to reject exploratory research as a basis for modification.

RAIEU

Recall that the RAIEU formula expresses the annual amount of inanimate energy use per capita. However, the term "use" is somewhat misleading, for the amount includes energy lost in the production, conversion, transmission, or distribution, much of it as unused heat. Estimates of the amount lost (however lost) in recent decades are approximately 25 percent, but that percentage is by no means internationally uniform (see Dunkerley, 1980); and that variation creates the problem in question. If the *proportionate* loss were even more or less internationally uniform, energy loss could be ignored.

If the amount of loss for each type of energy were known, the RAIEU referential formula could be altered by simply redefining the E_2 variable, such that it denotes all energy of the type in question exported, stored, *or* somehow lost. The RAIEU referents would more nearly express inanimate energy used *effectively*, and the corresponding concept itself should be altered accordingly.

Unfortunately, published data on energy loss are limited to a few types of inanimate energy and a few countries; hence, the change in question would drastically reduce the formula's empirical applicability (the feasibility dimension). Nonetheless, the problem of energy loss should be confronted eventually in future work on the theory.

Priority of Exploratory Work on Temporal Quantifiers. The major problem in choosing among alternative lines of work is that future tests with diachronic (lagged) temporal quantifiers could have quite different outcomes from those reported in Chapter 8, even though all other features of the theory remain unchanged. Yet alterations of the referential formulas could enhance the theory's predictive accuracy even though the temporal quantifiers remain synchronic. Nevertheless, there are two reasons why exploratory work on the RAIEU temporal quantifiers should have priority over attempts to modify the formula (and possibly the concept). First, the prescribed data have been published *annually* for numerous countries over several decades, and that time range facilitates exploratory research on alternative temporal quantifiers.[6] Second, because the range of the CPAs is greatest for the RAIEU theorems, the outcome of exploratory research on the temporal quantifiers will be the most suggestive as regards the theory's predictive accuracy in general.

RDID and RDOD

More or less simultaneous observations on the referential formula for industry differentiation and the referential formula for occupational differentiation are justified. The formulas differ only as regards the kind of requisite data, and even the kind of data source is the same. Moreover, the contrast between the two pairs of alternatives (or versions), $RDID_1$ vs. $RDID_2$ and $RDOD_1$ vs. $RDOD_2$, is the same.

The Relevance of the Alternatives. Whatever the referential formula, an alternative is inconsequential if there is a very substantial positive correlation between a set of prescribed referents and another set computed in accordance with the alternative formula.[7] Given such a correlation, then the outcome of a test of any related theorem (e.g., Theorems 2, 3, 6, 13, and 14 in the case of RDOD) would not depend significantly on a choice between the prescribed kind of referents and the alternatives.

To illustrate the kind of work needed, a rank-order coefficient correlation (*rho*) between the $RDID_1$ referents and $RDID_2$ referents was computed for the 66 countries shown previously in Table 8–1 (Chapter 8, p. 211). The *rho* value is .940. Given a correlation of that magnitude, the test outcome would not have been appreciably different had the $RDID_2$ referents been used.

What has been said about $RDID_1$ and $RDID_2$ applies without qualification to $RDOD_1$ and $RDOD_2$. In the latter case *rho* is .938.

Despite the two findings, the research should be construed as illustrative rather than conclusive. At least one more investigation of the same subject is needed. The same kind of international industry and occupational data are available in the same kind of sources for a period roughly thirty years prior to the present referents (i.e., prior to *circa* 1980), and those earlier data can be used to throw light on the awful possibility of historical relativity in one or both of the two relations.

Alternative Kinds of Data. Reconsider the evidence that the choice between $RDOD_1$ and $RDOD_2$ or between $RDID_1$ and $RDID_2$ is inconsequential. Although comforting, that evidence is based on the same kind of data for all four referentials—gross categories, occupations or industries.

There is an alternative data source, the census publications of individual countries; and in virtually all cases some of the data are much more detailed than those reported by international organizations, meaning a much greater number of occupations and industries. Over a thousand occupations or industries are reported in the census publications of some countries, but in no country does the number of "census" occupations or industries remotely approach the true number. Because international variation in the census number appears to be clearly an artifact (specific occupations or industries are recognized more in the census reports for some countries than others), it is imperative that the referential formula somehow eliminate the influence of that variation. However, international variation in the distributional dimension of differentiation (i.e., the amount of distributional uniformity *relative* to the maximum possible given the number of categories) appears much greater for detailed occupations or industries than for gross categories. For that matter, it could be that the choice between $RDID_1$ and $RDID_2$ or between $RDOD_1$ and $RDID_2$ does have real consequences when those formulas are applied to detailed data, and that possibility illustrates the need to coordinate what could be independent lines of exploratory research.

Utilization of the alternative data source would not entail a substantial reduction in the number of countries. Nor would the cost of the research be prohibitive, especially if the investigators have access to a library known for an extensive foreign census collection.

RVDA₂

The most desirable alternative to $RVDA_2$ is not $RVDA_1$. Rather, it is the coefficient of variation (CV) as it applies to individual death ages (i.e., *not* to deaths grouped by age intervals, such as 0–4, 5–9...84, because of the open-ended upper age group and international variation in that age group and some of the younger age groups). Although conventional, the CV formula can be applied correctly only to individual death ages on "mortality tapes," which are readily available for only a few countries.

No Real Alternative. Given the character of readily available data, there is only one feasible alternative to $RVDA_2$. That alternative was identified in Chapter 7 as $RVDA_1$, the formula being $1-[(\sum Pr-1)/(Na-1)]$, where *Pr* is the proportion of all deaths in an age group and all older age groups, and *Na* is the number of age groups.

The $RVDA_1$ formula can be applied to data from the same sources as those used here to compute the $RVDA_2$ referents, but additional countries could be considered by using publications of national agencies (i.e., official reports of vital statistics). However, whatever the source, all of the age groups should be uniform internationally; and for that reason the $RVDA_2$ formula can be applied to published data on more countries than can the $RVDA_1$ formula (i.e., the latter formula is less feasible, a dimension of empirical applicability).

Further contemplation of the use of $RVDA_1$ referents rather than $RVDA_2$ referents is pointless in light of the correlation between them among 53 of the 66 countries (Table 8–1, same years and data sources); again, *rho* is .980 and *r* is .958. As for the possibility that both formulas are inappropriate (i.e., their use invalidates Transformational Statement 6), there is contrary evidence. Reconsider the use of official mortality tapes to compute the coefficient of variation (CV) in individual death ages for each state in the U.S. (N=50) as of

1980. The relevant correlations between those CV values and $RVDA_1$ referents are $rho=.896$ and $r=.918$, while the corresponding correlations in the case of the $RVDA_2$ referents are $rho=.802$ and $r=.832$.

In light of the foregoing, there is no real basis to question the association asserted in Transformational Statement 6; hence, attention shifts to Postulate 7, and in that case doubts are clearly justified. Even granting that variation in death ages is reduced primarily through effective biotic control (disease prevention through public health measures particularly), effective inanimate control may prevent numerous deaths directly (i.e., not through biotic control). The reduction of accidental deaths stemming from failures in inanimate control (e.g., automobile collisions) alone is probably substantial. Then ineffective human control is directly conducive (i.e., not through biotic control) to violent and accidental deaths (see, especially, Lane, 1979). The solution may be the simple alteration of Postulate 7 such that the construct is the extent and efficacy of control attempts *in general* rather than biotic control attempts alone. However, that change would necessitate the use of a *compound* concept and a *compound* referential. In the case of the compound referential it will be necessary to devise a formula for combining RPAI, RDID, RDOD, and RAIEU referents. That combination would result in the substitution of one theorem for what are now four theorems (numbers 4, 8, 11, and 13), but the predictive accuracy of that one theorem might be much greater than that of any of the four theorems it would replace. Work along that line need not be delayed until there are no serious doubts about the four formulas—RPAI, RDID, RDOD, and RAIEU.

RLEA

As described at length in Chapter 8, the tests outcomes create more doubts about the $RLEA_1$ referential formula than any other. Fortunately, there are various alternatives, and the same data source (UNESCO, 1990) can be used for several of them.

The most obviously possibilities have to do with commonly recognized levels of educational attainment, the three most conventional being: primary, secondary, and tertiary. The present RLEA formula ($RLEA_1$) pertains exclusively to the tertiary level; hence, there are various other possibilities, either combinations of two levels or a combination of all levels.

Still other possibilities have to do with the criterion for distinguishing population members. Regardless of the attainment level considered (primary, secondary, or tertiary), some population members are currently undergoing that level of educational experience (i.e., currently enrolled or currently attending), others have had at least some experience at that level, and still others have *completed* the level.

None of the possibilities will avoid the arbitrariness of the trichotomy (primary, secondary, tertiary). Arbitrariness could be reduced by using the median or average number of school years completed by individuals who are over (say) 24 years of age. That alternative might enhance the predictive accuracy of the RLEA theorems more than does any other alternative, but ostensibly comparable data are available (in published form) for only a few countries.

Despite the range of alternatives, the outcome of the exploratory research would be a simple matrix showing the international correlation between pairs of particular alternative sets of RLEA referents (any two sets would differ as regards the formula itself, the kind of data on level of educational attainment, and/or the source of such data). Hopefully, all of the correlation coefficients will approach unity, in which case the choice among the alternative RLEA formulas for tests of the theory would be inconsequential. If some of the coefficients do not approach unity, the question will be: which alternative results in the greatest average CPAs in tests of RLEA theorems. The choice of that alternative over others would be based on induction, but a theory can be based on the findings of exploratory research. The way a theory is stated (i.e., the mode of construction) has nothing to do with the origin of the constituent ideas.

Enhancing the Theory's Intensity

The notion itself is simple: a theory's intensity depends on the variety of types of space-time relations to which the theory pertains; the greater the variety, the greater the intensity. So a theory that pertains only to one type of space-time relation (e.g. cross-sectional and synchronic, longitudinal and diachronic, or longitudinal and synchronic) would have minimal intensity.

The present theory's unit phrase indicates more than minimal intensity, because the phrase means that the asserted relation in question holds both cross-sectionally (i.e., internationally) and over time (i.e., longitudinally). However, the distinction between "test" intensity and "potential" intensity should be recognized, and in light of that distinction the theory's longitudinal intensity is only potential. So future work should extend beyond replications of the present cross-sectional tests to longitudinal tests. Each test would be based on data for a particular country over time; but currently there is no alternative to the use of synchronic temporal quantifiers even in longitudinal tests, although longitudinal data would permit exploratory research on varying time lags. Should the longitudinal tests be negative, the theory would not be rejected until replaced with a theory that has greater predictive accuracy *both* cross-sectionally and longitudinally.

Given the sheer variety of possible space-time relations (see Gibbs, 1982), it may appear that no theory can ever have maximum intensity. However, the maximum is realized if a theory asserts that (1) particular designated types (perhaps only one) of space-time relations between the variables in the theorems are closer than are any other type or (2) the strength of the relations is not appreciably contingent on the space-time type (a remote possibility at best). The present theory does not assert any significant difference between the cross-sectional and longitudinal relations for any of the theorems, which makes future longitudinal tests all the more important. Should there be a substantial contrast in the outcomes of the two types of tests, the theory must be extended to an explanation of the difference or simply limited to one type of space-time relation. Finally, future work on the temporal quantifiers will take on special significance in connection with the intensity dimension of predictive power. Given evidence that a particular lag between the two sets of referents (not necessarily the same for all theorems) maximizes predictive accuracy, the temporal quantifiers would be altered accordingly. If that alteration is accompanied by the assertion that the relation is closer for those quantifiers than other possibilities, that assertion will further the theory's intensity.

Prospects for Expansion of the Theory

A theory can be expanded by increasing its range or increasing its scope. Either increase is desirable, but it is commonly the case that the prospects for expansion are much greater for scope.

Some Prospects for Expanding the Theory's Range

The only prospect for expanding the theory's range also holds forth the promise of improving predictive accuracy. However, the first step is to explain why there is only one prospect.

The Irrelevance of Intranational Territorial Units. As the theory now stands, its range is minimal. Recall that throughout the unit term is "countries"; but there is a mitigating consideration—any other unit term would reduce the theory's predictive accuracy enormously. The mitigation is actually only an assertion, one not made explicit in the premises or theorems; but in effect it extends the theory's range to all types of units. However, such an assertion pertains to theory's *qualified* range. Unless stipulated otherwise, the term "range" is to be understood in the ostensive sense, meaning the unit terms that are explicit in the premises and the theorems. Nevertheless, there is a need for exploratory research on what the theory denies.

The immediate justification for limiting the theory to countries (i.e., its *ostensive* range) has to do with the position of cities, urban areas, metropolitan areas, metropolitan regions, provinces, or states in the territorial division of labor at the national level. Those intranational territorial units tend to specialize in the production of particular kinds of commodities. That specialization *reduces* occupational and industry differentiation, and it may inflate or deflate the percentage of the economically active engaged in animate industries; but there is no corresponding decrease in the functional interdependence, the second major dimension of the degree of division of labor (differentiation being the other dimension). To the contrary, interdependence increases with specialization, including the territorial division of labor.

So if *intranational* tests were undertaken, there would be no basis to expect impressive support for any theorem, not even those pertaining to mortality and educational attainment. Residential mobility decreases the association between the educational level of a locality's population and other characteristics of the locality, including the extent and efficacy of control (all basic types). For that matter, a locality's age-mortality pattern may come to be determined much more by *external* public health measures and medical facilities than by local facilities.

Some intranational tests are needed because the anticipated contrast—much weaker associations at the intranational level—would be evidence of the theory's predictive power, its range in particular.[8] For that matter, although there is little prospect for acquiring the requisite energy data on intranational territorial units, intranational tests of the other theorems (those that do not pertain to RAIEU) may be more feasible than international tests. Be that as it may, intranational tests should not have priority in future work.

Toward a Third-Order Theory. The present theory is second-order in that each constituent generalization asserts a relation between two variables (i.e., a bivariate relation). Unfortunately, it is extremely unlikely that the predictive accuracy of any second-order theory in the social sciences will even remotely approach the maximum. A substantial improvement in predictive accuracy is most likely to be realized by qualifying the theory, and one of two principal means of qualification is the transformation of a second-order theory into a third-order theory. The other means is the wording of the unit phrase. Thus, a generalization commencing with "Among literate social units" has less range than one commencing with "Among social units."

Each constituent generalization in a second-order theory asserts a relation between two variables, X and Y (henceforth, a second-order generalization). A generalization in a second-order theory becomes third-order when the $X–Y$ relation is asserted to be contingent on either the magnitude of a third variable, Z, or on the amount of variance in that third variable.[9] In either case the unit phrase of the third-order generalization is "Among sets of U's," where U is the unit term in the original second-order theory. The extrinsic part of a third-order theory gives instructions (see, e.g., Gibbs, 1989:155–157) as to how sets of units are to be created either to maximize differences *among the sets* as regards the magnitude of the Z values (mean, median, mode, minimum and/or maximum) or the amount of variance (intraset) in the Z values.

The previous argument about intranational territorial units implies the need to transform the present theory into third-order. As international trade increases, the ecological autonomy of countries declines; and as a consequence countries come to be more and more like intranational territorial units in connection with exchange and specialization. The implication is that the theory's predictive accuracy would be greater if the tests were based on data for completely isolated units. Because no social unit is completely isolated, the condition is only an ideal; but some countries approximate it more than others in that they have less international trade. So, in brief, the expectation is that the predictive accuracy of some if not all of the theorems, especially those pertaining to occupational or industry differentiation and animate industries, is appreciably greater when each country in the set is characterized by a relatively low level of international trade (expressed in some uniform monetary unit per capita).[10] The rationale for that expectation cannot be fully stated without actually stating a third-order theory, but that formulation and tests of it are for future work (for more on third order theories, see Appendix, pp. 349–356).

Some Evidence. The foregoing expectation stems from more than sheer speculation. In an earlier line of research (Gibbs, 1989:158) on the international relation between RPAI referents (percent in animate industries) and RAIEU referents (inanimate energy use) the following coefficients of correlations (r's) were found for the following four sets of countries (N=26 for each set) arranged in order of U.S. dollar value of imports per capita: Set I, first quartile (greatest imports per capita), $-.433$; Set II, second quartile, $-.606$; Set III, third quartile, $-.733$; and Set IV, fourth quartile (least imports per capita), $-.809$.

Then there are findings concerning the international relation between RAIEU referents and each of the two differentiation referents, RDOD and RDID; and the findings indicate a decline *over time* in each relation. The first set pertains to 19 countries, *circa* 1960 (Gibbs, 1972:299); and the *rho* value is .904 for RDOD-RAIEU and .837 for RDID-RAIEU. Those coefficients decline to .746 and .741 in the second set, which pertains to 28 countries, *circa* 1970 (Gibbs, 1989:131). Still another decline is manifested in the present findings (66 countries, *circa* 1980), with the two coefficients being .570 and .702. The contrasts could be due to variation in the countries from one period to the next, and that possibility should be examined in exploratory research; but the decline is consistent with a global increase in international trade over the two decades (*circa* 1960 to *circa* 1980).

Exploratory research should focus on two generalizations. First, the greatest CPAs (coefficients of predictive accuracy) in tests of Theorem 3 (RAIEU and $RDOD_1$) and Theorem 10 (RAIEU and $RDID_1$) will obtain for the set of countries having the least average international trade per capita. Second, those CPAs will decline for any set of countries if international trade per capita increases for each country in that set. Should the research support the generalizations, the scene would be set for extending the theory to third-order; and the research should eventually extend to a consideration of the possibility that the CPAs of all of the theorems (not just Theorems 3 and 10) are contingent on the level of international trade per capita for the countries in question. If there is evidence of such an inclusive contingency, a total transformation of theory to third-order would be warranted.

An Acute Need for Additional Postulates

Neither the theory's form nor its content precludes additional premises, and there is an acute need for two more postulates. The postulates would enhance the theory's testability and parsimony, but those considerations are secondary to a particular structural shortcoming of the theory.

Toward Differentiation of Axioms 14 and 15

A glance at Figure 6–1 (Chapter 6, p. 175) is sufficient to reveal that Axiom 14 and Axiom 15 necessarily enter into the same theorems, numbers 3 and 10. Hence, it is fortunate that the tests outcomes do not even suggest that either theorem is false. If either theorem were known to be false, there would be no basis for a defensible inference as to which axiom, 14 or 15, is most likely to be false. The point is not that other premises entered into the derivation of Theorems 3 and 10; rather, there is simply no way that test outcomes could lead to the conclusion that one of the two axioms is possibly true and the other possibly false, and that will remain the case until "technological complexity" (a construct) is linked with some concept in what would be an additional postulate. Given that additional postulate, Axiom 14 would enter into at least one theorem independently of Axiom 15 and the reverse would be true.

The Principal Obstacles. The linking of technological complexity with a concept will serve no purpose unless the concept can be linked with a referential formula that promises appreciable empirical applicability (indeed, otherwise, it is not a concept). However, there are other crucial considerations. The postulate must be a genuine empirical generalization, and there must be a definite basis for assuming that the relation between the concept variable and the construct variable is very close (internationally and over time for any country). So there is need that cannot be met by exploratory research alone; the new postulate will require thought and imagination.

Thought and imagination are needed all the more because of the necessity of linking the concept to a referential formula, but knowledge of published data is also at a premium when contemplating that link. Whatever the formula contemplated, limited research resources will make it necessary to prescribe the use of published data when computing referents.

246

Extension of Observations on the Need

Everything said of Axioms 14 and 15 extends to Axioms 2 and 3. Recall that "amount of supernaturalism," a construct, is now linked *only* with other constructs; and until it is linked with a concept in what would be an additional postulate, test outcomes cannot possibly be such as to suggest that only one of the two axioms, 2 or 3, is possibly true and the other possibly false. Given that the two pairs of axioms, 14–15 and 2–3, are both instances of the same shortcoming of the theory, subsequent comments apply to both pairs.

An Ineffective Solution. When two axioms are linked but the linking construct is not linked to a concept, it may appear that the problem (i.e., differentiating the truth-falsity of the axioms in light of tests outcomes) can be solved by linking the intervening construct with another construct, meaning the addition of another axiom rather than another postulate. The addition would expand the theory's scope, but it would only compound the problem.

To illustrate, suppose that "amount of supernaturalism" is linked with third construct. Whatever that third construct, an axiom would be added and identified as Axiom 16. However, even if the new construct is in turn linked with a concept, the truth-falsity of Axioms 2 and 3 would remain undifferentiable; and that would be the case for two additional pairs of axioms, one being Axioms 2 and 16, and the other being Axioms 3 and 16.

A Gain in Parsimony. The immediate goal in adding the postulates in question would be to make it possible, in light of the outcome of future tests, to differentiate the truth-falsity of certain axioms. However, there would be a secondary gain in a dimension of predictive power that has nothing to do with testability or predictive accuracy.

That dimension is parsimony, expressed as the ratio of theorems to premises. The parsimony of the theory as it now stands (see Figure 6–1, p. 175) is .468, the ratio of 15 theorems to 32 premises (nineteen axioms, seven postulates, and six transformational statements). That amount is truly meaningful only compared with the amount for a contending theory; nevertheless, the addition of even one postulate and related transformational statement would increase parsimony to .618 (i.e., 21/34).

Exploratory Work with Test Procedures

In assessing a theory that has no testable contenders, the initial concern should be with this question: does the theory warrant retention if only with a view to its modification? That question should be answered on the basis of what the test outcomes reveal about the theory's *ordinal* predictive accuracy. Hence, the appropriate test procedure makes use of measures of ordinal association, but the rationale is not just that the related "retention criteria" is more realistic than one that requires predictions of absolute magnitudes. Additionally, measures of ordinal association are appropriate for identifying lines of exploratory work that need to be undertaken before more rigorous tests and the related use of powerful statistical techniques.

An Illustration of a Simple Extension of the Test Procedure

The foremost rationale for using measures of ordinal association is that the reliability of sociological data, even data gathered especially for tests of a theory, make impressive predictive accuracy most unlikely for any theory pertaining to quantitative variables.[11] Moreover, an ordinal association measure is sufficient to identify dubious transformational statements, in which case the immediate doubt is the adequacy (not just reliability) of the prescribed kind of data.

A Particular Troublesome Case. Recall that the CPA of Theorem 2 is .576. That coefficient is disturbing even though not the lowest of the 15 (i.e., one for each theorem); rather, Theorem 2 links $RDID_1$ and $RDOD_1$, and it suggests that the degree of industry differentiation and/or the degree of occupational differentiation are not closely associated with the degree of division of labor. However, that is the suggestion only if there are no serious doubts about the validity of Transformational Statements 3 and 4, and doubts are surely warranted. Even if the referential formulas themselves were known to be ideal, the prescribed kind of data may be inadequate, whatever their reliability. The industry and occupational categories are so gross that a substantial ordinal association holds between the referents ($RDID_1$ or $RDOD_1$) and the *true* amount of differentiation (industry or occupational) if and only if the countries differ sharply as regards those referents. Stating the argument more abstractly, when varience in the referents increases, the ordinal association between the referents and the true values (i.e., of the concept variables) is more likely to increase than is the cardinal association. Stating the argument in more conventional terms, the influence of measurement error can be reduced more by increasing variation when the association measure is ordinal (e.g., *rho*) rather than cardinal (e.g., *r*).

Some findings concerning the relation between $RDID_1$ and $RDOD_1$ illustrate the exploratory work that needs to be undertaken in connection with the forgoing argument as it applies to tests of all of the theorems. Note, however, that the argument may be especially relevant for $RDID_1$ and $RDOD_1$, because in both cases the referents are extremely skewed negatively. As evidence, 29 of the 66 countries have $RDID_1$ referents in the range .900–.956 (1.000 is the maximum possible value), and the corresponding number is 26 in the case of the $RDOD_1$ referents. The illustrative findings that follow pertain to some manipulations of the amount of variance (reckoned in terms of minimum divergence of values) in the $RDID_1$ referents, but the findings can be generalized to the $RDOD_1$ referents. Only four countries (Trinidad, Paraguay, Thailand, and Malawi) can be selected from the 66 (Table 8–1) such that their $RDID_1$ referents differ by at least .150 but by that amount as closely as possible. For those four the rank-order coefficient of correlation (*rho*) between $RDID_1$ referents and $RDOD_1$ referents is 1.00. By contrast, for the 33 countries selected such that their $RDID_1$ referents differ by at least .005 but as close to that value as possible, *rho* is .824.[12] Finally, recall that for all 66 countries, where the minimum divergence of values is zero (several countries have the same $RDID_1$ referent), *rho* is .576. So an increase in variance—again, reckoned in terms of *minimum* divergence—results in appreciably greater *rho* values (even a small increase in variance has that result). Lest that conclusion be construed as a rationale for using cardinal measures of association, they are less appropriate when there are serious doubts about the adequacy of the data precisely because they are less influenced by the amount of variance in one or both variables than are ordinal measures and, hence, less suited for making inferences about the adequacy of the data that entered into the values (whether identified as referents or measures). The assumptions conventionally made in the use of r— relational linearity and normal distributions of values—are still another reason for using an ordinal measure of association. Nonlinearity is not a serious problem in testing Theorem 2 ($RDID_1$ and $RDOD_1$), but it is in testing some of the other theorems. Furthermore, all of the six sets of referents are conspicuously skewed, with both the $RDID_1$ and the $RDOD_1$ referents being skewed negatively to an extreme degree.

The findings have implications not only for other $RDID_1$ theorems but also for all other theorems. Hence, in future research more should be done toward taking the amount of variance into account when testing any of the 15 theorems. It must suffice to say here that exploratory research has indicated that, with the exception of one set of theorems, the selection of countries so as to maximize variance in one or both of the two sets of referents *increases* the coefficient of predictive accuracy (CPA) for the theorem substantially. Hence, it appears that measurement error (the conventional designation) is so great that it cannot be overcome by an ordinal measure association, at least not without resort to selection of units of comparison so as to increase variance in the values of the variables.[13] The exception is any $RLEA_1$ theorem, meaning any theorem in which $RLEA_1$ is one of the two referentials. Recall that the *average* CPA is less for the five $RLEA_1$ theorems than for any other theorems; and when countries are selected so as to maximize variance in the $RLEA_1$ referents, the CPA's do not increase. To the contrary, there are instances of a substantial decrease, and these comparisons suggest that the $RLEA_1$ theorems cannot be readily attributed to questionable $RLEA_1$ referents of any one country (Costa

Rica and Equador are glaring possibilities). Consequently, doubts about the $RLEA_1$ formula transcend what is conventionally known as measurement error, and Postulate 1 (which asserts a positive association between amount of scientific activity and level of educational attainment) becomes all the more suspect. However, the postulate should not be abandoned before undertaking exploratory research on varying time lags in the temporal quantifiers of the referentials. Again, synchronic quantifiers may be less realistic for RLEA theorems than for any others, but exploratory research along that line should not be undertaken before eliminating doubts about the effect on test outcomes of questionable $RLEA_1$ values of particular countries.

The Eventual Use of More Powerful Statistical Techniques

Simple statistical techniques were used in the tests for two reasons. First, there are such serious questions about the adequacy of the data that more powerful techniques might have produced misleading results. Second, whereas conventional regression analysis assumes that some of the variables are "dependent" (ostensibly translatable as "effects of the other variables"), any such assumption would be inappropriate in testing the theorems, because all of the variables in the theorems are assertedly *mutual* effects of the extent and efficacy of control attempts. Those two considerations do not preclude the eventual use of more powerful statistical techniques, and both are relevant in contemplating prospects.

Evidence of Monistic Causation. The sheer number of premises tends to conceal a major feature of the theory. One way or another, the extent and efficacy of control (all basic types combined) is asserted to be the cause of all other variables. The very idea of such monistic causation is unfashionable in contemporary sociology, but objections to the idea itself are alien to the principle of parsimony and discourage efforts at syntheses. Be that as it may, the idea suggests the need for a particular statistical technique, one suitable for testing a *monocausal* argument about a set of variables. At one time there was only one well-known conventional technique—factor analysis. That technique warrants consideration in future work on the theory, but others of more recent vintage may prove more appropriate.

Whatever the technique used, evidence of monistic causation is bound to be controversial, the immediate reason being that the identification of the exclusive cause is likely to be disputed. Thus, in the case at hand, it could be claimed that there is an exclusive cause of all of the variables, but it is economic development rather than the extent and efficacy of control attempts. That claim is rejected here, the counterargument being that so-called economic development cannot be described independently of its alleged effects. Of course, a more elaborate counterargument is needed, but it does serve to indicate that future work should go beyond the use of more powerful statistical techniques and take up contending interpretations of the relations that hold in tests of the theorems.

The Ultimate Goal. Once research resources are such that doubts about the adequacy of the data are allayed, tests of the theory can be extended to the expression of the theorems as equations. That step will be a shift away from ordinal predictions to magnitude predictions. However, in turning to regression analysis there will be a more distant goal.

Because structural equations with latent variables can be used to estimate unknowns, they could prove to be strategic for inferences about the nature of the relations asserted in the theory's premises. Of course, at the theory stands now, there are far too many unknowns in those relations; but equations will become more feasible as postulates are added to the theory. The possibilities in that direction are by no means limited to the "missing" postulates previously discussed (linking amount of supernaturalism and technological complexity with concepts), and substantive expansion of the theory could be integrated with the use of more powerful statistical techniques in testing the theorems.

Notes

1. The direction (sign) of each association in the illustration need not be considered, meaning that the distinction between positive and negative causation is irrelevant.

2. Depending on the judgment of the theorist, the alternative diachronic expression could be "change in M over T_{0-6}" and "change in Q over T_{0-13}"; and either change could be absolute or proportionate, again depending on the theorist's judgment. Note, however, that the distinction between "lagged time points" and "lagged changes over periods" is only one of several that sociologists rarely recognize in observations on causal evidence.

3. The most obvious complexity is the sheer variety of *kinds* of lags. Briefly illustrating, each X value and each Y value may be for particular time points or periods, meaning that neither expresses some amount of change; or each X value and each Y value may be the amount of change over some period; or each X value may pertain to some time point or period and each corresponding Y value may be the amount of change over some subsequent period. Still another complexity is that the optimal lag (the interval that maximizes the association between the variables) depends not only on the kind of lag but also on the kind of comparison of units, cross-sectional or longitudinal. Such complexities may make it necessary to have alternative versions of the theorems, with each version having a distinctive unit phrase and/or distinctive temporal quantifiers; but such complexities do not necessarily pose insoluble problems. Nonetheless, the notion of causal evidence cannot be taken seriously without confronting the complexities described here. For an extensive elaboration, see Gibbs, 1982.

4. Comparability and reliability are both explicable in terms of referential formulas and the congruence dimension of empirical applicability. Two or more values are *comparable* if and only if they were computed by the application of the same referential formula (including data instructions) to more than one unit or what is taken as the same unit at more than one time point or period. A value is *reliable* to the extent that it equals other values that were computed independently by application of the same referential formula (again, including data instructions) to the same unit at approximately the same time. Very little is known about the reliability of census data because for all practical purposes there are never two independent but simultaneous censuses of the same population. There are isolated instances of "census checks," but they are less defensible than independent censuses; and no definition of reliability or related assessment procedure will justify a generalization about all census data.

5. In all countries individuals below some stipulated age are assumed for census purposes to be economically inactive (not in the labor force), but that minimum varies considerably internationally. Observe that all of these data problems would be reduced if it were feasible to gather data for the referential formulas (especially two or more independent projects for each unit being compared) rather than rely on published data.

6. The time range is all the more important because annual data are not readily available for any of the other referential formulas (the RVDA formula, either version, is somewhat an exception), and the most appropriate diachronic temporal quantifier for RAIEU is likely to depend on the theorem in question (i.e., on the other referential in the theorem). Should that prove to be the case, the theorems will have to be restated so that the RAIEU temporal quantifier is not the same for all theorems.

7. Of course, each pair of referents must be for the same unit, and the unit must be of the type designated in the theory's unit phrase (countries in the present case).

8. Recall that a theory's range is a matter of the types of units or types of conditions to which it pertains; the greater the variety of types, the greater the range. However, a theory may pertain to more types of units than are recognized in the unit phrases (its ostensive range). If the theory explicitly asserts, as the present theory does, that the relations in question are closer for one particular type of unit (here, countries) than for any other type, in that sense the theory pertains to all types of units. But one type of unit term in the premises or theorems does not necessarily entail such an assertion. The theorist may stop short of explicitly asserting that the relations in question are closer for the designated type of unit.

9. The relation would be third-order also if the X–Y relation is asserted to be contingent on the magnitude or amount of variance in the X values and/or the Y values. Such third-order statements are particularly relevant when it comes to nonmonotonic relations.

10. Note that in formulating a third-order theory the theorist is able to introduce the notion of an ideal condition, and yet realize a testable theory.

11. The argument is particularly relevant when contemplating predictive magnitude rather than directional congruence, especially given any possibility of nonlinear but monotonic relations.

12. To be sure, there are alternative procedures for maximizing or minimizing variance and even divergent conceptions of variance. So as another illustration, consider

252

the selection of 11 of the 66 countries such that a particular country comes closer to one of these $RDID_1$ values than does any of the other 55 countries: .149, .230, .311, .392, .473, .554, .635, .716, .797, .878, and .959. For those ".081–interval" countries, *rho* between $RDID_1$ and $RDOD_1$ is .982.

13. Recall the rationale for using an ordinal measure of association: measurement error reduces the magnitude of an ordinal measure of association (e.g., *rho*) less than the magnitude of a cardinal measure of association (e.g., *r*).

10

The Notion of Control
Reconsidered

The theory in Chapters 3–7 is particularly relevant in answering this question: could control be sociology's central notion? A central notion, whatever it may be, should be judged principally by its products, theories especially; and when a central notion candidate is used to formulate a theory, the theory's merits and shortcomings are bound to reflect that notion's character. Although one theory is insufficient for assessing the advantages and disadvantages of a central notion candidate, tentative judgments are in order, especially with a view to future work on that theory or other theories.

Major Problems in Formulating
Control Theories

The principal problem when stating or modifying a theory is introduced by this question: how can the theory's predictive power be maximized? That goal—maximization of predictive power—can be pursued by considering two conspicuous features of the control theory in Chapters 3–7.

Extreme Heterogeneity and Extreme Aggregation

Each axiom in Chapters 3–6 is indicative of the theory's abstract quality, but all theories are abstract. Nor is it constructive to allege that a theory is too abstract. In a sense no theory can be too abstract; but if only because "abstract" suggests a qualitative distinction, it is better to speak of the *heterogeneity* of a class of things, events, or properties. That term more nearly suggests a continuum, and the term "heterogeneous behavior" is more intelligible than "abstract behavior."

The related problem is posed by a question about any theory in which each constituent construct or concept denotes an extremely heterogeneous class: is it feasible to generalize about causes, effects, or even correlates of such classes? The question is most relevant in the case of a class denoted by a construct or concept, but a theory's unit term is relevant also. If it denotes a type of unit that typically has numerous members, the theory's constructs and concepts refer to an astronomical number of acts by diverse individuals. Such extreme aggregation is not avoided by glib references to society or culture, and it is rarely feasible to reduce the sheer volume of behavior by shortening the time period. The frequency of control attempts during a calendar year in even a small country must be reckoned in billions, and any interval less than an all-seasons period (a calendar year being one instance) is likely to be grossly unrepresentative. So a depressing conclusion: the aggregation level can be such as to preclude measures of properties or dimensions of attempted control. Even if the present funding of the social sciences should increase enormously, ethical-legal barriers (e.g., respecting privacy) and technical difficulties pertaining to data gathering procedures would severely limit various kinds of control research.

Toward Reduction of Heterogeneity

The term "attempted control" denotes extremely heterogeneous behavior, but the conceptualization in Chapter 2 demonstrates that the notion is not vague. For that matter, if the behavior were not extremely heterogeneous, there would be doubts about control as a candidate for sociology's central notion. Nonetheless, there must be doubts about any generalization concerning the causes or effects of attempted control when various distinctions as to types or kinds are ignored.

The problem can be illustrated by contemplating an ostensible impossibility: for several countries a defensible measure of the extent and efficacy of control attempts *in general* and a corresponding measure for each of the three basic types (biotic, inanimate, and control over human behavior). Despite the part-whole character of the relation, the international statistical association between the generic measure and each basic-type measure could be far from truly close, and the same is true for the association between measures for any two of the basic types. Indeed, it is easy to think of *isolated* negative evidence. The moon landing required efficacious inanimate control on a massive scale; but it was realized by a nation in which annually there are millions of violent crimes, each representing a failure in attempted behavior control. For that matter, contemplate the effectiveness of laser surgery and the seeming intractability of AIDS or cancer.

The Principal Means of Reducing Heterogeneity. There are three comforting consideration. First, the heterogeneity problem haunts theory construction in all fields, though perhaps more in sociology than in any other. Second, the level of heterogeneity can be reduced by formulating special theories, those that deal with narrower subjects. Third, if the central notion used in formulating theories has been conceptualized properly, the conceptualization itself is a basis for reducing heterogeneity.

Elaborating on the third consideration, a proper conceptualization extends to typologies and recognition of properties and dimensions.[1] The ultimate defense of a typology is its use in theories; but the proper conceptualization of a central notion sets the scene for a variety of theories, some much broader than others. The conceptualization in Chapter 2 points the way to theories about types, properties, and dimensions of control much narrower than those recognized in Chapters 3–7. Unfortunately, space limitations permit only brief treatments of a few examples.

Legal Punishments and the Deterrence Doctrine. Although not commonly recognized, the deterrence doctrine is a control theory. The doctrine is grossly oversimplified in the typical summary, such as: certain, severe, and swift legal punishments of crime reduce the crime rate. Although "swift" suggests an exclusive concern with *actual* legal punishments, it would be rash to ignore statutory penalties. Unfortunately, more than the actual-statutory distinction should be recognized. Whereas the summary identifies only certainty, severity, and celerity, six properties of each of the two types of legal punishments—statutory and actual—could be relevant (Gibbs, 1986).

Deterrence occurs when an individual contemplates commission of what would be a crime but refrains in whole or in part because he/she perceives and fears some threat of punishment. The definition applies regardless of the punishment or the behavior, but tradition will be followed by speaking largely only in reference to criminal justice.

Virtually all writers recognize the distinction between specific deterrence (all too briefly, the deterrent impact of actually being punished) and general deterrence (again all too briefly, the deterrent impact of the threat of punishment on those who have not been punished). Another distinction is rarely recognized. In the case of *absolute* deterrence the individual under consideration has refrained each time that he/she has contemplated commission of a crime and refrained in whole or in part because of fear of punishment. By contrast, restrictive deterrence occurs when an individual *only curtails* his/her commissions of an act with a view to reducing the probability and/or severity of punishment.

The distinctions are important if only because evidence that bears on one type of deterrence has no necessary bearing on other types. Thus, evidence that convicts are more prone to commit crimes after incarceration than before would raise serious doubts about specific deterrence, but the amount of general deterrence realized by the threat of imprisonment would be another question. Then while absolute deterrence may be extremely rare, it could be that the greatest amount of deterrence obtains among so-called professional criminals; but that possibility is likely to be overlooked if the distinction between restrictive and absolute deterrence is ignored.

There is a pressing need to translate the deterrence doctrine into a sophisticated theory, especially one which avoids the horrendous evidential problems that haunt attempts to test deterrence generalizations (Gibbs, 1986). Perhaps the most serious problem is the need to somehow take *extralegal* determinants of criminality into account when testing deterrence generalizations.[2] No one argues that legal punishments are the only determinants of the crime rate; but even the identification of extralegal determinants is extremely disputable, largely because there is no accepted theory on the etiology of crime or delinquency.

Characterizing the deterrence doctrine as a control theory does not solve problems, but it illustrates how a control theory can pertain to behavior that is far less heterogeneous than Chapters 3–7 suggest. For that matter, the conceptualization of control (Chapter 2) directs attention to several inconspicuous but important features of the doctrine. Although the doctrine pertains to a very special kind of attempted control, it is not sufficient to identify the kind as "punitive." Punishment is a subclass of proximate control and also of vicarious social control. That recognition underscores the distinction between specific deterrence (effective punitive proximate control) and general deterrence (effective punitive vicarious social control), and the conceptual linkage alone suggests that the deterrence doctrine comprises at least two distinct and all the more narrow control theories.

Other conceptual linkages suggest that the deterrence doctrine is an all too narrow theory, and the suggestion is consistent with negative research findings. In particular, there have been repeated reports of a negligible correlation among U.S. states between average or median length of imprisonment (severity of actual punishment) for a type of crime (e.g., robbery) and the rate for that type (for some references, see Gibbs, 1986, and Chamlin, *et. al.*, 1992). An interpretation should go beyond the obvious possibility that the correlation is negligible because the researchers failed to take into account several other properties of legal punishment, such as imprisonment's *certainty* as perceived by potential offenders (i.e., perceived certainty). Regardless of the number of properties taken into account, three considerations are commonly ignored. First, virtually any crime is itself an attempt at control (contemplate robbery and rape), and political units probably differ appreciably as to the opportunities for realizing the same goals (e.g., money, sexual experience) though legitimate control attempts. Second, as traditionally interpreted, the deterrence doctrine erroneously implies that rewards or benefits are irrelevant means of control (i.e., only punishment is relevant). Third, even if a substantial *negative* correlation between length of prison sentence and the crime rate were found, it could be attributed to prison's incapacitating effect rather than to deterrence, which is to say that incarceration is a means of control (coercive) apart from its punitive quality. The first two considerations pertain to extralegal determinants of crime, and they are more informative than the usual criticism of the doctrine—that it ignores social and cultural factors.

In one sense the deterrence doctrine is much too narrow, but in another it is perhaps far too broad. For all practical purposes, criminal law applies to everyone; and in that sense the *range* of legal punishment (i.e., as a means of attempted control) approaches the maximum. Yet it is incredible that any means of control, punitive or otherwise, is equally effective, even approximately, for all social unit members. Similarly, the *scope* of legal punishments is far greater than it may appear, because in the typical political unit there is an astonishing variety of crimes. Hence, legal punishments may be much less effective as a means of preventing (one of many "control" terms) some kinds of crimes than others. So an analysis of the deterrence doctrine in terms of control dimensions underscores the importance of two questions when stating the doctrine as a theory. First, how should the statement treat individual differences as regards responses to punishment or the threat of it? Second, how should it treat differences among types of crimes?

Control dimensions are all the more important because the deterrence doctrine is actually a theory about the *effectiveness* of a particular kind of attempted control, and a related ambiguity haunts the doctrine. Stating the ambiguity as a question: does the doctrine assert that extant legal punishments (actual and/or statutory) are such that they actually deter crime or does it only identify the properties of legal punishment (e.g., objective certainty) that determine varying levels of deterrence? The distinction is essentially between "what is" and "what could be." Even granting the need for research on extant legal punishments, the "what could be" question has far greater policy implications. So the deterrence doctrine illustrates not only how a control theory can pertain to much less heterogeneous classes of phenomena than is suggested by Chapters 3–7 but also have enormous policy implications, far more obvious and immediate than does the theory in those chapters.

Advertising. Sociologists have scarcely contributed to the vast literature on advertising, leaving its scientific study largely to economists and psychologists. For that matter, in those few cases where sociologist have written on the subject, they regard advertising as so aesthetically or ethically objectionable that their "analysis" is little more than a shrill condemnation (e.g., Schudson, 1984).

Despite the vast literature, there is no well-known theory about the extent or efficacy of advertising. Steps toward a theory are not taken here; rather, the purpose is to identify possible common features of an advertising theory and a deterrence theory. Because of those features, a synthesis of the theories will be a realistic prospect; and despite previous observations on the heterogeneity problem, the ultimate goal could be an inclusive theory about control. For that matter, the heterogeneity problem can be reduced by pursuing an inclusive theory through syntheses of special theories, and the theory in Chapters 3–7 would inspire greater confidence had it been such a synthesis.

A synthesis of the two theories, one about advertising and the other about deterrence, will be a real prospect not just because both necessarily pertain to behavior control. Specifically, both are theories about the *efficacy* of control attempts. Research on both subjects does indicate a focus on effectiveness; but the concern should extend to efficiency, if only because the amount of time and human energy invested in control attempts commonly translates as monetary costs, an essential ingredient of any policy consideration.[3] Indeed, a theory on either subject, deterrence or advertising, is likely to have much more policy implications if it pertains to both effectiveness and efficiency (i.e., efficacy).

Considered as attempts at control, advertising and legal punishment are much more similar than they appear, especially as regards range and scope. Their ranges are similar if only because in both cases the targets are an indefinite and seemingly infinite category—all potential offenders or all potential consumers. The scope similarity is less but substantial nonetheless. Whereas legislators select particular kinds and magnitudes of punishment for particular types of crimes, so is advertising tailored for particular commodities. True, each type of punishment (incarceration, fines, etc.) is used to prevent various types of crimes, but each advertising media (television, newspapers, etc.) is used to promote sales of various commodities. The range and scope similarities pose a major challenge in formulating either theory, because in both cases one major presumptive question is something like this: why does the efficacy of a means of attempted control depend on the target and the kind of behavior? No one is likely to doubt the presumption, it should be added.

Propaganda. At one time sociologists devoted considerable attention to propaganda, usually in connection with collective behavior and social movements; and that interest was shared with psychology and political science.[4] Hence, it is puzzling that there has never been a well-known theory on the subject. The point, though, is not that acceptance of control as sociology's central notion would promote theories on *all* subjects, not even those that clearly have something to do with control. To the contrary, whatever the field, theoreticians must be very selective in their choice of subjects. Perhaps the most pertinent consideration is heterogeneity. If a concept or construct denotes an extreme variety of things or events, doubts about causal homogeneity are inevitable. Stating the matter as a question: is it credible to assume that extremely heterogeneous things and events have a common cause or consequence?

The question poses a dilemma, for a confident affirmative answer is unlikely. Nevertheless, the ultimate defense of any term is its use in an impressive theory, and terminological choices must be made very early when pursuing a theory, albeit on a largely intuitive basis. The decision to use a term depends appreciably on the way it is defined, and definitional difficulties are bound to create doubts about using the term for any purpose. Even if the term in question can be defined satisfactorily, when using it a theorist may discover that he/she cannot think readily about the denoted class of events or things, especially as regards possible empirical associations with other events or things. All such considerations underscore the utility of a central notion. The notion can be used to define the field's terms, and extensive use to that end promotes conceptual integration. Perhaps more important: however a term is defined, the denoted things or events can be described and thought of in terms of the field's central notion, thereby facilitating the detection of empirical associations and conceptual connections. Thus, as just indicated, *specific* similarities between legal punishments and advertising become more evident when describing and thinking about each as attempted control.

The subject takes on special significance in the case of propaganda. For one thing, the literature clearly suggests great difficulties and controversies in defining the term (even the relevance of the truth-falsity distinction is debatable). All definitions indicate that propaganda is an attempt at control, but beyond that characterization nothing can be said with confidence. True, most definitions suggest that a propagandist's goal is to maintain or alter internal behavior (e.g., values, ideology, etc.); but no one would argue that the goal never pertains to overt behavior, voting and donations in particular. For that matter, even if the goal could be described exclusively in terms of internal behavior, no definition even suggests that all attempts to alter or maintain internal behavior are propaganda.

If there is any common element in definitions, descriptions, or identifications of propaganda, it reduces to something like this: propaganda is used to realize political ends. Unfortunately, few terms in the social sciences have a vaguer meaning than "political," and the meaning of "political ends" is even more nebulous. But vagueness is not the only problem. Political violence (even terrorism) and political appointments are rarely identified as propaganda, but both have political goals. As for restricting propaganda to communication in its narrowest sense, that limit does not clarify "political ends." Surely it would be disputable to stretch the meaning to include attempts by religious leaders or employers to sway followers or employees, but it would be even more disputable to deny that such attempts could be propaganda.

In light of the foregoing, "propaganda" is nothing more than a term that people commonly use to identify and thereby tacitly condemn particular attempts at behavior control (indeed, the condemnation itself may be an attempt at behavior control). Even the reference to control is somewhat misleading. No extant conceptualization of attempted control suggests a defensible definition of propaganda, and describing or thinking about propaganda in terms of control forces recognition of the heterogeneity problem. It must suffice to illustrate by identifying three instances of what would be identified as propaganda by one definition or another. First, Hitler's derogation of Jews in his campaign speeches appear to have been largely referential social control. Second, particularly in the 1950s many American writers were accused of being communists; and those accusations were allegative social control if made in the belief that employers and publishers would discharge those accused or reject their work, *but* vicarious social control if made in the belief that the accusation would discourage other writers from "radical" lines of work. Third, time and again in human history rioting mobs have been pacified by the promise of food or money, proximate control or referential social control in either case. Those illustrations indicate that propaganda is such a hodgepodge that a defensible theory about it is a remote prospect at best.

The conclusion may appear puzzling, for it runs contrary to previous claims about the benefits of taking control as sociology's central notion; but there is no real contradiction. Describing and thinking of phenomena, including the meaning of terms, facilitate the formulation and syntheses of theories; yet, no less important, such activity may discourage—indeed, should discourage—the pursuit of theories along particular lines.

Toward Reduction of Aggregation

Several premises in Chapters 3–6 presumably hold only when comparing countries. So there are no real prospects for expanding the theory's range, which is a serious limitation because countries make the extreme aggregation problem *(supra)* worse. Stating the matter in more conventional sociological terms, extremely aggregated variables are characteristic of macro units; and control cannot be a candidate for sociology's central notion if control theories are not feasible at both levels, macro and micro.[5] However, should extremely macro control theories prove infeasible, there are strategies for reducing the level of aggregation; and they are best introduced in connection with specific problems.

Problems in Gathering Data. Level of aggregation is a crucial consideration in sociological research because it largely determines the feasibility of gathering data through particular procedures. Briefly, it is doubtful that a systematic procedure can be based on anything like direct observations of behavior (control attempts or otherwise) in even a small city, let alone a country. As for observations on a sample of instances of specific kinds of behavior (e.g., commands, requests, applying for a position, preparing meals, repairing equipment), not even astronomical research resources would assure ostensibly representative sample in the case of macro units, countries particularly. True, surveys are an alternative to direct observation; and, appearances to the contrary, it may prove possible to gather data on a wide variety of control attempts in large social units through surveys. Contemplate three illustrative survey questions. First, have you ever applied for a loan, a mortgage, or credit of some kind? Second, when was the last time? Third, did you get what you requested? Unfortunately, there is a difficult problem: even ignoring the difficulties of sampling and the declining response rate in surveys, the scope of the surveys would have to be far beyond present research resources. Limiting research and theories to subtypes of attempted control (e.g., proximate) is far from a sufficient reduction of the aggregation level. Hence, research on attempted control in micro units would not only make direct observations more feasible; it also would reduce the resources needed for gathering data through surveys, with the schedules or questionnaires designed so as to get at various kinds of control. But the suggestion is not that the problem is somehow peculiar to research on control. For that matter, sociology's central notion should be such as to force recognition of this question: given limited research resources, how can reliable data be gathered on the requisite scale? Until sociologists confront that question, wittingly or unwittingly they will allow the availability of data (including published data) to dictate their research, a sure way to sterilize any field.

Three Strategic Types of Social Units. Direct and systematic observations on control attempts are feasible in at least three contexts—organizations, families (or households), and what is loosely identified as primary groups other than nuclear families. Even sociologists who work at the macro level would admit that those three types occupy important positions in the field's history; and comments on them in connection with control are needed, though they must be all too brief.

Unfortunately, many organizations (e.g., corporations, companies, associations) are so large that direct and systematic observations on all organizational behavior of all members are not feasible even for short periods, if only because of limited research resources. However, the tradition of organizational research is rich with illustrations of observational techniques and survey procedures. That tradition alone suggest the possibility of gathering data on the major features of the principal kinds of control in at least a few organizations. Such research would have merit even if only exploratory, meaning conducted along the lines of studies in the natural history tradition. No central notion can eliminate the need for that tradition, and the theory in Chapters 3–7 suffers because not informed by precisely that kind of exploratory research.

When a theory's unit phrase is "Among organizations and for any organization over time," gathering data on actual control behavior and perceptions of control capacity becomes all the more feasible, because requisite data for tests of the theory can be limited to a few kinds of control. That point is better appreciated on recognition that in the present theory (Chapters 3–7) only one *concept* variable, "use of inanimate energy," pertains to control in the immediate, direct sense. By contrast, all of the concept variables in a theory about control in organizations could pertain to control in that sense.

Families. The tradition of research through direct observation is even richer in the sociology of the family, and the use of schedules or questionnaires has been so extensive that family research is characterized by standard measurement procedures. There are even standard measures pertaining to parental control; and there have been several systematic cross-cultural comparisons of parental control, with evidence of substantial coder's agreement even when using anthropological literature as the data source (see, e.g., Rohner and Rohner, 1981). So family research offers an enormous potential for systematic analyses of attempted control, especially in connection with attempts by children to control their siblings and their parents.

Although research on control in families would avoid the excessive aggregation problem, critics are a virtual certainty. For one thing, the belated rediscovery by sociologists of the "State" has reinforced doubts about the family's importance, doubts already widespread because of the traditional concern in sociology with society as the premier social unit. Another source of skepticism is the belief that the family has ceased to be paramount in socialization, having surrendered much of that activity to schools and popular culture.

In reply, beliefs pertaining to the decline in the family's importance rest all too much on general observations, and the proposed control research would contribute to a systematic assessment of such beliefs. True, retrospective historical studies of control in the family context would be difficult, but the arguments underlying the beliefs in question clearly suggest that the family's importance will continue to decline; and that suggestion can be assessed systematically through research focused on familial control.

Two lines of family research illustrate reduction of the level-of-aggregation problem in theories and research on control. One is research on the association between delinquency and the extent-intensity of parental control (especially Larzelere and Patterson, 1990, and Wilson, 1980.) The findings clearly indicate that the association is negative and much more robust than is suggested by conventional etiological theories, most of which reflect the traditional preoccupation of sociologists with class and such nebulous notions as anomie.

The other line of research pertains to educational achievement, especially at the primary and secondary level. One surprising finding indicates that various "objective" features of a school (e.g., ratio of teachers to pupils) are not closely associated with educational achievement (e.g., reading skill, proficiency in mathematics). It scarcely taxes credulity to interpret the finding as suggesting that educational achievement is highly contingent on the extent and efficacy of various kinds of parental control.

Questions about delinquency and educational performance should head the agenda for research on control in families. At all levels, official or unofficial, Americans appear much concerned with preventing delinquency and elevating educational achievement. Anticipating the argument that the research would have no policy implications because parental control cannot be altered, the argument itself is about control and little more than conjecture. Moreover, evidence that delinquency or educational failure is closely associated with the character of parental control would indicate that present policies are misdirected at best, for they have little bearing on parental control.

Other Kinds of Primary Groups. The nuclear family is only one of many types of primary groups.[6] As examples of other kinds, there are work teams, infantry squads, cliques, gangs, and lovers.

Sheer variety is only one of three reasons why primary groups could be strategic in work on control, apart from alleviating the level-of-aggregation problem. The second reason pertains to a particular tradition in sociological research, one of the few akin to a natural history stage. Several studies of primary groups, such as neighborhood gangs or cliques, were based on extensive direct observations (participant or otherwise) over long periods; and some of those studies are now sociological classics (e.g., Whyte, 1981 [1943]). Unfortunately, the tradition appears to have become less honored in sociology, but the literature awaits use as a general guide for natural history studies of control in primary groups. Indeed, those studies could revive a tradition, and that possibility takes on special significance if one assumes, as this writer does, that sociology suffers enormously for not having gone through a genuine natural history stage. Theorists occupied canter stage from the outset, and the field borrowed much of its vocabulary from the humanities.

The third reason for regarding primary groups as strategic is simple but controversial. At least approximations of primary groups can be created in experiments, and the experimenters can manipulate the character of control in and over those groups. Research along that line will be controversial because of the common belief among sociologists that findings of experiments on anything social cannot be generalized readily, if at all, to the "real world." Although many experimental studies in the literature bear on a control question more than their terminology indicates, the extent to which experimental research on control can blunt traditional criticisms is debatable. However, whatever the outcome, some control questions are answerable (if at all, perhaps) only through experimentation. A recent example is the experimental work of Stafford, *et al.* (1986), on punishment. The point is not just they manipulated properties of punishment (e.g., perceived certainty) that are central in the deterrence doctrine; more important, it may be that the requisite kind of manipulation cannot be realized in a "real" criminal justice system. The same may prove to be true of various other kinds of attempted control in the real world, including advertising.

Less Inclusive Properties and Dimensions
of Attempted Control

The principal variable in the present control theory (Chapters 3–7) is "extent and efficacy of attempted control." The term is a *compound* construct;

and, as indicated in Chapter 3, both extent and efficacy are extremely general properties of attempted control. While separation of the two properties is one route to narrower and perhaps more realistic control theories, there is no prospect of identifying either property as a concept and linking it (as a concept must) to an empirically applicable formula. Such would be the case even if the focus were limited to some institutionalized nexus of control, criminal law being one. No one is likely to identify either the extent or the efficacy of attempted control through criminal law as a concept rather than a construct. However, narrower control theories can be pursued by focusing on specific dimensions, such as distinctions pertaining to the frequency, range, scope, and intensity in the case of *extent* of attempted control or effectiveness, efficiency, and indispensibility in the case of the *efficacy* of attempted control.

To make the proposal more realistic, think of the "*normative scope* of attempted control through criminal law." There are two bases for identifying that term as a concept. First, it can be defined fairly clearly; it refers to the number of types of behavior for which some kind of punishment is prescribed in a particular set of criminal laws (commonly designated as a "code"). Second, a count of those types for many countries or states is feasible because criminal statutes are published (the notion of "dead laws" gives rise to a troubling question, but the answer is a matter for a theorist to decide).

Lest the prospect of focusing on normative scope of criminal law appear unimportant, contemplate two considerations. First, a multitude of informed writers (e.g., Sheleff, 1975:33) have suggested that the *expansion* of criminal law is virtually universal, a suggestion far from consistent with Durkheim's arguments (1949 [1893]) about the evolutionary course of "repressive law." Second, if there is ever a theory about the efficacy of criminal law, *normative scope* is very likely to be recognized as one determinant of the effectiveness and/or efficiency of criminal law. Given that a defensible theory about the efficacy of criminal law is certain to have definite policy implications, the normative scope dimension takes on even more importance. However, the immediate point is that there are real prospects for theories about properties or dimensions of attempted control much narrower (less inclusive) than those on the present theory.

Some Conspicuous Gaps in the Theory

Despite the theory's scope (six concepts and eleven constructs), the vast majority of sociological subjects are excluded; but it scarcely suffers in that regard when compared to sociological theories in general.[7] Nevertheless, even though an inclusive theory was not the goal, some comments on excluded subjects are appropriate; and the rationale is not just the bearing on future work concerning the theory. If excluded subjects cannot be described and thought of in terms of control, their eventual incorporation in *any* theory becomes more unlikely. Because of space limits, only some illustrative exclusions can be examined; and the comments in each case must be all too brief.

Stratification

The exclusion of stratification is all the more serious because the subject (including status attainment) is becoming sociology's paramount concern. Fortunately, there is no barrier to the extension of control theories to stratification; indeed, there are at least two paths to that end.

Conceptual Considerations. The sheer volume of research on stratification indicates that the subject is not bedeviled by conceptual problems, a genuine rarity in sociology. True, the immediate reason for the voluminous research is ready access to data (even from census reports) on income, occupations, and educational achievement; but such access in itself suggests that the term "stratification" has a fairly clear meaning.

The only conspicuous conceptual problem is indicated by the focus of stratification research on income differences and status attainment. That focus would remain too narrow even if there is an expansion of research on occupational composition (in conjunction with differential prestige) and on educational achievement. There is no alternative to a definition of stratification something like this: the amount of variation among members of some designated population as regards their enjoyment of or access to conditions that members in general value or consider desirable. Whatever the population, the members are likely to value various conditions *in addition to* money (or wealth), occupational prestige, and educational achievement. In many social units such conditions would include at least health, affection, friendship, respect, and security. Agreement on a precise and inclusive list is not really needed to justify the definition of stratification; but given the diversity of valued conditions, it is pointless to presume that the term denotes a mensurable phenomena (i.e., that it is possible to compute one value as representing all kinds or dimensions of stratification). So stratification must be identified as a construct and linked through postulates to concepts, each of which may denote some particular kind or dimension of stratification (e.g., income inequality); but those links are the office of substantive theory, not conceptualization.

The Relevance of Control. Like all sociological subjects, there are two "most general" questions about stratification, the first pertaining to its causes and the second to its consequences. There have been numerous sociological studies on each question; but apart from Marx there is no well-known theory (as distinct from a perspective or line of research) about either question, and an impressive theory is unlikely until sociologists commence describing and thinking about stratification in terms of control. The point of departure could be this generalization: in any social unit, members attach the greatest value to control itself or conditions that can be realized only through efficacious and perhaps extensive control.

Whenever the "valued condition" in question, it does not vary substantially among population members unless the members differ as to the extent and efficacy of control attempts. Think, for example, of great contrasts as regards income or wealth (whatever the form). How could such contrasts obtain if there were no correlative differences in control? The difference may be something as simple as the range of control, with the central question in comparing individuals being: what are the principal kinds of things that each individual attempts to control? An answer for a particular individual is commonly indicative of his/her occupation, and in many countries income variation stems largely from occupational differences. To illustrate, in numerous countries there is an enormous difference between the reported incomes of surgeons and farmers; and they differ sharply as to what they attempt to control, even though both are engaged primarily in biotic control.

Why does one kind of control result in a greater income than others? That question warrants serious consideration eventually, but it is grossly unrealistic to demand that a control theory of stratification (any theory, for that matter) identify ultimate causes. However, although this chapter is not even a step toward a control theory of stratification, thinking toward that end can go far beyond the control-occupation-income connections; but one additional consideration must suffice.

Why do occupations differ as to prestige? Differential income is a part of the answer, at least for many social units; but there is a related question: why is income correlated with prestige? Control itself is generally a valued condition but more for some social unit members than others (see Burger, 1992, and his earlier work on variability in the desirability of control). Moreover, social unit members perceive the interrelations among income, occupation, and control; and they bestow prestige accordingly, though again perhaps more for some members than others. Supporting evidence comes in many forms, one being Marsh's observations (1971) that indicate a substantial positive association between an occupation's prestige and the amount of control exercised by incumbents. Still other evidence is a *major exception* to the positive association between occupational prestige and income. At least at one time in the U.S., judges, priests, ministers, and rabbis enjoyed prestige beyond their incomes; but there is reason to presume that individuals in those occupations are perceived as exercising considerable control over human behavior.

Space limits preclude additional illustrations of the control-stratification connection, but two caveats are imperative. The first pertains to what the illustrations may suggest—that income-wealth differences among population members are somehow justified, ethically defensible, etc., because they stem from control. To the contrary, in at least some social units a valued condition may be enjoyed through inheritance without any effort whatever. Nonetheless, if social unit members did not differ as regards their control attempts (both extent and efficacy), there would be no real contrasts as regards inheritance. Indeed, a will in itself is an attempt at control.

The other caveat is that it oversimplifies to characterize all aspects of stratification as *consequences* of control. Some of those aspects are actually means of control in themselves. In particular, money (however defined or whatever the form) may have been a much more revolutionary means of control than casual observations suggest. Be that as it may, an impressive theory about money is unlikely without fuller recognition that money *is* a means of control.

Two Routes for Extending the Theory. The amount of stratification could be largely if not entirely a consequence of one particular major property of attempted control, but it is doubtful that any of the control properties recognized in Chapters 3–7 could be such a determinant. Extent and efficacy of control are not determinants, because neither property refers to *variation* among social unit members (a major dimension of attempted control not recognized in the theory). Stratification cannot be appreciable if there is no variation among social unit members as regards any property of attempted control, but the relations is very complex. For instance, there is no reason to presume that the enormous difference in the median income of farm laborers and neurosurgeons reflects the greater efficacy of the latter's control attempts. Instead, farm laborers and neurosurgeons engage in quite different kinds of control, though both of the same basic type (biotic). So it appears that the amount of stratification depends not on variation in the extent and efficacy of control in the abstract but, rather, variation in the specific nature of what social unit members attempt to control. Yet it could be that various dimensions of stratification, income and prestige especially, are predominantly determined by both the range and the scope of attempted control over human behavior (both formal properties). Many of Marx's argument about capitalism can be so interpreted.

Social Class. Whereas conceptual issues and problems are rare in the stratification literature, they abound in the social class literature. It must suffice to recognize three distinct approaches to the definition of social classes and the identification of class members—the objective, the subjective, and the reputational—and to note that there are six versions of the objective approach, including the Marxist version (for elaboration, see Gibbs, 1989:294–301). There is scarcely any prospect that any one of the approaches or versions will eventually triumph, because each is either extremely vague or gives rise to problems that can be solved only by embracing grossly arbitrary distinctions.

The perennial problem in delimiting social classes (defining them and identifying their members) is that the conventionally relevant variables, including ownership of the means of production, are clearly quantitative; and in the face of a continuum one can speak of social classes rather than stratification only if the distribution of population members along that continuum is *multimodal*. When it comes to income, educational achievement, and occupational prestige, there is no evidence of a conspicuous and consistent multimodal distribution of social unit members.[8] Therein lies the possibility that a conceptualization of social classes in terms of control would be more defensible than are conventional contenders. Of course, until it is possible to systematically assess variation among social unit members as regards the extent of attempted control, social classes must be treated as theoretical entities; but that treatment would be an advance over grossly arbitrary delimitations of classes in terms of occupational prestige, income, level of educational achievement, or number of employees, all of which can be subsumed under the notion of stratification.

Regardless of social class's conceptualization, the present theory (Chapters 3–7) can be extended readily by an axiom that asserts a negative association between the degree of division of labor and the *distinctiveness* of social classes. The rationale is simple, and it pertains to two of Marx's great mistakes. His conceptualization of the division of labor in terms of mental vs. manual occupations or activities is a grotesque oversimplification, and he did not recognize that a high degree of division of labor makes the "proletariat" an extremely heterogeneous category as regards occupations, income, and education. Sympathetic commentaries on Marx's treatment of the division of labor (e.g., Rattansi, 1982) have not even suggested how Marx's mistakes should be corrected.

In contemplating the addition of an axiom, the presumption is that "distinctiveness of social classes" must be a construct. Even so, the axiom can enter into the derivation of theorems without a measure (or referential formula) of distinctiveness. One illustrative possibility is a postulate that links the construct to a concept pertaining to occupational mobility (negative association), and another is a postulate linking the construct with a concept pertaining to the incidence of political violence (positive association). Whatever the postulate, it will not negate the idea of a close connection between control and social classes, including their distinctiveness. In particular, the division of labor requires extensive control over human behavior (recall Chapter 5); and it is manifested in occupational differentiation, which could be associated closely with amount of contrast in the range and scope of control among social unit members (unlike occupational differentiation, control range or scope may be a property of a social unit or of individual members).

Control and Conflict

A theory about control long the lines in Chapters 3–7 is vulnerable to two disputable interpretations. First, the theory implies that human behavior is predominantly rational. Second, the theory implies that social life is harmonious. The first interpretation is objectionable because there is no defensible extant definition of "rational"; and, whatever the definition, the interpretation perpetuates a pernicious tradition in sociology—armchair assessments of theories, meaning assessments not informed by tests. The second interpretation ignores two possibilities: (1) that certain kinds and amounts of control generate conflict and (2) that certain amounts of other kinds of control are necessary to prevent or terminate conflict.

Control Generates Conflict. The relation between control and conflict could not be clearly synthetic if control were defined in terms commonly used in connection with power, such as "overcoming resistance" or "thwarting someone's will." Moreover, the *possible* empirical relations are so varied that a thorough treatment of the subject would require a book in itself. Yet only one sociologist, Austin Turk (1982), has argued at length that control generates conflict (meaning, as here, social conflict).

Turk's argument is suggested by this quote (1982:251): "*Control* is... behavior intended to establish and maintain an unequally beneficial relationship." The blanket characterization (note the suggested imagery: control is an evil) has merit in what it implies—that resisting control transforms it into conflict. However, the argument will not really point the way to a theory about control or conflict without the pursuit of two questions in future work. First, for any given type of control, under what conditions are instances most likely to be resisted?[9] Second, under what conditions is resistance of control attempts most likely to result in conflict? Constructive pursuit of either question will require natural history studies, some retrospective and based in part on published accounts of cases of conflict, and others tracing continuous attempts at control, especially in connection with social movements (e.g., the current anti-abortion and pro-life movements in the U.S.).

The Prevention or Termination of Conflict Through Control. Far from viewing conflict as a threat to social order, many sociologists ostensibly believe that conflict contributes to social order, perhaps is necessary for it. That belief may be a reaction to the excesses of functionalism or perhaps an attempt to modify functionalism (see, especially, Coser, 1956); in any case, it ignores numerous instances where a social unit did not survive a conflict, the latest major case being Yugoslavia. Then many sociologist appear to believe that instances of conflict will end without efforts to terminate them, meaning without attempts at control. The present theme runs contrary to both beliefs in the way of three claims. First, granted that some kinds of conflict may contribute to social order, there are kinds that result in the disintegration of the social unit. Second, even highly organized attempts to prevent or terminate conflict are common, in part because those who engage in them perceive the conflict (rightly or wrongly) as socially disruptive. Third, there are conditions in which some kinds of conflict cannot be prevented or terminated without attempts at behavior control to that end.

Even if valid, the three claims are a far cry from a theory or even suitable components. They cannot be transformed into axioms, postulates, or propositions without answers to several questions, and the following three are only illustrative. First, is it defensible to assume substantial differences not only among social units but also among members of the same unit as regards perceptions of the potential consequences of conflict and, if so, what are the determinants of those differences? Second, what are the determinants of the perceived need to prevent or terminate conflicts? Third, what determines success or failure when attempts to prevent or terminate conflict are made? Truly defensible answers will require a theory, but a theory without exploratory research is a remote prospect.

The Bearing on Explanatory Mechanisms. At least three types of explanatory mechanisms should be recognized in sociology and perhaps other social and behavioral sciences (for an elaborate treatment, see Elster, 1983:15–88, or Gibbs, 1989:192–197, 280–283). They are designated here as causal, teleological (or telic), and functional; but even the labels are debatable. If only because of diverse and disputable interpretations of a teleological explanation, it might be better to use the label "purposive."[10] That use is all the more justified because in the social or behavioral sciences teleological explanation are commonly characterized by an emphasis on the human behavior's purposive quality.

Then perhaps it would be better to speak of a selective survival explanation rather than a functional explanation. The rationale is something that most functionalists in sociology ignore—a functional explanation cannot be defended unless it entails at least implicit reference to selective survival (for elaboration, see Gibbs, 1989: chp. 9).

Finally, it is difficult to identify the distinctive features of a causal explanation, the immediate reason being that the notion of causation enters into the other two types of explanation. So it must suffice to say that a causal explanation comprises at least one causal claim but without emphasis on either the purposive quality of human behavior and/or selective survival.

The foregoing problems need not be resolved to make the point that the notion of control is compatible with all three types of explanations. If the conceptualization of control in Chapter 2 is accepted, any explanation that uses the term control has both a causal and a teleological quality.[11] Then because neither humans nor human societies can survive without certain kinds and amounts of control, control notions can be used to explain some phenomena in terms of selective survival.[12] To illustrate, unless one is prepared to deny that internal conflict can eliminate a social unit, certain kinds of control may be absent in some kinds of social unit because those kinds of control generate disintegrative conflict; and certain kinds of control may be present in some kinds of social units because those kinds of control are *necessary* to prevent or terminate one or more kinds of disintegrative conflict. Of course, the argument is not a theory or even a suitable component, and it will never become either one without extensive exploratory research; but the argument is a step toward a theory.

Environmental Problems

For decades there has been an ever increasing concern with environmental problems. A truly satisfactory generic definition of that term would be difficult, but it is not needed for present purposes. The following list is by no means exhaustive, though it does include those problems that are perceived as real dangers by a multitude of writers in various countries: atmospheric pollution of such quantity and quality as to threaten human health at various places on the globe; unsustainable annual losses of topsoil; diminution of the earth's ozone layer; widespread loss of natural vegetation, rain forests in particular; widespread pollution of ground and surface water, including seas and oceans; a potential increase in global temperature that will result in cataclysmic weather changes (droughts in some regions, flooding in others) and destructive increases in sea levels.

Inanimate Energy Reconsidered. The notion of control is more relevant than any other sociological notion when contemplating research and theories on environmental problems, but space limitations dictate a focus on one basic type of attempted control. Inanimate control was chosen because it is the most immediately relevant in connection with the theory in Chapters 3–7. Indeed, the theory can be expanded by a simple generalization that purports to identify the chief source of one of the major environmental problems: among countries and for any country over time, the amount of inanimate energy use is the asymmetrical, positive, bidirectional and paramount determinant of atmospheric pollution. The generalization is consistent with the argument that environmental problems are largely if not entirely technological consequences. Though widely accepted and probably valid, the argument is informative only when reduced to generalization like the one just stated; and the generalization is all the more important because corroboration would surely indicate that a high price is being paid for an efficient technology.

The generalization's position in the theory will depend on its identification as being either a postulate or a proposition. The latter identification would require (1) a complete and clear definition of the term "atmospheric pollution" and (2) a link (transformational statement) between the term and a referential formula that promises appreciable empirical applicability. Even if various difficult questions (e.g., whether the amount of pollution is to be expressed relative to the country's surface area) could be answered such that a defensible formula can be articulated, the resources required to apply it are likely to be prohibitive. As for reducing the requisite resources by narrowing the meaning of the term, steps in that direction will raise doubts about the appropriate notion itself. For instance, it could be argued that in comparing countries the term "point of maximum atmospheric pollution" is realistic because inanimate energy use is highly localized. The counterargument is that atmospheric pollution is most serious when diffused, a condition not described by measures for particular localities.

With a view to at least partially avoiding such issues and reducing the problem of limited resources, it may prove necessary to identify "amount of atmospheric pollution" as a construct. If so, the generalization *(supra)* will be a postulate rather than a proposition, which would make it imperative to link the term with a concept rather than with an empirically applicable formula. There are various alternatives in the way of concepts, such as terms that denote particular kinds or dimensions of atmospheric pollution. For that matter, the concept could denote some alleged consequence of atmospheric pollution, such as a particular kind of mortality or morbidity (human or otherwise). Nevertheless, the choice among alternatives will be both difficult and controversial.

Whatever the eventual status of the generalization, whether identified as a postulate or a proposition, tests that bear on it are very likely to indicate only moderate predictive accuracy. Indeed, it may be that the generalization can be retained only if extended to third-order assertions, each being a claim about the conditions under which maximum or minimum predictive accuracy will obtain. Such extensions will have important policy implications, perhaps much more than does the original generalization. For instance, should it be found that the generalization's predictive accuracy is much greater in the case of geographically isolated countries, that outcome would support the argument that atmospheric pollution is truly an *international* environmental problem. Then should it be found that relation asserted by the generalization holds much better for particular types of inanimate energy sources (e.g., coal vs. petroleum), that finding would have more policy implications than does the original generalization.

Even purely exploratory research not undertaken with a view to modifying a theory could have policy implications. For instance, should it be found that the generalization's predictive accuracy is much greater for international comparisons based on, say, 1890-1910 data, that finding would undermine the argument that there are only two alternatives—greater technological efficiency and more atmospheric pollution or less technological efficiency and less atmospheric pollution.[13] Then it might be discovered that the generalization holds better for some countries over time than for others, thereby suggesting two possibilities: first, that certain geographical features make some countries less vulnerable to atmospheric pollution regardless of amount of inanimate energy use; or second, that some countries have realized much "cleaner" energy use than have others. Subsequent international comparisons could further knowledge of the kinds of technological change that reduce atmospheric pollution, perhaps with no decline in the use of inanimate energy.

Supremacy of Control over Human Behavior. Environmentalists commonly appear unaware of the basic source of resistance to their proposals. That source is not merely the threat of an employment decline in particular industries (the understandable fear of "job loss") or even a less viable economy in general. Most environmental problems stem from technology; hence, any solution will require either a change in the use of particular technological items *or* a change in technology itself. Change in amount of use is likely to reduce certain kinds of activities (e.g., foregoing vacations in the family car) and/or increase the human energy or time previously invested in the activities. Thus, less use of cars and greater use of public transportation in family vacations would increase only travel time, while use of bicycles rather than cars would increase both time and energy. A qualitative technological change designed to alleviate an environmental problem is likely to have the same consequences as a change in the amount of use of particular technological items. Thus, at least initially, abandoning petroleum powered cars (a qualitative change) is likely to increase the monetary cost of operating a private car and/or travel time per distance unit. If either increase is appreciable, a substantial decline in the use of private cars is unlikely.

The argument reduces to this generalization: any proposal to alleviate an environmental problem by changing technology or its use will be resisted because of perceived energy-time "losses," and the resistance intensity will be roughly proportionate to the perceived losses. There is no implicit denial of the importance of the reluctance to forego conventional activities; rather, with increases in requisite human energy and time, the activities will be abandoned or reduced, grudgingly in either case. Nor is the suggestion that humans react to proposals of technological change by calculating time-energy gains and losses, but humans are *sensitive* to time-energy considerations. Above all, the argument does not belittle economic consequences (actual or perceived) of technological change. Although economists are not prone to emphasize the connection, technology is the foundation of any economy; therefore, techno-logical changes, particularly the kinds commonly proposed in connection with environmental problems, influence the employment rate, real income, and the standard of living.

Because resistance to virtually any proposed means for alleviating an environmental problem is certain, the *ultimate* concern is behavior control rather than inanimate control or biotic control. No one questions that some resistance to environmental programs can be overcome (at least in anything like a liberal democracy) only through law, regulatory law in particular. However, the problem is not just promoting compliance with environmental laws; overcoming resistance to enactments may be even a greater challenge. Be that as it may, no sociological notion rivals control when it comes to relevance in research and theories about regulatory law.

The notion of control is especially relevant even when coping with the difficulty of defining regulatory law. Those difficulties are rarely confronted in the literature, and four questions must suffice to indicate the nature of the difficulties (for a more elaborate but still too brief treatment, see Gibbs,

1989:405–406). First, what is the difference, if any, between regulatory law and sumptuary law? Second, were the various legal controls over production and consumption in feudal England regulatory law? Third, to what extent and in what sense, if any, does legal coercion or its threat of it distinguish regulatory law from other types of law, criminal law in particular? Fourth, can regulatory law exist in a country where the state owns the means of production?

The notion of control is relevant in defining regulatory law not merely because the enactment and administration of regulatory law is an attempt at control. After all, the same may be said of criminal law. However, accepting that enactment and/or administration of regulatory law (including enabling legislation) necessarily involves the participation of experts or authorities, then two types of social control are especially relevant when conceptualizing regulatory law but not various other types of law, criminal law in particular. Those two are (1) modulative social control, as when legislators use the influence of an expert or authority in a particular industry; and (2) prelusive social control, as when legislators solicit judgements from an expert or authority as to whom or what should be controlled.

The notion of control is relevant beyond the obvious conceptual link (i.e., regulatory law is an attempt at control). If a theory includes the division of labor as a construct variable, Durkheim (1933) set the scene for this axiom: among political units or for a political unit over time, the degree of division of labor is the asymmetrical, positive, bidrectional, and paramount cause of the amount of restitutive law.[14] However, what Durkheim designated as "restitutive law" should be redesignated as "regulatory law," if only to avoid conceptual problems that Durkheim never confronted (for elaboration, see Gibbs, 1993a). Recognize also that Durkheim made no use of control notions because he did not depict the division of labor as creating problems that legislators attempt to solve by creating regulatory agencies. Instead, Durkheim wrote as though legislators are robots, mere reflections of the "collective conscience" and seemingly unconcerned with controlling human behavior.

Placating Interpretive Sociologists

Interpretive sociologists—symbolic interactionists, phenomenologists, and ethnomethodologists in particular—are likely to view the theory in Chapters 3–7 as contrary to their brand of sociology. They are not known for explicit generalizations, let alone formally stated theories, nor are they prone to grant the quantitative character of most sociological variables (constructs or concepts). Nonetheless, if attempted control is conceptualized along the lines in Chapter 2, no control theory will be truly contrary to interpretive sociology.

Although any identification of interpretive sociology's maxims is disputable, no one would deny some merit in this candidate: sociological terminology must be such that it can be used to interpret particular human actions. Advocates of interpretive sociology argue that an interpretation must be compatible with actors' perceptions and that most of sociology's major terms (e.g., anomie, social integration, class conflict, and social structure) fail that criterion.

What has been said about major sociological terms does not extend to control (again, though, as conceptualized in Chapter 2). That claim cannot be substantiated by a mere reading of the theory in Chapters 3–7. The claim is more nearly supported by a simple assertion: each premise expresses a conclusion reached by thinking about phenomena in terms of control. That assertion cannot be corroborated or refuted because it is private, and it has significance only in the way of a suggestion—that other sociologist can think about subjects that interest them in terms of control. However, the suggestion is not limited to the formulation of theories, and it does bear on the maxim *(supra)* of interpretive sociology. Surely thinking about and describing a particular human action in terms of control is an interpretation of that action.

Avoiding a Perennial Dilemma

Apart from recognition of dimensions of predictive power other than predictive accuracy, there is a noteworthy argument against making tests of sociological theories decisive. Any sociological theory is based on various presuppositions or assumptions that are not explicit components of the theory; indeed, the theorist may be at most only dimly aware of them, and it is doubtful that all of them can be made truly explicit (i.e., fully expressed).

To illustrate, because Durkheim was at great pains to deny the relevance of internal behavior (perception, intention, motives, etc.), his argument (1933) that increases in population density cause increases in the division of labor ostensibly *presumes* selective survival. A society is more likely to disintegrate from competition that escalates into lethal conflict if the division of labor does not (for one reason or another) increase more or less concomitant with and proportionate to increases in population density. That argument is quite different from one that postulates recognition by social unit members (at least elite members) of a need for the division of labor as population density increases, but Durkheim never made the assumption of selective survival explicit.

The point is not that a presumption is somehow less valid if left implicit, nor that implicit presumptions somehow invalidate a theory. Thus, some components of the present theory (Chapters 3–7) are based on the assumption that occupations are first and foremost regular means by which the incumbents attempt to control; but that assumption is not made explicit in any of the premises or theorems. Again, though, any theory is a study in implicit assumptions or presuppositions.

Advocates of interpretive sociology and the *new* "received view" in the philosophy of science would agree, perhaps with relish; and it would be difficult to exaggerate the importance of the subject, if only because tests of a theory cannot bear on all of its presuppositions or even on all of its auxiliary assumptions (see, especially, Harding, 1976). Yet two distinct possibilities should be recognized. First, theories differ as to the plausibility of their presuppositions or assumptions, explicit or implicit. Second, a theory's plausibility is largely determined by its central notion.[15] The presuppositions or assumptions of any control theory are much more plausible because the notion of control can be used to describe and think about all or virtually all of human behavior. As a case in point, suppose there are two contending theories about robbery, one of which implicitly depicts robbery as "anomic behavior" and the other implicitly depicts robbery as "control behavior." Who could confidently assess the plausibility of the first depiction, and who would deny that robbery is attempted control?[16] The point is not that theories should be assessed on the basis of plausibility rather than tests; but it is ludicrous to claim that a test of a sociological theory bears on all implicit presuppositions or assumptions, and no less ludicrous to deny that sociologists commonly assess a theory on the basis of plausibility and entirely apart from reported tests. So the only issue is the relative emphasis on the two bases for assessing theories. The argument is not that the notion of control somehow eliminates the need for tests of theories; rather, it makes implicit assumptions or presuppositions more plausible than does any contending notion.

Notes

1. The point bears on contending candidates for sociology's central notion, such as values, norms, conflict, interaction, social relations, and forces of production. None of those notions have been conceptualized so as to facilitate the formulation of theories at varying levels of heterogeneity.

2. This problem haunts research on any type of deterrence, but there are special problems in connection with each type. Comparisons of social units with regard to perceptual properties of punishment (e.g., the probability of execution for a capital crime as perceived by potential offenders) and in connection with general deterrence require enormous resources. Even in the case of objective properties of legal punishment, there are horrendous complexities concerning the temporal character of the relation between those properties and the crime rate (see, e.g., Chamlin., et al., 1992). As for specific deterrence, there is a substantial association between previous criminal history and the severity of sentence on last conviction; and while that association should be taken into account when conducting research on specific deterrence, there are ethical reasons why it cannot be eliminated by a full randomization of punishments as regards severity.

3. Whatever the major dimension or subdimension of attempted control (e.g., extent vs. efficacy, effectiveness vs. efficiency, scope vs. range), there are two quite different questions. First, what are the causes of variation in the dimension? Second, what are the consequences of that variation? There are several theories about the causes of variation in the severity of legal punishments (see Grabosky's survey, 1984), and there could be a corresponding theory about the determinants of variation in the extent of advertising.

However, the deterrence doctrine pertains to the effectiveness of legal punishments, and the prospects of a synthesis are greater if a theory about advertising also pertains only to effectiveness.

4. The decline of work on the subject was conspicuous even 25 years ago. For example, there is a section on propaganda in the *International Encyclonedia of the Social Sciences* (Smith, 1968), but less than 10 percent of the cited literature was published (originally) after 1963. Then note that there is no section on propaganda in *The Social Science Encyclopedia* (Kuper and Kuper, 1985).

5. The macro-micro distinction is invoked here with reservations. Sociologists treat the distinction uncritically, and it appears destined to remain either vague or arbitrary; but the distinction is useful if treated as pertaining to average or typical social unit size (number of members in particular).

6. The traditional distinction between a primary group and a secondary group is that all members of a primary group interact on a face-to-face basis.That distinction entails more arbitrariness than appears to be the case, but that problem is not pertinent for present purposes.

7. When discursively stated sociological theories are restated formally, commonly it becomes obvious that their scope is far less than the discursive version suggests.

8. Even in the case of ownership of the means of production, the evidence is disputable, especially if it is recognized (as avowed Marxist's appear loath to do) that there is no accepted and empirically applicable definition of the means of production and that the self-employed should not be ignored. Nonetheless, it is not difficult to see why Marxists cling to the belief that social classes are distinguished by ownership of the means of production. The connection between ownership and control alone justifies the belief, but control is the broader and much more important notion. Ownership of the means of production does not distinguish employers and the self-employed; rather, the distinction lies in control over the behavior of others, whether slaves, serfs, or employees. For a much more elaborate treatment of these subjects, see Gibbs, 1989:293–304.

9. Note the bearing on control efficacy (effectiveness in particular), assuming that resistance is conducive to failures in control attempts. Indeed, even anticipation of resistance may discourage a control attempt. Such observations are not suitable components of a theory (i.e., an axiom, postulate, or proposition), but they are steps in that direction.

10. For instance, Catton (1966) alleges that a teleological explanation reverses the usual temporal sequence in that it has the effect preceding its cause.

11. Such is not the case if control is defined without any reference to internal human behavior (perception, beliefs, etc.). However, one criticism of that kind of definition deserves repeating because of its special bearing on explanatory mechanism. Briefly, if the term "control" has no necessary connection with the internal behavior, why not speak of causation or influence and thereby avoid conceptual redundancy?

12. The possibilities are even greater than they may appear, because selective survival need not be interpreted as literally a life or death matter. After all, no one is puzzled when reference is made to a particular marriage, business firm, or occupation as surviving or not surviving.

13. Of course, the finding would not be evidence of a decline in atmospheric pollution in this century, but it might point to ways of decreasing atmospheric pollution without a decrease in technological efficiency.

14. The term "political units" refers to any territorial unit that is a governmental entity; but for reasons explicated in Chapter 4, the unit term should be "countries" if the premise asserts a relation between the division of labor and either occupational differentiation or industry differentiation.

15. What of a theory not based on a central notion? The plausibility of its implicit assumptions or presuppositions is likely to suffer enormously.

16. Restating the question: who would know how to test any statement about anomie, and who would think it necessary to test the statement that robbery is a kind of control?

Appendix: A Formal Mode of Theory Construction for Sociology

A mode of theory construction is a set of rules for stating a theory, with those rules pertaining to the theory's form rather than its content. In the discursive mode the rules are nothing more than the conventions of a natural language (e.g., English, German). By contrast, some or all of the rules of a formal mode were designed for stating theories; as such, the rules transcend natural language conventions.

Subsequent comments further clarify the discursive-formal distinction, but sociologists scarcely need further clarification. Virtually all sociological theories were stated in accordance with the discursive mode. While the substantive terminology of those theories is technical, their *form* does not differ from that of a novel. Hence, should "discursive" appear inappropriately pejorative, "conventional" can be substituted without altering the principal argument: the discursive mode is defective in so many respects that sociologists will never realize effective consensus in assessing theories unless they adopt formal theory construction. However, the use of a formal mode is only *necessary* for realizing effective consensus; and the principal argument (*supra*) entails two assumptions: first, progress in any scientific field is largely a matter of an increase in the number of accepted theories or in the range and scope of accepted theories; and, second, such progress requires effective consensus in assessments of contending theories.

Before prescribing a particular a formal mode of theory construction, several caveats are in order. One is a denial of any necessary relevance for fields other than sociology. The mode was designed to reduce sources of dissensus in assessments of theories, and some of those sources may be peculiar to sociology. For that reason alone, it will not do to look to an advanced science (e.g., physics) or to the philosophy of science for a mode of theory construction.

Another caveat relates to subsequent commentaries (commonly in footnotes) on issues in sociology. The comments are distinct from the mode of theory construction itself, and they are made only to further its understanding. Yet it is not assumed that the mode will somehow resolve sociology's most controversial and crucial issue, one introduced by this question: what are the appropriate criteria for assessing sociological theories? The mode presumes that a sociological theory should be judged solely by reference to its predictive power *relative to that of contending theories.* Many sociologists will reject that presumption, perhaps even if they recognize that testability and predictive accuracy are only two of seven dimensions of predictive power. Nonetheless, the foremost rationale for formal theory construction is its furtherance of assessments of theories by reference to their predictive power. So if a sociologist is determined to assess sociological theories in terms of presuppositions, preconceptions, or ideological considerations, he/she should cling tenaciously to the discursive mode of theory construction. That mode is truly essential for rhetoric, which from the field's beginning has been the principal conventional medium for assessing sociological theories.

Still another caveat: a formal mode of theory construction is not a logic of discovery, presuming that there can be such a thing. Instead, any formal mode is irrelevant unless a theorist has some ideas—the content of a prospective theory—and needs some format to state those ideas so as to clarify their logical interrelations and bring evidence to bear on them. So a formal mode does not even suggest how sociologists come to have ideas.

The penultimate caveat is that the prescribed mode cannot be used unless the theorist's ideas pertain to quantitative properties of social units. Yet it is not claimed that the *qualitative* properties are less important, and sociology truly needs a formal mode for stating qualitative theories. Nevertheless, the quantitative-qualitative issue is a red herring. It diverts attention from the question about appropriate criteria for assessing theories (*supra*), and for that reason alone the issue cannot have a constructive outcome.

Finally, there are contending formal modes in sociology (for references and a brief discussion of some contrasts, see Gibbs, 1993b), and their existence indicates disagreements as to what a formal mode should comprise. Nevertheless, because *any* extant formal mode would be a constructive departure from convention, differences among contending formal modes are less important than they may appear.

Distinguishing the Two Principal
Parts of a Theory

Most sociologists give at least lip service to testing theories, but some components of virtually any theory are untestable. In particular, the notion of a "real" definition notwithstanding, definitions are untestable; and perhaps in no field is the meaning of all major terms so conventional that they need not be defined when used in stating a theory. But for present purposes the most relevant notion is broader than a definition. An *analytic statement* is either true or false solely as a consequence of the very meaning of its constituent terms.[1] Connversely, while a *synthetic statement* also may be true or false, it is neither solely as a consequence of the very meaning of its constituent terms.The analytic-synthetic distinction is pertinent here if only because all sociological theories ostensibly comprise some analytic statements; hence, some components of those theories are not testable, *not even in principle*. The emphasis indicates that a statement may be untestable for reasons unrelated to observability, mensurability, technical problems, ethical-legal barriers, or limited research resources. Thus, none of those considerations enter into the judgment that "any two members of a primary group have a social relation" is analytic and, therefore, untestable. But the analytic-synthetic distinction is not exhaustive; some types of statements (e.g., imperative, interrogative) are neither analytic nor synthetic. For that matter, some synthetic statements are testable only in principle, meaning that the considerations in question (e.g., limited research resources) make a test impractical if not impossible. Contemplate the practical problems in attempting to falsify or corroborate this synthetic statement: the frequency of social interaction during the past calendar year was greater in San Francisco than in Cleveland.

Endless examples could be given to demonstrate that it is difficult and debatable to apply the analytic-synthetic distinction to statements in the typical sociological theory. Two quotes must suffice (for others, see Gibbs, 1972:82).

> To the extent that a society is stable, adaptation type I—conformity to both cultural goals and institutionalized means—is the most common and widely diffused. (Merton, 1957:141)
>
> Power is the resource that permits an individual or group to coordinate the efforts of many others, and legitimate authority is the resource that makes possible a stable organization of such coordinated effort on a large scale. (Blau, 1964:222)

Difficulties in applying the analytic-synthetic distinction should not be equated with doubts about the distinction itself. The naysaying commenced primarily with Quine (e.g., 1960), and it is much in keeping with the flowering of rabid antipositivism in the social sciences and philosophy since then. Moreover, Quine's argument can be interpreted at least two ways. If interpreted as meaning that *no* statement can be labeled incontrovertibly as either analytic or synthetic, then an army of scientists have wasted much of their life attempting to corroborate or falsify some particular empirical generalization; and the assertion "throughout 1990, Chicago, Illinois, was spatially larger than Muleshoe, Texas" is no more or less testable (subject to refutation, susceptible to falsification, etc.) than is "two plus three equals five." Yet if Quine is interpreted as arguing that the analytic-synthetic distinction is neither somehow objectively given nor indisputable in all instances, only the incorrigibly naive would voice misgivings. Indeed, if so interpreted, Quine's argument underscores the need for sociologists to state theories in such a way that there can be no doubt as to which of the theory's constituent statements are *to be taken* as analytic and which as synthetic. There can be no doubt if two major parts of a theory are set apart and labeled.

The Intrinsic Part vs. the Extrinsic Part

It is difficult to imagine a sociological theory that is testable even though bereft of definitions (i.e., the field's conventions are such that definitions are not needed); and it is commonly argued that a scientific or empirical theory—the exclusive concern here—necessarily comprises at least one synthetic statement (see Gibbs, 1990, for a treatment of the issue). So it is appropriate to designate one of the two principal parts of a theory as "intrinsic" and the other "extrinsic." The distinction is clarified by subsequent examinations of each part's content (see Glossary, pp. 357–359, for explicit definitions of the formal mode's principal terms); so a few general observations will suffice.

The Intrinsic Part. An empirical or scientific theory is commonly defined (for elaboration, see Gibbs, 1990) such that some or all of its constituent synthetic statements are logically interrelated generalizations about at least one *infinite* class of events or things, meaning a class with no temporal and/or spatial limits. Accepting such a definition, it is insufficient to say that a theory's intrinsic part comprises synthetic statements, for some synthetic statements pertain to events or things that are or were limited both in space and time (e.g., the French revolution). The identification of such a synthetic statement as singular, unique, or instantial indicates that it refers to a *finite* class of events or things.

The prescribed formal mode presumes that all intrinsic statements (i.e., those in a theory's intrinsic part) are empirical generalizations, each of which pertains to at least one infinite class. However, it suffices to characterize the intrinsic statements as synthetic, because that identification signifies that the theorist must regard all of the statements as true (or valid) even though it is logically possible for them to be false (or invalid). As for the argument that a theory should be defined such that it *may* comprise *only* analytic statements, the issue cannot be resolved (for elaboration, see Gibbs, 1990). Nonetheless, the prescribed formal mode presupposes that a theory comprises at least two interrelated synthetic statements; so an isolated empirical generalization, even one about infinite classes, does not qualify as a theory.

The Extrinsic Part. This part cannot be described as comprising only definitions; it comprises also formulas and stipulations of requisite *kinds* of data, including an acquisition procedure, and statements about test procedure. Indeed, if a theory makes assertions about quantitative properties (commonly identified as "variables"), defensible tests are unlikely if the extrinsic part does not include formulas and data stipulations.

The label "extrinsic" does not mean inessential; far from it. Again, although one can imagine a field in which all terms have a sufficiently clear meaning without definitions, that condition is totally alien to sociology.

Statement of the Rule

The foregoing is summarized by Rule 1: *In formulating a theory, the theorist must identify each constituent statement as being a component of the theory's intrinsic part or a component of the theory's extrinsic part.* There are various ways to realize such identifications, the most feasible being the literal physical (spatial) division of the theory into two labeled parts.

Issues. Rule 1 is hardly a convention of the English language, but advocates of discursive theory construction are likely to argue that the rule is inconsequential. Those who so argue have never struggled with a discursive sociological theory in an attempt to determine which component statements are analytic and which synthetic. Surely compliance with the rule may avoid confusion, and compliance cannot be harmful. True, a theorist may be unable to decide whether a particular statement is analytic or synthetic; but, if so, the theory's promulgation would be premature.

If one is determined to assess theories without regard to tests, Rule 1 will appear to be only another burden for theorists. As for the objection that compliance will not insure defensible tests, even contemplating a test is pointless unless the theory's synthetic statements can be identified confidently.

Reducing Ambiguity. Compliance with Rule 1 will not engender sterile arguments about either the analytic-synthetic distinction or its application in particular instances. The rule enables the theorist to say, in effect: treat these statements as analytic and treat those statements as synthetic. The theorist's judgment may be debatable, but the prospect of sterile arguments are even greater when a theorist ignores the analytic-synthetic distinction.

Nevertheless, Rule 1 and many that follow run contrary to a theme that has come to have a large following in the scholarly world: because ambiguity, subjectivity, and vagueness are inevitable, efforts to reduce them are feckless. The logic of the theme appears to be something like this: if something cannot be totally overcome, then wallow in it.

Principal Components of the Intrinsic Part:
Types of Terms

Although terms are elements of a theory, none expresses an assertion, claim, or generalization. So statements are the basic components of a theory; but *some* kinds of synthetic statements are untestable, with testability being primarily contingent on the character of a statement's constituent terms. Consequently, the proposed mode of theory construction prescribes a particular typology of statements *based on* a particular typology of terms (again, see Glossary, pp. 357–359, when needed).

Types of Property Terms: Constructs

When a theorist uses a construct in stating a theory, he/she may or may not define the term; and if left undefined, the construct is a primitive term.[2] Should the construct be defined, the theorist may not regard the definition as complete or clear. Described otherwise, the theorist does not claim that the term or its definition is empirically applicable, and that may be the case even though the theorist regards the term's definition as being clear and complete (i.e., a clear and complete definition is only necessary for empirical applicability).

The Notion of Empirical Applicability. The notion is central because, assuming an intelligible syntax, a synthetic statement's testability depends entirely on the empirical applicability of the statement's constituent terms. As regards the empirical applicability of a term *or* its definition, the ultimate concern is the amount of congruence realized when independent investigators use the term to identify or describe the same events or things.[3] Briefly illustrating, suppose someone formulates a definition of "upper class" and two sociologists independently attempt to apply the term, so defined, to the same list of individuals. In each application the investigator makes inquiries to answer this question: given the definition, is this individual upper class? Now suppose that, even though working independently, the investigators never disagree in their answers.[4] If so, the agreement in identifying class members would be evidence of the definition's empirical applicability, though not conclusive.

Despite occasional suggestions here to the contrary, empirical applicability is virtually always a matter of degree. However, a theorist may treat a term as though not empirically applicable to any degree, which may be the case. Additionally and obviously, the outcome of future examinations of a definition's empirical applicability cannot be known; but if a critic demands certainty, he/she should have no truck with the notion of empirical applicability or theories or even science.

Although congruence is the ultimate consideration, two other dimensions of empirical applicability have priority. First, no definition can be applied if incomprehensible; hence, *intelligibility* is absolutely essential for the application of a definition. Second, even if a definition is intelligible, investigators may report that its application is not *feasible*.

Feasibility judgments reflect an assessment of the field's research resources, but monetary cost is only one consideration. Application of a definition may require instruments and/or aptitudes (skills, expertise, etc.) that few if any possess, and various kinds of legal or ethical barriers (e.g., respect for privacy) may preclude research. Such facets of *feasibility* preclude a simple characterization of constructs as terms that denote unobservable phenomena. Assume that instances of social interaction are observable; even so, try to imagine a definition that would make "national volume of social interaction" empirically applicable.[5] So even though a theorist may realize a complete and clear definition of "volume of social interaction," he/she is not likely to believe that the definition can be applied to countries or even smaller social units. That limitation would force identification of the term as a construct when using it in stating a theory. Finally, whereas congruence is closely associated with the conventional notion of reliability, the feasibility dimension of empirical applicability is distinct from reliability.

Empirical applicability is relevant whether the term in question denotes something qualitative or quantitative. The paramount question in particular qualitative cases: is the event or thing an instance of the class denoted by the term? The question pertains to identification and calls for a categorical response ("yes" or "no"), but there is another consideration when extending the notion of empirical applicability to a quantitative property of an entity. In that case both identification and description are relevant, and measurement is a kind of description; but independent investigators are not likely to report congruent values (measures, quantities, etc.) as descriptions of a particular property of a particular entity unless they have applied the same formula to the same kind of data or observations. Thus, two investigators are extremely unlikely to report the same residential population density value for Chicago as of a particular date if they have used different formulas and applied them to different kinds of data.

Any quantitative property term (e.g., crude birth rate) in the theory's intrinsic part can be linked to a formula in the theory's extrinsic part, but the linkage is whimsical unless the theorist regards the term's definition as complete and clear. Moreover, the notion of empirical applicability extends to formulas as well as terms and definitions. As for terms, the immediate consideration concerning constructs is introduced by Rule 2: *If an intrinsic term denotes a property of instances of some designated class of events or things but the theorist does not assert that the term is sufficiently empirically applicable, it must be designated as a construct.*

Rule 2 and those that follow do not mean that terminological distinctions are objectively given. Specifically, whether a given term is identified as a construct depends entirely on the theorist's judgment, but the judgment has crucial consequences. If the theorist identifies all of the theory's property terms as constructs, he/she tacitly admits that the theory is untestable.

Another Rule. Still another way to characterize a construct is suggested by Rule 3: *A quantitative property term in a theory's intrinsic part must be identified as a construct if it is not linked in that part to a symbol denoting a formula in the extrinsic part of the theory, one which the theorist asserts to be sufficiently empirically applicable.* The possibility that a construct may be left undefined is irrelevant; and even if defined, the theorist may not regard the definition as complete and clear. Those considerations suggest the most common reason why the theorist cannot link a construct with a symbol (a referential) that denotes a formula in the theory's extrinsic part.

The following four examples of constructs are consistent with Rule 3 (*supra*). However, that point cannot be fully understood without examining a simple illustrative theory (*infra*) in which there are examples of constructs.

First Example: Population Concentration. Assuming that the term refers to residential patterns, "population concentration" can be defined such that its meaning is regarded as complete and clear. It is the reciprocal of the mean, median, or modal distance between each occupied place of residence in some designated territorial unit and all others in that unit at some designated time point. So defined, the term can be linked with a formula; and if it were feasible for independent investigators to apply the formula to each of several territorial units, there is every reason to anticipate substantial congruence of the reported values, especially if the meaning of some of the key words in the definition were clarified through auxiliary definitions (e.g., households in the same building are separate residences).[6] But it is pointless to stipulate a formula and requisite kinds of data, because sociology's resources at present funding levels would not permit an application to a large city, let alone a country.

The term "population concentration" illustrates the importance of *feasibility* as a dimension of empirical applicability. Eventually the field's research resources may be such that population concentration need not be identified as a construct; nevertheless, formulating theories on the basis of what sociological researchers may be able to do eventually only adds to the mountain of untestable theories.

Second Example: The Degree of Division of Labor. Durkheim's (1933) conceptualization of the division of labor is defective in several respects. Far from offering an explicit definition, Durkheim merely suggested that the degree of division of labor is reflected in the number of occupations.[7] The immediate objection is that, Watson (1929) notwithstanding, the notion of an occupation scarcely applies to foraging populations (e.g., the nomadic hunter–gatherers of the Kalahari desert). Adult members do not engage regularly in a particular kind of sustenance activity throughout the working day and from one season to the next, let alone some kind that is socially recognized as differentiating members (i.e., such that there are occupational titles).

Even in the case of literate social units, it will not do to define the division of labor in terms of number of occupations (or industries); and the primary problem would not be remedied entirely by recognizing a dimension of occupational differentiation that Durkheim ignored—the *distribution* of population members among occupations. It is imperative to recognize also the relevance of functional interdependence. The division of labor is not just a matter of differentiation; it also involves human symbiosis. Accordingly, a definition that applies to foragers as well as to countries and does not ignore relevant dimensions must be something like this: the degree of division of labor refers to the amount of differences among members of some designated population as regards their sustenance activities at some designated time point and the related amount of functional interdependence among the members at that time.

Even if the foregoing definition could be construed as complete and clear, no one has suggested a related formula. Moreover, should anyone ever advance an intelligible formula, research resources would not permit extensive application, if any at all.

Third Example: Organic Solidarity. Following Durkheim, sociologists think of the division of labor and organic solidarity as related, but the connection scarcely clarifies the latter notion's meaning. Durkheim (1933) suggested that organic solidarity is based on functional interdependence, but in what sense, if any, is the relation between the division of labor and organic solidarity *synthetic*? Whatever the answer, the term "organic solidarity" is not needed to state Durkheim's theory about the division of labor (see Gibbs, 1993a).

The relation between the division of labor and organic solidarity is synthetic if the latter notion is defined as the amount of functional interdependence *perceived* by social unit members. Yet there is scarcely any prospect of a measurement procedure and even less prospect of the research resources needed to apply it. For that matter, Durkheim's followers are likely to balk, rightly recognizing that the definition is contrary to his rejection of what he took as psychological notions.

Fourth Example: Political Stability. When contemplating the possibility of an empirical relation between organic solidarity and political stability, the immediate problem is conceptual. The difficulties and issues may be greater in the case of political stability than for organic solidarity. Political stability is scarcely a technical term, and it is used frequently by scholars, social scientists, and journalists without an explicit definition. Yet the usage does suggest that various terms or phrases could be relevant in defining political stability, such as: lawful, orderly, socially accepted, peaceful, and institutionalized. Many of those terms or phrases are vague; and, more serious, each suggests only a partial definition of political stability, with seemingly infinite possibilities as to completion of the definition. The possibilities appear infinite even when attempting a *negative* definition of political stability, meaning by reference to the *rarity* of riots, political protests, assassinations, revolutions, rebellions, insurgencies, civil wars, terrorism, and so forth. The "and so forth" is, of course, one of the conceptual problems.

Given the foregoing, an argument could be made for leaving "political stability" undefined; and that option illustrates how a mode of formal theory

288

construction can ease the theorist's burdens. A theorist need not struggle to
define a construct, and an eventual definition is always a possibility. Indeed,
uses of an undefined construct point the way to its definition.

how does it metastasize.

Types of Property Terms: Concepts

In a sense, a concept is the opposite of a construct. When using a term the
theorist identifies it as a concept only if he/she has defined the term and regards
the definition as complete and clear, which is a necessary for asserting that the
definition is *sufficiently* empirically applicable (i.e., the theory's predictive
accuracy will not be exceeded by that of a contending theory because the
definition's empirical applicability is less than maximum). However, if the term
denotes a quantitative property, it cannot be identified as a concept unless
linked with a formula and stipulations as to requisite kinds of data, including
an acquisition procedure (henceforth, unless indicated otherwise, the formula
and related data stipulations are considered inseparable). The linkage itself is
made in the theory's intrinsic part, and the formula appears only in the extrinsic part.

Statement of the Rule. The prescribed identification is formulated as Rule
4: *A quantitative property term in the theory's intrinsic part is identified by the
theorist as a concept if and only if it is linked in that part with a symbol that
denotes a formula in the theory's extrinsic part, a formula which the theorist
asserts to be sufficiently empirically applicable.* To simplify, the rule makes no
reference to two requirements: (1) that the concept be defined and (2) that the
theorist regards the definition as complete and clear. Unless those
requirements are met a link between the term and the formula is bound to
be whimsical.

The example concepts that follow are constituents of the illustrative
formally stated theory (*infra*). They were selected especially for that use,
and in the illustrative theory each concept is linked to one of the example constructs (*supra*).

The First Example: Degree of Urbanization. It is the percentage of some
designated population who at some designated time point resided in some
designated type of urban unit. The definition is construed as complete and
clear, but auxiliary definitions of an urban unit and the three types—cities,
urban areas, and metropolitan areas—are needed to link the concept with a
formula and data stipulations.

The emphasis on formulas does not imply that only quantitative concepts
are important. All manner of important terms in sociology's vocabulary—
society, cities, interaction, social relation—are prime concept candidates
even though commonly construed as entailing qualitative distinctions. Both
qualitative concepts and quantitative concepts are asserted to be empirically

applicable, but in the case of a quantitative concept the assertion is warrantless unless the term is linked with a formula. The point is not made merely to clarify. Those sociologists who decry "quantification" are especially likely to reject formal theory construction, but there is no necessary connection. For that matter, the carping about quantification is a red herring. It conceals an indifference if not hostility to assessing theories solely in terms of tests and predictive power, the very kind of assessment that is facilitated by formal theory construction.

Second Example: Degree of Industry Differentiation. The term is defined as the number of industries in some designated population at some designated time point and the uniformity or evenness of the distribution of population members among those industries at that time, excluding those members who cannot be described as working or seeking work in a particular industry. That definition is construed as complete and clear, but those qualities are only necessary for identifying the term as a concept. Additionally, the term must be linked to a formula, one asserted to be empirically applicable; but the link is intuitive unless the theorist regards the term's definition as complete and clear.

The possibility of an alternative is not denied, nor is there ever any need for a theorist to demonstrate that the definition in question is complete and clear in some objective sense. To be sure, if a theorist identifies terms cavalierly and/or links them to formulas whimsically, the theory's predictive accuracy (perhaps even its testability) will suffer; but it is unrealistic to demand that the theorist justify his/her identification of a quantitative term as a concept *beyond linking it with a formula.*

Third Example: Political Violence Death Rate. This concept is defined as the number of deaths from political violence of members of some designated population over some designated period as a ratio to the average daily number of members over that period. The phrase "deaths from political violence" means all deaths caused by coercive actions taken to maintain or alter a political arrangement or situation. Such auxiliary definitions clarify; but when the term denotes a quantitative property, as here, there is really only one question: is the definition such that the theorist can link the term to an empirically applicable formula?

The primacy of the concept-formula link stems from the prescribed procedure (*infra*) for testing theories. To follow that procedure, investigators need not fully understand the theory's constructs and concepts; but they must understand the formulas.

Types of Property Terms: Referentials

A referential is an acronym in the theory's intrinsic part that denotes a formula in the extrinsic part. Were it not cumbersome to introduce formulas in the intrinsic part, referentials would not be needed. Nonetheless, because a concept is connected with a referential in the theory's intrinsic part, it is, unlike a construct, linked with a formula (i.e., through a referential).

Given that the connection between a referential and the formula is purely analytic, a synthetic relation between a concept and its referential may appear impossible. For that matter, it may appear misleading to identify a referential as a property term, meaning that it refers to characteristics of entities. In reply, a referential denotes not only a particular formula but also the values that are computed *when the formula is applied correctly*. The concept also denotes values, in the last example the *true* (actual) number of deaths per capita from political violence. That number is unknown and unknowable, but the relation between it and the value denoted by the referential (the value that would be computed by correct application of the formula to the prescribed kind of data) is not analytic, meaning not true by definition. The relation can never be known with anything like certainty, but the intrinsic statement that connects a concept and a referential has a synthetic character.

Statement of the Rule. The foregoing terminology and notions are necessary to understand Rule 5: *Each constituent concept of a theory must be connected in the theory's intrinsic part with a referential.* The rule can be fully understood only in conjunction with a subsequent rule about transformational statements, each of which connects a concept and a referential.

The prescribed mode of construction applies only when the theory's property terms denote quantitative characteristics, and some of the mode's rules reflect that limitation. If the mode applied to theories about qualitative characteristics (i.e., no quantitative variables), there would be no referentials. There would be data stipulations and other components of a prescribed test procedure in the extrinsic part, just as there are in a quantitative theory, but no formulas (hence, no need for referentials).

Types of Terms: Unit Terms and Unit Phrases

Just as a sentence without a subject is incomplete, so is an intrinsic state-ment without a unit term. Consider this phrase: the greater the per capita income, the less the interpersonal violence rate. Both property terms suggest that the generalization does *not* apply to individuals, but what kind of entities should be compared when to testing it? There are various possibilities—neigh-borhoods, cities, metropolitan areas, and countries being some; but it taxes credulity to presume that any sociological generalization holds for all types of units, let alone that holds equally well for all types.

An explicit unit term in an intrinsic statement is not sufficient clarification, because there are two basic types of comparisons: (1) cross-sectional, where two or more instances of some type of unit (e.g., organizations, countries) are compared and (2) the longitudinal, where what is taken as the same unit is compared at two or more time points or periods. If only to avoid ambiguity, an intrinsic statement must indicate the relevant comparison. Both types may be relevant, but avoiding ambiguity is not the only consideration. It could be that the theorist believes that the relation in question holds only or much better for one type of comparison; and in that sense the unit phrase, which includes the unit term, qualifies the generalization.

Statement of Two Rules. The subject is especially pertinent for sociology, a field having an astonishing variety of unit terms (e.g., individuals; primary groups, including families; organizations; statuses, including occupations; cities; and countries). That variety alone indicates a need for a special treatment of unit phrases, including unit terms. There is no special treatment in a discursively formulated sociological theory; consequently, it is commonly difficult to identify the unit phrases and terms with confidence (for examples, see Gibbs, 1972: 94–95).

A formal mode does not even suggest the appropriate unit terms for a theory; it is entirely a matter of the theorist's substantive interests. So a formal mode should accommodate any unit term, and that is the interpretation of "X" in Rule 6: *The initial phrase in each intrinsic statement (those in the theory's intrinsic part) must be "Among X's," "For any X over time," or "Among X's and for any X over time."*

The following illustration makes a previous generalization intelligible: Among cities, the greater the per capita income, the less the interpersonal violence rate. The unit phrase clearly indicates that "cities" should be the units compared in any test of the generalization, but the unit phrase is an implicit denial of a longitudinal relation between the two variables.

As for empirical applicability, a unit term is like a qualitative concept. It is not linked to a formula, but a theorist is not likely to assume that a unit term is sufficiently empirically applicable without a definition. Stating the matter as Rule 7: *Each unit term must be defined in the theory's extrinsic part; and if a unit term is generic (e.g., social unit, population, territorial unit), each specific type (e.g., organizations, age groups, cities) must be identified and also defined.* Note particularly that the rule does not even suggest how any unit term should be defined.

Unit Terms and Phrases as Qualifications of the Theory. Unless the unit term is totally generic (i.e., all inclusive as far as the field's subject matter goes), it qualifies or limits the theory. No sociologist is likely to doubt that the predictive accuracy of an unqualified theory is bound to suffer, but unit terms can qualify a theory in several ways.

Some unit terms can be thought of as denoting subclasses, as in the case of "organizations," a subclass of social units. When any such subclass term is used as a unit term, it implicitly qualifies the theory. The theorist may or may not offer a rationale for the qualification; but if he/she believes that it prevents the use of unreliable data in tests, he/she should make that rationale explicit.[8]

Unless there is a special and explicit rationale for qualifying a theory through the choice of a particular unit term, the qualification implies this generalization: the empirical relations asserted in the theory are greater for instances of the stipulated type of unit than for instances of any other type.

The subject bears on "range" as a dimension of predictive power. Described most simply: the greater the variety of unit terms in a theory, the greater the theory's range. The use of a generic unit term (e.g., social units) is indicative of a substantial range, though how much depends on the definition of the generic term and the explicit identification of types. In any case, a distinction should be drawn between explicit and implicit range. The latter pertains, as suggested earlier, to the claim (implied unless explicitly denied) that the illustrative theory holds better for the stipulated type of unit (e.g., countries) or types than for any other, a claim that in effect maximizes the theory's range.

A theorist can ill afford to assume that those who test the theory need not be instructed as to the definition of types of units or the identity of subtypes. The general point is that the theory's intrinsic statements must clearly identify the type or types of units that are to be compared when testing the theory.

Whatever the unit term, the unit phrase may both clarify and qualify the theory. Indeed, the phrases "Among X's" and "For any X over time" are major qualifications.[9] Either phrase reduces the theory's predictive power (i.e., relative to the unit phrase "Among X's *and* for any X over time"), but a reduction is better than the dismissal of a theory because of negative test outcomes that could have been avoided by a qualification.

Types of Terms: Relational Terms

In the typical discursively stated sociological theory long passages commonly end with a sentence in which the initial phrase is something like this: "It follows that..." Ordinarily, close examination of the passage does not permit a confident identification of the premises from which the conclusion was supposedly deduced, let alone how (for examples, see Gibbs, 1972:99–106). The point is that sociologists rarely employ explicit rules of deduction, and they use such a variety of relational terms in stating a theory that deduction rules are precluded. One paragraph of a discursive sociological theory may include these relational terms: influences, is based on, causes, depends on, varies directly with, determines, is positively associated with, and stems from.

As the examples suggest, a relational term connects the property terms of a synthetic statement, such that the statement asserts some kind of empirical relation.[10] Two illustrations must suffice. First, among U's and for any U over time, X causes Y. Second, among U's and for any U over time, the greater X, the less Y.

The variety of *possible* relational terms is seemingly infinite; and, again, in the discursive mode of theory construction they are so diverse as to preclude comprehensible rules of deduction. However, sociologists may need far more relational terms than the two illustrations (*supra*) suggest, perhaps even more than are subsequently introduced; but the prescribed formal mode is flexible in that regard. A theorist can devise additional or alternative relational terms if needed, provided that he/she defines them in the theory's extrinsic part and relates them to some deduction rule, perhaps a special rule.

A Relational Term Signifying Covariation. Although some sociologists (e.g., Blalock, 1969) demand the use of a causal language in theory construction, they ignore numerous issues and problems pertaining to causation.[11] As a case in point, a term is needed to link a theory's concepts with something akin to measurement and/or research procedure, and a causal language is inappropriate. For that matter, there is substantial consensus in the philosophy of science that some scientific laws are not causal. The general point is that covariational relational terms are needed for several reasons, including the possibility that (in the tradition of Bertrand Russell and Ernst Mach) a theorist eschews a causal language in stating theories.

The relevant terminology is introduced by Rule 8: *In an intrinsic statement that asserts covariation, the relational term must be "greater...greater" or "greater...less."* Briefly illustrating, should a theorist wish to assert a positive association between two variables, the form of the intrinsic statement is: Among U's, the greater X, the greater Y.[12] The form in the case of a negative association between the constituent variables (property terms) is: Among U's, the greater X, the less Y.

The relational term (greater...greater or greater...less) is treated as signifying only the direction of the asserted relation (of course, the *actual* direction may or may not be consistent with the assertion); and while the direction is always asserted to be monotonic, it may or may not be linear. The relevant terminology is introduced by Rule 9: *If the linear-nonlinear distinction is relevant, it must be recognized in a intrinsic statement by the use of the term "nonlinearily" immediately after the unit phrase.* Intrinsic statements that assert *nonmonotonic* relations are treated subsequently in connection with third-order theories, meaning a theory in which at least one premise asserts that the relation between two variables is contingent on a third variable (but possibly one of the two variables in the asserted relation).

Causal Relational Terms. Sociologists who prescribe a causal language in theory construction never recognize that the language cannot be both simple and clear. Contemplate an assertion about two quantitative variables in this form: X causes Y. Does it preclude the possibility that a change in Y causes a change in X? So a causal assertion is ambiguous if it does not speak to the distinction between symmetrical or reciprocal causation and asymmetrical or nonreciprocal causation.

Even if the original assertion were modified to recognize the distinction, would it mean that increases in X cause an increase in Y or that increases in X

cause decreases in Y? So an assertion of a causal relation between quantitative variables is ambiguous unless it speaks to the *direction* of causality; positive if a change in the alleged causal variable is supposedly followed by a change in the same direction (increase or decrease) of the alleged effect variable, and negative if the change in the effect variable is in the opposite direction.

The positive-negative distinction clarifies but oversimplifies. If increases in X cause increases in Y, it does not necessarily follow that decreases in X cause decreases in Y. Similarly, if increases in X cause decreases in Y, decreases in X do not necessarily cause increases in Y. In both cases the second causal assertion follows only if the causation is *bidirectional*. As for *unidirectional* causation, there are four possibilities: first, in the case of positive unidirectional causation, increases in X cause increases in Y but decreases in X do not cause decreases in Y; second, in the case of positive-negative unidirectional causation, increases in X cause decreases in Y but decreases in X do not cause increases in Y; third, in the case of negative unidirectional causation, decreases in X cause increases in Y but increases in X do not cause decreases in Y; and, fourth, in the case of negative-positive unidirectional causation decreases in X cause increases in Y but an increase in X does not cause a decrease in Y.

Are there instances of unidirectional causation? The possibility has been stressed by Leiberson (1985), though he did not employ the present terminology or recognize the four types of unidirectional causation.[13] As for evidence, many instances may have gone undetected because most social-behavioral scientists appear insensitive to the possibilities.

Returning to the original causal assertion, X causes Y, does it mean that X is the exclusive cause or a partial cause of Y? The question's terminology is conventional, but a distinction between *exclusive* and *paramount* causation is warranted. When a theorist speaks of X as being the paramount cause of Y, he/she implies that other causes are so insignificant that they need not be recognized *in the theory* to realize a level of predictive accuracy in tests exceeding that of contending theories. If the theorist regards other causes of Y as significant, they will be components of the theory and the theorist will speak of X as a *partial* cause.

All of the foregoing distinctions are recognized in Rule 10: *In formulating a synthetic statement so as to make a causal assertion, the theorist must use the term "determinant" and qualify it as being: (1) reciprocal or nonreciprocal, symmetrical or asymmetrical; (2) positive, negative, positive-negative, or negative-positive; (3) bidirectional or unidirectional; and (4) exclusive, paramount, or partial.* The rule cannot be fully understood until it is used in stating an illustrative theory (*infra*), and here three examples must suffice. First, among U's, X is the asymmetrical, positive, unidirectional, and paramount cause of Y.[14] Second, among U's, X is the reciprocal, negative, bidirectional, and paramount cause of Y; and Y is the reciprocal, negative, bidirectional, and partial cause of X. Third, among U's, X is the symmetrical, negative, bidirectional, and paramount cause of Y.

The first example may appear contradictory, because X is described as the paramount cause of Y and yet the second and third causal typifications ("positive, unidirectional") in that example must be translated this way: an increase in X causes an increase in Y but a decrease in X does not cause a decrease in Y. Note, however, that the "paramount" typification refers only to the "positive, unidirectional" (i.e., no claim is made about causes of a decrease in Y). Then note that the second example comprises two sets of causal typifications (four in each set), the reason being that they are not the same for each of the two reciprocal causal relations (X is asserted to be the *paramount* cause of Y but Y is asserted to be a *partial* cause of X). By contrast, in the third example there is only one set of causal typifications, and the term "symmetrical" is employed rather than "reciprocal" to signify that the typification describes the causation of X by Y as well as the causation of Y by X. So the term "nonreciprocal" need not be used (it is treated as equivalent to "asymmetrical"), and "symmetrical" is used to avoid repetition of the causal typification when they are identical for the causation of Y by X and the causation of X by Y.

Despite the diverse causal typifications, they are not exhaustive. In keeping with conventional terminology as regards causal relations among quantitative variables, the distinction between a necessary causes and a sufficient cause is ignored. But "exclusive" and "paramount" are to be construed as akin to causes that are both necessary and sufficient, while two or more asserted partial causes of some variable are to be construed as having additive effects on that variable but not necessarily even approximately of the same magnitude. Then the typifications do not extend to the possibility that increases or decreases in X are sufficient but not necessary causes or necessary but not sufficient for increases or decreases in Y. All such causal typifications can be introduced as relational terms, but in introducing them the theorist should define them clearly and specify criteria of causal evidence as well as related rules of deduction (all in the theory's extrinsic part).

Components of the Intrinsic Part:
Types of Intrinsic Statements

There is general agreement that statements are the meaningful constituents of empirical or scientific theories, and it appears that the vast majority of philosophers and scientists presume, as here, that each empirical or scientific theory comprises some synthetic statements in the form of generalizations about infinite classes. However, there is far less consensus when it comes to recognizing types of synthetic statements as components of a theory. The labels axiom, postulate, proposition, theorem, and hypothesis suggest a typology, but sociologists use those labels uncritically (for examples, see Gibbs, 1972:- 86–93).[15] For that matter, there is scarcely a standard terminology in the philosophy of science literature.

The argument that a statement's position in a theory determines its typification begs three questions. First, what positions should be recognized? Second, what determines position? Third, for any position what is the appropriate label for the statement type? Those questions are circumvented here by a simple prescription—that the typification of a synthetic statement in a theory depends entirely on the identification of its constituent property terms, as constructs, concepts, or referentials.[16] As for the notion of "position in a theory," it reduces to the distinction between premises (axioms, postulates, propositions, and transformational statements) and conclusions (theorems); but all of those distinctions are based on the typology of terms, and the ultimate consideration is not so much position as testability.

The First Type of Intrinsic Statement: Axioms

An axiom's definition is implied by Rule 11: *A statement in which all of the property terms are constructs must be designated as an axiom.*[17] Despite the rule's simplicity, there are some complexities, issues, and problems, all of which can be introduced best in connection with illustrations. The examples of axioms, along with examples of other types of premises, constitute a version of a *part* of Durkheim's theory about the division of labor (1933). Although space limitations preclude an elaborate version, it is more than just an illustration; and there is a major issue. This version of Durkheim reflects a rejection of traditional exegetical sociology. Restatements of sociology's classical theories are sterile unless made in accordance with some formal mode; otherwise, the restatement will suffer from the most basic flaw of the original theory—it cannot be tested defensibly, if at all.

A formal restatement of a discursive theory is compatible with this argument: the ultimate question in restating a theory is not exegetical but, rather, how can the theory's predictive power be maximized? The question is not a belittlement of the grand theorists. Rather, sociologists should celebrate the genius of Durkheim, Marx, Pareto, Simmel, and Weber; then *get on with it.*

The First Example: Axiom 1. Although Durkheim did not make his reasoning explicit, his assertion of a positive association between "material" density and the division of labor is an extension of a biological argument about the amount of animal life that a distinctive geographic area (e.g., a mountain range, a swamp) will sustain. Briefly, the amount depends on the variety of animal species; the greater the variety, the greater the amount of animal life the area will support, because conspecifics exploit the same environmental elements and the ensuing competition limits their numbers. However, just as jackals, giraffes, and hippos are not commensalistic competitors, so is that true of farmers, cobblers, and bakers (to mention only three ancient occupations). Described otherwise, if population density increases without an increase in the division of labor, the potential for lethal competition and ensuing social disintegration increases. The argument is most understandable in contemplating the consequence of continuous and substantial density increases when population members remain hunters or agriculturalists, but the argument is not truly limited to those sustenance activities.

So interpreted, Durkheim's argument is plausible; but indisputable tests have never been undertaken.[18] The most obvious reason is that general observations in the way of international comparisons do not suggest a positive association between population density and the division of labor. Think about these two sets of countries: (1) Australia, Canada, and the United States vs. (2) China, Sri Lanka, and Thailand. Population density is substantially greater for the second set, but no one would argue that the division of labor is greater for any country in the second set than for any country in the first set.

If it is claimed that a positive relation between population density and the division of labor holds only for a society over time (i.e., longitudinally), casual comparisons are consistent with that claim much more than in the case of the cross-sectional relation.[19] However, the suggested limitation would reduce the theory's intensity, meaning the *variety* of asserted space-time relations.[20] Yet even that limitation is preferable to a common interpretation of Durkheim; that his causal variable is moral (or social) density and not material density. There are three objections to that interpretation. First, Durkheim not only used the term "material density" time and again but also claimed (1933:257) that material density can be used to measure moral density; hence, the validity of this part of his theory cannot depend on the choice of one term over the other. Second, the meaning of material density is much clearer because Durkheim used the term such as to justify equating it with "residential population density." Third, whereas Durkheim's argument about material density and the division of labor is plausible, in the case of "moral density" the argument is obscure; indeed, assuming that the term refers to the frequency of interaction (if not, the meaning is hopelessly vague), it denotes something that could be determined *by* the division of labor, a reversal of the causation.

The only way to salvage this part of Durkheim's theory is to replace his density terms with "population concentration." In stating his theory Durkheim occasionally used the latter term, though less than density; and evidently he did not appreciate the difference.[21] Two areas may have identical levels of residential population density, and yet in one area no two residences are separated by more than, say, 100 meters, while in the other no two are that close.

Durkheim's argument is a functional explanation in that he evidently assumed selective survival, meaning that instances of a particular type of society—high material density and low degree of division of labor—tend to be eliminated. Like most contemporary functionalists in the social sciences, Durkheim did not make the assumption of selective survival explicit, nor did he recognize alternatives (functional equivalents) to the division of labor for avoiding the socially disruptive consequences of increases in density and/or checking the increases. Emigration and expansion of the population's boundary (perhaps militaristically) are obvious possibilities.

Whatever the reasons for the ostensible invalidity of Durkheim's functional explanation, the present version of his theory involves more than a switch from density to population concentration. Durkheim's antireductionism led him to rely (implicitly) on selective survival as an explanatory mechanism, for at no point did he attribute the increase in the division of labor to perceptions of population members of the consequences of escalating density.[22] By contrast, it is assumed here that as population concentration increases numerous population members become convinced that they cannot enjoy a previous standard of living without more differentiation in sustenance activities. For that matter, insofar as there is anything like survival conditions, a high degree of population concentration could be just as necessary for a high degree of division of labor as the latter is necessary for the former (see Gibbs and Martin, 1958, 1962). The division of labor requires efficient transportation and communication, but population concentration reduces the time and energy invested in that requisite. Contrary to Durkheim's robotic sociology, it is assumed that a sufficient number of population members are aware of the advantages of proximity and act accordingly in matters pertaining to spatial arrangements.

All of the foregoing arguments are summarized in Axiom 1: *Among countries and for any country over time, population concentration is the symmetrical, positive, bidirectional, and paramount determinant of the degree of division of labor.*[23] The generalization's most questionable feature is the "paramount" causal typification. The implied exclusion of technological efficiency alone is reason for doubts, but it is assumed that both population concentration and the division of labor are positively associated with technological efficiency (Gibbs and Martin, 1962); hence, the axiom could hold without taking technological efficiency into account. Should evidence invalidate that assumption, it may be necessary to extend the theory from second-order to third-order; but the only immediate purpose is the illustration of a formally stated second-order theory.

Second Example: Axiom 2. Durkheim's book (1933 [1893]) is the exclusive rationale for Axiom 2: *Among countries and for any country over time, the degree of division of labor is the asymmetrical, positive, bidirectional, and exclusive determinant of organic solidarity.* However, unless organic solidarity is defined in a way contrary to Durkheim's brand of sociology, the axiom cannot be construed as a genuine empirical generalization. Durkheim never defined organic solidarity explicitly, one of many problems with the notion (see Pope and Johnson, 1983); but time and again (1933) he indicated that organic solidarity is solidarity based on functional interdependence. Yet if the term is so defined, then any statement like Axiom 2 becomes at least somewhat tautological, because the division of labor is defined partially in terms of functional interdependence. The most obvious way to avoid any tautological quality is to define organic solidarity as the amount of functional interdependence as *perceived* by population members.

Even accepting the proposed definition of organic solidarity, general observations raise doubts about the typification of the causation as exclusive. Relatives and friends commonly perceive themselves as interdependent, perhaps in some economic sense, even in cases where they have the same occupation or engage in the same kinds of sustenance activities (i.e., no differentiation). For that matter, cooperative activity does not require or imply differentiation, but cooperation is functional interdependence and probably so perceived by the participants.

There are two counterarguments against the suggested change in the causal typification from exclusive to paramount or partial. First, the perceptions just noted do not necessarily play a role as regards differences among countries, and the causation in question pertains only to those differences. Second, as far as the rules of deduction (*infra*) are concerned, the distinction between exclusive and paramount causation is inconsequential; and only the assertion of partial causation creates a problem.

The Third Example: Axiom 3. Although most commentators on Durkheim's theory treat organic solidarity as central, Durkheim scarcely used the term to formulate specific empirical generalizations; and the theory can be stated without using the term (see Gibbs, 1993a). Thus, while Durkheim characterized restitutive law as an external index or symbol of organic solidarity (1933:64), that characterization adds nothing to the argument that increases in the division of labor cause increase in restitutive law (by itself or relative to repressive law). Moreover, granted that increases in the division of labor lessen the punitiveness of criminal law through the erosion of normative consensus (Gibbs, 1993a), reference to organic solidarity need not be made.

If organic solidarity is defined in terms of perceived functional interdependence, it can enter into a causal argument never made explicit by Durkheim: organic solidarity is conducive to political stability. Leaders of contending interest groups perceive the nation as functionally integrated to the point that major divisions of producers or consumers cannot be coerced effectively, much less eliminated. Described partially in terms used extensively by John Higley (most recently: Burton, Gunther, and Higley, 1992), organic solidarity is conducive to a consensual unity of elites, the principal basis being the elites' belief that those who compete for power must do so not only by nonviolent means but also in accordance with certain political arrangements. The entire argument is summarized by Axiom 3: *Among countries and for any country over time, organic solidarity is the asymmetrical, positive, bidirectional, and paramount determinant of political stability.*

Because Durkheim's interests were so predominantly apolitical, Axiom 3 cannot be described as an interpretation of his theory. Indeed, he actually did very little in the way of extending his famous distinction between mechanical solidarity and organic solidarity to the formulation of clear-cut empirical generalizations. He obviously thought of the two as (by definition) inversely related and each determined by the degree of division of labor, but he did not recognize that the relation makes the *amount* of solidarity, ignoring the type, a *constant* (i.e., if both types of solidarity were mensurable by the same metric, the sum of the two measures would be approximately invariant across societies or for any society over time). As such, the notion of solidarity cannot be used to explain variation among societies with regard to political stability or anything else. However, if it is assumed that mechanical solidarity and organic solidarity have positive interactive (multiplicative) effects on political stability, then there is a significant implication.[24] Briefly, solidarity's stabilizing effect is at an absolute maximum when and where the degree of division of labor is at the scale's midpoint (.5 if the minimum is .00 and the maximum is 1.00). More specifically, up to the midpoint increases in the division of labor generate political stability but beyond that further increases generate political instability.

Durkheim might have agreed with the first part of the generalization; but given his near veneration of mechanical solidarity and obvious doubts about the efficacy of organic solidarity as a basis for social order, it is difficult to imagine him agreeing that increases in the division of labor are infinitely conducive to political stability. Nevertheless, Durkheim notwithstanding, Axioms 2 and Axiom 3 taken together imply a positive monotonic association between the division of labor and political stability, which is an implicit denial that mechanical solidarity (a low degree of division of labor) is conducive to political stability. Of course, when evidence is brought to bear on those axioms, the possibility of a *nonmonotonic* relation between the division of labor and political stability should be examined. Evidence of an inverted U-shape relation (political stability on the vertical axis), would indicate that both types of solidarity are relevant but their effects on political stability are interactive (multiplicative rather than additive). Still another possibility—a monotonic *negative* association between the division of labor and political stability would force abandonment of Axiom 2 and/or Axiom 3, and it would underscore Durkheim's seeming doubts about the efficacy of organic solidarity as a basis for social order.

The Second Type of Intrinsic Statements: Postulates

Rule 12: *A synthetic statement in which a construct and a concept are the constituent property terms must be designated as a postulate.* Although the rule makes an explicit definition of a postulate unnecessary (see Glossary, p. 358), examples are needed for clarification.

First Example: Postulate 1. The resources required to measure population concentration at anything like the macro level are prohibitive, but general observations suggest a mensurable correlate. The degree of urbanization has been defined (*supra*) as the percentage of the population of some designated spatial entity who resided in some type of urban unit at some designated time point; and the residents of instances of the three types—cities, urban areas, metropolitan areas (see Gibbs, 1977)—are a highly concentrated population. So the very nature of urban units suggest a relation between the degree of urbanization and population concentration. The summary generalization is Postulate 1: *Among countries and for any country over time, the greater the population concentration, the greater the degree of urbanization.*

The postulate is synthetic because it could be false. In both of two countries the degree of urbanization could be, say, 70.0, and yet it would be *logically possible* for one country to have only one urban unit while in the other there are numerous and widely dispersed urban units. If so, the two would have the same degree of urbanization but differ sharply as to level of population concentration.

Despite the covariational relational terms in Postulate 1, it may appear that population concentration is the cause or a cause of the degree of urbanization. However, doubts transcend the most obvious consideration—that the definition of an urban unit (whatever the type) does not entail reference to some minimum residential proximity. Even if increases in population concentration eventually cause increases in the degree of urbanization, urban residents enjoy certain amenities—utilities, sewer lines, paved roads, etc.—that may attract rural emigrants, thereby causing more population concentration. Yet the point is not just that the causal relation must be reciprocal; rather, a theorist may be uncertain about some intrinsic statements, perhaps not even totally confident as regards the analytic-synthetic distinction.[25] So while the testability requirement adds to a theorist's burden, it is reduced by enabling him/her to choose between a covariational assertion and a causal assertion when formulating an axiom, postulate, or proposition. There are cases where an argument can be made to support this assertion: whatever the causal relation between the two variables, variation in one is closely related (however defined) to variation in the other.

Second Example: Postulate 2. By definition, the degree of division of labor (*supra*) is the product or sum of two variables: (1) the amount of differences among population members as regards their sustenance activities and (2) the related amount of functional interdependence. Although the definition does not imply any empirical association between the two variables, a casual relation is implied by Postulate 2: *Among countries and for any country over time, the degree of division of labor is the asymmetrical, positive, bidirectional, and paramount determinant of the degree of industry differentiation.*[26] The generalization is extralogical in that it *implies* two positive empirical associations: first, between the amount of functional interdependence and the amount of differentiation in sustenance activities; and, second, between the amount of that differentiation and the degree of industry differentiation.

The positive association between differentiation in sustenance activities and the degree of industry differentiation can be thought of as asymmetrical causation. As members come to differ more and more in their sustenance activities, the contrast increases the social identification of population members with particular types of products (what economists label as commodities, benefits, goods, or services); and the increase is manifested in greater industry differentiation. So the explanatory mechanism is in part simple causation.

The explanatory mechanism is different for functional interdependence and differentiation in sustenance activities. Exchange is the key notion in connection with functional interdependence, and specialization in connection with differentiation. Products are not exchanged extensively unless someone is producing a surplus, but humans are telic creatures; hence, specialization is undertaken or arranged with a view to producing a surplus and exchange. Described another way, both production and exchange necessarily involve attempts at control, which alone means that the relation between functional interdependence and differentiation is telic.

Given that Durkheim virtually equated the division of labor with the variety of occupations and industries, Postulate 2 is entirely consistent with his theory. However, he failed to recognize that the notions of occupation and industry are alien to some populations, foragers especially. Hence, any generalization like Postulate 2 simply does not apply to all social units. Because the notion of an industry is not alien to countries, the unit phrase of Postulate 2 has been worded accordingly.

Still another rationale for the unit term "country" pertains to the flow of products across territorial boundaries. That flow indicates territorial specialization; and highly specialized territorial units tend to have less industry differentiation as a consequence but not less functional interdependence. Such exceptions to Postulate 2 are especially common among intranational territorial units (e.g., cities), which is to say that *ecological autonomy* is appreciably greater for countries. However, there is an international flow of products, and that is a rationale for identifying the division of labor as the paramount rather than the exclusive determinant of industry differentiation.

Third and Final Example: Postulate 3. When a construct is defined vaguely or not at all, it is especially difficult to link with any concept. In the case of quantitative property terms, the difficulty is exacerbated by the required subsequent linkage of the concept (through a referential) with a formula. The difficulty is exemplified by Postulate 3: *Among countries and for any country over time, political stability is the asymmetrical, negative, bidirectional, and paramount determinant of the political violence death rate.*

Whatever the causal relation between the two variables, political violence does not necessarily result in deaths. Ideally, then, the concept would be "political violence," but that change will not be feasible as long as the news media (newspapers especially) are the major source of global data on political violence. Those data are much more complete (hence, reliable in that sense) for lethal than nonlethal political violence. Revolutions, civil wars, rebellions, or insurgencies are virtually certain to be reported in the world press, but they are so rare that a count of them for a period less than several generations might grossly *overestimate* the political stability of many countries. For that matter, instances of collective domestic political violence—riots, revolutions, etc.—are by no means equally violent; and deaths from political violence may well be the most defensible gauge.

Even if deaths from political violence were known to be perfectly correlated with a more inclusive measure, there would be doubts about each causal typification in Postulate 3, save "negative." Most obvious, it could be argued that political violence lessens political stability and, hence, the causal relation is asymmetrical (nonreciprocal), though in the opposite direction. Then increases in political stability cannot reduce deaths from political violence below the absolute minimum (zero value), a relational quality alien to unlimited bidirectionality. Finally, international terrorism alone suggests partial rather than paramount causation. Because none of the foregoing arguments can be rejected confidently, only exceptionally positive tests of derivative theorems will eliminate doubts about Postulate 3.

More than any other premise, Postulate 3 illustrates how a theory's formal statement erroneously suggests absolute confidence and finality. To the contrary, whether stated discursively or formally, any sociological theory is continuously subject to revision.

Types of Statements: Transformational Statements

A quantitative concept is empirically applicable only through its link with a symbol, a referential, that denotes a formula. That link is made in accordance with Rule 13: *An intrinsic statement in which the property terms are a concept and a referential must be designated as a transformational statement.* The formulas subsequently denoted by referentials are set forth in the illustrative theory's extrinsic part; hence, the treatment of transformational statements can be brief.

First Example: Transformational Statement 1. The initial issue has to do with a hoary argument: a link between a concept and anything like a research procedure, including formulas, is not established justifiably unless the procedure is somehow deduced from the concept's definition. Stated more conventionally, the link must be made in accordance with transcendent "rules of correspondence."[27] The argument takes on special significance in connection with Transformational Statement 1: *Among countries and for any country over time, the greater the degree of urbanization, the greater the RDU at T_{0-1}*. The acronym RDU (referential of degree of urbanization) denotes a particular formula in the theory's extrinsic part, and the temporal quantifier "at T_{0-1}" signifies any point during some type of time period (in this case, any calendar year) stipulated in the extrinsic part. The value computed by applying the formula is the percentage of the total (national) population who at some time point during a designated calendar year were residents of a city, an urban area, or metropolitan area. As such, the formula appears equivalent to the concept and, hence, the concept-referential link appears entirely consistent with the rule-of-correspondence notion. The appearance is misleading.

An explication of a referential formula should go beyond a definition of its constituent symbols (variables) to a stipulation of the requisite *kind* of data and acquisitional instructions, possibly including the use of published sources. Those data stipulations are extensions of the formula in that correct application of the formula requires compliance with the stipulations. Contemplate this illustrative possibility: in recognition of the field's limited research resources, a theorist stipulates that when testing the theory in question investigators are to apply the RDU formula to census data on urban areas but not census data on cities or metropolitan areas. Such a stipulation probably reflects a judgment about the international comparability of the three kinds of data; but, whatever the basis of the stipulation, how could it possibly be given by or correspond to the concept (degree of urbanization) or its definition? Indeed, how could the use of census data somehow correspond to any concept?

Those questions are totally ignored in Costner's (1969) treatment of rules of correspondence, the reason being that he confuses correspondence rules with criteria for judging the adequacy of a theory in light of tests. The notion of rules of correspondence is controversial precisely because, unlike Costner, its other advocates (e.g., Wilson and Dumont, 1968) write as though test outcomes do not and cannot justify the link between concepts and research procedures.

It is hardly surprising that advocates of rules of correspondence have never set forth specific rules, for it is difficult to imagine any rule that implies the appropriate kind of requisite data (including judgments as to feasibility) for each particular theory. Should it be argued that no theory should comprise data stipulations, imagine someone saying: "The outcome of tests of this theory will not be contingent on the kind of data employed." Credulity is taxed only slightly less by the claim that investigators need no instructions to agree on the requisite kind of data for tests of a sociological theory.

On the whole, what has been said about the notion of rules of correspondence extends to the notion of validity as it applies to anything like transformational statements. As commonly used in criticisms of theories, invoking either notion implies an unrealistic demand. Indeed, the unrealistic demand is essentially the same in both cases: that instances of a particular type of component be justified *independently* of any test outcome. The type of component is any statement that asserts or claims some association or connection between a construct or concept and some research procedure, measure, or formula (a transformational statement being an instance).

The immediate problem with the notion of validity (again, in reference to transformational statements) is drawing and maintaining the distinction between it and the notion of reliability (e.g., contemplate *demonstrating* that an unreliable measure is valid). However, the foremost objection is that the notion of validity conventionally translates so as to suggest that a procedure, measure, or formula can be "validated" by some technique that is distinct from a test of the theory. To the contrary, in the social and behavioral sciences most of what passes for evidence of validity is nothing less than a test of an implicit theory. Contemplate the common practice of "validating" a purported intelligence test by reporting a correlation for a particular set of individuals between test scores and grades achieved in school. Such reports commonly ignore this question: why expect a positive correlation between such values? The question forces recognition that the reported correlation is actually a test of a generalization. The generalization is implied by two postulates, one that asserts a positive association between intelligence (a construct) and test scores and one that asserts a positive association between intelligence and grades achieved in school. So the reported correlation is actually a test of an implicit theory. Indeed, if the correlation does not hold, there would be no basis to reject both postulates or identify only one of them as false. The general point should be obvious: the belief that the validity of the kind of statement in question can be validated or invalidated apart from any theory is a vast illusion.

Second Example: Transformational Statement 2. The notion of a transformational statement potentially entails issues other than data stipulations. Each issue is likely to stem from a misconception—that the relation between a concept and a referential is purely logical, meaning that a transformational statement is analytic and, hence, unfalsifiable even in principle. To the contrary, any transformational statement has an extralogical quality, meaning synthetic and subject to falsification in principle. The argument can be elaborated readily in connection with Transformational Statement 3: *Among countries and for any country over time, the greater the degree of industry differentiation, the greater the RDID at T_{0-1}.*

In the illustrative theory's extrinsic part (*infra*) there are two versions of the RDID referential formula, $RDID_1$ and $RDID_2$. Multiple versions further testability; but two referential formulas may appear identical and yet differ as to requisite kinds of data, perhaps including instructions as to the acquisitional procedure. Consequently, if investigators cannot acquire one of the two kinds of data, the other kind may be possible. However, a theorist may set forth multiple versions of a referential formula not to maximize testability but, rather, because he/she does not know which version will maximize predictive accuracy. Eventually, tests may justify eliminating some versions, but that possibility is not created by a logical relation between the concepts and the formulas.

Even when the theorist prescribes only one version of a referential formula, he/she is likely to concede that some other version (the formula itself and/or different kinds of data) might result in greater predictive accuracy. Indeed, when formulating a transformational statement, the theorist in effect makes a claim something like this: although I do not know the ideal formula (the one that would maximize predictive accuracy), if the referential formula is applied correctly to completely reliable data for each of several units, the correlation between the computed referents and the "true" referents would be substantial. The claim is not testable but possibly false nonetheless. Even if the prescribed formula is identical with the ideal formula, it may have been applied to unreliable data, even though the data were acquired exactly as stipulated. When a theorist stipulates how data are to be acquired, he/she claims that such data will be sufficiently reliable; but that claim may be unwarranted. So whereas the concept refers to the ideal formula *and* completely reliable data, the same is not necessarily true of the formula (including the stipulated kind of data) denoted by the referential in the transformational statement.

In the case of Transformational Statement 2, no one can know the true amount of industry differentiation for any country at any time. Nonetheless, the statement in effect asserts that those amounts would be closely correlated among countries with the computed referents if the RDID formula has been applied correctly to the prescribed kind of data.

Last Example: Transformational Statement 3. Some advocates of the rule–of–correspondence notion might grant all previous points about data but then argue that the *form* of the measurement procedure (formulas especially) must correspond to the definition of the related concept. The argument is especially pertinent when contemplating Transformational Statement 3: *Among countries and for any country over time, the greater the political violence death rate, the greater RPVDR for T_{0-30}.*

The referential, RPVDR, denotes a formula in the extrinsic part of the theory (*infra*) that appears equivalent to the concept's definition. That appearance lends credence to the rule-of-correspondence argument; but it is misleading, and the reason has nothing to do with the point that a concept's definition scarcely prescribes any particular kind of data. All referentials have temporal quantifiers. For RPVDR it is "for T_{0-30}," which translates as "any period of between 25 and 35 calendar years." So if in a test the other temporal quantifier ("at T_{0-1}" in Transformational Statements 1 and 2) is taken as any point during calendar 1960, then "for T_{0-30}" must be translated as a period of calendar years not shorter than 1960-1985 or longer than 1960-1995.

A temporal quantifier is not necessary for a concept or construct, but unless one is attached to each referential formula the theorems are either ambiguous or vacuously true.[28] However, even when a concept's definition refers to a "period," as in the present definition of the political violence death rate, it does not stipulate any particular length. The point is not that "for T_{0-30}" identifies the period that maximizes the theory's predictive accuracy. The only claim is that "0–30" approximates that ideal period, and exploratory research may be necessary for greater confidence (indeed, the illustrative theory suffers because the temporal quantifiers are not based on exploratory research). However, a temporal quantifier is not given or implied by the concept to which the referential is linked, and that consideration alone creates doubts about anything like rules of correspondence that transcend particular theories. Even an interpretation of a transformational statement as a rule of correspondence in itself would be dubious, for that interpretation ignores the extralogical quality of the relation between the concept and what the referential denotes.

Types of Intrinsic Statements: Theorems

A theory's intrinsic part ends with theorems; but further clarification of the term's meaning is needed, especially to indicate why theorems are the only intrinsic statements that enter directly into tests. As before, a rule implies the definition, in this case Rule 14: *If an intrinsic statement has been deduced and its constituent property terms are referentials, the statement must be designated as a theorem.*[29] The only property terms in theorems are referentials; and because referentials are the only empirically applicable property terms in a quantitative theory, only theorems enter directly into tests of such a theory.

Examples of theorems cannot be understood apart from premises. Taken together, the illustrative theory's premises (axioms, postulates, and transformational statements) imply three theorems. Repeating the premises seriatim (*infra*) will further understanding of each theorem's deduction; but the repetition does not reveal the deduction rules, and it is best to delay stipulating them.

The Intrinsic Part of the Illustrative
Theory as a Whole

The illustrative intrinsic part comprisess only four axioms, three postulates, three transformational tatements, and three theorems. The brevity touches on an issue. Being accustomed to discursive theories that run for hundreds of pages, sociologists may think of a formally stated theory as trivial, pedestrian, unimportant, etc. Such tacit invidious comparisons confuse verbosity with profundity and fail to recognize that a theory's logical structure is obscure if the theory exceeds a few pages. Yet discursive and formal theory construction are not totally incompatible. As done here, the theorist can use a natural language to introduce each constituent idea, provided that he/she commences or ends the introduction with a formally stated premise. That combination of the two modes has advantages; but it should not be a prop for a traditional sociological belief—that rhetoric is somehow a satisfactory substitute for systematic tests. For that matter, if the two modes are mixed, the theory's logical structure (including analytic-synthetic distinctions) is bound to be less than clear if the components of the intrinsic part (axioms, etc.) are not arranged seriatim, as follows.

Axiom 1: Among countries and for any country over time, population concentration is the symmetrical, positive, bidirectional, and paramount determinant of the degree of division of labor.

Axiom 2: Among countries and for any country over time, the degree of division of labor is the asymmetrical, positive, bidirectional, and exclusive determinant of organic solidarity.

Axiom 3: Among countries and for any country over time, organic solidarity is the asymmetrical, positive, bidirectional, and paramount determinant of political stability.

Postulate 1: Among countries and for any country over time, the greater the population concentration, the greater the degree of urbanization.

Postulate 2: Among countries and for any country over time, the degree of division of labor is the asymmetrical, positive, bidirectional, and paramount determinant of the degree of industry differentiation.

Postulate 3: Among countries and for any country over time, political stability is the asymmetrical, negative, bidirectional, and paramount determinant of the political violence death rate.

Transformational Statement 1: Among countries and for any country over time, the greater the degree of urbanization, the greater the RDU at T_{0-1}.

Transformational Statement 2: Among countries and for any country over time, the greater the degree of industry differentiation, the greater the RDID at T_{0-1}.

Transformational Statement 3: Among countries and for any country over time, the greater the political violence death rate, the greater RPVDR for T_{0-30}.

Theorem 1 (from Axiom 1, Postulates 1 and 2, Transformational Statements 1 and 2): Among countries and for any country over time, the greater the RDU at T_{0-1}, the greater the RDID at T_{0-1}.

Theorem 2 (from Axioms 2 and 3, Postulates 2 and 3, Transformational Statements 2 and 3): Among countries and for any country over time, the greater the RDID at T_{0-1}, the less the RPVDR for T_{0-30}.

Theorem 3 (from Axioms 1–3, Postulates 1 and 3, Transformational Statements 1 and 3): Among countries and for any country over time, the greater the RDU at T_{0-1}, the less the RPVDR for T_{0-30}.

Other Types of Intrinsic Statements and the Rules of Deduction

Four types of intrinsic statements have yet to be introduced because none enters into the illustrative theory. They are introduced here in recognition that some are relevant in the subsequent formulation of deduction rules.

Types of Intrinsic Statements: Propositions

A theory may commence not with axioms and/or postulates but, rather, with propositions or a combination of propositions and axioms and/or postulates. That type of intrinsic statement—a proposition—is in effect defined by Rule 15: *If the constituent property terms of a premise are concepts, the statement must be designated as a proposition.*

Two Illustrations. Propositions are much to the liking of staunch empiricists in sociology, especially those who take a dim view of terms that might qualify as constructs. So they would limit sociology's property terms to concepts. But no matter how clear or complete a term's meaning, if it denotes a quantitative property, it is illusionary to presume some inherent connection between the term and any particular research procedure, measurement or otherwise. Even when a term comes to be equated by convention with a procedure (or anything akin, such as a referential formula), a theory about the relation between quantitative properties is enthymematic (i.e., incomplete premises) without transformational statements or equivalents.

Another illusion is that quantitative propositions can be tested without deriving theorems. The belief would be defensible if a negative test outcome could stem only from a false proposition, meaning in each case it is known that (1) the formulas or measures could not be otherwise (i.e., no alternative would support the proposition more) and (2) the kind of data used in the tests are reliable. Such knowledge is alien to sociology and perhaps any field.

A Sterile Issue. Should a theory commence with propositions or with axioms and postulates?[30] The question cannot be answered by any mode of theory construction, and it introduces a sterile issue.

Consider Figure A–1, a diagram of the illustrative theory. It may appear that the theory could have commenced with two propositions, one linking the degree of urbanization and occupational differentiation, and the other linking occupational differentiation with the political violence death rate. Had the theory so commenced, the same theorems could have been deduced from the

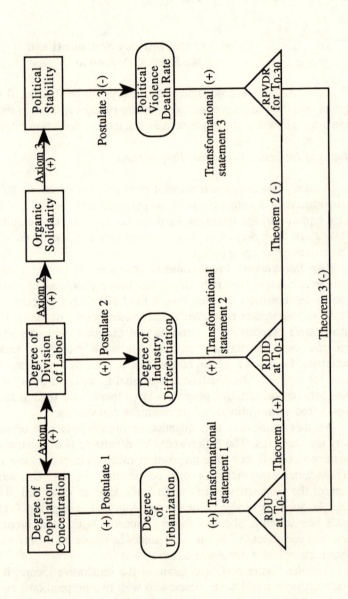

Figure A-1: DIAGRAM OF A VERSION OF DURKHEIM'S THEORY ABOUT THE DIVISION OF LABOR

propositions and the same three transformational statements. The suggestion is that the propositions would make the axioms and postulates superfluous; and the extreme argument would be something like this: once theorems can be deduced from propositions, the original axioms and postulates should be abandoned.

Yet the illustrative theory did not commence with the two propositions in question, and it might never have been formulated without the constructs, axioms, and postulates. Furthermore, if those components were abandoned in preference for propositions, it would reduce opportunities for expanding the theory. As the theory stands now, one can think of other possible correlates of the four constructs and three concepts; and abandoning the axioms and postulates would limit such thinking to the concepts. Indeed, given a theory that commences with propositions, the immediate challenge is to deduce the same theorems from axioms and postulates. If such a change does not necessarily result in additional (new) theorems, it may appear pointless.[31] However, granted that additional theorems are highly desirable, deducing what were originally propositions from axioms and/or postulates is worthwhile even if it yields no additional theorems.

Again, axioms and postulates pose opportunities for expanding the theory, and they increase the theory's scope, another dimension of predictive power.[32] Moreover, deduction of the relation previously asserted by a proposition may contribute to the relation's explanation, but the argument stops short of the unrealistic demand that the premises be explained. Any theory leaves at least one question unanswered: if the premises are true, why? An attempt to answer leads to an infinite regression.

In light of the foregoing, should a theory that commences with propositions be avoided or rejected? Not at all. Just as any predictive power is better than none, then *a fortiori* any theory is better than none.

Three Remaining Types of Intrinsic Statements

Subsequent deduction rules apply not just to the relation between referentials (i.e., theorems) but also to the relation between constructs, between constructs and concepts, and between concepts. Such rules are needed if only to deduce what would appear to be an axiom, a postulate, or a proposition. Indeed, in light of the deduction rules that follow, if a theory comprises more than two constructs and/or more than two concepts, the premises imply more than theorems. To illustrate, as Figure A–1 indicates, Axioms 1, 2, and 3 taken together imply some kind of relation between population concentration and political stability. Another illustration pertains to Postulate 1, Axiom 1, and Postulate 2. Taken together those premises imply some relation between population concentration and the degree of industry differentiation.

The final example pertains to something alien to the illustrative theory. Suppose that the theory had commenced with two propositions, one linking the degree of urbanization with the degree of industry differentiation and the other linking the degree of industry differentiation with the political violence death rate. If so, those two propositions taken together would have implied a relation between the degree of urbanization and the political violence death rate.

Each of the three types of implied statements in question need not be defined individually. Rule 16 suffices: *Should a statement other than a theorem be deduced from a theory's premises, it must be designated as an implied axiom if the constituent property terms are constructs, an implied postulate if one of the property terms is a construct and the other a concept, and an implied proposition if both property terms are concepts.* There is no label for a deduced relation between a construct and a referential, and it is difficult to imagine a need for it.

Rules of Deduction

No aspect of the methodology of theory construction is more difficult than deduction rules, especially when the premises assert causation and, hence, are untestable unless translated into assertions of covariational relations (as theorems do in the proposed mode). Although Hume's critics appear reluctant to grant the point, one never observes causation; rather, it is *inferred* from space-time associations (or conjunctions). Hence, if a theory's premises assert causation, defensible tests require the deduction of covariational conclusions. Such deduction is a thicket of issues and problems, for it involves criteria of causal evidence. Far from having reached agreement as to those criteria, sociologists are prone to ignore the issue and problems (for elaboration, see Gibbs, 1982, and note a major exception: Sobel, 1994). Paradoxically, those sociologists who prescribe a causal language in theory construction (e.g., Blalock, 1969) or advocate path analysis (e.g., Duncan, 1966) have never stated criteria of causal evidence, nor formulated deduction rules. What has been said of sociologists applies also to those who have influenced the methods and techniques of sociology pertaining to causation, notably Herbert Simon (especially 1952 and 1968) and Sewall Wright (especially 1934).

"Causes" Defined and Criteria of Causal Evidence. Prior to defining "causes" and stating a criterion of causal evidence, four criticisms of common features of extant alternatives warrant recognition (for a much more extensive treatment, see Gibbs, 1982). First, in defining causation the practice of using synonyms, such as "produces" or "determines," merely reduces the definition's empirical applicability. Second, at least as far as the social and behavioral sciences are concerned, it is unrealistic to define causation such as to suggest that a variable is either *the* cause of another variable, *a* cause of it, or *neither* (i.e., as though causation must be thought of trichotomously rather than as a

matter of degree). Third, a definition of causation scarcely furthers consensus in assessments of particular causal assertions unless coupled with criteria of causal evidence. Fourth, extant criteria of causal evidence tend to be (1) vague, (2) arbitrary, (3) grossly unrealistic as far as the condition of research and findings in sociology are concerned (e.g., there is nothing like a consistent and even near maximum association between any two variables), and/or (4) patently alien to conventional conceptions of causation.[33] Yet the four objectionable features of extant criteria of causal evidence are secondary to the point that most sociologists, even those who write on causation, ostensibly see no need for any criteria.

The term "causes" is defined here in connection with quantitative variables as follows: in some designated kind of condition or all conditions, one variable, X, is *the* asymmetrical or nonreciprocal cause of another variable, Y, to the *extent* that the proportion of instances where a change in X is followed by a change in Y during some stipulated period length in some stipulated spatial context *exceeds* the proportion of instances where a change in Y is followed by a change in X during any stipulated period length and in any stipulated spatial context. Space limitations permit only two statements in defense of the definition. First, those who object to the exclusive reliance on a terminology of space-time association are reminded that Hume's argument has survived its critics. Second, although the definition is subsequently translated into criteria of causal evidence, that evidence can never be conclusive; and those who demand conclusive evidence should avoid any connection with science.

There is only one criterion of causal evidence (Ca) in the case of an asserted asymmetrical (nonreciprocal) causal relation between quantitative variables:
$Ca = /S/M([X]>[Y]) - \{M[(Y)>(X)]\}$,
where $/S/$ is $+1$ if positive causation is asserted and -1 if negative causation is asserted; M is some stipulated kind of association measure (e.g., a standardized regression coefficient) pertaining to the X–Y or the Y–X relation; $[X]$ or $[Y]$ are static values of the variable at any time point or a change value (absolute or proportional) of the variable over a period of some stipulated length (perhaps any length, a minimum, a maximum, or both); $>$ signifies temporal sequence, with the first variable's value preceding the second variable's value by some stipulated interval (perhaps any length, a minimum, a maximum, or both); (X) or (Y) is a static value of the variable at any time point or a change value (absolute or proportional) of the variable over a period of any length; and $\{\}$ signifies zero if the two M values (one to the left and one to the right of the minus sign) do not have the same sign, positive or negative.[34] The stipulations in question are set forth by the individual making the assertion that X is the direct or indirect cause of Y; but no temporal stipulations are allowed in the case of the second relation, $(Y)>(X)$, as they could be such as to virtually preclude any association, thereby assuring that the $[X]>[Y]$ relation is greater (closer) than is the $(Y)>(X)$ relation.

The individual making the assertion must identify the appropriate kind of association measure, M, because he/she stipulates the kind of data to be used in testing causal claim and can select the most appropriate measure in light of judgments of the prospective data's quality (reliability and the nature of the related metric—ordinal, interval, ratio, etc.—in particular).[35] Nothing precludes additional stipulations, such as the identification of other variables, especially other asserted causes of variation in the Y variable, and instructions as to how they are to be controlled or otherwise taken into account. Such instructions are to be construed as an identification of the kind of condition under which variation in X is *the* cause of variation in Y, meaning exclusive rather than paramount or partial causation. Correlatively, with or without such instructions, to the extent that Ca is less that 1.0, it is evidence of only paramount or partial causation; and to the extent it approaches .00, it is evidence of no causation whatever.

Another criterion (Cs) is needed when symmetrical (reciprocal) causation is asserted. Using the same notational system as in the case of Ca, the criterion is:
$$Cs=[/S/M([X]>[Y])+/S/M([Y]>[X])]/2-|[/S/M([X]>[Y]-[/S/M([Y]>[X])]|.$$
Note that there is no instance of (Y)>(X), and the length of the lag interval must be stipulated for [Y]>[X] as well as [X]>[Y]. However, the observations in the case of Ca (asymmetrical or nonreciprocal causation) pertaining to the recognition of other causal variables are also relevant in the case of Cs (symmetrical or reciprocal causation). But in the case of Cs the crucial question is more complex: is variation in X the exclusive, paramount, or partial cause of variation in Y and is variation in Y the exclusive, paramount, or partial cause of variation in X? With or without an assertion of other causal variables as part of the theory, variation in X is the exclusive cause of variation in Y and variation in Y is the exclusive cause of variation in X to the extent that the Cs value approaches 1.0. Conversely, to the extent that Cs is less than 1.0, variation in X and/or variation in Y is the paramount cause or a partial cause of variation in the other variable; and a Cs approaching .00 is evidence that neither variable, X or Y, is even a partial cause of the other variable.

Still another criterion is needed when the asserted relation pertains to unidirectional rather than bidirectional causation. To simplify, only two versions of the unidirectional criterion are stated. The first pertains to positive unidirectional causation, Cpu, where it is asserted that an increase in X is the cause or a cause of an increase in Y but not that a decrease in X is the cause or a cause of a decrease in Y. The second version, Cnu, pertains to negative unidirectional causation, where it is asserted that an increase in X is the cause or a cause of a decrease in Y but not that a decrease in X is the cause or cause of an increase in Y. The two versions are:
$$Cpu=[A/(A+B)]-[(.5-|[C/(C+D)]|)+(.5-|[E/(E+F)]|)+(.5-|[G/(G+H)]|] \text{ and}$$
$$Cnu=[B/(A+B)]-[(.5-|[D/(C+D)]|)+(.5-|[F/(E+F)]|)+(.5|[H/(G+H)]|],$$
in which A = the number of observed instances where an increase in X was

followed by an increase in Y; B = the number of observed instances where an increase in X was followed by a decrease in Y; C = the number of observed instances where a decrease in X was followed by a decrease in Y; D = the number of observed instances where a decrease in X was followed by an increase in Y; E = the number of observed instances where an increase in Y was followed by an increase in X; F = the number of observed instances where an increase in Y was followed by a decrease in X; G = the number of observed instances where a decrease in Y was followed by a decrease in X; and H = the number of observed instances where a decrease in Y was followed by an increase in X.

Some Qualifications and Caveats. Six points are crucial for understanding and applying the criteria. First, again to simplify, the *Cpu* criterion and the *Cnu* criterion are stated such that an instance of no discernible change in either X or Y is to be ignored. Second, for any asymmetrical (nonreciprocal) criterion, whereas the length of the interval between change in X and subsequent change in Y must be stipulated by the theorist, the interval between change in Y and subsequent change in X (if any) can be an interval of any length as long as it is the same for all observations. Third, all previous observations about recognizing other causal variables in connection with *Ca* apply to *Cpu* and *Cnu*. Fourth, the unidirectional criteria (i.e., *Cpu* and *Cnu*) are not truly complete if only because they pertain to increase or decreases (i.e., as dichotomies) and ignore the degree of association between the amount of change in the two variables. Fifth, *Ca*, *Cs*, *Cpu*, and *Cnu* are to be applied only in longitudinal research; specifically, the data pertain to change in the values of the variables. Sixth, neither *Cpu* or *Cnu* is worded such that it applies when it is asserted that (1) a decrease in X is the cause or a cause but not that an increase in X is the cause or a cause of an increase in Y or (2) that a decrease in X is the cause or a cause of an increase in Y but not that an increase in X is the cause or a cause of a decrease in Y. The last point can be remedied readily by substituting the following letters in the *Cpu* and *Cnu* criteria: C for A and A for C, D for B and B for D, G for E and E for G, and H for F and F for H.

There are no statements of criteria for assessing causal assertions that combine the bidirectional-unidirectional distinction and the symmetric-asymmetric distinctions (or the reciprocal-nonreciprocal distinction). Such criteria are excluded for two reasons. First, four combinations (asymmetric-bidirectional, asymmetric-unidirectional, symmetric-bidirectional, and symmetric-unidirectional) would have to be treated, and each is very complicated. Second, sociological theories have not developed to the point that a theorist is likely to make causal assertions that combine the two distinctions. For that matter, an assertion of unidirectional causation can be treated as though bidirectional in tests of the theory if it is assumed (justifiably, of course) that changes in the values of the causal variable have been monotonic—all increases or all decreases—and in the direction indicated by the relevant causal assertion.

Despite recognition of types of causation, it must be stressed that causation is treated as a matter of degree or extent rather than in terms of the traditional trichotomy (X is the cause of Y, X is a cause of Y, or neither). Note, however, that there is a connection between *some* recognized types of causation and the conception of causation as a matter of degree or extent. Specifically, bidirectional causation can be translated as meaning "more" causation than is the case for unidirectional causation; and the translation is no less obvious in the case of exclusive vs. paramount vs. partial causation. Although a characterization of causation as both necessary and sufficient means "more" causation than does only necessary or only sufficient, no criterion pertaining to the necessary-sufficient distinction has been introduced. Granted the possible need for such a criterion, the distinction becomes exceedingly complex when an attempt is made to extend it from qualitative to quantitative variables. For that matter, it is doubtful that the necessary-sufficient distinction can be made independently of the exclusive-paramount-partial distinctions.

Whatever the criterion, one application is hardly a sufficient basis for assessing a causal assertion, but any stipulation of a minimum number would be grossly arbitrary and perhaps clearly unrealistic. Still another bar to conclusive evidence is the virtual certainty that no test will provide maximum support for the causal assertion (a criterion value of +1.0); hence, any test is simply indicative of the *amount* of the assertion's predictive accuracy. If critics reject the strategy and demand a criterion of conclusive evidence, they should contemplate abandoning the notion of causation, especially in connection with the social and behavioral sciences.

Causal criteria need not be applied and perhaps cannot be applied when deducing assertions of space-time relations between variables from causal premises. Consider two assertions of positive and bidirectional causation in these forms: $X{\rightarrow}Y$ and $Y{\rightarrow}Z$. If in both instances the causation is assertedly exclusive or paramount (i.e., not partial), then surely the deduction of a positive measure of association between X and Z would be justified (assuming they are mensurable variables). Moreover, evidence could be brought to bear on the deduced relation without applying a criterion of causal evidence to the three relations (X–Y, Y–Z, and X–Z), even assuming that it would be possible.

If a theory makes causal assertions, an assessment of its predictive power is incomplete until a criterion of causal evidence has been applied; but the application is not necessary for the deduction of theorems in accordance with subsequent rules. Indeed, should the theorist be unable or unwilling to formulate temporal quantifiers such that the measures of association in tests of the theorems pertain to lagged referents, the test outcomes have only a problematical bearing on the causal criterion. To illustrate, in the X–Y–Z case (*supra*) the theorist may have no confident belief about the appropriate time lag for both asserted causal relations ($X{\rightarrow}Y$ and $Y{\rightarrow}Z$). If so, he/she may be willing to assume that the lag is so short that some support for the theory can be realized by attaching synchronic temporal quantifiers to the referentials (i.e., in the theorems).

Even if the theorist does have a confident belief as to the length of the temporal lag for both causal relations (in the illustrative case, X–Y and Y–Z), he/she may also believe that specifying the appropriate temporal quantifiers would make the theory untestable (i.e., investigators would not be able to acquire the requisite data); and, again, the theorist may resort to synchronic temporal quantifiers. Whatever the rationale for synchronic temporal quantifiers, tests of the theorem cannot be construed as an application of the causal criterion (*supra*). Again, though, it is possible to deduce theorems with synchronic temporal quantifiers, provided that the theorist explicitly assumes that the causal lags are not so long as to preclude at least moderate association measures in tests of the theorems. If in testing such a synchronic theorem the association measure proves to be negligible, it will not be known whether the outcome is due to an unjustified assumption about the lengths of the causal lags or a false casual assertion; but the tests will not have been pointless, because the outcome is negligible predictive accuracy, whatever the reason.

Terminology. To realize general rules of deduction, the term "variable" is used subsequently not only in a quantitative sense but also as meaning a construct, a concept, or a referential. Therefore, a deduced statement may be a theorem, an implied proposition, an implied postulate, or an implied axiom. In each case the statement is deduced from the premises in the theory's intrinsic part; and, once deduced, the statement becomes a component of that intrinsic part (i.e., another intrinsic statement). However, it is necessary to identify each intrinsic statement, whether a premise or a deduction, as being either causal (the relational term is "determinant" or "determinants") or covariational (the relational term is either "greater...greater" or "greater...less"). In either case the reference is always to a statement *about* a relation and not the actual relation itself; so the truth of the statement (i.e., its consistency with the actual relation) is only asserted.

In subsequent deduction rules extensive use is made of four terms: circuit, incomplete circuit, incomplete causal circuit, and incomplete covariational circuit. Each term refers to two or more interrelated statements, interrelated in that each shares a constituent variable with at least one of the others.

The Sign of a Statement. The subsequent deduction rules apply only if the statements in question have the relational terms prescribed earlier. That point is particularly relevant in the case of Rule 17: *If the phrase "positive... determinant" or "greater...greater" is a constituent of a statement, the statement is identified by a plus (+) sign; and if the phrase "negative... determinant" or "greater...less" is a constituent, the statement is identified by a minus (–) sign.*

For purposes of deduction, signs need not be actually shown in the premises; but they should be recorded in a theory's diagram (see Figure A–1, *supra*). Indeed, while not mandatory, a diagram facilitates application of deduction rules, promotes understanding of the theory, offers a succinct summary of it, and may lead the theorist to recognize features of the theory that might otherwise not have been detected readily (if at all).

Illustrations of Various Forms of Incomplete Circuits. Each broken line in the six illustrations that follow represents a statement which connects two variables. A pointed line (i.e., an arrow) signifies causation, and other lines signify covariation. In either case the line is broken to show the statement's sign (i.e., the direction of the asserted relation). Each series of connected lines is to be construed as a theory's premises; as such, each variable is a construct, a concept, or a referential. Although the deduction rules were designed primarily to deduce theorems, they apply also in deducing implied propositions, implied postulates, or implied axioms. Accordingly, a deduced statement can be thought of as a conclusion (i.e., a generic designation).

The six series, I–VI, that follow illustrate causal paths, covariational paths, and mixed paths.

Series I: $Z \leftarrow (+) - Y \leftarrow (-) - X - (+) \rightarrow W - (+) \rightarrow V$
Series II: $Z - (+) - Y - (-) - X - (+) - W - (+) - V$
Series III: $Z - (+) - Y \leftarrow (-) - X - (+) \rightarrow W - (+) \rightarrow V$
Series IV: $Z \leftarrow (-) - Y \leftarrow (+) \rightarrow X - (+) - W - (-) - V$
Series V: $B - (+) \rightarrow X$
Series VI: $Z - (+) \rightarrow Y - (-) \rightarrow X \leftarrow (+) - W \ll \leftarrow (+) - V$

Series I is an incomplete causal circuit, Series II is an incomplete covariational circuit, Series III and IV are mixed incomplete circuits, Series V is not a complete or incomplete circuit, and Series VI comprises two incomplete causal circuits (variables Z–Y–X and variables V–W–X). Five definitions are needed to understand the differences and to clarify subsequent terminology.

First, an incomplete circuit is a series of three or more variables linked by two or more statements, such that (1) each statement relates only two variables; (2) each of two and only two of all of the variables in the series are constituents of only one statement (e.g., in Series I, *supra*, two and only two variables—*V* and *Z*—are constituents of only one of the four statements in the series); (3) at least one of the variables in the series is a constituent of two of the statements; (4) no variable in the series is a constituent of more than two statements; and (5) if the relational term of some or all of the statements is causal, one of the variables, designated as the distal variable, can be described as the cause—symmetrical or symmetrical, reciprocal or nonreciprocal, direct or indirect—of all of the other variables in the causal statements. Second, an incomplete causal circuit is an incomplete circuit in which there is a causal relational term in all of the statements linking the variables (i.e., each statement asserts causation). Third, an incomplete covariational circuit is an incomplete circuit in which the relational term in each statement is either "greater...greater" or "greater...less". Fourth, an incomplete mixed circuit is an incomplete circuit in which at least one statement is causal and at least one is covariational. Fifth, unless qualified, the term "incomplete circuit" refers to an incomplete causal circuit, an incomplete covariational circuit, or a mixed incomplete casual circuit.

The six series do not remotely reveal the variety of forms of incomplete circuits. For one thing the most simple incomplete casual circuit, $X \rightarrow Y \rightarrow Z$ (signs would be irrelevant), is not shown. Why is it, then, that Series I is not described as comprising *two* incomplete causal circuits (X–Y–Z and X–W–V)? Because if those two sets of statements appear in the same theory, they are components of *one* incomplete causal circuit. Then observe that some changes in each series would not alter the identification. Thus, if the X–W covariational relation in Series IV were changed to $X–(+) \rightarrow W$, the series would remain "mixed."

The six series are conducive to both an overestimation and an underestimation of the complexity of deduction. One example of overestimation must suffice. The plus and minus signs in the series have no bearing on the definition of an incomplete circuit or the types of circuits. As for underestimating complexity, the deduction rules do not apply to some types of causation, one being "unidirectional"; and even partial causation creates difficulties.

The Primary Deduction Rule. In a complete circuit each variable appears in two of the constituent statements, such that the circuit is "circular"; but the following illustration may appear puzzling, simple though it is: $X–(+)–Y–(+)–Z–(+)–X$. The illustration is not puzzling on recognition that the last statement, $Z–(+)–X$, can be deduced from the first two (X–Y and Y–Z). The deduction rule is stated subsequently, and the immediate point is that a deduction can be described as *closing* an incomplete circuit. However, a deduction presupposes and requires certain kinds of circuits.

What has been said applies to causal circuits (i.e., not just to covariational circuits), the corresponding illustration being: $X–(+) \rightarrow Y–(+) \rightarrow Z \leftarrow (+)–X$. The $Z \leftarrow (+)–X$ statement can be deduced from the first two statements in the sequence; as such, the statement closes an incomplete causal circuit.

The depiction of deduction as closing incomplete circuits is better understood by reconsidering Series I–IV (*supra*). Observe that each of the two *terminal* variables, Z and V, in all of the incomplete circuits (causal or covariational) appears in only one constituent statement. In each series the deduced statement would link Z and V.

The diagram of the illustrative theory, Figure A–1 (*supra*), serves to clarify the translation of deduction as the closing of an incomplete circuit of statements. Each theorem in the theory is a covariational statement, one that closes what would otherwise be an incomplete circuit. However, illustrations are not substitutes for rules of deduction, the primary one being Rule 18: *The sign of a deduced statement, one that links the terminal variables in an incomplete circuit and thereby closes that circuit, is negative if and only if an odd number of statements in the incomplete circuit have a negative sign; otherwise, the sign of the deduced statement is positive.*

Some Complexities. In the illustrations designated as Series I, III, IV, and VI (*supra*), each causal relation can be described as either exclusive or paramount causation. Stated otherwise, there is no instance of partial causation, meaning that no variable is depicted as being the asserted effect of two or more variables.[36] But contemplate the consequences of combining Series V with some of the other series. If all of the statements in Series V and Series I were premises in a theory, it may appear at first thought that there is still only one incomplete causal circuit but now a longer one, a new distal variable, B, having been added. Yet that would be contrary to the definition of an incomplete circuit, for X would appear in *three* statements: B–X, X–Y, and X–W. Moreover, the combination of Series V and Series I would result in three incomplete circuits: Series I as it is now shown (*supra*), then B–X–Y–Z, and then B–X–W–V. Series I would still be closed by a negatively signed statement linking V and Z; but one of the new incomplete circuits would be closed by a statement linking B and Z, and the other by a statement linking B and V.

When Series V is combined with Series IV, the outcome is equivalent to the combination of I and V (previously described). As before, there would be three incomplete circuits: the existing one, Z–Y–X–W–V (Series IV), would still be closed by a statement linking Z and V; one of the new circuits, B–X–W–V, would be closed by a statement linking B and V; and the other new circuit, B–X–Y–Z, would be closed by a statement linking B and Z. Note particularly that the outcomes of the two combinations—Series I and V, Series IV and V—are equivalent even though Series I is an incomplete causal circuit and Series IV is a mixed incomplete circuit. Note also that reciprocal or symmetrical causation, Y↔X in Series IV, is treated as asymmetrical or nonreciprocal causation in both directions (i.e., Y↔X=Y→X and Y←X) as far as closing incomplete circuits are concerned. But that is not the case if both variables are asserted to have additional determinants. Thus, Z←Y↔X→W is interpreted as an incomplete causal circuit, one that would be closed by a statement linking Z and W; but Z→Y↔X←W cannot be closed by that statement, though it could close Z→Y↔X→W or Z←Y↔X←W.

Partial causation is not just a matter of a variable being a constituent in two or more incomplete causal circuits in the same theory, as is X when Series I and Series V are combined; additionally, the variable must be an asserted direct *effect* of two or more determinants. That point is illustrated by Series VI (note again that the series comprises two incomplete circuits). No covariational relation between Z and V can be deduced without qualification.[37] It is not just a matter of X being a constituent in two incomplete causal circuits (Z→Y→X and X←W←V); additionally, the incomplete circuits are such that X is asserted to have two proximate determinants (Y and W) and two distal determinants (Z and V). So the deduction of a negative covariational relation between Z and X (thereby closing the Z–Y–X incomplete circuit) would have to be qualified something like this: eliminating the determination of X by W, then the greater Z, the less X. Similarly, the deduction of a positive covariational relation between V and X would have to be qualified something like this: eliminating the determination of X by Y, then the greater V, the greater X.

Further Consideration of Partial Causation. The prescribed relational terms require recognition of the distinction between partial causation and exclusive or paramount causation. Given that partial causation is not asserted in the illustrative theory (again, a glance at Figure A–1, *supra*, will suffice), Figure A–2 was designed to provide examples of partial causation and the ensuing problems in connection with deduction.[38] The complexities created by partial causation and the structure of the premises preclude the deduction of a theorem from any of the premises in the diagram.

It may appear that Rule 18 prescribes a positive theorem that links R1 and R2 (both referentials) in Figure A–2; but Postulates 1 and 3 create doubts, for they indicate that Constructs I and II are both *partial* determinants of Concept II, and yet causal connections between those constructs and Concept I are not asserted.[39] So how could the covariational relation between Concepts I and II (as asserted by Proposition I) be close? The question introduces another deduction problem, one dealt with by Rule 19: *A statement that links the terminal variables in an incomplete circuit and thereby closes the incomplete circuit cannot be deduced without qualification unless the relation asserted by each constituent statement in that circuit is assumed to be close and/or the error terms in the relations asserted by those constituent statements are correlated negligibly at most.* The need for the rule can be illustrated by reference to two product-moment correlation coefficients, r_{xy}=+1.0 and r_{yz}=+1.0. Whatever the three variables may be, if the coefficients are based on the same units (e.g., all of the 50 United States), on the basis of a principle akin to Rule 19 one can deduce that r_{xz} is +1.0 or approaches that value. The immediate problem is that the closeness of the relations asserted in the premises of a theory cannot be known in any direct sense. At most it can be inferred from tests of theorems, and even then the inference cannot be precise (e.g., deducing a particular value of some conventional measure of association, such as a correlation coefficient).

Another problem is introduced by this question: how close must the relations in an incomplete circuit be to justify a deduction that closes the circuit? For present purposes, there can be only one answer: close enough to deduce correctly the sign (positive or negative) of the covariational association between the terminal variables. That answer is crucial in assessing a theory's predictive accuracy. If the direction (the sign) of the actual or "true" relation (though perhaps unknown and unknowable) is inconsistent with the deduced statement

Figure A-2: THE FORM OF A THEORY THAT ILLUSTRATES DEDUCTION PROBLEMS*

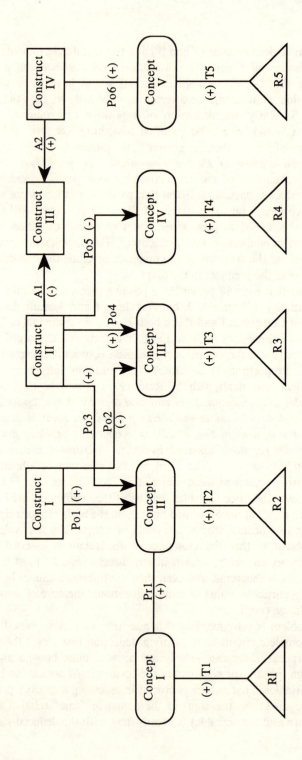

*A = an axiom; Pr = a postulate; R = a referential; T = a transformational statement

(i.e., what the relation should be if the premises are valid), one or more premises must be false. However, there are complexities, stemming primarily from recognition that the actual relations among the variables in the premises can be only inferred. Indeed, if the actual relations in the premises could be known without deduction, then theorems would not be essential; but theorems are deduced and tested primarily with a view to assessing the validity of the premises.

It is not possible even to estimate precisely how close the unknown relations among the variables in the incomplete circuit (i.e., the premises) must be for the deduced relation between the two terminal variables to be consistent with the associations revealed subsequently in tests. The minimum closeness depends not just on the number of relations (premises) in the incomplete circuit but also on the correlation of the error terms from one relation to the next. So there are really two unknowns.

Advocates of causal relational terms appear blissfully unaware that those terms do not solve any of the problems in question. In particular, if a statement asserts exclusive or paramount causation, the assertion suggests that the covariational relation between the statement's two constituent variables is close; but that suggestion no more justifies deduction or solves problems than does the simple assertion that the covariational relations in the premises are close, whatever their causal connections may be. Nonetheless, when partial causation is asserted or implied, it does create a need to qualify deductions.

Returning to Figure A–2, Pr1 (Proposition 1), T1 (Transformational Statement 1), and T2 make up an incomplete circuit, one that could be closed by a theorem linking R1 (a referential) and R2 (another referential). But, again, it is difficult to see how the actual relation between Concept I and Concept II could be sufficiently close given that (1) both Construct I and Construct II are causes of Concept II but not of Concept I and (2) Concept II is not the asserted cause of Concept I. So the deduction of a theorem linking R1 and R2 would be dubious without somehow taking R3 into account, for the R3 referents supposedly reflect both Constructs I and II (see Postulate 2, Postulate 4, and T3 in Figure A–2).

The prospect of a R2–R3 theorem is far more complex. If the theorem were deduced from Po1 (Postulate 1), Po2, T2, and T3, the deduction would have to be qualified so as to recognize Construct II as a partial cause of both Concept II and Concept III. Similarly, the R2–R3 theorem closing the other incomplete circuit—Po3, Po4, T2, and T3—would have to be qualified so as to take Construct I into account; but there would be no indisputable way without an expansion of the theory such that some concept is linked with Construct I but not Construct II. The same problem would arise when attempting to deduce a R2–R4 theorem or a R3–R4 theorem, the problem being that no referential reflects Construct I independently of Construct II.

The negative sign of Po2 precludes deduction of a theorem linking R2 and R3. Should it be deduced from Po1, Po2, T2, and T3, the theorem's sign would be negative; but its sign would be positive in the case of a deduction from Po3, Po4, T2, and T3. If the sign of Po2 were positive, it would be possible to deduce the same R2–R3 theorem from Po1–Po2–T2–T3 or Po3–Po4–T2–T3. The two incomplete circuits include all asserted causes of Concepts II and III, and the deduction of the same theorem from two or more incomplete circuits means that all of the variables in those circuits are (in effect) taken into account. Such would not be the case if Pr1 (Proposition 1) asserted that Concept I is a cause of Concept II, for that would make Concept I an exogenous variable.

Finally, the prospect of deducing a theorem linking R4 and R5 illustrates the most obvious problem in Figure A–2: the theorem could be deduced only from A1, A2, Po5, Po6, T4, and T5, a sequence that does not qualify as an incomplete causal circuit.[40] Indeed, for the same reason R5 cannot be linked with any of the other referentials.

Final Deduction Rules. Three rules are needed to summarize the observations made in connection with Figure A–2. Scant attention has been given to the illustrative theory's diagram (Figure A–1) because there is no need to qualify the deduction of any theorem.

Some of the deduction rules refer to an "exogenous variable"; and that term is defined by Rule 20: *A variable is exogenous if it is asserted to be the cause or a cause of one or more variables in an incomplete circuit but is not a constituent of that circuit.* Note that the term is defined relative to the notion of an incomplete circuit (causal, covariational, or mixed), and the definition does not necessarily apply in other contexts.

Although not illustrated by Figure A–1 or Figure A–2, a theory may be such that one and the same theorem can be deduced from two or more incomplete circuits. That situation is governed by Rule 21: *If the same asserted relation between two terminal variables can be deduced from two or more incomplete circuits and there is no variable exogenous to any of those circuits, the deduction need not be qualified.*

The situation necessitating a qualified deduction is recognized by Rule 22: *If the statement that links two terminal variables is deduced from an incomplete circuit in which one or more of the constituent variables is asserted to be an effect of an exogenous variable and Rule 21 does not apply, the deduction must be qualified by a reference to the exogenous variable or variables.* It is particularly important to recognize four possibilities: (1) more than one of the endogenous variables (those in the incomplete circuit) may be caused by an exogenous variable; (2) there may be more than one exogenous variable; (3) if more than one exogenous variable, they may or may not be asserted causes of the same endogenous variable; and (4) an exogenous cause cannot be exclusive or paramount (i.e., it must be identified as partial).

While application of any deduction rule does not require a diagram of the theory, a diagram does facilitate application; and that is especially true of Rule 22. In any case, the reference to an exogenous variable when qualifying a deduction must be consistent with Rule 23: *The qualification of a deduction must not only identify the relevant exogenous variables but also stipulate that they are to be taken into account, though how they are to be taken into account is not part of the qualification itself.* Because an exogenous variable is either a construct or a concept, it cannot be taken into account literally and directly. Only referents can be statistically controlled or otherwise taken into account; so referentials are the pertinent property terms when qualifying a deduction.

The appropriate form for qualifying a deduction is stipulated by Rule 24: *A qualified theorem should be stated in this form: Among U's and/or for any U over time, taking referential X into account, the greater referential Y, the greater (or less) referential Z.* More than one referential can be taken into account, but each must be linked with a concept or indirectly (through a postulate) with a construct, an exogenous variable in either case. Finally, the theorist must stipulate (in the theory's extrinsic part) how referents are to be taken into account when testing the qualified theorem, meaning that the stipulation is not given by the mode. There are various alternative procedures or techniques for taking variables into account (e.g., partial correlation), and the choice among alternatives is so contingent (e.g., on what is known or assumed about the distribution of the values of the variables) that it cannot be governed by a rule. Therefore, the theorist is the best judge for selecting a test procedure or technique so as to maximize a qualified theorem's predictive accuracy.

To be sure, the foregoing rules are somewhat complex and difficult, perhaps irritatingly so. Be that as it may, the notion of causation is complex; and nothing is gained by ignoring or tacitly denying those complexities, though that is precisely what advocates of causal models and path analysis in sociology have done. It will not do for those advocates to claim that the creators of the related statistical techniques imported by sociologists, notably Sewall Wright (e.g., 1934) and Herbert Simon (e.g., 1968), solved problems and resolved issues in formulating criteria of causal evidence. For all practical purposes, they ignored the problems and issues.[41] The more general point is that the conspiracy of silence in sociology about problems and issues concerning the notion of causation is bound to make the rules of deduction appear excessively complex.

The Sign-Rule Issue. Difficulties in formulating deduction rules are exacerbated in the case of quantitative variables because the only alternative to mathematics is the controversial "sign rule." That controversy cannot be ignored if only because Rule 18 is a version of the sign rule (for a more elaborate version, see Gibbs, 1972: 190–196).

Costner and Leik have created doubts about the sign rule; but their statements are puzzling, one being (1964:824): "Nothing in our present discussion can be construed as validating the sign rule for symmetric propositions." It is not clear how their discussion does *invalidate* the sign rule; and they do not deny that a sign-rule deduction is justified if the relations in the premises are assumed to be close, nor do they deny that the correlation between error terms from one relation to the next in the premises is relevant.

What has been said about Costner and Leik applies to the Turner and Wilcox's critique (1974). Freese and Sell (1980:283) describe the critique as relegating the sign rule to "decent oblivion"; but contemplate what Turner and Wilcox (1974: 586) actually say: "The system based on the 'high correlations' assumption lacked the deductive power of the standard system." It is not clear what they mean by the standard system, but neither that statement nor any other in their conclusions is a clear-cut declaration that the sign rule is unjustified regardless of the assumptions made. If their arguments are interpreted as claiming that the sign rule is not justified unless there is a unity (1.0) correlation between the variables in the premises, there are conditions (notably the correlation between error terms and the number of variables in the premises) in which the sign of the correlation between the terminal variables can be deduced with confidence even when the deduction is based on correlations in the premises that are far less than unity.

Remarkably, critics of the sign rule do not advance alternatives. True, Blalock and Costner argue as though deduction problems are avoided by the use of a causal language in theory construction, but that language is in no sense a substitute for deduction rules. For that matter, critics of the sign rule have yet to confront even the principal problems and issues concerning criteria of causal evidence (for elaboration, see Gibbs, 1982), let alone stipulate rules for deducing covariational conclusions (theorems or otherwise) from causal premises.

Critics of the sign rule may be tacitly arguing for statements of premises as equations; but while equations would make deduction unambiguous, several problems would not be avoided. Most obvious, a mathematical language and a causal language are quite different; but the contrast appears lost on Costner and Blalock (1972:834), who speak of causal notions coming "to be represented in mathematical terms" without identifying any such term. Causal premises may be translated as equations, though the strategy requires defensible criteria of causal evidence and what are really rules of deduction (i.e., translating a causal assertion into a covariational assertion entails deduction, explicit or implicit). Advocates of the strategy have yet to formulate such deduction rules, perhaps because they are unable or unwilling to confront the problems and issues pertaining to causation, evidential criteria in particular.

The idea of using mathematics as a mode of theory construction in itself is disputable. To be sure, such use is formal theory construction; and the ultimate goal in the development of a quantitative theory is a mathematical rendition of the theorems and perhaps even the premises. However, tests of a theorem are needed before reducing it to an equation, if only to have some basis for estimating the constants; and advocates of mathematical sociology persistently ignore the argument that a formal *verbal* version is needed as the first step. If that argument is accepted, then the sign rule or something akin to it is needed for the verbal version.

Some Limitations. It cannot be claimed that the prescribed deduction rules apply regardless of the causal terminology in the premises. In particular, the rules do not apply automatically unless the word "bidirectional" is a component of the relational term. They can be applied to theories in which the word "unidirectional" is a component of the relational term but *only if* the theorist assumes that changes in the relevant variables have been monotonic and in the direction (positive or negative) asserted.

What has been said about unidirectional causation extends to premises asserting that a change (increase or decrease) in some variable is necessary but not sufficient or sufficient but not necessary for change in some other variable. Such causation is not recognized by the proposed mode for two reasons: first, the appropriate deduction rules are bound to be complex; and, second, they are likely to give rise to theorems that cannot be tested by conventional methods.

The proposed mode will be incomplete until it comprises deduction rules and relational terms that apply to all identifiable kinds of causal relations between quantitative variables, but the incompleteness is not crippling. Should a theorist contemplate some kind of causal relation that is alien to the deduction rules or to the prescribed relational terms, he/she can devise what is needed as additions to the mode and set forth the additions in the extrinsic part of his/her theory.

Two Fallacious Problems. The commentary on limitations has no bearing on misgivings of many sociologists about assessing a theory's empirical validity or predictive accuracy by testing generalizations (theorems or conclusions) deduced from the theory's premises. Those critics never pose an alternative, perhaps because they are reluctant to declare that premises should be tested directly (i.e., without deductions). In any case, it is totally unconstructive to argue (see, e.g., Maris, 1969:51) that tests of a theorem cannot verify the premises. The argument is correct as far as it goes; but generalizations about infinite classes never can be verified, not even if they can be tested directly. Moreover, the critics ignore the point that tests of theorems may falsify the premises, or at least indicate that the theory's predictive accuracy is less than some acceptable level.

An even more fallacious problem with deduction is created by a charge akin to the fallacy of affirming the consequence. Even if the critics of deduction should grant that the premises can never be proven true (and concluding that the premises are true because the theorems are true does entail the fallacy), they could argue that the tests of theorems are irrelevant in the absence of a demonstration that the theorems can be deduced *only* from the premises in question. The critics ignore not only the possibility that the tests may yield evidence that the premises are false but also that a unique deduction or derivation can never be demonstrated, if only because the alternative premises for deducing the same theorem are seemingly infinite. The point is that demanding the impossible cannot be constructive criticism.

The Extrinsic Part of the Illustrative Theory

The illustrative theory's extrinsic part would be incomplete without definitions of unit terms and property terms, a few of which have been defined in the discursive introduction of the premises (*supra*). For that matter, some of the definitions that follow duplicate those given in Chapter 7, but avoiding duplications might make the illustrative theory's extrinsic part confusing.

Definitions of the Unit Term and the Unit Phrase

A country is a politically sovereign, autonomous, and unified territorial unit, though not necessarily continuous or contiguous, in that a particular set of inhabitants and only that set make decisions as to (1) military actions by the inhabitants and (2) coercive control attempts concerning who and what may cross the unit's boundary. If there are political divisions of a territorial unit (as in the case of, e.g., Latin America) and such decisions are made by two or more distinct sets of inhabitants, that unit is not a country, though a country's territorial parts are not necessarily coterminous.

Although the requisite data for tests are to be obtained from published sources (e.g., a *Demographic Yearbook*), tables in those sources are not the criterion for identifying countries, because they commonly list—in addition to countries—colonies, possessions, or mandated territories. If any criterion other than the definition is used, it must be the specific identification of territorial units as countries or nations in the publications of international organizations (e.g., the Organization of American States) or in a series of publications commonly recognized as pertaining to political features of or events in territorial entities throughout the world (e.g., *The Statesman's Yearbook*). No territorial unit is to be identified as a country if any such publication contradicts that identification.

The unit phrase "Among countries" denotes two or more countries, whether at the same historical time or not (e.g., 1980 for all or 1986 for one, 1980 for another, 1991 for still another, etc.). By contrast, the unit phrase "For any country over time" denotes any country considered at three or more time points or periods.

Property Terms: Constructs and Concepts

There are four constructs and three concepts in the theory's intrinsic part. All seven terms denote quantitative properties of countries, but unless stipulated otherwise the following definitions apply also to all types of populations or social units (including some types of intranational territorial divisions).

Constructs. Definitions of the four instances are arranged alphabetically because there is no rationale for any other order. No particular significance should be attached to the presence or absence of auxiliary (supplementary) definitions.

The "degree of division of labor" refers to the amount of differences among members of some designated population as regards their sustenance activities at some designated time point and the related amount of functional interdependence among the members at that time. Occupations and industries are indicative of differentiation in sustenance activities, but the differentiation must be socially recognized in the way of titles or other labels for divisions of population members. A sustenance activity is the expenditure of a human's energy and time in the production of what could be a commodity, good, service, or benefit, though not necessarily material or for exchange. Sustenance activities include all activities associated with work or gainful employment, but they are not limited to activities of persons identified as in the labor force, employed, or economically active.

"Organic solidarity" is the amount of functional interdependence among members of some designated population *as perceived by the members* at some designated point in time. The definition departs from Durkheim in that he did not describe organic solidarity as being a perceptual phenomenon.

"Political stability" is left essentially undefined. Its meaning can be illustrated by reference to the *rarity* of collective protests, assassinations, schisms within political parties, the emergence of political parties, insurrections, rebellions, revolutions, or civil war; but the list is only illustrative.

"Population concentration" is the reciprocal of the mean, median, or modal distance between each occupied place of residence in some designated territorial unit and all others in that unit at some designated time point. Two or more households in the same building are separate residences.

Concepts. Some of the three concepts are defined by a primary *definiens* and one or more auxiliary (supplementary) *definiens*. As in the case of constructs, the definitions are arranged alphabetically.

"Degree of industry differentiation" is the number of industries in some designated population at some designated time point and the uniformity or evenness of the distribution of the members among those industries, excluding those members who cannot be described as working or seeking work in a particular industry. An industry consists of (1) a particular and distinctive type product, (2) the related production activities, and (3) those who engage in the activities. The product may or may not be material, and instances may or may not be produced for exchange. In any case, there are no industries unless there are conventional designations in the population's language (e.g., in English-speaking populations: manufacturing, agriculture, banking) of one or more of the three components.

"Degree of urbanization" is the percentage of some designated population who at some designated time point resided in some designated type of urban unit. An urban unit is a city, an urban area, or a metropolitan area.

"Political violence death rate" is the average annual number of deaths resulting from political violence in a population during some designated period expressed as a ratio to the average daily number of population members. Political violence is (1) coercive behavior, including coercive threats, in an attempt to alter or maintain some political arrangement or (2) violence result-ing from such an attempt, as in the case of retaliation.

Property Terms: Referentials and Referential Formulas

Each of the three referentials (RDU, RDID, and RPVDR) in the theory's intrinsic part designates at least one formula. If more than one, each formula is a *version* of the referential (e.g., RDU_1, RDU_2); but two versions may differ only as regards stipulations of requisite data, the kinds and/or the acquisition procedure. Whatever the contrast in data instructions (if any), the referential formula itself may or may not be the same for two versions.

RDID. The first of two alternative referential formulas is:
$$RDID_1 = (1-[\Sigma X^2/(\Sigma X)^2])/(1-[1/Nc]),$$
where X is the number of members of a country's population in a *specific* industry (e.g., railroad transportation) or industry *category* (e.g., transportation), and Nc is the number of such specific industries or industry categories in the country. In this and a subsequent version of the RDID formula, the temporal quantifier is "at T_{0-1}," meaning any time point in any calendar year.

The unemployed are to be included in the total—ΣX—if and only if they have been assigned to particular industries or industry categories (along with the employed); otherwise, where the unemployed are reported as one separate category, they must be excluded from the total. If "students" and "retired" are reported in the source table, they must be excluded from the total. Finally, individuals identified as "industry unknown" or a similar designation are to be excluded from the total.

The second alternative referential formula is:
$$RDID_2 = 1-([\Sigma|X-M|/2]/[\Sigma X-M]),$$
where $M = \Sigma X/Nc$, and X and Nc are as defined previously in connection with

$RDID_1$. All observations made on particular categories (e.g., the unemployed) in connection with $RDID_1$ apply also to $RDID_2$.

Any test of a RDID theorem (one in which that referential is a variable) can be based on referents computed by application of either $RDID_1$ or $RDID_2$. However, *only one* of the two formulas is to be used in each particular test. The claim is that both formulas will support the theorem; but should research eventually demonstrate that one formula provides substantially more support than the other, this part of the theory must be reformulated.

Because there is no possibility of gathering data on the industry composition of even a few countries, the stipulation of a data-gathering procedure (e.g., through surveys) would serve no constructive purpose. Hence, in each test the $RDID_1$ or $RDID_2$ formula is to be applied to industry data obtained from one and only one of two kinds of sources: (1) official census reports of countries or (2) publications of international organizations, such as the *Labour Yearbooks* of the International Labour Office or the *Demographic Yearbooks* of the United Nations.

In the publications of international organizations, industry data for countries are commonly reported only in terms of eight, nine, or ten broad categories (e.g., manufacturing, services). However, the number of categories is less for a few countries because two or more categories have been combined, and no country should enter into a test of a RDID theorem if the source reports data on less than five inclusive industry categories in that country.

As for official census reports, the most detailed list of industries or industry categories (the table listing the greatest number) is to be used in computing $RDID_1$ or $RDID_2$ referents. There is considerable international variation in the number of "detailed census industries," and such variation is clearly an artifact of differential but arbitrary census practices. The number reported for any country is undoubtedly far less than the true number, and the discrepancy is probably substantially greater for some countries than others; hence, there is a need to eliminate the influence of variation in the number. Both $RDID_1$ and $RDID_2$ were so designed.

RDU. There is only one referential formula:

$RDU=[(Ur/P)]100$,

where *Ur* is the total number of individuals residing in one of the country's urban units at some time point, and *P* is the country's total number of residents at that time. Consistent with the definition, the temporal quantifier "at T_{0-1}" means any point in any calendar year.

There are three versions of the formula, with the only difference being the *type* of urban unit. In the case of RDU_1, *Ur* is the total number of individuals residing in any metropolitan area having at least 100,000 residents; for RDU_2, *Ur* is the total number residing in any urban area having at least 50,000 residents; and for RDU_3, *Ur* is the total number residing in any city having at least

20,000 residents. In each test of a RDU theorem, the formula is to be applied only to urban units of the same type, meaning that all referents are to be instances of RDU_1, RDU_2, or RDU_3 rather than a mixture of types.

Each *Ur* number is to be acquired from (1) any official publication (e.g., a census report, statistical abstract, or yearbook) of one of the country's government agencies (2) any publication by an international organization (e.g., the United Nations' *Demographic Yearbook* series), or (3) any scholarly or scientific publication that reports *Ur* numbers as one outcome of an attempt to delimit urban areas or metropolitan areas by applying some uniform procedure internationally. Whereas all *Ur* numbers in a test are to be acquired from the same kind of source (i.e., one of the three but not a mixture), the *P* numbers are to be acquired from either the first or second source.

If English is not the major language of the country, the terms designating the three types of urban units are to be translated as indicated by any multilingual dictionary. However, if only to facilitate translations, three brief definitions are in order. A *city* is territorial unit with an official (i.e., legal, administrative, governmental) boundary, one originally drawn so as to include most or all of an extant or anticipated urban area; and the boundaries of instances (unlike other civil divisions, such as states or counties in the U.S.) are not necessarily coterminous even when separations by water are ignored. An *urban area* comprises space used from some definite purpose *other than* resource extraction (including agriculture, forestry, hunting, fishing, or mining) and is the location of at least two nonextractive facilities (stores, hospitals, factories, cemeteries, etc.) *and* two or more residences. Observe that the separation of nonextractive facilities and the separation of residences by space under extractive use is indicative of the dispersed mode of spatial organization (i.e., the extreme case being *no* urban areas). Finally, a *metropolitan area* consists of a central urban area and the surrounding territory (perhaps including additional urban areas) in which a substantial proportion of residents commute to work in the central urban area and/or serves as a place of employment for a substantial proportion of the central urban area residents.

Data from the first two kinds of sources (government publications or publications by international organizations) appear much more reliable and comparable than was once supposed (for evidence, see Gibbs and Davis, 1958); but minimum size limits are desirable because the official minimum varies substantially among some countries, the primary reason why the official definition of urban is not recognized in a referential formula. The minimum size limits also reduces the amount of rural territory and population in any instance of the type of urban units, but the limit is not so large as to result in a zero RDU referent for any country.

RPVDR. There is only one referential formula:

RPVDR=[(Td/Ny)/P] 1,000,000,

where *Td* is the total number of deaths from political violence occurring in a country over a period not less than 25 nor more than 35 years, Ny is the number of years in that period, and P is the country's population size at any point over the period. The temporal quantifier, "for T_{0-30}," is to be understood as meaning any period of not less than 25 years not more than 35. The most appropriate period, the one that would maximize predictive accuracy, is unknown. Less than 25 years might make the rate far too unstable for some countries, while a period longer than 35 years might remove the rate too much temporally removed from the RDU and RDID referents.

P is to be obtained from the same kind of sources stipulated in connection with the RDU formula. Td is to be computed from the contents of two newspapers, both published outside the country in question, a requirement thought to reduce the influence of governmental interference in domestic journalism. One newspaper is to have the world's greatest international circulation (but excluding newspapers published in the country), and the other is to have the greatest international circulation of all other newspapers published in the neighboring countries or the closest country if none are contiguous. Newspaper can be compared as regards *total* circulation only if separate figures for *international* circulation are not available. Finally, no event is to be counted as an instance of Td unless the event is reported in both newspapers and in such a way as to lead to the conclusion in both cases that the event qualifies.

Special Instructions for Tests of the Theorems

The test need not comply fully with all stipulations; but all departures from the stipulations should be noted in reporting the test outcomes, as should any ambiguity in the stipulations. All data sources and/or acquisition procedures must be reported.

One benefit of conducting tests in accordance with a particular stipulated procedure is that various features of that procedure (e.g., epistemic statements, deduction rules) need not be explained when reporting test outcomes. However, exploratory research, including the use of referentials formulas not identified here, is encouraged. Indeed, regardless of the theory, there is always a real need for a particular kind of exploratory research: the computation of a correlation between two sets of referents, with the only contrast being that each set was computed (independently) by different investigators. Such a correlation would bear on the assertion that the referential formula in question, including data instructions, is sufficiently empirically applicable. The only qualification of the need for exploratory research is that the findings must be reported apart and distinct from the test outcomes.

The Selection of Countries and Years. There is no particular criterion for selecting countries. Data availability is the foremost consideration, and the only prohibition is the selection of a particular country in the belief that it is especially consistent with or contrary to one or more of the theorems. Nothing precludes a random selection among countries for which the requisite data are available, but it is more compelling evidence when a cross-sectional test is based on all countries for which the requisite data are available over some time span (e.g., 1950–1960 for the RDID and RDU referents, and 1950–1985 for RPVDR). Whatever the RDID and RDU year (it must be the same for RDID and RDU because the temporal quantifier of both is "at T_{0-1}"), the years for RPVDR must be the following subsequent 25–35 years. Thus, if the available data are such that "at T_{0-1}" for a particular country is taken to be any point during 1955, then "for T_{0-30}" in that case must be 1955–1980 or some longer period within the 1955–1990 time span. The exact years may vary internationally, and for any particular country they depend on what is taken as T_{0-1}.

Comments on selecting countries for cross-sectional tests apply also to longitudinal comparisons (e.g., the U.S., each census year since 1899). However, whatever the country, the historical year taken as T_{0-1} determines the other historical years; and a decennial series of RDID and RDU referents is desirable. Thus, if in longitudinal comparisons 1910 is taken as T_{0-1}, then the corresponding (but lagged) RPVDR referent could be for 1910–1935, the next RDID and RDU referents would be for 1920 and the corresponding RPVDR referent would be for 1920–1945, and so forth. The temporal stipulations are not made with confidence, because at present there is no evidence as to what lag length for RPVDR maximizes predictive accuracy; so there is a very special need for exploratory research on the question.

Measures of Statistical Association. Only two association measures are to be used: the rank-order coefficient of correlation (*rho*) or Kendall's *tau*. The second measure must be used when comparing the theory's predictive accuracy with that of a contending theory. *Rho* is the more conventional measure of ordinal association, and it can be computed more readily; but *tau* is more amenable to a precise interpretation (in terms of proportionate reduction in prediction errors), and for that reason alone it is less ambiguous when comparing the ordinal predictive accuracy of contending theories.

The use of a bivariate ordinal association measure is contrary to conventional sociology. Observe, however, that the concern is with *initial* tests of the theory, and a test of a theory differs from the fishing expeditions of sociologists under the guise of "modeling." The more important point is the need for simple tests to justify retention, modification, or rejection of the theory. After all, if even the sign of an ordinal association is not predicted correctly by a theory, why even bother to compare the theory with contenders to justify its rejection? As for the magnitude of ordinal associations, any magnitude in the predicted direction is better than none at all, at least until there is a superior contending theory.

Should simple tests justify retaining the theory (with or without modifications), more sophisticated association measures will be needed in subsequent tests. Thus, if the present theory should survive initial simple tests, in subsequent tests special attention should be devoted to the relation between population concentration and political stability (hardly an obvious relation, be it noted). As Figure A–1 indicates, the first variable is supposedly related to the second only through their mutual relation with the division of labor. Hence, the question: what happens to the association between RDU referents and RPVDR referents when RDID referents are taken into account? Obviously, something other than an ordinal measure of bivariate association is needed for an answer.

More on Test Procedure and an Application

There are two illusions in sociology concerning tests: first, that most sociologists judge a theory's merits by reference to test outcomes; and, second, that no particular procedure is needed to realize defensible tests. Those two illusions make formal theory construction all the more important. A formal mode should be coupled with a test procedure if only because the foremost rationale for the mode's use is *to further assessment of theories in terms of their predictive power relative to that of contenders.*

Testability is a pivotal dimension of predictive power if only because all other six dimensions depend on it one way or another (e.g., systematic assessments of a theory's predictive accuracy require tests), but testability is more difficult to analyze than any other dimension. The immediate problem is that even a clearly synthetic statement may be testable only in principle, and judgments of testability without regard to actual tests are inherently conjectural to some extent. Yet the number of actual tests is irrelevant unless the tests were defensible, and most sociologists appear insensitive to the difficulties in identifying the essential features of a defensible test. Confidence in the empirical applicability of the theory's referentials, congruence particularly, is only a necessary condition. Additionally, there must be a systematic procedure by which the theorems of a theory can be linked with the data employed in a test, and the conventional reliance of sociologists on the language of operational definitions or indicators is a far cry from such a procedure.

A formal mode of theory construction need not stipulate a particular test procedure to the exclusion of others. Therefore, the following procedure is not stated in terms of rules; but that admission does not make a test procedure any less important, and defensible tests are not the only consideration. Each theory could extend to a full prescription of the test procedure (i.e., not just special instructions); but a general procedure, one that applies to all theories stated in accordance with some particular mode, eases the burden on a theorist and conserves space in reporting tests.

The prescribed test procedure is illustrated by applying it to the theory used as an example (*supra*) in explicating the mode of theory construction. Because the simultaneous introduction of a test procedure and a detailed illustrative application would tax a reader's patience, the details of the application are slighted.

Three Referents for Each of 45 Countries

In a sense, any test of a theory is illustrative, but those reported subsequently are doubly so. Because of extremely limited research resources, only one of the three prescribed referentials formulas was actually applied, and in all three instances the data were not originally gathered to test the theory. Rather, data in two publications were used to approximate the tests called for in the theory's extrinsic part. Such use qualifies the tests, but there is a special justification. Research resources are so limited in sociology that use of published data in tests, especially of macro theories, should be encouraged. Those tests provide a low-cost basis for assessing the theory; and while a cautious interpretation of each outcome is imperative because of the use of secondary data, there is really only one real danger. If a theory is stated such that tests of it must rely on data in a *particular set* of publications, the tests cannot be constructive. Even if the tests are positive, the theory would have to be modified to realize future tests; and that modification creates doubts about the relevance of the initial tests. Fortunately, the tests of the illustrative theory reported here by no means exhaust the possibilities.

The RDU Referents. To comply in the early 1990s with the stipulation of data on deaths from political violence over a period of 25–35 years for each several countries, the RDU and RDID referents must be for some year during the 1950s or 1960s. Fortunately, what are subsequently identified as RDU_1 and $RDID_3$ referents were published (Gibbs and Martin, 1962) for each of 45 countries, *circa* 1950 data. Those referents are shown in Table A–1.

With only one minor qualification, the RDU_1 referents (Column 1, Table A–1) are totally consistent with the instructions in the illustrative theory's extrinsic part. The qualification is that Gibbs and Martin (1962) made use of a published report (International Urban Research, 1959) of the number of residents in the world's metropolitan area, the outcome of a near global application of a uniform delimitation procedure. There are questions, of course, about the adequacy of that procedure, but such questions are virtually inevitable.

RDID Referents. These referents (Column 2, Table A–1) were not computed strictly in accordance with instruction. The referential formula is:
$$RDID_3 = 1 - [\Sigma X^2 / (\Sigma X)^2],$$
where X is the number of individuals in each of nine industry categories, including "not classifiable elsewhere." That formula differs from $RDID_1$ (as in the theory's extrinsic part) only in that it excludes the $RDID_1$ denominator,

Table A-1

REFERENTS OF DEGREE OF URBANIZATION (RDU$_1$), *CIRCA* 1950;
REFERENTS OF DEGREE OF INDUSTRY DIFFERENTIATION (RDID$_3$), *CIRCA*
1950; AND REFERENTS OF POLITICAL VIOLENCE DEATH RATE (RPVDR),
1948-1977: 45 COUNTRIES

Countries and Years of Referents in Columns 1 and 2	RDU$_1$: Degree of Urbanization*	RDID$_3$: Degree of Industry Differentiation**	RPVDR$_2$: Death Rate from Political Violence, 1948-1977***
	Col. 1	Col. 2	Col. 3
Argentina, 1947	44.6	.8147	23.79
Australia, 1947	55.4	.8348	0.00
Austria, 1951	37.7	.7911	0.05
Belgium, 1947	41.4	.7969	0.32
Canada, 1951	42.7	.8197	0.03
Colombia, 1951	19.3	.6624	26.41
Costa Rica. 1950	19.9	.6565	3.16
Cuba, 1953	26.1	.7420	23.97
Denmark, 1950	37.3	.8007	0.11
Dominican Republic, 1950	11.2	.6293	72.04
Ecuador, 1950	14.9	.6793	2.07
Egypt, 1947	19.6	.6394	1.08
El Salvador, 1950	11.9	.5689	2.41
Finland, 1950	17.0	.7193	0.03
France, 1954	34.7	.8100	0.13
Greece, 1951	22.0	.7114	40.79
Guatemala, 1950	10.5	.5086	5.96
Haiti, 1950	6.0	.3010	3.84
Honduras, 1950	7.3	.3029	4.80
India, 1950	7.8	.4788	0.70
Ireland, 1951	27.5	.7631	0.56
Israel, 1948-52	55.8	.8187	3.21
Japan, 1950	36.6	.7055	0.02

Table A-1 (*continued*)

Countries	RDU$_1$	RDID$_3$	RPVDR$_2$
Malaya, 1947	12.7	.5500	88.91
Mexico, 1950	20.6	.6303	1.01
Netherlands, 1947	45.5	.8132	0.05
New Zealand, 1951	43.6	.8256	0.00
Nicaragua, 1950	13.3	.5140	16.27
Norway, 1950	21.8	.8098	0.01
Pakistan, 1951	5.1	.4033	303.49
Panama, 1950	23.9	.6956	4.47
Paraguay, 1950	15.6	.6549	5.24
Peru, 1940	11.0	.5816	5.70
Philippines, 1948	10.3	.5418	24.26
Portugal, 1950	19.6	.7073	0.26
R. of South Africa, 1951	29.9	.7059	4.49
Spain, 1950	25.5	.7014	0.26
Sri Lanka, 1946	9.5	.6723	27.80
Sweden, 1950	22.4	.8007	0.28
Switzerland, 1950	28.9	.7762	0.00
Thailand, 1947	6.8	.2735	3.00
Turkey, 1950	9.5	.4082	0.43
United Kingdom, 1951	71.5	.7687	0.97
United States, 1950	55.9	.8130	0.10
Venezuela, 1950	25.2	.7597	11.49

*Percentage of the country's population residing in metropolitan areas. Figures from Gibbs and Martin, 1962: 671.

**See text for formula. Figures from Gibbs and Martin, 1962: 671.

***Average annual per 1,000,000 population at year shown in row heading. Number of deaths from Taylor and Jodice, 1983: Table 2.7.

1–(1/Nc), where Nc is the number of industry categories. The exclusion is not serious because the denominator eliminates the influence of variation in Nc (a variation stemming from arbitrary census practices), and the countries in Table A–1 do not differ as regards industry categories in the data source (United Nations, *Demographic Yearbook, 1956*). So for those countries there was no need to eliminate Nc variation.

Inclusion of "not classifiable elsewhere" is a more serious departure from instructions in the theory's extrinsic part. Nonetheless, some sample computations indicate that the international correlation between the $RDID_3$ referents and the $RDID_1$ or $RDID_2$ referents approaches unity. Indeed, although systematic research is needed, it appears that the correlation between any two versions of the referential formula (even some not considered here) for any set of countries will be substantial; and demonstration would further confidence in Transformational Statement 2.

The RPVDR Referents. Had Taylor and Jodice (1983) not attempted counts of deaths from political violence in 136 countries over 1948–1977, prospects for tests of Theorem 2 or Theorem 3 would be diminished greatly. However, the counts were not made from exactly the kind of sources stipulated in the illustrative theory's extrinsic part; rather, they were made on the basis of the *New York Times Index* and various other sources (e.g., *Keesing's Contemporary Archives*) that rely partially on numerous national newspapers.

The referents in Column 3 of Table A–1 were computed by the referential formula previously designated as RPVDR, and the $RPVDR_2$ designation in the column heading indicates only that the data were not acquired fully as stipulated by the theory.[42] Yet it does not follow that the death counts are less reliable than the counts that would have been made had it been feasible to make them exactly as stipulated by the theory. Given Taylor and Jodice's vast experience, their counts might well be more reliable.

Selection of the 45 Countries. Although the countries are not a random global sample, they represent a wide range of various characteristics (e.g., as to predominant religion). Moreover, they could not have been selected with a view to support or refute the theory, for they were identified (as a set) in one of the source publications (Gibbs and Martin, 1962) long ago.

Insofar as the countries are unrepresentative, it is due primarily to international variation in the availability of requisite industry data in the *Demographic Yearbook, 1956* (Gibbs and Martin's source, 1962). Given the extensive global coverage of deaths from political violence and metropolitan residents, selectivity is scarcely a major problem as far as those data are concerned.

Epistemic Statements, Hypotheses, and Descriptive Statements

Regardless of the data used, tests are indefensible without a procedure for linking the data with predictions derived from the theory. Sociologists traditionally speak of operational definitions or indicators, but both languages fail to recognize any distinction akin to that between transformational statements and epistemic statements.[43] Moreover, neither language is suited for an answer to this question: is the link between a theory and test data synthetic and, if so, in what sense?

Epistemic Statements. In conducting a test, an epistemic statement is made to link a referential in a theorem with referents allegedly computed by applying the referential formula in question. The three following examples pertain to the illustrative theory.

Epistemic Statement 1: Among the countries shown in Table A–1, the greater the RDU_1 for a country, the greater the country's referent in Column 1 of that table.[44]

Epistemic Statement 2: Among the countries shown in Table A–1, the greater the $RDID_3$ for a country, the greater the country's referent in Column 2 of that table.

Epistemic Statement 3: Among the countries shown in Table A–1, the greater the $RPVDR_2$ for a country, the greater the country's referent in Column 3 of that table.

Far from being true by definition or pedantic, an epistemic statement makes a crucial assertion; it claims that the referential formula in question has been applied correctly to the prescribed kind of data. Obviously, application errors and even deliberate misapplications (perhaps total fabrications) are possibilities, and the data may not have been acquired as stipulated by the theory.

To appreciate the implications, suppose that for each country there are several RDU_1 referents, with any two having been reported by different and ostensibly independent investigators (an individual or a team). Now suppose little if any disagreement between any two RDU_1 referents. Such congruence would indicate that the RDU_1 data were acquired as stipulated by the theory and that the formula was applied without error in all instances.[45] Described otherwise, the congruence would corroborate the empirical applicability of the RDU_1 referential formula. Yet no matter how many referents are compared, it would be incorrect to identify any of them as the "true value."[46] The "true" referents are unknown and unknowable, but someone who demands certainty should eschew science. Moreover, far from solving the problem, the language of operational definitions or indicators merely conceals it.

Hypotheses. When investigators compute two sets of referents (e.g., one set of RDU_1 referents and one set of $RDID_3$ referents, both for the same countries), the relation between the two sets is unknown; and a test of a hypothesis is essentially an examination of the truth or falsity of a prediction about something taken as an unknown.[47] However, a prediction is not relevant unless deduced from the theory's intrinsic statements by an objective procedure (i.e., one that promotes agreement when followed by two or more individuals working independently). Such a prediction takes the form of a hypothesis, meaning a possibly true or a possibly false statement about the relation between two particular sets of referents. The three following examples pertain to the illustrative theory (*supra*).

Hypothesis 1 (from Epistemic Statement 1, Epistemic Statement 2, and Theorem 1): Among the countries shown in Table A–1, the greater the value in Column 1, the greater the value in Column 2.

Hypothesis 2 (from Epistemic Statement 3, Epistemic Statement 2, and Theorem 2): Among the countries shown in Table A–1, the greater the value in Column 2, the less the value in Column 3.

Hypothesis 3 (from Epistemic Statement 1, Epistemic Statement 3, and Theorem 3): Among the countries shown in Table A–1, the greater the value in Column 1, the less the value in Column 3.

As just indicated, a hypothesis is a prediction deduced from a theorem and two epistemic statements in accordance with an explicit rule.[48] It is the sign rule as previously explicated.

Figure A–3 facilitates understanding both the prescribed test procedure and the deduction rule. However, three major components of the diagram have not been introduced.

Descriptive Statements. No theory is falsifiable unless hypotheses can be deduced from it and judged as either true or false. Agreement in such judgments requires a particular procedure, one which calls for investigators to make a statement about referents that is either clearly contrary to or consistent with the hypothesis in question. Such a statement is labeled descriptive rather than factual. The notion of a fact as "that known with certainty" is largely alien to science, and that point is illustrated by descriptive statements.[49] Regardless of how many descriptive statements are made by different investigators about two particular sets of referents and regardless of the amount of agreement, there is always the possibility of a computational error or a deliberate distortion. Nevertheless, a descriptive statement is as close to "that known with certainty" as science ever comes.

Three examples of a descriptive statement follow.

Descriptive Statement 1: The rank-order coefficient of correlation between the referents in Column 1 of Table A–1 and the referents in Column 2 of that table is +.909.

Descriptive Statement 2: The rank-order coefficient of correlation between the referents in Column 2 of Table A–1 and the referents in Column 3 of that table is –.572.

Descriptive Statement 3: The rank-order coefficient of correlation between the referents in Column 1 of Table A–1 and the referents in Column 3 of that table is –.530.

Summarizing the Test Outcomes. An interpretation of test outcomes should be based on two or more series of tests (in a series there is one test of each theorem). The interpretation may be nothing more than a summary of the

342

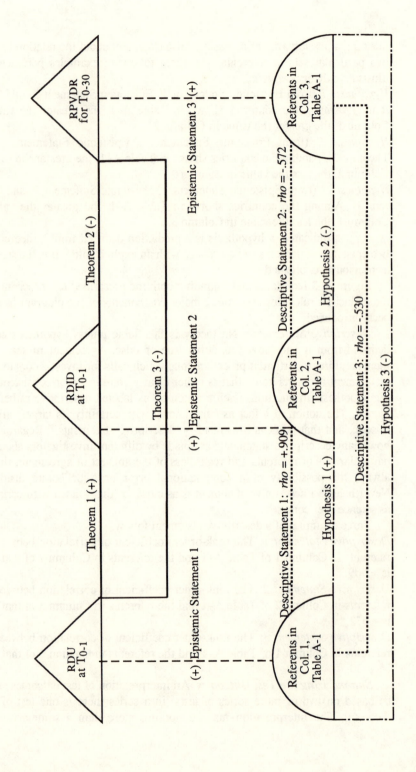

Figure A-3: DIAGRAM PERTAINING TO TESTS OF THE ILLUSTRATIVE THEORY

outcomes; and in this case it is brief: all descriptive statements are consistent with the corresponding hypothesis. If the theorist anticipates a certain minimum level of predictive accuracy, the summary of tests outcomes should speak to the magnitude of the association measure in each descriptive statement. No particular minimum level is anticipated in the present case, and any stipulation along that line will be arbitrary unless it pertains to a contending theory and tests of it (e.g., Robinson and London, 1991).

Although the subject is controversial, a theorist may anticipate that association measures will reach some particular level of statistical significance (e.g., <.05), and the practice of reporting the level regardless of the nature of the sample of units (e.g., random or not) is virtually a convention. So if only because of their *possible* relevance, levels of significance should be reported as a test outcome. Each of the three previously reported *rho* values is significant at the .01 level in a one-tail test (because the direction of the association is as predicted).

Discriminatory Power. Special test instructions may include a generalization about variation in the predictive accuracy of the theorems. Should the theorist not formulate such a generalization, the theory has no *discriminatory power*, the least commonly recognized dimension of predictive power. The generalization should be based on a principle that has potential applicability to other theories, and the theorist should make the principle explicit when stating the discriminatory generalization in the extrinsic part of the theory. For the illustrative theory the principle is: the greater the time lag between two referentials, the greater the probability of divergence from the true time lag (that which would maximize association) and the less the magnitude of the association measure in the corresponding descriptive statement. The rationale for the principle is that the stipulation of a very long time lag is especially likely to be little more than a guess and, hence, subject to considerable error.

The three example tests are largely consistent with the discriminatory generalization. The most substantial *rho* value pertains to Theorem 1, where there is no time lag between the two referentials (i.e., the temporal quantifier is the same for both). Then there is little difference between the *rho* values pertaining to Theorem 2 and Theorem 3. The negligible contrast is consistent with the discriminatory generalization because the two theorems have the same time lag (i.e., between the two referentials), and it is substantial.

Commentary and Exploratory Research on the Illustrative Theory

The prescribed procedure for reporting tests (*supra*) is largely alien to sociology, because sociologists are accustomed to critiques of theories rather than reports of tests. However, the procedure does not preclude special commentaries in light of the tests outcomes or exploratory research beyond the tests, and both are needed in the case of the illustrative theory.

Durkheim Reconsidered. Although Durkheim (1933) did not devote more attention to mechanical solidarity than to organic solidarity, numerous passages could be quoted as evidence that he had more doubts about organic solidarity's efficacy as a basis for social order. Despite Durkheim's astonishing indifference to political conflict (indeed, conflict in general), he did not deny that social order encompasses the political sphere. Hence, the test outcomes bear on an implication of the illustrative theory—that mechanical solidarity is *irrelevant* when contemplating determinants of political stability. Stated differently, only organic solidarity is relevant.

If *both* mechanical solidarity and organic solidarity are positive determinants of political stability but their effects are interactive (multiplicative) rather than additive, the form of the relation between the RDID referents (industry differentiation) and the RPVDR referents (political violence death rates) would resemble an inverted "U."[50] When those referents (Table A–1) are plotted in a scatter diagram, there is nothing like that form. Therefore, whatever the role of mechanical solidarity in the creation and maintenance of other dimensions of social order, it appears irrelevant as far as political stability is concerned. Of course, that conclusion is contingent on the validity of Postulates 2 and 3, Axioms 2 and 3, and Transformational Statements 2 and 3 in the illustrative theory, but the test findings are consistent with those premises. Anticipating the argument that Postulate 3 and Transformational Statement 3 (pertaining to political stability and violence) are alien to Durkheim's theory, those additional premises are necessary if organic solidarity is to have any real predictive implications beyond Durkheim's focus on restitutive law.

Further Exploratory Research. The previous argument about the *irrelevance* of mechanical solidarity can be translated such that it has additional predictive implications. Specific predictions can be made by computing referents of *extreme industry differentiation,* henceforth REID, and interpreting them as correlates of extreme division of labor, *meaning extremely high or extremely low.* Given the RDID formula employed to compute the referents in Column 2 of Table A–1, the absolute maximum possible value is .8889 and the absolute possible minimum value is .000.[51] So the midpoint of the scale is approximately .4445; hence, $REID=|RDID_3-.4445|$. Observe that a country having no industry differentiation (.0000) and one having the maximum amount (.8889) would have the same REID referents, .44 in both cases.

The rank-order coefficient of correlation between the REID referents (not show in any table) and the $RPVDR_2$ referents (Column 3, Table A–1) is –.582, which scarcely differs from the coefficient in the case of $RDID_3$ and $RPVDR_2$ (–.572). The virtual equivalence of the two coefficients suggests that both mechanical solidarity and organic solidarity are relevant, but there are only five countries with $RDID_3$ values *less than* .4445, the midpoint of the $RDID_3$ scale. For those five countries the rank-order coefficient of correlation between the

$RDID_3$ referents and the $RPVDR_2$ referents is not negative, as it should be if more mechanical solidarity (*less* industry differentiation) is conducive to political stability and reduces political violence. To the contrary, the coefficient is .000 for those five countries. By contrast, for the remaining 40 countries (those above the midpoint of the $RDID_3$ scale) the correlation between the $RDID_3$ referents and the $RPVDR_2$ referents is $-.602$. So, again, it appears that organic solidarity is a determinant of political stability but mechanical solidarity is irrelevant.

Of course, it could be argued that a much lower degree of division of labor than shown for any country in Table A–1 is needed for political stability. Yet that argument is akin to Durkheim's astonishing indifference to political instability and violence throughout much of human history, including many antiquarian societies (e.g., ancient China), where the degree of division of labor must have been far less than in any contemporary country. Nevertheless, as indicated by the findings on the five countries with $RDID_3$ values less than .4445, it could be that below some level the division of labor ceases to have a positive relation with political stability; and that possibility warrants further attention.

Interpretation of Test Outcomes

Again, an interpretation of tests should be based on at least two series. Any *greater* minimum number would reek with arbitrariness, and no mode of theory construction or principle of interpretation assures consistency in test outcomes from one series to the next (i.e., the dilemma of induction cannot be overcome). Consequently, it is unrealistic to demand interpretations that culminate in an irreversible conclusion. Such conclusions are particularly unrealistic when the theory's constituent variables are quantitative and, hence, each descriptive statement reports an instance of an association measure that varies (perhaps from -1.0 to $+1.0$). But in each case the hypothesis may be either consistent or inconsistent with the descriptive statement; so one can speak of predictive congruence or predictive incongruence as a possible test outcome. However, if predictive congruence is realized (i.e., the hypothesis is consistent with the descriptive statement), then predictive *magnitude*—the value of the association measure in the descriptive statement—becomes relevant. The two facets of predictive accuracy can be combined in the coefficient of predictive accuracy (CPA), which is the measure of association signed positively if the hypothesis and the descriptive statement are consistent and signed negatively if they are inconsistent.

The foregoing distinctions are necessary to understand two problems that haunt an interpretation of tests, problems that transcend the dilemma of induction (i.e., no one can know what future tests will reveal). First, it would be

346

grossly unrealistic to reject a theorem, let alone the entire theory, because of only one instance of predictive incongruence; but any criterion as to a minimum number or proportion would be extremely arbitrary. Second, the specification of any particular minimum predictive magnitude, whether for one test or an average, would be extremely unrealistic if the absolute maximum (usually +1.0) is specified but clearly arbitrary if less. The only constructive alternative is to judge the theory's predictive accuracy relative to that of contending theories.[52] That alternative is not a panacea, but it an illusion to suppose that the problems are somehow created by formal theory construction. Indeed, they are exacerbated by the discursive mode, and that mode virtually precludes any *systematic* revision of a theory in light of tests.

Preamble to Some Principles

Space limitations make it necessary to treat the subject largely in terms of a few principles. They are not exhaustive; and each must be introduced briefly (for a more elaborate treatment, see Gibbs, 1972:310–365), commencing with the most general: test outcomes should be interpreted with a view to retaining the theory for further tests (quite different from declaring it valid), modifying it before additional tests, or abandoning it.

The other principles presuppose that after two or more *series* of tests one of four labels has been assigned to each theorem. The first label is *true in the "A" sense*, meaning (1) no instances of predictive incongruence and/or proportionately less than for the foremost contending theory and (2) an average coefficient of predictive accuracy equal to or greater than .50 of the maximum for the kind of association measure in question and/or greater than the foremost contending theory.[53] The second label is *true in the "B" sense*, meaning (1) some instances of predictive incongruence but less than 50 percent and/or less than for the foremost contending theory and (2) an average coefficient of predictive accuracy less than .50 of the maximum for the kind of association measure in question and/or less than that for the foremost contending theory. The third label is *false in the "C" sense*, meaning (1) some instances of predictive congruence but less than 50 percent and/or less than the percentage for the foremost contending theory and (2) on average a negative coefficient of predictive accuracy less than .50 of the absolute maximum for the kind of association measure in question and/or ignoring the sign less than the coefficient for the foremost contending theory. The fourth label is *false in the "D" sense*, meaning (1) no instances of predictive congruence and (2) on average a *negative* coefficient of predictive accuracy greater than .50 of the absolute maximum for the kind of association measure in question and/or ignoring the sign greater than the coefficient for the foremost contending theory.

The labels cannot be applied to the three theorems of the illustrative theory because the reported tests constitute only one series. If the outcome of future tests is similar, all three theorems will be labeled true in the "A" sense; but should an attempt be made to improve the theory's predictive accuracy the modifications would be made as though Theorem 2 and Theorem 3 have been labeled true in the "B" sense.

First Principle. If all theorems are labeled "A," the theory may be retained unmodified; but if all either "C" or "D," abandonment of the theory should be entertained. Retention without modification does not necessarily indicate satisfaction with the theory's predictive accuracy; rather, that decision may reflect the judgment that more tests are needed to identify questionable components with greater confidence.

The rationale for abandoning a theory will not be fully understood until some examples are considered. It must suffice to say now that abandonment is advisable when extensive modifications appear necessary but with no clear basis for selecting particular components for modification.

Second Principle. When a particular transformational statement enters *only* into the deduction of "B" or "C" theorems (i.e., no "A" or "D" theorems), an attempt should be made to revise the referential formula. It may be revised by modifying the formula itself and/or the related data instructions (designations of the kind of data and/or the acquisition procedure). Returning to the illustrative theory, should future tests lead to "B" labels for Theorems 2 and 3 but "A" for Theorem 1, then modification of the $RPVDR_2$ referential formula would be in order.

The principle's rationale is that the relation asserted by a transformational statement may not be substantial but its sign (positive or negative) is virtually certain to be correct. True, a relation asserted by an axiom, postulate, or proposition may not be substantial, but such premises can be modified only by reversing the relational term (e.g., from "positive determinant" to "negative determinant"). The only alternative to that modification is to abandon the premise in question or extend it to third-order.

Third Principle. If both of two transformational statements entered into the deduction of at least one "B" theorem in common and both entered into the deduction of at least one "A" or "D" theorem (though not necessarily in common), modify the referential formula in the transformational statement that has the lesser average coefficient of predictive accuracy. The principle bears on a major problem in interpreting tests outcomes with a view to prescribing modifications. Tests may clearly indicate that a theorem is "B" because of *one or both* of the two referential formulas, but there may be doubts as to which of the three possibilities is most likely. As the principle suggests, the choice should be made by reference to other theorems deduced *in part* from each of the two transformational statements in question.

The illustrative theory (a glance at Figure A–1 will suffice) can be used as an example if it is supposed that two or more series of tests has resulted in these labels: "A" for Theorems 1 and 2 but "B" for Theorem 3. In such a case there is only one obvious possibility: the relation asserted either by Transformational Statement 1 or by Transformational Statement 3 is close enough to result in an "A" theorem that closes a short causal circuit (as in the case of Theorem 1 or 2) but not close enough to result in an "A" theorem that closes a long circuit (the circuit closed by Theorem 3, which includes all premises save Postulate 2 and Transformational Statement 2). Hence, a comparison of the average coefficient of predictive accuracy of Theorem 1 and Theorem 2 should reveal the "weakest" of the two transformational statements and thereby identify the referential formula that should be modified (here, RDU_1 or $RPVDR_2$). However, if the two average coefficients do not differ substantially (as in the present case), the theorist should modify both referential formulas; but the modification should not reduce the average coefficient of predictive accuracy for any theorem that has been labeled true in the "A" sense.

Fourth Principle. If an axiom, postulate, or proposition entered into the deduction *only* of "D" theorems, reverse the sign (positive to negative or negative to positive) of that premise. Reconsider the illustrative theory in connection with the principle, and suppose that the test outcomes were such that Theorems 1 and 2 are labeled as false in the "D" sense but Theorem 3 is labeled true in the "A" sense. Nothing more than the reversal of the sign of Postulate 2 would be needed to make the test outcomes consistent with the theory.

The fourth principle is more complicated than it may appear if only because a "D" theorem could be due to any one of at least two premises, perhaps a mixture of axioms, postulates, and propositions. When so, the premises most likely to be false in the "D" sense is in this order: axioms, postulates, propositions, and transformational statements.

Fifth Principle. A premise's sign, positive or negative, is irreversible if it would alter the sign of one or more "A" theorems. The principle recognizes one of many complexities in the interpretation of test outcomes. When there are multiple theorems, each premise enters into the deduction of more than one; and changing a premise has consequences for more than one theorem.

Suppose that after several series of tests Theorems 1 and 2 (the illustrative theory) have been labeled true in the "A" sense but Theorem 3 false in the "D" sense. Reversing the sign of any premise *other than* Postulate 2 and Transformational Statement 2 would make Theorem 3 true in the "A" sense, but the reversal would make Theorem 1 or 2 false in the "D" sense. Such a situation is indicative of a deduction error or an error in conducting or reporting a test.

Sixth Principle. Rather than abandon the theory totally, retain those premises that entered into at least one theorem labeled true in the "A" sense and abandon all other premises. The common belief that a theory is either true or false notwithstanding, some of its components may be true and others false.

Suppose that tests of the illustrative theory eventually lead to the labeling of Theorem 1 as true in the "A" sense but Theorems 2 and 3 as false in the "C" sense. For various reasons, some suggested by the previous principles, modification of the theory so as to retain all of it would not be feasible. However, according to the sixth principle, Transformational Statements 1 and 2, Postulates 1 and 2, and Axiom 1 should be retained along with Theorem 1, and the remaining premises abandoned along with Theorems 2 and 3.

Examples

Unfortunately, the six principles do not encompass all possible interpretations of test outcomes, nor are they complete criteria for deciding to retain, modify, or abandon the theory. The limitations of the principles can be appreciated best by close examination of Table A–2, which shows all possible outcomes of tests of a type 3–3–0–3–3 theory. Like the illustrative theory, all instances of that type comprise three axioms, three postulates, no propositions, three transformational statements, and three theorems.

The Character of the Suggested Changes. It is not feasible to do more here than *suggest* changes in a theory, given certain test outcomes. Just as a theorist must rely extensively on his/her imagination and intuition in formulating a theory, that is also the case when contemplating its retention, modification, or abandonment after tests.

Several suggested changes in Column 15 of Table A–2 merely point to choices that a theorist must make. Thus, for example, the choice between reversing Axiom 1 or reversing Postulate 1 in a type 3–3–0–3–3 theory cannot be governed by anything like a firm rule. Above all, the decision to abandon a theory should depend appreciably on the merits of contending theories.

Other Types of Theories. Although the interpretive principles apply to any theory stated in accordance with the proposed formal mode, the suggested changes in Column 15 of Table A–2 do not apply to all theories regardless of type. The theory must have the same structure as that of the illustrative theory, even the same signs of the premises. Otherwise, the test interpreter should prepare a table like Table A–2. Only then is he/she truly forced to assess test outcomes in light of all logical possibilities.

Neither the interpretive principles nor the suggested changes in particular types of theory extend to a discursively stated theory, but the implication is not that special principles are needed in the case of discursive theories. To the contrary, it is doubtful whether tests of a discursive theory can be interpreted in any systematic way, meaning such that independent interpreters are likely to agree as to the retention, modification, or abandonment of the theory.

Third-Order Theories

Up to this point the proposed mode has been limited to second-order theories, those in which there are only two property terms in each intrinsic

Table A-2

POSSIBLE ASSESSMENTS OF THE PREMISES OF A TYPE 3-3-0-3 THEORY IN LIGHT OF AT LEAST ONE SERIES OF TESTS AND SUGGESTED CHANGES IN THE THEORY

Judgments of the Three Theorems: 1, 2, 3*				Average Coefficient of Predictive Accuracy	Possible Assessments of the Premises in Light of Judgments of the Theorems*									Suggested Changes in the Theory**
True in "A" Sense	True in "B" Sense	False in "C" Sense	False in "D" Sense		Axioms			Postulates			Transformational Statements			
Col. 1	Col. 2	Col. 3	Col. 4	Col. 5	A1 Col. 6	A2 Col. 7	A3 Col. 8	P1 Col. 9	P2 Col. 10	P3 Col. 11	Tr1 Col. 12	Tr2 Col. 13	Tr3 Col. 14	Col. 15
1,2,3				Irrelevant	A	A	A	A	A	A	A	A	A	None
	3			1>2	A/B	A/B	A/B	A/B	A	A/B	A	A	A/B	Revise Tr3 referential formula
	3			2>1	A/B	A/B	A/B	A/B	A	A/B	A/B	A	A/B	Revise Tr1 referential formula
		3		1>2	A/C	A/C	A/C	A/C	A	A/C	A	A/C	A/C	Abandon A2, A3, P3, Tr3, Th2, Th3
		3		2>1	A/C	A/C	A/C	A/C	A	A/C	A/C	A	A/C	Abandon A1, P1, Tr1, Th1, Th3
			3	Irrelevant	A/D	A/D	A/D	A/D	A	A/D	A/D	A	A/D	None; deduction error or test error
	2			1>3	A	A/B	A/B	A	A/B	A/B	A	A/B	A/B	Revise Tr3 referential formula
	2			3>1	A	A/B	A/B	A	A/B	A/B	A	A/B	A/B	Revise Tr1 referential formula
		2		1>3	A	A/C	A/C	A	A/C	A/C	A	A/C	A/C	Abandon A2, A3, P3, Tr3, Th2, Th3
		2		3>1	A	A/C	A/C	A	A/C	A/C	A	A/C	A/C	Abandon P2, Tr2
			2	Irrelevant	A	A/D	A/D	A	A/D	A/D	A	A/D	A/D	None; deduction error or test error
	1			2>3	A/B	A	A	A/B	A/B	A	A/B	A/B	A	Revise Tr1 referential formula
	1			3>2	A/B	A	A	A/B	A/B	A	A/B	A/B	A	Revise Tr2 referential formula
		1		2>3	A/C	A	A	A/C	A/C	A	A/C	A/C	A	Abandon A1, P1, Tr1, Th1, Th3
		1		3>2	A/C	A	A	A/C	A/C	A	A/C	A/C	A	Abandon P2, Tr2, Th1, Th2
			1	Irrelevant	A/D	A	A	A/D	A/D	A	A/D	A/D	A	None; deduction error or test error
1,2,3				Irrelevant	B	B	B	B	B	B	B	B	B	Revise all referential formulas
3	1,2			Irrelevant	A/B	A/B	A/B	A/B	B	A/B	A/B	B	A/B	Revise Tr2 referential formula
1,2		3		Irrelevant	B/C	B/C	B/C	B/C	B	B/C	B/C	B	B/C	Abandon the theory

Table A-2 (continued)

Judgments of the Three Theorems: 1, 2, 3*				Average Coefficient of Predictive Accuracy	Possible Assessments of the Premises in Light of Judgments of the Theorems*									Suggested Changes in the Theory**
True Sense in "A"	True Sense in "B"	False Sense in "C"	False Sense in "D"		Axioms			Postulates			Transformational Statements			
					A1	A2	A3	P1	P2	P3	Tr1	Tr2	Tr3	
Col. 1	Col. 2	Col. 3	Col. 4	Col. 5	Col. 6	Col. 7	Col. 8	Col. 9	Col. 10	Col. 11	Col. 12	Col. 13	Col. 14	Col. 15
	1,2		3	Irrelevant	B/D	B/D	B/D	B/D	B	B/D	B/D	B	B/D	Abandon the theory
2	1,3			1>3	B	A/B	A/B	B	A/B	A/B	B	A/B	A/B	Revise Tr3 referential formula
2	1,3			3>1	B	A/B	A/B	B	A/B	A/B	B	A/B	A/B	Revise Tr1 referential formula
	1,3	2		Irrelevant	B	B/C	B/C	B	B/C	B/C	B	B/C	B/C	Abandon the theory
	1,3		2	Irrelevant	B	B/D	B/D	B	B/D	B/D	B	B/D	B/D	Abandon the theory
1	2,3			2>3	A/B	B	B	A/B	A/B	B	A/B	A/B	B	Revise Tr3 referential formula
1	2,3			3>2	A/B	B	B	A/B	A/B	B	A/B	A/B	B	Revise Tr2 referential formula
	2,3	1		Irrelevant	B/C	B	B	B/C	B/C	B	B/C	B/C	B	Abandon the theory
	2,3		1	Irrelevant	B/D	B	B	B/D	B/D	B	B/D	B/D	B	Abandon the theory
3		1,2		Irrelevant	A/C	A/C	A/C	A/C	C	A/C	A/C	C	A/C	Abandon P2, Tr2, Th1, Th2
	3	1,2		Irrelevant	B/C	B/C	B/C	B/C	C	B/C	B/C	C	B/C	Abandon the theory
		1,2	3	Irrelevant	C/D	C/D	C/D	C/D	C	C/D	C/D	C	C/D	Abandon the theory
2		1,3		Irrelevant	C	A/C	A/C	C	A/C	A/C	C	A/C	A/C	Abandon A1, P1, Tr1
	2	1,3		Irrelevant	C	B/C	B/C	C	B/C	B/C	C	B/C	B/C	Abandon the theory
		1,3	2	Irrelevant	C	C/D	C/D	C	C/D	C/D	C	C/D	C/D	Abandon the theory
1		2,3		Irrelevant	A/C	C	C	A/C	A/C	C	A/C	A/C	C	Abandon A2, A3, P3, Tr3, Th2, Th3
	1	2,3		Irrelevant	B/C	C	C	B/C	B/C	C	B/C	B/C	C	Abandon the theory
		2,3	1	Irrelevant	C/D	C	C	C/D	C/D	C	C/D	C/D	C	Abandon the theory
3			1,2	Irrelevant	A/D	A/D	A/D	A/D	D	A/D	A/D	D	A/D	Reverse P2***
	3		1,2	Irrelevant	B/D	B/D	B/D	B/D	D	B/D	B/D	D	B/D	Abandon the theory
		3	1,2	Irrelevant	C/D	C/D	C/D	C/D	D	C/D	C/D	D	C/D	Abandon the theory

Table A-2 (continued)

Judgments of the Three Theorems: 1, 2, 3*					Possible Assessments of the Premises in Light of Judgments of the Theorems*									
					Axioms			Postulates			Transformational Statements			
True in "A" Sense	True in "B" Sense	False in "C" Sense	False in "D" Sense	Average Coefficient of Predictive Accuracy	A1	A2	A3	P1	P2	P3	Tr1	Tr2	Tr3	Suggested Changes in the Theory**
Col. 1	Col. 2	Col. 3	Col. 4	Col. 5	Col. 6	Col. 7	Col. 8	Col. 9	Col. 10	Col. 11	Col. 12	Col. 13	Col. 14	Col. 15
2			1,3	Irrelevant	D	A/D	A/D	D	A/D	A/D	D	A/D	A/D	Reverse A1 or P1***
	2		1,3	Irrelevant	D	B/D	B/D	D	B/D	B/D	D	B/D	B/D	Abandon the theory
		2	1,3	Irrelevant	D	C/D	C/D	D	C/D	C/D	D	C/D	C/D	Abandon the theory
1			2,3	Irrelevant	A/D	D	D	A/D	A/D	D	A/D	A/D	D	Reverse A2, A3, or P3***
	1		2,3	Irrelevant	B/D	D	D	B/D	B/D	D	B/D	B/D	D	Abandon the theory
		1	2,3	Irrelevant	C/D	D	D	C/D	C/D	D	C/D	C/D	D	Abandon the theory
1	2	3		Irrelevant	A/C	B/C	B/C	A/C	A/B	B/C	A/C	A/B	B/C	Abandon A2, A3, P3, Tr3, Th2, Th3
1	2		3	Irrelevant	A/D	B/D	B/D	A/D	A/B	B/D	A/D	A/B	B/D	Abandon A2, A3, P3, Tr3, Th2, Th3
1		3	2	Irrelevant	A/B	B/C	B/C	A/B	A/C	B/C	A/B	A/C	B/C	Abandon A2, A3, P3, Tr3, Th2, Th3
1		3	2	Irrelevant	A/B	B/D	B/D	A/B	A/D	B/D	A/B	A/D	B/D	Abandon A2, A3, P3, Tr3, Th2, Th3
2	1		3	Irrelevant	B/C	A/C	A/C	B/C	A/B	A/C	B/C	A/B	A/C	Abandon A1, P1, Tr1, Th1, Th3
2	1		3	Irrelevant	B/D	A/D	A/D	B/D	A/B	A/D	B/D	A/B	A/D	Abandon A1, P1, Tr1, Th1, Th3
2	3		1	Irrelevant	B/C	A/B	A/B	B/C	A/C	A/B	B/C	A/C	A/B	Abandon A1, P1, Tr1, Th1, Th3
2	3		1	Irrelevant	B/D	A/B	A/B	B/D	A/D	A/B	B/D	A/D	A/B	Abandon A1, P1, Tr1, Th1, Th3
3	1		2	Irrelevant	A/B	A/C	A/C	A/B	B/C	A/C	A/B	B/C	A/C	Abandon P2, Tr2, Th1, Th2
3	2		1	Irrelevant	A/C	A/B	A/B	A/C	B/C	A/B	A/C	B/C	A/B	Abandon P2, Tr2, Th1, Th2
3	1		2	Irrelevant	A/B	A/D	A/D	A/B	B/D	A/D	A/B	B/D	A/D	Abandon P2, Tr2, Th1, Th2
3	2		1	Irrelevant	A/D	A/B	A/B	A/D	B/D	A/B	A/D	B/D	A/B	Abandon P2, Tr2, Th1, Th2
1		2	3	Irrelevant	B/D	C/D	C/D	B/D	B/C	C/D	B/D	B/C	C/D	Abandon the theory
1		3	2	Irrelevant	B/C	C/D	C/D	B/C	B/D	C/D	B/C	B/D	C/D	Abandon the theory
2		1	3	Irrelevant	C/D	B/D	B/D	C/D	B/C	B/D	C/D	B/C	B/D	Abandon the theory

Table A-2 (continued)

Judgments of the Three Theorems: 1, 2, 3*				Average Coefficient of Predictive Accuracy	Possible Assessments of the Premises in Light of Judgments of the Theorems*									Suggested Changes in the Theory**
True in "A" Sense	True in "B" Sense	False in "C" Sense	False in "D" Sense		Axioms			Postulates			Transformational Statements			
Col. 1	Col. 2	Col. 3	Col. 4	Col. 5	A1 Col. 6	A2 Col. 7	A3 Col. 8	P1 Col. 9	P2 Col. 10	P3 Col. 11	Tr1 Col. 12	Tr2 Col. 13	Tr3 Col. 14	Col. 15
2	3	3	1	Irrelevant	C/D	B/C	B/C	C/D	B/D	B/C	C/D	B/D	B/C	Abandon the theory
3	1	1	2	Irrelevant	B/C	B/D	B/D	B/C	C/D	B/D	B/C	C/D	B/D	Abandon the theory
3	2	2	1	Irrelevant	B/D	B/C	B/C	B/D	C/D	B/C	B/D	C/D	B/C	Abandon the theory
1		2	3	Irrelevant	A/D	C/D	C/D	A/D	A/C	C/D	A/D	A/C	C/D	Abandon A2, A3, P3, Tr3, Th 2, Th3
1		3	2	Irrelevant	A/C	C/D	C/D	A/C	A/D	C/D	A/C	A/D	C/D	Abandon A2, A3, P3, Tr3, Th 2, Th3
2		1	3	Irrelevant	C/D	A/D	A/D	C/D	A/C	A/D	C/D	A/D	A/D	Abandon A1, P1, Tr1, Th1, Th3
2		3	1	Irrelevant	C/D	A/C	A/C	C/D	A/D	A/C	C/D	A/D	A/C	Abandon A1, P1, Tr1, Th1, Th3
3		1	2	Irrelevant	A/C	A/D	A/D	A/C	C/D	A/D	A/C	C/D	A/D	Abandon P2, Tr2, Th1, Th2
3		2	1	Irrelevant	A/D	A/C	A/C	A/D	C/D	A/C	A/D	C/D	A/C	Abandon P2, Tr2, Th1, Th2
		1,2,3		Irrelevant	C	C	C	C	C	C	C	C	C	Abandon the theory
			1,2,3	Irrelevant	D	D	D	D	D	D	D	D	D	Abandon the theory

*"A" = Actual relation is most likely in direction asserted and most likely substantial; "B"=actual relation most likely in direction asserted but most likely in direction not substantial; "C"= actual relation most likely not in direction asserted and most likely not substantial; "D"=actual relation most likely not in direction asserted but most likely substantial.

**The suggested changes, reversals of asserted direction in particular, apply only for a 3-3-0-3-3 theory in which the premises are signed (positive and negative) in a structure exactly like that shown in Figure A-1.

***Change relational term from positive to negative or from negative to positive if a causal premise. Change relational term from "greater ... greater" to "greater ... less" or from "greater ... less" to "greater ... greater" if the premise is stated in the covariational form.

354

statement (i.e., a bivariate relation), neither of which combines or relates what would otherwise be distinct terms.[54] Of the three other types of quantitative theories distinguished by order, two need not be considered, one being a first-order theory. In a theory of that type there is at least one statement in this form: All U's are X's. First-order theories need not be taken seriously *in sociology* because first-order synthetic statements either tax credulity (e.g., "All primary groups have five members.") or border on uninformative tautologies (e.g., "All social groups have a communication system.").

The other type of theory that need not be considered is fourth-order. In that case there is at least one intrinsic statement in this form: Among sets of U's, the greater the positive W–X relation among the units in a set, the greater the positive Y–Z relation among the units in that set.[55] Fourth-order statements are simpler than they appear, because each merely asserts that a relation between two variables is contingent on another relation (its magnitude and/or variance among sets of units).

Whereas there is no prospect for first-order theories becoming important, there is a real prospect for fourth-order theories, even though second-order sociological theories have not developed to the point where extension to fourth-order is an immediate realistic possibility. Hence, were space not so limited, an elaborate treatment of fourth-order theories would be undertaken.

A Brief Introduction of Third-Order Theories

In a third-order theory at least one intrinsic statement takes the form of "Among sets of U's, the greater the minimum X value for the U's in a set, the greater the positive relation between Y and Z among the U's in that set" *or* "Among sets of U's, the greater the variance in the X values of the U's in a set, the greater the positive relation between Y and Z among the U's in that set." Five points need to be made for clarification. First, reference may be made to the mean, median, modal, or maximum X value in a set rather than the "minimum X value." Second, the relational term in a third-order statement may be "greater...less" rather than "greater...greater." Third, the phrase "less positive" extends to negative measures of association; thus, just as a correlation coefficient of .44 is less positive than is than is .67, so is –.73 less positive than is –.17. Fourth, a theorist may assert that the Y–Z relation is contingent on both the magnitude and the amount of variance in X. Fifth, contrary to the previous illustrative forms, the contingent variable (X in the illustrations) may be one of the other two variables, as when a theorist asserts that the X–Y relations depends on the magnitude of X and/or on the amount of variance in X. The fifth point is particularly relevant when the X–Y relation is asserted to be nonmonotonic.

The Purpose of a Third-Order Theory. Although a theorist could state a third-order theory *de novo*, it is most appropriate given evidence that (1) the relation asserted by a premise in a second-order theory varies substantially and (2) the relation's magnitude and perhaps even its sign are contingent on some identifiable third variable (whether a construct or concept). The theorist does not think of the contingency as stemming from differential causation by the third variable (i.e., X is a cause of one of the two variables, Y or Z, but not both). If that were the case, the second-order theory would be expanded by simply adding a bivariate causal premise. Instead, the theorist believes that X influences the Y–Z relation over and beyond any X–Y or X–Z relation.

Extension of a second-order theory to third-order is one of two ways that a theorist may qualify a second-order relation. The other way is by the wording of the unit phrase in a second-order theory.[56] However, a third-order qualification does something that cannot be realized by qualifying the unit term of a second-order theory: a third-order qualification is a way to recognize some *ideal* condition and still have a testable theory. For example, in no country do all families (or households or individuals) have the same income, but sets of countries can be created such that the sets differ systematically as to the estimated amount of income equality among families in each constituent country; and if the Y–Z relation (whatever Y and Z may be) reaches its maximum or minimum only under a condition of absolute equality, then the relation should vary systematically from one set of countries to the next.

A Brief Illustration. As international trade increases, countries tend to specialize in the production of particular commodities. That specialization reduces industry differentiation but not functional interdependence. Accordingly, the validity of Postulate 2 in the illustrative theory (*supra*) appears contingent along the line expressed by this third-order postulate: Among sets of countries, the greater the minimum international trade per capita in a set, the less positive the relation between the degree of division of labor and the degree of industry differentiation in that set.[57] The second property term (a "relational" property term) expresses a relation that entered into the deduction of Theorem 2 in the original theory; hence, that term can be linked to a relational referential—"RDID at T_{0-1} and RPVDR for T_{0-30}."

Evidence can be brought to bear on the third-order postulate only in conjunction with two transformational statements.

Transformational Statement 1: Among sets of countries, the greater the minimum international trade per capita in a set of countries, the greater the RMITPC during T_{0-1} for that set.

Transformational Statement 2: Among sets of countries, the greater the positive relation between the degree of division of labor and the degree of industry differentiation in a set of countries, the less positive the relation between RDID at T_{0-1} and RPVDR for T_{0-30} for that set.

In accordance with the sign rule, the third-order postulate and the two transformational statements taken together imply this third-order theorem: Among sets of countries, the greater the RMITPC during T_{0-1} for a set of countries, the more positive the relation between RDID at T_{0-1} and RPVDR for T_{0-30} among countries in that set. Note that "more positive" translates as "less negative," because the original theory (second-order) anticipates a negative relation between RDID and RPVDR. Accordingly, the predictive magnitude of the second-order theorem (Theorem 2) that asserts the negative relation should be greatest in that set of countries where international trade per capita is the *least*.

As the illustration indicates, the *form* of third-order intrinsic statements and the rule of deduction are not different from second-order counterparts; and much of the second-order theory's extrinsic part is used when expanding the theory to third-order. However, something must be added—instructions for creating sets of units, including specification of ranges in the number of sets and the number of units in each set (see Gibbs, 1989: 155–157). When the goal is creation of sets such that they differ maximally with regard to the magnitude of the contingent variable (RMITPC in the illustration), the set instructions pose no real problem; but they are difficult when it comes to creating sets such that they differ maximally with regard to amount of *intraset variance* in the values of the contingent variable, one reason being that there are various alternatives and even different ways of expressing variance.

Implications for the Original Illustrative Second-Order Theory

The third-order illustration has been greatly simplified, but it would be misleading even if formulated at great length. Specifically, the second-order theory was extended to third-order by focusing on the contingent relation between the division of labor and industry differentiation, the relation asserted in Postulate 2 of the second-order theory without recognition of any contingency. That postulate entered into deduction of the RDID-RPVDR relation (Theorem 2 in the second-order theory), but it entered also into the deduction of the RDU-RDID relation (Theorem 1) in the same theory. Accordingly, the RDU-RDID relation should be contingent on the level of international trade no less than is the RDID-RPVDR relation. Yet given the *rho* of +.909 between RDU referents and RDID referents for the 45 countries (Table A–1), there is no obvious basis for assuming that the relation is *appreciably* contingent on international trade (or anything else for that matter).

So, granted the need to improve the second-order theory's predictive accuracy, extending it to third-order along the line just indicated would be questionable at the outset. Modifying the RPVDR referential formula would be much more promising. However, because there are no obvious alternatives to the RPVDR referential formula (either the formula itself or the requisite kind of data), it is more realistic to contemplate expanding the concept in Postulate 3, "political violence death rate," to "political disturbances." But that change would make Postulate 3 tautological. The solution is to exclude the construct "political stability" altogether, and revise Postulate 3 such that it asserts a negative relation between organic solidarity (a construct) and political disturbances (e.g., riots, protests, political strikes). The present formula can be used by substituting "political disturbances" for "political violence death rate" and data are available (Taylor and Jodice, 1983) for exploratory research along that line. The research will be a resort to induction as the basis for improving a theory's predictive accuracy, but no mode of formal theory construction eliminates the need for exploratory research.

Glossary of the Formal Mode's Principal Terms

Analytic statement: A statement that is either true or false solely as a consequence of the very meaning of its constituent terms.

Axiom: An axiom is (1) a statement in the intrinsic part of a theory, (2) a premise in the form of an empirical generalization about at least one infinite class of events or things, and (3) such that all of the statement's constituent property terms are identified in the theory's extrinsic part as constructs.

Concept: A concept is a term that when used by a theorist in stating a theory (1) denotes a particular property or characteristic of all instances of some type of unit (e.g., "residential population density" in the case of cities); (2) is defined by the theorist in the theory's extrinsic part; (3) the theorist regards the definition as complete and clear; (4) the theorist also regards the definition as sufficiently empirically applicable; and (5) if the term denotes a quantitative property or characteristic, it is linked in a transformational statement with a referential.

Construct: A construct is a term that when used by a theorist in stating a theory (1) denotes a particular property or characteristic of all instances of some type of unit (e.g., "extent of class conflict" in the case of countries); (2) may or may not be defined by the theorist in the theory's extrinsic part; (3) if defined, the theorist does not regard the definition as complete or clear; (4) the theorist does not regard the term or its definition (if defined) as sufficiently empirically applicable; and (5) if the term denotes a quantitative property or characteristic, it is not linked in a transformational statement with a referential.

Descriptive statement: A statement that purportedly describes the association between two designated sets of values, referents or otherwise.

Empirical applicability: In the case of a term, definition, formula, or procedure, empirical applicability refers to the extent that researchers or investigators working independently (1) indicate that they regard it (the term, definition, formula, or procedure) as sufficiently intelligible, (2) report that its use is feasible when describing (including, perhaps, the computation of numerical values) or identifying events, things, or properties; and (3) realize congruence when identifying the same event or thing or when describing a particular property of the same event or thing.

Epistemic statement: A statement made in testing and reporting a test of a theory, with the statement worded such that it asserts a connection between a referential and a designated set of referents (values) ostensibly computed for use in the test by application of the formula corresponding to the referential and in accordance with instructions in the theory's extrinsic part.

Extrinsic part of a theory: That part of a theory which comprises (1) whatever definitions the theorist sets forth as components of the theory; (2) referential formulas; (3) prescriptions as to requisite kinds of data for tests of the theory and procedures for their acquisition, possibly including designations of kinds of data sources; (4) an identification of the formal mode of theory construction used in stating theory or a description of a formal mode; (5) an explication of a test procedure if not given by the mode; and (6) comments on any feature of the theory or test procedure not governed by the mode or features that represent departures from the mode.

Hypothesis: A statement made in conducting and reporting a test of a theory, with the statement worded such that it takes the form of a prediction as to the association between designated sets of referents (values), a prediction deduced from a theorem and epistemic statements.

Intrinsic part of a theory: That part of a theory which comprises all of the theory's constituent empirical generalizations (synthetic statements) about at least one infinite class of events or things, be those generalizations premises (axioms, postulates, propositions, and transformational statements) or conclusions (theorems).

Postulate: A postulate is (1) a statement in the intrinsic part of a theory, (2) a premise in the form of an empirical generalization about at least one infinite class of events or things, and (3) such that some (perhaps only one) of its constituent property terms are identified in the theory's extrinsic part as constructs and the remainder (again, perhaps only one) are so identified as concepts.

Property term: A term that denotes some set of mutually exclusive attributes (e.g., colors, homicide rates) of all instances of at least one class of events or things (e.g., cities, human individuals).

Proposition: A proposition is (1) a statement in the intrinsic part of a theory, (2) a premise in the form of an empirical generalization about at least one infinite class of events or things, and (3) such that all of the statement's constituent property terms are identified in the theory's extrinsic part as concepts.

Referent: A value for some designated unit (e.g., a particular organization) at some designated time point or period, one assertedly computed by the application of some designated referential formula.

Referential: An acronym in a transformational statement or theorem, one that denotes a particular formula and related instructions as to kinds of data in the extrinsic part of a theory.

Referential formula: A formula that is (1) denoted by a referential in the intrinsic part of theory and (2) set forth in the extrinsic part of the theory along with prescriptions as to requisite kinds of data and the procedure for acquiring such data, possibly including designations of kinds of data sources.

Relational terms: Any term in a statement that connects the statement's constituent property terms, such as to make some assertion about an empirical association between the phenomena denoted by the property terms, with the illustrative form of the assertion being "X causes Y" or "the greater X, the greater Y."

Synthetic statement: A statement that is neither true nor false solely as a consequence of the very meaning of its constituent terms.

Theorem: A theorem is (1) a statement in the intrinsic part of a theory, (2) an empirical generalization about at least one infinite class of events or things, (3) deduced from the theory's premises (also in the theory's intrinsic part), and (4) such that all of the constituent property terms are identified in the theory's extrinsic part as referentials.

Theory: A set of logically interrelated statements, at least two of which are in the form of empirical generalizations about at least one infinite class of events or things.

Transformational statement: A transformational statement is (1) a statement in the intrinsic part of a theory, (2) a premise in the form of an empirical generalization about at least one infinite class of events or things, and (3) such that some (perhaps only one) of the statement's constituent property terms are identified in the theory's extrinsic part as concepts and the remainder (again, perhaps only one) are so identified as referentials.

Unit phrase: The initial phrase in each constituent statement of a theory's intrinsic part, the form of the phrase being "Among X's" or "For any X over time" or "Among X's and for any X over time," where X is a unit term (e.g., cities, city, occupations, occupation).

Unit term: A unit term is a term in a unit phrase that denotes an infinite class of events or things (e.g., cities, city, occupations, occupation), including entities in the form of individuals or populations or territories.

Notes

1. One example must suffice: any two members of a primary group have a social relation.

2. An undefined construct is a theoretic primitive; as such, unlike empirical primitives, a construct does not enter into the definition of other terms.

3. Everything said about the empirical applicability of a term's definition applies to

the term itself and vice versa, but a theorist may regard a term as empirically applicable even though left undefined. Indeed, when an undefined term enters into definitions (i.e., the term is an empirical primitive), it is assumed that the term is empirically applicable without a definition; and in all theories there are undefined terms, some or all of which denote theoretical notions

4. The illustration runs contrary to an astonishing argument about social classes, one most likely to be embraced by avowed Marxists: the reality of a social class has nothing to do with the identification of its members (see, e.g., Poulantzas, 1975:17). Stating the argument another way, a class need not be defined such that its members can be identified. If Marxists would grant that the term social class is a construct, the argument might be defensible. Some terms denote purely theoretical notions, though their importance is not diminished by identifying them as constructs. However, Marxists persist in writing as if social classes are not just theoretical, meaning as though the term is empirically applicable.

5. For that matter, the notion of observability has little relevance for sociology, not even for research at the micro level. The truth is that the vocabulary of the sciences is a warehouse of terms that do not denote observable "things." Thus, no one will ever see, touch, hear, or smell a personality or group cohesion, and one may observe gravity's effects but not gravity itself.

6. Nothing said up to this point precludes auxiliary definitions. Indeed, sociologists should abandon the seemingly widespread belief in the field that a major sociological term can be defined completely and clearly in one brief sentence. However, when reference is made here to a complete and clear definition, auxiliary definitions (if any) are considered to be parts of the initial definition.

7. Isolated observations by Durkheim (1933) suggest that the number of industries could be relevant also, but that consideration does not remedy any defect of his conceptualization.

8. For example, a theorist may believe that the theory holds both for countries and for cities within the same country, but he/she believes also that international data are insufficiently reliable or comparable. If so, the theorist should state the second belief as a rationale for using "Among cities within the same country" as the unit phrase. If nothing else, the audience would be alerted to the possibility of eventually broadening the theory by making the unit term more inclusive.

9. If either phrase is used by a theorist in the belief that available data for the other type of comparison are unreliable, that rationale for the qualification should be made explicit.

10. The exception is a first-order synthetic statement, in which case the relational term connects a property term and the unit term, just as a verb connects a predicate and the subject of a sentence. Consider two illustrations. First, all primary groups have five members. Second, all groups have a system of communication. First-order statements receive little attention here because they either tax credulity (as in the first illustration) or appear tautological (second illustration).

11. Contemplate Blalock's strategy for confronting issues and problems (1964: 9): "it indeed may turn out wise to treat the notion of causality as primitive or undefined."

12. The illustration could commence with the unit phrase "Among U's and for any U over time" or "For any U over time."

13. Leiberson (1985:63-69) makes parenthetical use of the terms "bidirectional" and

"unidirectional," but only to opt for "symmetric" and "asymmetric" without recognizing that the latter two terms are commonly used as the equivalents to the distinction between reciprocal and nonreciprocal causation. He further muddies the conceptual water by subsequently switching to the distinction between irreversible and reversible causation. So Lieberson's causal terminology is conducive to confusion.

14. Unless the theorist explicitly states otherwise, any assertion in the form "X causes Y" is to be understood as referring to *changes* in X and *changes* in Y.

15. Both the failure of sociological theorist to identify synthetic statements as to type and the lack of agreement in the use of relevant labels is a conspicuous feature of the discursive mode of theory construction.

16. Henceforth, unless explicitly disclaimed, the term "statement" refers to a synthetic statement as a component of a theory's intrinsic part; and an "intrinsic statement" is a statement in the theory's intrinsic part. However, an empirical theory should not be defined as though it comprises *only* synthetic statements, for such a definition denies the possibility (if not the necessity) of some analytic statements as components of a theory (for elaboration, see Gibbs, 1990).

17. A more elaborate version of this and subsequent rules pertaining to types of premises would recognize that each premise is (1) a component of a theory's intrinsic part, (2) synthetic, and (3) pertains to one or more infinite classes.

18. The closest approximation is Land's research (1970). Even that research is disputable because Land focused on *urbanization* rather than *density*, and his identification of features of technology as major variables is not truly consistent with Durkheim. For elaboration, see Gibbs, 1993a.

19. Although Durkheim was virtually obsessed with the notion of a society, the term is defensible only if defined such that countries *and* tribes are instances. Because systematic research is more feasible at the international level than at the intertribal level, the term "countries" is used here rather than "societies."

20. Intensity is a dimension of predictive power; and the variety of space-time relations is primarily determined by a theory's unit phrase: among U's, for any U over time, among U's and for any U over time.

21. For a much more elaborate treatment of Durkheim's theory, see Gibbs, 1993a.

22. Functional explanations may be truly justified in the social sciences; but they have no rationale unless the explanatory mechanism of selective survival is made explicit, an extremely rare practice in sociology. Whatever the reason, "nonsurvival" need not be equated literally with death. Thus, no one is confused by the statement that some occupations and marriages do not survive.

23. Note the interpretation of the causal assertion: the positions of the two property terms could be reversed, meaning that either one is the positive, bidirectional, and paramount cause of the other.

24. Although the possibility of a reciprocal (positive) causal relation between organic solidarity and political stability should be entertained, the same theorems would be derived from the theory even if Axiom 3 were revised so as to assert reciprocal causation.

25. Again, however, a theory's intrinsic part is to be construed this way: these statements are to be taken as synthetic. The analytic-synthetic distinction is crucial only in the case of theorems (*infra*); and even in that case there is only one question: is it logically possible (including mathematical possibility) for the theorem to be false?

26. The same generalization appears in Chapter 5 as Postulate 5, and the companion postulate concerning occupational differentiation would be used also were it not for the need to simplify the illustrative theory.

27. Advocates of the notion are likely to stop short of demanding that the research procedure be *deduced* from the concept's definition. They prefer to argue that the two must "correspond" or be "homologous," but either term's meaning is far too vague for constructive argumentation.

28. Consider this generalization: increases in X are always followed by increases in Y. Whatever X and Y may be, an increase in the former is virtually certain to be followed by an increase in the latter *sooner or later*.

29. Because referentials are constituents only of theories having quantitative property terms, a theorem would be defined differently (if recognized at all) in a mode of theory construction for *qualitative* variables.

30. Bear in mind various other possibilities: a theory having postulates but no axioms, or a mixture of propositions and postulates, or a mixture of propositions, postulates, and axioms. However, some possibilities are precluded, at least as for as testable quantitative theories are concerned, such as a theory having axioms but no postulates or a quantitative theory bereft of transformational statements.

31. The change may appear worse than pointless, because it will reduce parsimony, a dimension of predictive power. Parsimony is the ratio of conclusions (theorems in the present mode) to premises. Alternative criteria are far too vague; but, whatever the criteria, the parsimony of a discursively stated theory is difficult to judge with confidence if only because of uncertainty in identifying premises and theorems.

32. A theory's scope is simply the number of constituent constructs and concepts (referentials need not be counted, as they equal the number of concepts), but various distinctions should be recognized. Thus, insofar as dependent variables can be identified, only the constructs and concepts that denote those variables should be counted when reckoning *explanatory* scope. Then in the case of *test* scope, the count is limited to those constructs and concepts that have entered into the deduction of one or more theorems that have been tested at least once. Finally, the "test" distinction applies also to all dimensions of predictive power except testability and predictive accuracy.

33. Consider, for example, Simon's statement (1952:518): "We shall avoid the usual assumption that the asymmetry of cause and effect has something to do with sequence in time."

34. No criterion need stipulate anything about the spatial character of the asserted causal relation. Such stipulation is not needed because the spatial context is specified by the unit phrase in the causal assertion.

35. The only restraint on selection is that the association measure must have values ranging from -1.0 to +1.0, or can be so adjusted.

36. The same may be said of multiple causation, but partial and multiple causation are not distinguished here because one implies the other.

37. All relations deduced from incomplete circuits—causal, covariational, or mixed—are expressed in the covariational form; hence, the order of the variables in the deduced relation is not relevant. The rationale is that the translation of causal relational terms into covariational relational terms is a necessary step for tests of the theory.

38. Again, the rules are worded such that they extend to the deduction of what has been previously identified as implied axioms, implied postulates, or implied

propositions; but the primary concern is the deduction of theorems, for those deductions are essential for tests of any theory stated in accordance with the prescribed mode.

39. When interpreting statements about Figure A–2, bear in mind that all of the constructs, concepts, and referentials pertain to quantitative variables. Moreover, when one speaks of one variable determining (or causing) another, it would be more accurate to speak of changes in one variable (increases or decreases in its value) determining changes in the other variable.

40. No significance should be attached to the covariational character of Po6; it serves only as a reminder that premises, even axioms or postulates, need not be causal assertions.

41. Space limitations preclude confronting all of the problems and issues here; but some of them have been confronted elsewhere (Gibbs, 1982), and the rules of deduction as well as other features of the proposed mode of theory construction (e.g., the temporal quantifiers and the relational terms) reflect that confrontation.

42. The *P* values were taken from United Nations, *Demographic Yearbook: Historical Supplement* (1979) or from the 1948, 1949, or 1955 *Demographic Yearbook*.

43. Sociologists use the label "operational definitions" grotesquely. To illustrate briefly, sociologist commonly define middle class by reference to some income range and then characterize the definition as "operational." Even ignoring the definition's arbitrariness, what is "operational" about it?

44. It is desirable but not imperative that all referents be shown tabularally in the test report. If that presentation is not feasible, the table need show only some illustrative referents, with the understanding that a complete version could be prepared.

45. Actually, even weaker evidence—proportionate congruence, a substantial international correlation between referents—would be comforting.

46. The data's reliability is crucial in contemplating the relation between a concept and a referential, but in the case of referents the only question is whether the investigators acquired the data *in the way prescribed* and applied the formula correctly. When setting forth a referential formula the theorist implicitly or explicitly claims that instances of the prescribed kind of data are sufficiently reliable, but the claim may be invalid. That possibility cannot be ascertained by examining the congruence between referents reported by independent investigators. However, if the data are congruent but the referents incongruent, one or both of the investigators did not apply the referential formula correctly.

47. As for the test itself, ignoring any concern with assessing empirical applicability, it makes no difference whether each referent was computed by a separate investigator or all by the same investigator. Indeed, the distinction between an individual and a team of investigators is irrelevant.

48. One need not invoke the term "retrodiction" to argue that a theory makes predictions. If by "prediction" one means a statement about the future and not a statement about an unknown, then a prediction derived from a theory must always be a conditional statement (e.g., if X increases such-and-such by the year 2000, then Y will increase such-and-such by that time). However, any testable theory makes at least one prediction about the future in this form: if investigators do such-and-such, they will report having experienced such-and-such.

49. The more general point is that scientists and philosophers tend to use the term "fact" uncritically and in such a way as to make it a dubious notion.

50. If the effect of mechanical solidarity and the effect of organic solidarity were additive, political stability would be a constant. When there is negligible division of labor, mechanical solidarity approaches the maximum; and when the division of labor approaches the maximum, so does organic solidarity. So if both types of solidarity generate political stability interactively (multiplicatively) but not additively, then political instability and deaths from political violence should approach the minimum when and where there is a *moderate* degree of division of labor.

51. The absolute maximum possible value is: $1-(1/Nc)$, where Nc is the number of industry categories (nine in the present case).

52. The advantage of the predictive power criterion is not just that contending theories can be judged in terms of it; additionally, that criterion promises more consensus when making invidious comparisons than does any alternative. Predictive power is clearly an amount or degree, and it is pointless to contemplate a certain minimum as necessary or sufficient for retaining the theory under consideration. Moreover, the criterion avoids something about Popper's falsifiability principle that makes it entirely unrealistic for sociology and perhaps several other fields. Examine Popper's statement (1965:86): "Thus a few stray basic statements contradicting a theory will hardly induce us to reject it as falsified. We shall take it as falsified only if we discover a *reproducible effect* which refutes the theory." The idea of *consistently* negative evidence is no more realistic for sociological theories than is the idea of consistently positive evidence. Yet Popper's principle is not totally rejected by any means; rather, it is one thing to say that a theory should be falsifiable but quite a different matter to say that a particular theory has been falsified. The dictum that a theory should be falsifiable is retained by recognizing testability and predictive accuracy as distinct dimensions of predictive power, but without entertaining the idea of consistently negative evidence.

53. All contending theories must have a constituent generalization comparable to the theorem in question, and only those that have been subjected to at least one test of that comparable generalization are considered in the comparisons. An absolute standard should not be used when assigning any one of the labels—*A*, *B*, *C*, or *D*—unless there are no contending theories that qualify for a comparison.

54. A property term may be a combination of what could be treated as distinct constructs or concepts, as illustrated by the following: population size and density, frequency and regularity of interaction, stratification and residential mobility. Such *compound* property terms should not be confused with "relational" property terms, such as "positive relation between population size and density." In the latter case, a relation (association) between variables is treated as a variable in itself.

55. The alternative is "the less the positive Y–Z relation," and "less positive" may translate as "more negative."

56. The unit term in a third-order theory is always "sets," but it may be qualified (e.g., "Among sets of cities within the same country," "Among sets of industrialized countries)."

57. The reference is not to the amount of trade among countries in a set but, rather, the amount for any country in the set with other countries, whether in the set or not.

References

Albas, Daniel and Cheryl Albas. 1989. "Modern Magic: The Case of Examinations," *Sociological Quarterly*, 30 (No. 4) 603–613.

Alcorn, Paul A. 1986. *Social Issues in Technology*. Englewood Cliffs, NJ: Prentice-Hall.

Altheide, David L. 1990. "Controlling the Urge for a Central Sociological Concept," *Social Science Journal*, 27 (No. 1) 69–74.

Atkinson, Paul. 1987. "Teaching Students about Science," *Social Studies of Science*, 17 (February) 189–192.

Bandura, Albert. 1982. "Self-Efficacy Mechanism in Human Agency," *American Psychologist, 37* (February) 122–147.

Banner, Michael C. 1990. *The Justification of Science and the Rationality of Religious Belief*. Oxford, England: Clarendon Press.

Barbour, Ian G. 1980. *Technology, Environment, and Human Values*. New York: Praeger.

Bellah, Robert N. 1968. "The Sociology of Religion." Pp. 406-414 in Sills, 1968–XIII.

Beniger, James R. 1986. *The Control Revolution*. Cambridge, MA: Harvard University Press.

Bickman, Leonard. 1974. "The Social Power of a Uniform," *Journal of Applied Social Psychology*, 4 (January-March) 47–61.

Bimber, Bruce. 1990. "Karl Marx and the Three Faces of Technological Determinism," *Social Studies of Science*, 20 (May) 333–351.

Black, Donald. 1976. *The Behavior of Law*. New York: Academic Press.

_____, ed. 1984a. *Toward a General Theory of Social Control*, 2 vols. New York: Academic Press.

_____. 1984b. "Social Control as a Dependent Variable." Pp. 1-36 in Black, 1984a–I.

_____. 1984c. "Crime as Social Control." Pp. 1-27 in Black, 1984a–II.

Blalock, Hubert M., Jr. 1964. *Causal Inferences in Nonexperimental Research*. Chapel Hill: University of North Carolina Press.

_____. 1969. *Theory Construction*. Englewood Cliffs, NJ: Prentice-Hall.

Blankstein, Kirk R., and Janet Polivy, eds. 1982. *Self-Control and Self-Modification of Emotional Behavior*. New York: Plenum.

Blau, Peter M. 1964. *Exchange and Power in Social Life*. New York: Wiley.

Blocker, T. Jean and Darren E. Sherkat. 1992. "In the Eyes of the Beholder: Technological and Naturalistic Interpretations of a Disaster," *Industrial Crisis Quarterly*, 6 (No. 2) 153–166.

Blumer, Herbert. 1969. *Symbolic Interactionism*. Englewood Cliffs, NJ: Prentice-Hall.

Boudon, Raymond. 1980. *The Crisis in Sociology*. New York: Columbia University Press.

Braun, Tibor, *et al*. 1985. *Scientometric Indicators*. Singapore: World Scientific.

Brinberg, David. 1979. "An Examination of the Determinants of Intention and Behavior," *Journal of Applied Social Psychology*, 9 (November-December) 560–575.

Brooke, John H. 1991. *Science and Religion*. New York: Cambridge University Press.

Brooks, Harvey. 1980. "Technology, Evolution, and Purpose," *Deadalus*, 109 (Winter) 65–81.

Bruce, Robert V. 1987. *The Launching of Modern American Science, 1846–1876*. New York: Knopf.

Burger, Jerry M. 1992. "Desire for Control and Academic Performance," *Canadian Journal of Behavioural Science*, 24 (April) 147–155.

Burns, Tom. 1958. "The Forms of Conduct," *American Journal of Sociology*, 64 (September) 137–151.

Burton, Michael, *et al*. 1992. "Introduction" to John Higley and Richard Gunther (eds.), *Elites and Democratic Consolidation in Latin America and Southern Europe*. New York: Cambridge University Press.

Cancian, Francesca M. 1990. "What Is Feminist Theory?," *Footnotes*, 18 (October) 5.

Carlson, John B. 1990. "America's Ancient Skywatchers," *National Geographic*, 177 (March) 76–107.

Carpenter, Mark P. and Francis Narin. 1981. "The Adequacy of the Science Citation Index (SCI) as an Indication of International Scientific Activity," *Journal of the American Society for Information Science*, 32 (November) 430–439.

Catlin, George and Seymour Epstein. 1992. "Unforgettable Experiences: The Relation of Life Events to Basic Beliefs About Self and the World," *Social Cognition*, 10 (Summer) 189–209.

Catton, William R., Jr. 1966. *From Animistic to Naturalistic Sociology*. New York: McGraw–Hill.

Chalmers, Alan. 1990. *Science and Its Fabrication*. Minneapolis: University of Minnesota Press.

Chamlin, Mitchell B., *et al*. 1992. "Time Aggregation and Time Lag in Macro–Level Deterrence Research," *Criminology*, 30 (August) 377–395.

Chattopadhyaya, D. P. 1990. *Anthropology and Historiography of Science*. Athens: Ohio University Press.

Cohen, Stanley. 1985. *Visions of Social Control*. Cambridge, England: Polity Press.

Collingridge, David and Colin Reeve. 1986. *Science Speaks to Power: The Role of Experts in Policy Making*. London: Pinter.

Coser, Lewis A. 1956. *The Functions of Social Conflict*. New York: Free Press.

Costner, Herbert L. 1969. "Theory, Deduction, and Rules of Correspondence," *American Journal of Sociology*, 75 (September) 245–263.

_____ and Hubert M. Blalock, Jr. 1972. "Scientific Fundamentalism and Scientific Utility," *Social Science Quarterly*, 52 (March) 827–844.

_____ and Robert K. Leik. 1964. "Deductions from 'Axiomatic Theory'," *American Sociological Review*, 29 (December) 819–835.

Dahl, Robert A. 1968. "Power." Pp. 405–515 in Sills, 1968–XII.

_____. 1982. *Dilemnas of Pluralist Democracy*. New Haven, CT: Yale University Press.

Dahlitz, Julie. 1983. *Nuclear Arms Control*. London: George Allen and Unwin.

Delamont, Sara. 1987. "Three Blind Spots? A Comment on the Sociology of Science by a Puzzled Outsider," *Social Studies of Science*, 17 (February) 163–170.

Dennis, Michael A. 1987. "Accounting for Research: New Histories of Corporate Laboratories and the Social History of American Science," *Social Studies of Science*, 17 (August) 479–518.

Devlin, Judith. 1987. *The Superstitious Mind: French Peasants and the Supernatural in the Nineteenth Century*. New Haven, CT: Yale University Press.

Dillon, Richard G. 1980. "Violent Conflict in Meta' Society," *American Ethnologist*, 7 (November) 658–673.

Duncan, Otis D. 1966. "Path Analysis: Sociological Examples," *American Journal of Sociology*, 72 (July) 1–16.

Dunkerley, Joy. 1980. *Trends in Energy Use in Industrial Societies*. Washington, D.C.: Resources for the Future.

Dunsire, Andrew. 1978. *Control in a Bureaucracy*. New York: St. Martin's Press.

Durbin, Paul T. 1988. *Dictionary of Concepts in the Philosophy of Science*. New York: Greenwood Press.

Durkheim, Emile. 1933 [1893]. *The Division of Labor in Society*. New York: Macmillan.

_____. 1938 [1895].*The Rules of Sociological Method*. Chicago: University of Chicago Press.

_____. 1951 [1897]. *Suicide*. New York: Free Press.

Eckhardt, Christopher I., et al. 1992. "Religious Beliefs and Scientific Ideology in Psychologists: Conflicting or Coexisting Systems?," *Psychological Reports*, 71 (August) 131–145.

Edgerton, Robert B. 1985. *Rules, Exceptions, and Social Order*. Berkeley: University of California Press.

Eliade, Mircea. 1978, 1982, 1985. *A History of Religious Ideas*, 3 vols. Chicago: University of Chicago Press.

Elster, Jon. 1983. *Explaining Technical Change*. Cambridge, England: Cambridge University Press.

Emerson, Richard M. 1962. "Power–Dependence Relations," *American Sociological Review*, 27 (February) 31–41.

Emerson, Robert M. and Sheldon L. Messinger. 1977. "The Micro–Politics of Trouble," *Social Problems*, 25 (December) 121–134.

Ervin, Delbert J. 1987. "Interdependence and Differentiation as Components of the Division of Labor," *Social Science Quarterly*, 68 (March) 177–184.

Etzioni, Amitai. 1968. "Social Control." Pp. 396–402 in Sills, 1968–XIV.

Fein, Helen. 1990. "Genocide: A Sociological Perspective," *Current Sociology*, 38 (Spring) 1–126.

Felson, Richard B. and George Gmelch. 1979. "Uncertainty and the Use of Magic," *Current Anthropology*, 20 (September) 587–589.

Ferris, Timothy. 1988. *Coming of Age in the Milky Way*. New York: William Morrow.

Festinger, Leon. 1981. "Human Nature and Human Competence," *Social Research*, 48 (Summer) 306–321.

Feyerabend, Paul. 1975. *Against Method*. London: New Left Books.

Fiske, Susan T. and Shelley E. Taylor. 1991. *Social Cognition*, 2nd ed. New York: McGraw–Hill.

Freese, Lee and Jane Sell. 1980. "Constructing Axiomatic Theories in Sociology." Pp. 263–368 in Lee Freese (ed.), *Theoretical Methods in Sociology*. Pittsburgh: University of Pittsburgh Press.

Freuchen, Peter. 1961. *Book of the Eskimos*. Cleveland: World.

Friedman, Myles I. and George H. Lackey, Jr. 1991. *The Psychology of Human Control*. New York: Praeger.

Fries, Sylvia. 1984. "The Ideology of Science during the Nixon Years: 1970–76," *Social Studies of Science*, 14 (August) 323–341.

Frisbie, W. Parker, and Clifford J. Clarke. 1979. "Technology in Evolutionary and Ecological Perspective," *Social Forces*, 58 (December) 591–613.

Gabe, Jonathan, and Susan Lipshitz–Phillips. 1984. "Tranquillisers as Social Control?," *Sociological Review*, Series 2, 32 (August) 524–546.

Gallup, George, Jr., and Jim Castelli. 1987. *The People's Religion: American Faith in the 90's*. New York: Macmillan.

Garner, Roberta and Larry Garner. 1991. "Socio–Economic Security and Insecurity in Socialist and Capitalist Political Economies," *Science and Society*, 55 (Spring) 5–25.

Gecas, Viktor. 1989. "The Social Psychology of Self–Efficacy," *Annual Review of Sociology*, 15 (annual) 291–316.

Geertz, Clifford. 1968. "Religion: Anthropological Study." Pp. 398–406 in Sills, 1968–XIII.

_____. 1990. "A Lab of One's Own," *New York Review of Books*, 37 (November 8) 19–23.

Gendron, Bernard. 1977. *Technology and the Human Condition*. New York: St. Martin's Press.

Gerstein, Dean R., *et al.*, eds. 1988. *The Behavioral and Social Sciences: Achievements and Opportunities*. Washington, DC: National Academy Press.

Gibbs, Jack P. 1968. "The Issue in Sociology," *Pacific Sociological Review*, 11 (Fall) 65–74.

_____. 1972. *Sociological Theory Construction*. Hinsdale, IL: Dryden

_____. 1977. "Types of Urban Units." Pp. 216–266 in Kent Schwirian, *et al.*, *Contemporary Topics in Urban Sociology*. Morristown, NJ: General Learning Press.

_____. 1979. "The Elites Can Do Without Us," *American Sociologist*, 14 (May) 79–85.

_____. 1981. *Norms, Deviance, and Social Control*. New York: Elsvier.

_____. 1982. "Evidence of Causation," *Current Perspectives in Social Theory*, 3 (Annual) 93–127.

_____. 1986. "Deterrence Theory and Research." Pp. 87–130 in Gary B. Melton (ed.), *The Law as a Behavioral Instrument*. Lincoln: University of Nebraska Press.

_____. 1989. *Control: Sociology's Central Notion*. Urbana: University of Illinois Press.

_____. 1990. "The Notion of a Theory in Sociology," *National Journal of Sociology*, 4 (Fall) 129–158.

_____. 1993a. "A Formal Restatement of Durkheim's Division of Labor Theory," unpublished paper.

_____. 1993b. "Sources of Resistance in Sociology to Formal Theory Construction." Forthcoming in Jerald Hage (ed.), *The Methodology of Theory Construction in Sociology*. Albany: State University of New York Press.

_____. 1993c. "Durkheim's Heavy Hand in the Sociological Study of Suicide." Forthcoming in David Lester (ed.), *Centennial of Durkheim's Le Suicide*. Philadelphia: Charles Press.

_____ and Kingsley Davis. 1958. "Conventional Versus Metropolitan Data in the International Study of Urbanization," *American Sociological Review*, 23 (October) 504–514.

_____ and Walter T. Martin. 1958. "Urbanization and Natural Resources: A Study in Organizational Ecology," *American Sociological Review*, 23 (June) 266–277.

_____ and Walter T. Martin. 1959. "Toward a Theoretical System of Human Ecology," *Pacific Sociological Review*, 2 (Spring) 29–36.

_____ and Walter T. Martin. 1962. "Urbanization, Technology, and the Division of Labor: International Patterns," *American Sociological Review*, 27 (October) 667–677.

Glenn, Norval D. 1987. "The Trend in 'No Religion' Respondents to U. S.

National Surveys, Late 1950s to Early 1980s," *Public Opinion Quarterly,* 51 (Fall) 293–314.

Goffman, Erving. 1961. *Encounters.* Indianapolis: Bobbs–Merrill.

_____. 1963. *Behavior in Public Places.* New York: Free Press.

_____. 1974. *Frame Analysis.* Cambridge, MA: Harvard University Press.

Golden, William T., ed. 1991. *Worldwide Science and Technology Advice to the Highest Levels of Government.* New York: Pergamon.

Grabosky, Peter N. 1984. "The Variability of Punishment." Pp. 163–189 in Black, 1984a–I.

Greenspan, Stanley I., and George H. Pollock, eds. 1989. *The Course of Life,* 2 vols. Madison, CT: International Universities Press.

Guthrie, Stewart. 1980. "A Cognitive Theory of Religion," *Current Anthropology,* 21 (April) 181–194.

Halfpenny, Peter. 1982. *Positivism and Sociology.* London: George Allen and Unwin.

Hallet, Jean–Pierre. 1965. *Congo Kitabu.* New York: Random House.

Hames, Raymond B. 1979. "A Comparison of the Efficiencies of the Shotgun and Bow in Neotropical Forest Hunting," *Human Ecology,* 7 (September) 219–252.

Hannay, N. Bruce, and Robert E. McGinn. 1980. "The Anatomy of Modern Technology," *Deadalus,* 109 (Winter) 25–53.

Harding, Sandra G., ed. 1976. *Can Theories Be Refuted?* Boston: D. Reidel.

Harris, Marvin. 1977. *Cannibals and Kings.* New York: Random House.

_____. 1979. *Cultural Materialism.* New York: Random House.

Hazen, Robert M. and James Trefil. 1991. *Science Matters.* New York: Doubleday.

Henslin, James M. 1967. "Craps and Magic," *American Journal of Sociology,* 73 (November) 316–330.

Hirschi, Travis. 1969. *Causes of Delinquency.* Berkeley: University of California Press.

Holdren, John P. 1990. "Energy in Transition," *Scientific American,* 263 (September) 156–163.

Hull, David L. 1988. *Science as a Process.* Chicago: University of Chicago Press.

Hurtado, A. Magdalena and Kim Hill. 1989. "Expiremental Studies of Tool Efficiency among Machiguenga Women and Implications for Root–Digging Foragers," *Journal of Anthropological Research,* 45 (Summer) 207–217.

International Labour Office. 1980, 1981, 1982, 1983, 1984, 1985, 1990. *Year Book of Labour Statistics* (the year in the title is the same as the year of publication, except *1989/90* was published in 1990). Geneva: International Labour Organization.

International Urban Research. 1959. *The World's Metropolitan Areas.* Berkeley: University of California Press.

Kevles, Daniel J. 1991. "The Final Secret of the Universe?," *New York Review of Books*, 38 (May 16) 27–32.

Kimmelman, Barbara A. 1983. "The American Breeders' Association: Genetics and Eugenics in an Agricultural Context, 1903–13," *Social Studies of Science*, 13 (May) 163–204.

Klausner, Samuel Z., ed. 1965. *The Quest for Self-Control*. New York: Free Press.

Kuhn, Thomas S. 1962. *The Structure of Scientific Revolutions*. Chicago: University of Chicago Press.

Kuper, Adam and Jessica Kuper, eds. 1985. *The Social Science Encyclopedia*. London: Routledge and Kegan Paul.

Land, Kenneth C. 1970. "Mathematical Formalization of Durkheim's Theory of Division of Labor," *Sociological Methodology, 1970* (annual) 257–282.

Lane, Roger. 1979. *Violent Death in the City*. Cambridge, MA: Harvard University Press.

Larzelere, Robert E. and Gerald R. Patterson. 1990. "Parental Management," *Criminology*, 30 (May) 301-323.

Lehmann, Arthur C. and James E. Myers, eds. 1985. *Magic, Witchcraft, and Religion: An Anthropological Study of the Supernatural*. Mountain View, CA: Mayfield.

Lieberson, Stanley. 1985. *Making It Count: The Improvement of Social Research and Theory*. Berkeley: University of California Press.

Lenski, Gerhard, and Jean Lenski. 1987. *Human Societies*, 5th ed. New York: McGraw–Hill.

Lesthaeghe, Ron and Johan Surkyn. 1988. "Cultural Dynamics and Economic Theories of Fertility Change," *Population and Development Review*, 14 (March) 1–45.

Lewontin, R. C. 1977. "Caricature of Darwinism," *Nature*, 266 (March 17) 283–284.

Liebow, Elliot. 1967. *Tally's Corner*. Boston: Little, Brown.

Madsen, Douglas. 1987. "Political Self–Efficacy Tested," *American Political Science Review*, 81 (June) 571–581.

Malinowski, Bronislaw. 1954. *Magic, Science and Religion and Other Essays*. Garden City, NY: Doubleday.

Maris, Ronald W. 1969. *Social Forces in Urban Suicide*. Homewood, IL: Dorsey Press.

Marsh, Robert M. 1971. "The Explanation of Occupational Prestige Hierarchies," *Social Forces*, 50 (December) 214–222.

_____ and Hiroshi Mannari. 1981. "Technology and Size as Determinants of the Organizational Structure of Japanese Factories," *Administrative Science Quarterly* 26 (March) 33–57.

Masterman, Margaret. 1970. "The Nature of a Paradigm." Pp. 59–89 in Imre

Lakatos and Alan Musgrave (eds.), *Criticism and the Growth of Knowledge*. London: Cambridge University Press.

Maze, J.R. 1983. *The Meaning of Behaviour*. London: George Allen and Unwin.

McFarland, Andrew S. 1969. *Power and Leadership in Pluralist Systems*. Stanford, CA: Stanford University Press.

Mele, Alfred R. 1985. "Self–Control, Action, and Belief," *American Philosophical Quarterly*, 22 (April) 169–175.

Merry, Sally E. 1984. "Rethinking Gossip and Scandal." Pp. 271–302 in Black, 1984a–I.

Merton, Robert K. 1957. *Social Theory and Social Structure*. New York: Free Press.

Miller, Howard S. 1970. *Dollars for Research*. Seattle: University of Washington Press.

Miller, Richard W. 1987. *Fact and Method*. Princeton, NJ: Princeton University Press.

Morris, Norval. 1966. "Impediments to Penal Reform," *University of Chicago Law Review*, 33 (Summer) 627–656.

Morris, Robert, ed. 1990. *Science Education Worldwide*. Paris: UNESCO.

Nagel, Jack H. 1975. *The Descriptive Analysis of Power*. New Haven, CT: Yale University Press.

National Science Board. 1991. *Science and Engineering Indicators–1991*. Washington, D.C.: U. S. Government Printing Office.

O'Brien, Conor C. 1986. "Thinking about Terrorism," *Atlantic*, 257 (June) 62–66.

OECD. 1984. *Science and Technology Indicators: Basic Statistical Series: Recent Results: Selected S and T Indicators, 1979–1984*. Paris: Organization for Economic Co–Operation and Development.

O'Keefe, Daniel L. 1982. *Stolen Lightning: The Social Theory of Magic*. New York: Continuum.

Oppenheim, Felix E. 1961. *Dimensions of Freedom*. New York: St. Martin's Press.

Oswalt, Wendell H. 1976. *An Anthropological Analysis of Food–Getting Technology*. New York: Wiley.

Palgi, Phyllis and Henry Abramovitch. 1984. "Death: A Cross–Cultural Perspective," *Annual Review of Anthropology*, 13 (annual) 385–417.

Pareto, Vilfredo. 1935. *The Mind and Society*. 4 vols., continuous pagination. New York: Harcourt, Brace.

Parsons, Talcott. 1951. *The Social System*. New York: Free Press.

Pawson, Ray. 1989. *A Measure for Measures: A Manifesto for Empirical Sociology*. London: Routledge.

Pfohl, Stephen. 1991. "Postmodernity as a Social Problem," *SSP Newsletter*, 22 (No. 3) 9–14.

Pitts, Jesse R. 1968. "Social Control." Pp. 381–396 in Sills, 1968–XIV.

Polhemus, Ted, and Lynn Procter. 1978. *Fashion and Anti–Fashion*. London: Thames and Hudson.

Pope, Harrison G. 1985. "Psychopharmacology." Pp. 670–671 in Kuper and Kuper, 1985.

Pope, Liston. 1942. *Millhands and Preachers*. New Haven, CT: Yale University Press.

Pope, Whitney and Barclay D. Johnson. 1983. "Inside Organic Solidarity," *American Sociological Review*, 48 (October) 681–692.

Popper, Karl R. 1965. *The Logic of Scientific Discovery*. London: Hutchinson.

Poulantzas, Nicos. 1975. *Classes in Contemporary Capitalism*. London: NLB.

Powell, Walter W. 1989. "The Whole is not Greater than the Sum of its Parts, But Some of the Parts are Pretty Darn Good!," *Contemporary Sociology*, 18 (July) 490–493

Power, Richard. 1984. "Mutual Intention," *Journal for the Theory of Social Behaviour*, 14 (March) 85–102.

Quine, W. V. 1951. "Two Dogmas of Empiricism," *Philosophical Review*, 60 (January) 20–43.

_____. 1960. *Word and Object*. Cambridge, MA: MIT Press.

Radder, Hans. 1986. "Experiment, Technology and the Intrinsic Connection Between Knowledge and Power," *Social Studies of Science*, 16 (November) 663–683.

Rattansi, Ali. 1982. *Marx and the Division of Labour*. London: Macmillan.

Reddy, Amulya K. N. and Jose Goldemberg. 1990. "Energy for the Developing World," *Scientific American*, 263 (September) 110–118.

Richter, Maurice N., Jr. 1982. *Technology and Social Complexity*. Albany: State University of New York Press.

Ridgeway, Cecilia L., and Joseph Berger. 1986. "Expectations, Legitimation, and Dominance Behavior in Task Groups," *American Sociological Review*, 51 (October) 603–617.

Ridley, Jasper. 1984. *Henry VIII*. London: Constable.

Robinson, Thomas D. and Bruce London. 1991. "Dependency, Inequality, and Political Violence," *Journal of Political and Military Sociology*, 19 (Summer) 119–156.

Rock, Paul. 1973. *Making People Pay*. London: Routledge and Kegan Paul.

Rohner, Ronald P. and Evelyn C. Rohner. 1981. "Parental Acceptance–Rejection and Parental Control," *Ethnology*, 20 (July) 245–260.

Rolston, Holmes. 1987. *Science and Religion*. Philadelphia: Temple University Press.

Ross, E. A. 1901. *Social Control*. New York: Macmillan.

Rubinson, Richard and John Ralph. 1984. "Technical Change and the Expansion of Schooling in the United States, 1890–1970," *Sociology of Education*, 57 (July) 134–152.

Russell, Bertrand. 1938. *Power*. London: George Allen and Unwin.

Salam, Abdus, and Azim Kidwai. 1991. "A Blueprint for Science and Technology in the Developing World." Pp. 61–79 in Golden, 1991.

Schein, Edgar H. 1956. "The Chinese Indoctrination Program for Prisoners of War," *Psychiatry*, 19 (May) 149–172.

Schelling, Thomas C. 1984. *Choice and Consequence*. Cambridge, MA: Harvard University Press.

Schudson, Michael. 1984. *Advertising, the Uneasy Persuasion*. New York: Basic Books.

Scott, John F. 1971. *Internalization of Norms*. Englewood Cliffs, NJ: Prentice–Hall.

Searle, John R. 1983. *Intentionality*. London: Cambridge University Press.

Sheleff, Leon S. 1975. "From Restitutive Law to Repressive Law," *European Journal of Sociology*, 16 (No. 1) 16-45.

Shils, Edward. 1985. "Sociology." Pp. 799–811 in Kuper and Kuper, 1985.

Sills, David L., ed. 1968. *International Encyclopedia of the Social Sciences,* 17 volumes. New York: Macmillan.

Simon, Herbert A. 1952. "On the Definitiion of the Causal Relation," *Journal of Philosophy*, 49 (No. 16) 517–528.

_____. 1968. "Causation." Pp. 350–356 in Sills, 1968–II.

Sites, Paul. 1973. *Control*. New York: Dunellen.

Skinner, B. F. 1971. *Beyond Freedom and Dignity*. New York: Knopf.

_____. 1974. *About Behaviorism*. New York: Knopf.

_____. 1978. *Reflections on Behaviorism and Society*. Englewood Cliffs, NJ: Prentice–Hall.

_____. 1983. *A Matter of Consequences*. New York: Knopf.

Smelser, Neil J., ed. 1988. *Handbook of Sociology*. Newbury Park, CA: Sage.

Smith, Adam. 1952. *An Inquiry into the Nature and Causes of the Wealth of Nations*. Chicago: William Benton.

Smith, Bruce L. 1968. "Propaganda." Pp. 579–589 in Sills, 1968–XII.

Sobel, Michael E. 1994 (forthcoming). "Causal Inference in the Social and Behavioral Sciences." Chp. 1 in Gerhard Arminger, *et al.*(eds.), *A Handbook for Statistical Modeling in the Social and Behavioral Sciences*. New York: Plenum.

Sorokin, Pitirim A. 1975. *Hunger as a Factor in Human Affairs*. Gainesville: University Presses of Florida.

Soysal, Yasemin N. and David Strang. 1989. "Construction of the First Mass Education Systems in Nineteenth-Century Europe," *Sociology of Education*, 62 (October) 277–288.

Sperry, R. W. 1988. "Psychology's Mentalist Paradigm and the Religion/Science Tension," *American Psychologist* 43 (August) 607–613.

Stafford, Mark C., *et al.* 1986. "Modeling the Deterrent Effects of Punishment," *Social Psychology Quarterly*, 49 (December) 338–347.

Stark, Rodney. 1992. *Sociology*, 4th ed. Belmont, CA: Wadsworth.

Stinchcombe, Arthur L. 1983. *Economic Sociology*. New York: Academic Press.

Susskind, Charles. 1973. *Understanding Technology*. Baltimore: Johns Hopkins University Press.

Swann, William B., Jr., *et al.* 1981. "Curiosity and Control," *Journal of Personality and Social Psychology*, 40 (April): 635–642.

Tallman, Irving. 1984. Book review, *Social Forces*, 62 (June) 1121–1122.

Taylor, Charles L. and David A. Jodice. 1983. *World Handbook of Political and Social Indicators*, 3rd ed., Vol. 2, *Political Protest and Government Change*. New Haven, CT: Yale University Press.

Taylor, Frederick W. 1911. *The Principles of Scientific Management*. New York: Harper and Brothers.

Thoresen, Carl E. and Michael J. Mahoney. 1974. *Behavioral Self-Control*. New York: Holt, Rinehart and Winston.

Tolpin, Marian, and Heinz Kohut. 1989. "The Disorders of the Self." Pp. 229–253 in Greenspan and Pollock, 1989–II.

Turk, Austin T. 1982. "Social Control and Social Conflict." Pp. 249–264 in Jack P. Gibbs (ed.), *Social Control*. Beverly Hills, CA: Sage.

Turner, Stephen and William C. Wilcox. 1974. "Getting Clear about the 'Sign Rule'," *Sociological Quarterly*, 15 (Autumn) 571–588.

UNESCO. 1990. *Statistical Yearbook, 1990*. Paris: UNESCO.

United Nations. 1948, 1949, 1955, 1956, 1982a, 1984, 1985a, 1986a, 1987, 1990. *Demographic Yearbook* (respective year in title: *1948, 1949, 1955, 1956,1980, 1982, 1983, 1984, 1985, 1988*). New York: United Nations.

_____. 1979. *Demographic Yearbook: Historical Supplement*. New York: United Nations.

_____. 1983a, 1985b, 1986b, 1988. *Statistical Yearbook* (respective years in title: *1981, 1982, 1983/84, 1985/86*). New York: United Nations.

_____. 1983b. *1981 Yearbook of World Energy Statistics*. New York: United Nations.

Wagner, Jon. 1979. "Defining Technology," *Human Relations*, 32 (August) 719–736.

Waite, Robert G. L. 1977. *The Psychopathic God*. New York: Basic Books.

Wallace, Walter L. 1988. "Toward a Disciplinary Matrix in Sociology." Pp. 23–76 in Smelser, 1988.

Walter, Eugene V. 1969. *Terror and Resistance*. New York: Oxford University Press.

Watson, Walter T. 1929. "A New Census and an Old Theory: Division of Labor in the Preliterate World," *American Journal of Sociology*, 34 (January) 632–652.

Weber, Max. 1978. *Economy and Society*, 2 vols, continguous pagination. Berkeley: University of California Press.

Weinstein, Jay. 1982. *Sociology/Technology*. New Brunswick, NJ: Transaction Books.

White, Leslie A. (with Beth Dillingham). 1973. *The Concept of Culture*. Minneapolis: Burgess.

_____. 1975. *The Concept of Cultural Systems*. New York: Columbia University Press.

White, Lynn, Jr. 1962. *Medieval Technology and Social Change*. Oxford, England: Clarendon Press.

Whyte, William F. 1981 (1943). *Street Corner Society*, 3rd ed. Chicago: University of Chicago Press.

Williamson, Joel. 1984. *The Crucible of Race*. New York: Oxford University Press.

Willink, Bastiaan. 1991. "Origins of the Second Golden Age of Dutch Science after 1860: Intended and Unintended Consequences of Educational Reform," *Social Studies of Science*, 21 (August) 503–526.

Wilson, Harriet. 1980. "Parental Supervision," *British Journal of Criminology*, 20 (July) 203–235.

Wilson, William J. and Richard G. Dumont. 1968. "Rules of Correspondence and Sociological Concepts," *Sociology and Social Research*, 52 (January) 217–227.

Winkelman, Michael. 1982. "Magic: A Theoretical Assessment," *Current Anthropology*, 23 (February) 37–44.

Winner, Langdon. 1977. *Autonomous Technology*. Cambridge, MA: MIT Press.

Wright, Sewall. 1934. "The Method of Path Coefficients," *Annals of Mathematical Statistics*, 5 (September) 161–215.

Wrong, Dennis H. 1979. *Power*. New York: Harper and Row.

Wulff, David M. 1991. *Psychology of Religion*. New York: Wiley.

Wuthnow, Robert. 1992. *Rediscovering the Sacred*. Grand Rapids, MI: Eerdmans.

Yates, Aubrey J. 1980. *Biofeedback and the Modification of Behavior*. New York: Plenum.

Yates, JoAnne. 1989. *Control through Communications: The Rise of System in American Management*. Baltimore: Johns Hopkins University Press.

Name Index

Subject Index

About the Book and Author

Moving beyond his 1989 book, *Control: Sociology's Central Notion,* Jack Gibbs develops in this new book a comprehensive theory of control in all its biological, technological, and human dimensions. His treatment goes beyond conventional ideas about social control to show why self-control and proximate control are essential to understanding human interaction. He also argues that thinking of control in terms of the counteraction of deviance is insufficient.

Tests of Gibbs's control theory, based on data from sixty-six countries, add credence to his claim that control could be the central notion for sociology and perhaps for other social sciences.

Jack P. Gibbs is Centennial Professor Emeritus in the Department of Sociology at Vanderbilt University.